ABANDONED TO LUST

GENDER, THEORY, AND RELIGION

GENDER, THEORY, AND RELIGION

Amy Hollywood, Editor

The Gender, Theory, and Religion series provides a forum for interdisciplinary scholarship at the intersection of the study of gender, sexuality, and religion.

Martyrdom and Memory: Early Christian Culture Making, Elizabeth A. Castelli

When Heroes Love: The Ambiguity of Eros in the Stories of Gilgamesh and David, Susan Ackerman

ABANDONED TO LUST

Sexual Slander and Ancient Christianity

JENNIFER WRIGHT KNUST

Columbia University Press

NEW YORK

Columbia University Press
Publishers Since 1893
New York   Chichester, West Sussex
Copyright © 2006 Columbia University Press
All rights reserved

Library of Congress Cataloging-in-Publication Data
Knust, Jennifer Wright, 1966–
Abandoned to lust : sexual slander and ancient Christianity /
Jennifer Wright Knust.
p.   cm.   (Gender, theory, and religion)
Based on the author's thesis (doctoral) —
Columbia University, 2001.
Includes bibliographical references (p.   ) and index.
ISBN 0–231–13662–5 (alk. paper)—ISBN 0–231–51004–7 (e-book)
1. Sex—Religious aspects—Christianity—History of doctrine—
Early church, ca. 30–600. 2. Libel and slander—Religious
aspects—Christianity—History. 3. Sex—Rome. 4. Libel and
slander—Rome. I. Title. II. Series.

BR195.S48K58 2006
241'.66—dc22
2005049778

Columbia University Press books are printed on
permanent and durable acid-free paper.
Printed in the United States of America

c 10 9 8 7 6 5 4 3 2 1

For my grandmothers,
Lillian Meinardus Wright and Jean Thorson Nash

CONTENTS

ACKNOWLEDGMENTS

This project began as a dissertation written at Columbia University under the direction of Vincent L. Wimbush, currently professor of religion at Claremont Graduate University. One could not have asked for a better advisor; to him I remain forever in debt. Roger S. Bagnall, professor of history and classics at Columbia University, and Elizabeth A. Castelli, associate professor of religion at Barnard College, read numerous drafts, offering invaluable, extensive, and detailed advice. Their generosity as teachers and mentors is astonishing; I could not have completed either the dissertation or this book without them. While writing the dissertation, I was fortunate to be awarded an American Fellowship from the American Association of University Women; I remain grateful for this much-needed support.

Several working groups and seminars have been kind enough to offer both encouragement and rigorous critique of this project along the way. These include the Boston Area Patristics Group, the Paul and Politics Section of the Society of Biblical Literature, the Critical Biblical Studies Group of the Boston Theological Institute, and the Second Annual Graduate Studies Conference in the Classics at Columbia University. I am especially grateful to Annewies van den Hoek and Gregory Mobley for providing me with opportunities to present my work to colleagues in my new home, Boston. Richard Horsley, Neil Elliott, Cynthia Briggs Kittredge, and Simon Price offered welcome feedback following the presentation to the Paul and Politics Group.

My former colleagues at the College of the Holy Cross have created a wonderful intellectual community that I treasured while I was there. Alan Avery-Peck, Mary Ebbott, Mary Hobgood, Caroline Johnson Hodge, Alice Laffey, Frederick J. Murphy, and Joanne Pierce were particularly generous to me personally. Professor Johnson Hodge kindly read one chapter of the book, Professor Ebbott helped me clarify and improve one particular argument, and Professors Avery-Peck, Hobgood, Laffey, Murphy, and Pierce consistently provided voices of reason just when I needed them. My former student Kate Warren assisted in double-checking many of the classical references; her care and attention to detail are much appreciated.

I was honored to receive fellowships from the American Council of Learned Societies and the Radcliffe Institute for Advanced Study for the academic year 2003–04, providing me with the opportunity to devote myself full-time to research and writing. Thanks to that year, and the support of these fine institutions, I was finally able to complete all the major revisions and additions I had planned. The Radcliffe Institute provided an ideal setting for this work. The staff is exceedingly supportive and professional, the other fellows were tremendously energetic and engaging, and the resources made available to us are beyond compare. In this context, Caroline Elkins, Jane Gaines, Drew Gilpin Faust, Oded Goldreich, Fiona Griffiths, Meryl Hamilton, Soledad Loaeza, Dana Ron, I. Tony Rufo, Arielle Saiber, Paula Soares, Heike Trappe, Judith Vichniac, Tandy Warnow, and Irene Winter deserve my special thanks. Fiona Griffiths kindly read and discussed the final chapter with me at great length, providing very helpful comments. Jeremy Galen, my Radcliffe research partner, carefully checked the entire book manuscript for errors and infelicitous sentences. Jeremy, you are a star.

Numerous other colleagues have been generous readers and conversation partners; their comments, challenges, and advice have been much appreciated. Bart Ehrman kindly read and commented upon the entire dissertation and the new chapters composed for this book. His encouragement has meant a great deal to me. William V. Harris served on my dissertation committee and offered exceedingly helpful advice. He has been my teacher and my friend. Gay Byron, Laura Harrington, and Rosamond C. Rodman have been kindred spirits and colleagues since our Columbia days. I thank them for sharing their insights with me.

I am grateful to Columbia University Press for the professionalism and enthusiasm with which this project has been greeted. It has been a true pleasure to work with Wendy Lochner, senior executive editor; Amy Hollywood, Monrad Professor of Christian Studies at Harvard Divinity School and editor of the Gender, Theory, and Religion Series; and Michael Haskell, my manuscript editor. Professor Hollywood's recommendations regarding improvements to the manuscript were particularly detailed and helpful. Jennifer A. Glancy, professor of religious studies at Le Moyne College, also offered comments and suggestions regarding the final manuscript. I am so thankful for her important advice.

As is clear from this long list of acknowledgements, I have been very fortunate to have been challenged, encouraged, indulged, and prodded by an illustrious group of scholars and readers from a variety of disciplines throughout the course of this project. I have done my best to incorporate their recommendations. Any mistakes remain my own.

Finally, my family and friends have been loving, supportive and very, very patient with me as I labored on this project. Thanks to Elizabeth, Earl, Sarah, Hannah, and Nathanael Kooperkamp, to Helle Thorning, Bennet Wine, and Rebecca and Kaleb Thorning-Wine, to the Reverend Robert Castle, to the Reverend Suzanne Woolston Bossert, Pastor Carl Storms, and the Reverend Patricia Coughlin, to Bobbi and Rob Macdonald, to James Bailey, to Herbert and Christa Knust, and especially to my mother and father, Charles and Sandra Wright. My immediate family, Stefan, Axel, and Leander, have been my constant support and inspiration. My grandmothers Lillian Meinardus Wright and Jean Thorson Nash died while I was writing this book and I dedicate it to their memory. Grandma Billie and Grandma Jean, you are missed.

ABBREVIATIONS

Abbreviations follow the recommendations of *The Oxford Classical Dictionary*, 3rd ed., edited by Simon Hornblower and Antony Spawforth (Oxford: Oxford University Press, 1999); *The SBL Handbook of Style For Ancient Near Eastern, Biblical, and Early Christian Studies*, edited by Patrick H. Alexander, John F. Kutsko, James D. Ernest, Shirley A. Decker-Lucke, and David L. Petersen (Massachusetts: Hendrickson, 1999). When citing classical sources or standard classical reference works, I have preferred the recommendations of *The Oxford Classical Dictionary*. When citing biblical, pseudepigraphical, apocryphal, or other Jewish sources and the standard reference works associated with these documents, I have preferred *The SBL Handbook*. Translations of biblical passages are my own. When I quote a translation by others I have preferred the New Revised Standard Version (NRSV). I have also consulted the Revised Standard Version (RSV).

Ach. Tat.	Achilles Tatius
Aeschin. *In Tim.*	Aeschines *Against Timarchus*
ANRW	*Aufstieg und Niedergang der römischen Welt*
Anth. Pal.	*Anthologia Palatina*
Apoc. Ab.	*Apocalypse of Abraham*
Apoc. Bar.	*Apocalypse of Baruch*
2 *Apoc. Bar.*	*Second Apocalypse of Baruch*
Apoc. Pet.	*Apocalypse of Peter*
Apth. *Prog.*	Ap(h)thonius *Progymnasmata*
Apul. *Apol.*	Apuleius *Apologia*
Arist. *Apol.*	Aristides *Apologia*
Arist. *Eth. Nic.*	Aristotle *Ethica Nicomachea*

Arist. *Pol.*	Aristotle *Politica*
Arist. *Rh.*	Aristotle *Ars Rhetorica*
Arr. *Anab.*	Arrian *Anabasis*
Arr. *Epct. diss.*	Arrian *Epicteti dissertationes*
Athanasius *Apol.*	Athanasius *Apologia*
Athenagoras *Leg.*	Athenagoras *Legatio*
Barn.	*Epistle of Barnabas*
BAGD	W. Bauer, W. F. Arndt, F. W. Gingrich, and F. W. Danker, *Greek-English Lexicon of the New Testament and Other Early Christian Literature*, 2nd ed. (Chicago: University of Chicago Press, 1961).
BDF	F. Blass, A. Debrunner, and R. W. Funk, *A Greek Grammar of the New Testament and Other Early Christian Literature* (Chicago, 1961).
BGU	Berliner Griechische Urkunden (Ägyptische Urkunden aus den Klg. Mussen zu Berlin). 15 vols. Berlin, 1895–1983.
Caes. B *Gall.*	Caesar *Bellum Gallicum*
Cass. Dio	Cassius Dio
CD	Cairo Genizah copy of the *Damascus Document*
Cic. *Cael.*	Cicero (Marcus Tullius) *Pro Caelio*
Cic. *Cat.*	Cicero (Marcus Tullius) *In Catilinam*
Cic. *De or.*	Cicero (Marcus Tullius) *De oratore*
Cic. *Fam.*	Cicero (Marcus Tullius) *Epistulae ad familiares*
Cic. *Mur.*	Cicero (Marcus Tullius) *Pro Murena*
Cic. *Off.*	Cicero (Marcus Tullius) *De officiis*
Cic. *Phil.*	Cicero (Marcus Tullius) *Orationes Philippicae*
Cic. *Tusc.*	Cicero (Marcus Tullius) *Tusculanae disputationis*
Cic. *Verr.*	Cicero (Marcus Tullius) *In Verrum*
Clement *Strom.*	Clement of Alexandria *Stromateis*
1 Clem.	1 Clement
2 Clem.	2 Clement
D	*Digest of Justinian*
Dem.	Demosthenes
Dem. *De cor.*	Demosthenes *De corona*
Demetr. Eloc.	Demetrius *De Elocutione* = Περὶ ἑρμηνείας
Did.	*Didache*
Din.	Dinarchus
Dio Chrys. *Or.*	Dio Chrysostom *Orationes*

Diog. Laert.	Diogenes Laertius
Diogn.	*Epistle to Diognetus*
Dion. Hal. *Ant. Rom.*	Dionysius Halcarnassensis *Antiquitates Romanae*
Dio. Sic.	Diodorus Siculus
Epiph. *Pan.*	Epiphanius *Panarion*
Ep. Jer.	Epistle of Jeremiah
Eusebius *Hist. Eccl.*	Eusebius *Historia Ecclesiastica*
Gell.	Aulus Gellius
Gos. Thom.	Gospel of Thomas
Herm. *Mand.*	*The Shepherd of Hermas, Mandate*
Herm. *Sim.*	*The Shepherd of Hermas, Similitude*
Herm. *Vis.*	*The Shepherd of Hermas, Vision*
Hippolytus *Haer.*	*Refutatio omnium haeresium*
HNT	Handbuch zum Neuen Testament
Hor. *Carm.*	Horace *Carmina*
Ign. *Eph.*	Ignatius of Antioch *To the Ephesians*
Ign. *Magn.*	Ignatius of Antioch *To the Magnesians*
Ign. *Phld.*	Ignatius of Antioch *To the Philadelphians*
Ign. *Pol.*	Ignatius of Antioch *To Polycarp*
Ign. *Rom.*	Ignatius of Antioch *To the Romans*
Ign. *Smyrn.*	Ignatius of Antioch *To the Smyrnaeans*
Ign. *Trall.*	Ignatius of Antioch *To the Trallians*
Iren. *Adv. Haer.*	Irenaeus *Adversus Haereses*
Isoc.	Isocrates
Isoc. *C. soph.*	Isocrates *Contra sophistas*
Isoc. *Paneg.*	Isocrates *Panegyricus*
JAAR	*Journal of the American Academy of Religion*
JBL	*Journal of Biblical Literature*
JECS	*Journal of Early Christian Studies*
Jerome *Adv. Iovinian.*	Jerome *Adversus Iovinianum*
Jerome *Ep.*	Jerome *Epistulae*
JFSR	*Journal of Feminist Studies in Religion*
Joseph *AJ*	Josephus *Antiquitates judaicae*
Joseph *Ap.*	Josephus *Contra Apionem*
Joseph *Vit.*	Josephus *Vita*
JRS	*Journal of Roman Studies*
JSOT	*Journal for the Study of the Old Testament*
Justin *1 Apol.*	Justin Martyr *First Apology*
Justin *2 Apol.*	Justin Martyr *Second Apology*

Justin *Dial.*	Justin Martyr *Dialogue with Trypho*
Juv.	Juvenal
L.A.B.	*Liber antiquitatum biblicarum* (Pseudo-Philo)
LCL	Loeb Classical Library
LSJ	H. G. Liddell, R. Scott, and H. S. Jones, *A Greek English Lexicon*, 9th ed., with revised supplement (Oxford: Oxford University Press, 1996).
Lucian *De mort. peregr.*	Lucian *De morte peregrini*
Lucian *Dial. meret.*	Lucian *Dialogi meretricii*
Lucian *Nigr.*	Lucian *Nigrinus*
LXX	Septuagint
Macrob. *Sat.*	Macrobius *Saturnalia*
Mart.	Martial
M. Aur. *Med.*	Marcus Aurelius *Meditations*
Men. Rhet.	Menander Rhetor
MT	Masoritic Text
Muson.	Musonius Rufus
Minucius Felix *Oct.*	Minucius Felix *Octavius*
Nep. *Dion*	Cornelius Nepos *Vitae excellentium imperatorum. Dion*
NovT	*Novum Testamentum*
NRSV	New Revised Standard Version
ORF[A]	H. Malcovati, *Oratorum Romanorum Fragmenta*, 4th ed.
Petron. *Satyr.*	Petronius *Satyrica*
Philo *Abr.*	Philo Judaeus *De Abrahamo*
Philo *Contempl.*	Philo Judaeus *De vita contemplativa*
Philo *Decal.*	Philo Judaeus *De decalogo*
Philo *Ios.*	Philo Judaeus *De Iosepho*
Philo *Leg.*	Philo Judaeus *Legatio ad Gaium*
Philo *Mos.*	Philo Judaeus *De vita Mosis*
Philo *Post.*	Philo Judaeus *De posteritate Caini*
Philo *Quest. Gen.*	Philo Judaeus *Quaestiones et solutiones in Genesin*
Philo *Spec.*	Philo Judaeus *De specialibus legibus*
Philo *Virt.*	Philo Judaeus *De virtutibus*
Plato *Grg.*	Plato *Gorgias*
Plato *Leg.*	Plato *Leges*
Plato *Prt.*	Plato *Protagoras*
Plato *Rep.*	Plato *Respublica*

Plato *Soph.*	Plato *Sophista*
Plin. *HN*	Pliny (the Elder) *Naturalis historica*
Plin. *Ep.*	Pliny (the Younger) *Epistulae*
Plin. *Pan.*	Pliny (the Younger) *Panegyricus*
Plut. *Alex.*	Plutarch *Vita Alexander*
Plut. *Ant.*	Plutarch *Vita Antonius*
Plut. *Caes.*	Plutarch *Vita Caesar*
Plut. *Cat. Mai.*	Plutarch *Vita Cato Maior*
Plut. *Cic.*	Plutarch *Vita Cicero*
Plut. *Dem.*	Plutarch *Vita Demosthenes*
Plut. *Demetr.*	Plutarch *Vita Demetrius*
Plut. *Luc.*	Plutarch *Vita Lucullus*
Plut. *Lys.*	Plutarch *Vita Lysander*
Plut. *Mor.*	Plutarch *Moralia*
Plut. *Mor.* (Quaest. Rom.).	Plutarch *Moralia (Questiones Romanae)*
Plut. *Otho*	Plutarch *Vita Otho*
Plut. *Pomp.*	Plutarch *Vita Pompeius*
Plut. *Sol.*	Plutarch *Vita Solon*
Plut. *Them.*	Plutarch *Vita Themistocles*
Polemon *Phys.*	Polemon (Marcus Antonius) *Physiognomy*
Poly. *Phil.*	Polycarp *To the Philippians*
Polyb.	Polybius
Prop.	Propertius
Ps.-Philo.	Pseudo-Philo, *Liber antiquitatum biblicarum*
Quint. *Inst.*	Quintilian *Institutio oratia*
RG	*Res gestae divi Augusti*
Sall. *Cat.*	Sallust *Bellum Catilinae*
SB	*Sammelbuch griechishen Urkunden aus Ägypten*
Sen. *Ben.*	Seneca (the Younger) *De beneficiis*
Sen. *Clem.*	Seneca (the Younger) *De clementia*
Sen. *Contr.*	Seneca (the Elder) *Controversiae*
Sen. *Dial.*	Seneca (the Younger) *Dialogi*
Sen. *Ep.*	Seneca (the Younger) *Epistulae*
Sen. *Suas.*	Seneca (the Elder) *Suasoriae*
Sib. *Or.*	*Sibylline Oracles*
Sir.	Sirach
Suet. *Aug.*	Suetonius *Divus Augustus*
Suet. *Calig.*	Suetonius *Gaius Caligula*

Suet. *Claud.*	Suetonius *Divus Claudius*
Suet. *Dom.*	Suetonius *Domanitianus*
Suet. *Iul.*	Suetonius *Divus Iulius*
Suet. *Ner.*	Suetonius *Nero*
Suet. *Otho*	Suetonius *Otho*
Suet. *Tit.*	Suetonius *Divus Titus*
Tac. *Ann.*	Tacitus *Annales*
Tac. *Hist.*	Tacitus *Historiae*
Tatian *Or.*	Tatian *Oratio ad Graecos*
T. Benj.	*Testament of Benjamin*
Tertullian *Ad nat.*	Tertullian *Ad nationes*
Tertullian *Apol.*	Tertullian *Apologeticus*
Tertullian *Praesc. haeret.*	Tertullian *De Praescriptione Haereticorum*
Tertullian *Pud.*	Tertullian *De pudicitia*
Tertullian *Virg.*	Tertullian *De virginibus velandis*
Theophilus *Ad Auto.*	Theophilus *Ad Autolycum*
Thom. Cont.	*Book of Thomas the Contender*
T. Levi	*Testament of Levi*
T. Naph.	*Testament of Naphtali*
T. Reub.	*Testament of Reuben*
Val. Max.	Valerius Maximus
Xen. *Oec.*	Xenophon *Oeconomicus*
ZPE	*Zeitschrift für Papyrologie und Epigraphik*

ABANDONED TO LUST

INTRODUCTION

Who's on Top?

Sex Talk, Power, and Resistance

> For all of the titillation about thongs and cigars, the story of the impeachment and trial of William Jefferson Clinton was not so much about sex as it was about power.
> — Peter Baker, *The Breach: Inside the Impeachment and Trial of William Jefferson Clinton*

When has discourse about sex ever been exclusively about sex? Moreover, has there ever been a time when sex itself was not also about power? Peter Baker's observation that the Clinton scandal was about power states the obvious to those who have followed the debates of feminist and cultural critics over the last several decades.[1] Of course the impeachment was about power, power framed and negotiated in terms of accusations about sex. The trial of a former American president is only the most recent example of a long history of the intersection of sex and politics. Charges of sexual misconduct of various kinds against leaders of all sorts have frequently served as important rhetorical weapons. Indeed, at about the same time that former President Clinton was apologizing for misleading the American people about his extramarital affair, the deputy prime minister of Malaysia was arrested for sodomy and illicit sex with "numerous" men and women. The prime minister, Mahathir Mohamad, expressed disappointment with his deputy, noting that the arrest was necessary since "I cannot accept a man who is a sodomist as leader of the country."[2]

From ancient times until today, accusers have sought to undermine, embarrass, and even overthrow political leaders on the basis of their (real or alleged) sexual wrongdoing. Such charges do not appear only in the contentious realm of governmental power politics; sexual slander has also served as an important tool in the production of group boundaries.

Outsiders are accused of being sexually deviant in some way while insiders are described as sexually pure.[3] So, for example, European explorers and missionaries regularly denounced the sexual promiscuity of the native peoples of the Americas. They were described by one Jesuit missionary as "extremely lazy, gluttonous, profane, treacherous, cruel in their revenge, and given up to all kinds of lewdness, men and women alike, the men having several wives and abandoning them to others, and the women only serving them as slaves."[4] Similarly, a Spanish Renaissance humanist compared the "base" morals of the natives to the superior temperance of the Spaniards "in greed as well as lust." He concludes that the natives really are slaves by nature; their (alleged) moral turpitude proves it.[5] According to the logic of such discourse, colonization and Christianization were not only justified, they were absolutely necessary for the "good" of native and European alike. Sexual slurs are not only excellent weapons when attacking specific political rivals; they are also effective instruments for attacking entire groups, often to the benefit of a self-proclaimed elite.

Charges of sexual impropriety can be employed to further the interests of an elite; they can also be useful to those who wish to undermine the moralizing pretensions of their rulers. The "governing elite," as Peter Brown has suggested, must present themselves to themselves and to the world at large as "in truth governing";[6] claims about the excellent morals of the ruling class often figure into this process.[7] Thus, bawdy jokes, gossip, and sexual slander targeted at privileged "models of virtue" can serve to challenge these pretensions and the authority they were designed to validate. Vine Deloria, former executive director of the National Congress of American Indians, offers an amusing example in the form of a joke involving a missionary and an Indian interlocutor. The missionary was brought up short by the allegedly innocent confusion of his interlocutor over the differences between hell and the white man's city, Albuquerque, New Mexico. The story goes as follows: A missionary warned his Indian traveling companion that, without Christ in his life, he would soon be headed to a place full of sinners, where the "wicked dwell in the depths of their iniquities," and "sinful women who have lived a bad life go." When the missionary asked his potential convert the name of this place, instead of supplying the expected answer—hell—the Indian replied "Albuquerque."[8] The humor of this joke depends on white Christian claims about the superiority of "their" religion and civilization, displayed, in part, by "their" good women, and the absurdity of such claims given the "reality" of "sinful" white Albuquerque. Such an interchange reverses the expected categories, employing terms used to define Indians as outside of civilization to suggest that it is the white man who is incapable of the very civilization he enjoins on everyone else. Seen in this light, a joke is hardly "just a joke": it is a potent weapon capable of voicing the shared disdain of the dominated for their dominators.[9]

This book explores the use of sexualized slander by the earliest Christians and their contemporaries in the context of ancient rhetorical invective and in light of ancient assumptions about sex and gender.[10] Christian authors have at times been taken at their word when they accused others of sexual misbehavior; thus, the decline and fall of the Roman Empire has sometimes been attributed to a rotting from within brought about by excessive luxury and manifested in sexual degeneracy.[11] The outrageous emperor Caligula—guilty of incest and orgiastic sexual romps and labeled an effeminate—has been offered as a paradigmatic example of the evils that Roman luxury inevitably produced.[12] Some historians have adopted the views of church fathers, arguing that at least a few of the Christian heretics actually were sexually promiscuous promoters of orgies for Christ.[13] Such historical reconstructions fail to take into account the rhetorical and discursive functions of accusations of sexual depravity. Of course it is at least possible that Caligula had sexual intercourse with his sisters or that the heretical Simonian Christians collected seminal emission and menstrual blood for religious purposes.[14] As we now know, the American president in fact did have sexual relations with "that woman." Still, accurate or not, sexual slurs provide a window into more than the titillating sexual misdeeds of presidents, emperors, and heretics.

Charges of debauchery, unrestrained lust, and the like illuminate cultural assertions about sex and morality while providing evidence of competitive power relations between individuals and the groups they claim to represent. "Good" and "bad" sexual behavior is not given, natural, or obvious; these categories are produced and enacted within history. Definitions of sexual deviance change; there is no universal, generalizable category "the sexual"; and gender is not determined by some unalterable biological fact.[15] Therefore, sexual slander both describes and delimits ever-shifting definitions of sexual impropriety. Once the legitimacy of a position or a group has been linked to a particular definition of sexual virtue, accusations of sexual vice become a potent weapon for distinguishing insiders from outsiders, policing group boundaries, and eliminating rivals. Moreover, sexual slurs, whether by means of jokes, gossip, or outright accusations, can serve as an important resistance strategy: the pretensions of an elite are efficiently skewered by their (supposed) subordinates once the emptiness of their claims to virtue have been exposed.[16] As we shall see, early Christian authors employed sexualized invective for all of these purposes, defining virtue in such a way that they, and they alone, were capable of sexual self-mastery; everyone else was said to be incuraably debauched.

STATEMENT OF THE PROBLEM

Christianity was once nothing but a novel, deadly superstition, or so its detractors claimed. But Christians were accused of even worse: from incest to orgies, nocturnal religious rites, and the ceremonial murder of an infant, the followers of Jesus of Nazareth were said to pursue "a religion of lust" that venerates genitalia, tricks initiates into ritualized cannibalism, and serves as a cover for the indiscriminate sating of desire.[17] In one especially purple passage, the Latin Christian apologist Minicuius Felix recounted charges lodged against the Christians that he attributed to M. Cornelius Fronto, a Roman aristocrat:

> On the day appointed they gather at a banquet with all of their children, sisters, mothers, people of either sex and every age. There, after full feasting, when the blood is heated and drink has inflamed the passions of incestuous lust, a dog which has been tied to a lamp is tempted by a morsel thrown beyond the range of his tether to bound forward with a rush. The tale-telling light is upset and extinguished, and in the shameless dark lustful embraces are indiscriminately exchanged; and all alike, if not in act, yet by complicity, are involved in incest, as anything that occurs by the act of individuals results from the common intention.[18]

Apparently, by the mid-second century, Christians were widely suspected of such behavior. But Christians were not the only group accused of an addiction to illicit sex and other moral or religious crimes during this period: Jews were said to worship the head of an ass, perform human sacrifice, and pursue lust, despite their famously strict marriage customs.[19] Conversely, Jews characterized Greeks or Egyptians as profligate, perverse, and adulterous.[20] Greeks represented Persians as slavish and licentious;[21] yet, according to several Roman authors, it is the Greeks who are lascivious pleasure seekers.[22] In other words, Christian, Jew, Greek, Roman, they were all said to be guilty of sexual excess of one sort or another.

Early Christians were not averse to participating in this sort of name-calling. For example, in his letter to the church in Rome, the apostle Paul claimed that idolaters—those who do not worship the God of Israel—are inevitably guilty of sexual misbehavior. Idolaters "exchanged the glory of the immortal God for images resembling a mortal human being or birds of animals or reptiles" (Rom 1:23); therefore, they have been handed over "to immorality, to the degrading of their bodies among themselves" (Rom 1:24). In their depravity, their women engage in "unnatural" acts while their men become inflamed with lustful passion for one another (Rom 1:26–27). They are said to be guilty of a whole laundry list of atrocities, including envy, hatred of God, disobedience to parents, and greed (Rom 1:29–31). According to Paul, the rejection of (his) God leads to a predictable decline into immorality characterized, principally, by "unnatural" sexual excess. Second-century Christian apologists built upon and expanded this argument, gleefully describing the incestuous, adulterous, and lascivious behavior of the pagan gods and those who worship them.[23] Christian authors also turned these stereotypical charges against one another, arguing that the "heretics"—fellow Christians with whom they disagreed—were incapable of sexual restraint.[24] False Christians allegedly "pervert the grace of God into licentiousness" (Jude 4), capture "weak women" (2 Tim 3:6), or entice formerly faithful Christians into fornication (Rev 2:21). The second-century heresiologist Ireneaus summed it up: pseudo-Christians always "live licentious lives and hold godless doctrine."[25] Greek, Roman, Jew, Persian, Christian, and heretic were all accused of sexual impropriety of one sort or another; enemies were inevitably represented as sexually profligate whether the author of the charge was a first-century Greek speaking Jew or a second-century Roman aristocrat.[26]

Clearly, allegations of moral turpitude were standard fare in ancient rhetorical invective, available to any author interested in discrediting an opponent or set of opponents. The practice of charging one's intended victim with sexual misbehavior can be read as part of a rhetorical tradition extending back as least as far as fourth-century Athens. For example, in his famous speech *De Corona*, the Athenian orator Demosthenes attacked the origin, occupation, and character of his target Aeschines by suggesting that Aeschines' mother engaged in indiscriminate intercourse in a public latrine; Aeschines (allegedly) imitated her example by involving himself in suspect religious rituals, wearing exotic apparel, and associating with old women.[27] Writing some five hundred years later, the Roman orator

Cicero followed Demosthenes' example, accusing his opponents of family scandals, uncontrolled lust, and other "shameful deeds."[28] Political opponents, unpopular emperors, controversial philosophies, new religions, and "barbarian" cultures were all characterized as debauched, depraved, and perverse.[29]

Sexual slander, therefore, was a widespread practice in ancient polemics, and similar charges were deployed both against Christians and by Christians. Still, however widespread and stereotypical, charges of sexual misbehavior were hardly "mere rhetoric." Intended to malign and defame, these accusations were deployed in fierce struggles for identity, prestige, and power. When Paul asserted that those who reject Christ are by definition sexually repulsive, he was making a claim about the superiority of his own group, declaring that he and those who agree with him are sexually pure, and drawing boundaries between himself, his followers, and "idolaters," that is, "everyone else." Similarly, by telling stories of Christian orgies, Fronto and others like him reasserted the "true" piety of Rome—a piety that leads to sexual and religious decency, not incest and human sacrifice. These accusations do not offer straightforward evidence of sexual practice; rather, they indicate a conflict between the author and those whom he maligned. Luke Timothy Johnson's characterization of New Testament anti-Jewish slander is instructive: "the main thing that such slander signified, therefore, was that someone *was* an opponent."[30] Perhaps this is all a historian can conclude from charges of sexual immorality: those making the charges were opposed to those whom they charged. Nevertheless, the form in which the opposition was expressed remains revealing.

Two recent studies of one of the commonplace accusations of ancient invective—the charge of human sacrifice—offer further support to Johnson's view, while also demonstrating that such charges, no matter how stereotypical, carried considerable weight. As James Rives and Andrew McGowan have shown, reports about ritual murder and cannibalism, though clearly false, were employed by those who offered them to indicate a profound gap between themselves and the target of their rhetoric.[31] Stories about human sacrifice served as "a marker of cultural distance between the people who told the stories and the people about whom they were told."[32] In other words, accusations of murder and anthropophagy against Christians were false, historically speaking, but their message was true: Christians had distanced themselves from their cultural context.[33] Read in this way, Fronto's suggestion that Christians killed and consumed an infant during their initiation rites, as shocking and extreme as the charge seems, may be understood as entirely believable to his audience—not because the accusation was thought to be "true" but because it efficiently expressed a collective distaste for the characteristic Christian refusal to participate in the common culture of city and empire. Christians, as Minucius Felix and other apologists proudly proclaimed, refused to acknowledge or worship the gods of their ancestors, a practice that was interpreted as atheism and misanthropy by their neighbors. "Such people" (the Christians) can be expected to be guilty of all sorts of moral and religious crimes. From out-of-control lust to incest and the ritual sacrifice of infants, people who would reject the gods and the city must be guilty of the worst kinds of mischief.

Charges of sexual vice could operate in similar ways. According to Catharine Edwards, accusations of sexual immorality lodged by Romans against one another were central to the "agonistic rituals of Roman political life."[34] Designed to marginalize and exclude, moralizing accusations about the decadence, prodigality, and self-indulgence of target members of the male Roman elite justified the dominant position of some—said to embody proper Roman virtue—at the expense of others. Virginia Hunter made a similar observation in her survey of fourth- and fifth-century Athenian forensic discourse. Routine accusations of miserly contributions to public expenditure, cowardly performance in military service, poor treatment of family members, and, especially, reprehensible sexual conduct were forceful rhetorical devices employed by male citizens in a constant battle for status and privilege. These accusations, however stereotypical, delineated "good" from "bad" citizen in such a way that the political and sexual status quo was maintained.[35] Thus, both Athenian and (later) Roman males defined and defended their privilege by referencing their own sexual virtue and condemning their rivals for failing to live up to a sexual standard they both rearticulated and reinforced. What is a "Roman"? A man who controls himself. What is an "Athenian"? A man who is brave, generous, and moderate in the expression of desire. A man who fails to display these virtues must not be tolerated, or so it was claimed.

A comparable phenomenon may be found in the association between idolatry and prostitution in the Hebrew Bible, though the distinction here is between (pious) Israel and (idolatrous) Canaan. Throughout much of the Bible, idolatry—worship of any god other than YHWH—was described in sexual terms as "fornication" or "prostitution" (*znh* and cognates). Canaanites were said to "prostitute themselves to their gods" and were therefore guilty of both false religiosity and sexual licentiousness.[36] Though scholars have occasionally interpreted these passages as an indication that the

Canaanites included cult prostitution among their repertoire of religious practices, Phyllis Bird disagrees. She comments: "while prostitutes *may* have had functions at times in the cultic sphere ... and while hierodules *may* have had functions or duties involving sexual activity ... the terms used in the indigenous languages to describe these two classes never connect the sacred sphere with prostitution or prostitution with the cult." The association of *znh* with sacred prostitution, therefore, was a consequence of a polemical interpretation of Canaanite practice present throughout the Hebrew Bible rather than a report about Canaanite religious ritual. In other words, the claim that Canaanites promoted sacred prostitution was designed to differentiate "true" religion, figured as the worship of YHWH, and the truly pious, figured as Israel, from false religion, figured as the worship of Baal or other gods, and the impious, figured as the Canaanites.

Early Christian authors deployed sexual slurs to similar ends, consistently claiming virtue for themselves alone, especially sexual virtue, while vilifying their competitors as utterly vice-ridden, most often in terms of lack of sexual self-control. From the obscure comment in the Gospel of Matthew that some have made themselves "eunuchs for the kingdom of heaven," to the celebration of the 144,000 (male) virgins who did not "defile themselves with women" in the book of Revelation, the insistence that (true) Christians are sexually pure pervades this literature.[37] Paul, disciples of Paul, Ignatius, and Polycarp all warned against tolerating anything that might resemble improper sexual behavior among "the saints."[38] Aristides, Athenagoras, Justin Martyr, Tertullian, Tatian, Theophilus of Antioch, and numerous others asserted that the Christians are exceptionally chaste, especially the continent who never engage in sexual activity at all.[39] The quests of elite Christian women to remain sexually continent in face of the demands of family and city are central to the dramas of the stories preserved in the Apocryphal Acts.[40] Christian texts in a variety of genres from the first century onward declared that, above all, sexual self-control was the trademark of their movement.[41]

Christian authors did not agree regarding the content of this self-control—indeed, as Peter Brown and others have pointed out, Christians argued vociferously about the character and meaning of the sexual mores they recommended[42]—but they were certain that all "true" followers of Jesus must display sexual purity, however defined. Moreover, whatever the position taken on sexual renunciation, Christians repeatedly represented differences between themselves and others, outsiders or insiders, in sexual terms. Either one was a "true Christian," and therefore chaste, or one was depraved. For example, the second-century Christians Tatian and Irenaeus radically disagreed regarding Christian marriage—to Tatian marriage was incompatible with Christian life,[43] to Irenaeus an outright rejection of marriage involved a presumptuous rejection of God's creation[44]—yet both persistently contrasted the propriety of their behavior with the purported sexual impropriety of their enemies.[45] Opponents were demonized and denounced across a spectrum of Christian authors and points of view by means of elaborate descriptions of sexual vice: gentiles were said to be licentious lovers of luxury;[46] the pagan gods were described as perverse lovers of incest and adultery; "false" Christian teachers were represented as profligate pleasure seekers;[47] and "heretics" were widely associated with prostitutes, demon possession, and wicked desire.[48]

What did Christian authors seek to gain by employing such slurs? Sexual slander, as I have already observed, draws boundaries between "us" and "them." Arguments presented in terms of the bad sexual behavior of a target, such as those frequently put forward by early Christians, served to reinforce boundaries between those associated with the bad behavior and those who claimed that such behavior is abhorrent. Finding themselves in agreement, the bonds between an author and audience were strengthened and the targets of the accusation were pushed even further away. The author and his sympathizers discovered that they are "superior" since they, of course, engage only in "proper" sexual activity. In the case of early Christians, then, the claim that the true followers of Jesus practice self-control while "everyone else" remains uncontrolled can be read as part of an effort to produce and maintain a discernible Christian identity. Arguably, there were no "Christians" at all in the in the first-century, only followers of Jesus who defined themselves in various ways.[49] Though later authors did identify themselves and their associates as Christian, the boundaries of the group remained much more ill-defined than these writings would suggest.[50] Did each author understand the label Christian in the same way? Would each author draw the same boundaries around the group he sought to identify? Clearly the answer is no. The overwhelming impression left by reading early Christian writings is of tremendous diversity: diverse points of view regarding the significance of Jesus; diverse claims about how, precisely, Christianity ought to be related to Judaism; diverse and contradictory positions regarding the nature of flesh and matter. The category "Christian" was (and is) subjective, not fixed; sexual slander served to provide this label with the appearance of closure when, in fact, there was (and is) none.

By utilizing sexualized discourse to define the contours of their group, Christian authors adopted a common strategy. We have already noticed that Roman noblemen jockeyed for position by proclaiming their own superior virtue while decrying the vices of their rivals. By doing so, they were also engaged in a contentious project of defining "Rome" and "Romanness." As Rives has observed, the categories "Greek" and "Roman" ought to be viewed "more as subjects of a debate and polemic by contemporary actors than as objective qualities to be traced by modern scholars."[51] The "politics of immorality"—described so nicely by Edwards—participated in the project of shaping the contours of the ideal Roman, a malleable category rather than an identifiable thing in itself. Similarly, "Greek" and "Greekness" were not fixed identities but cultural markers that were performed and enacted and, as such, subject to change.[52] Moreover, "Jew" and "Judean" were not set identifiers, labels with a stable content upon which everyone agreed; like the other labels under consideration here, these terms were subjective.[53] By adopting these labels, therefore, I do not mean to imply that group boundaries were clear. Rather, whenever possible, I note how particular authors claimed these various identities for themselves, demarcating insiders and outsiders by means of a sexualized discourse of "us" and "them," among other strategies. Pierre Bourdieu commented, "there is no social agent who does not aspire, as far as his circumstances permit, to have the power to name and to create the world through naming: gossip, slander, lies, insults, commendations, criticisms, arguments, and praises are all daily and petty manifestations of the solemn and collective acts of naming."[54] Engaging in a "solemn act of naming," the followers of Jesus sought to define their group by representing themselves as sexually virtuous and their enemies as sexually degenerate. In the process, a "Christian" became someone who exhibits sexual self-mastery.

Christians were not the only group that grounded their claim to legitimacy, in part, on sexual restraint. According to an ancient and venerable tradition, a tradition at least as old as Plato, only good men can truly be kings.[55] Though a bad man may seem to be king—he may be called king by his subjects, he may call himself king—in actual fact, this is impossible. Enslaved to his passions, he is equally enslaved to his subjects, though he and his subjects may not realize it. In other words, men deserve to rule others when they demonstrate that they are capable of ruling themselves. Dio Chysostom attributed this theory to Homer:

> Homer, in the same manner as other wise and truthful men, says that no wicked or licentious or avaricious person can ever be a ruler or mas-

ter either of himself or of anybody else, nor will such a man ever be a king even though all the world, both Greeks and barbarians, men and women, affirm the contrary.[56]

With this theory in mind, Greek histories and biographies evaluated rulers and other illustrious men according to their relative virtues;[57] Roman rulers were similarly evaluated by how well they did (or did not) promote and display virtue during their reign.[58] Trading on this logic, Octavian, soon to be "Augustus,"[59] sought to present himself as the restorer of Roman mores by instituting a moral reform through legislation, building projects, and a revival of Roman religion at the expense of "foreign" cults.[60] In 27 B.C.E, the Senate recognized Augustus' exceptional political and moral achievements by praising his *virtus, clementia, iustitia,* and *pietas* and commemorating his restoration of the *res publica* on a golden shield.[61] Among later authors, Augustus came to set the standard for the "good emperor," a man in control of his passions who rules both himself and the empire well.[62] Augustus, Nero, and Trajan were all, at one time or another, said to personify virtue, at least in theory.[63] The ideal emperor "embodies in himself and ensures for all mankind [*sic*] the divine blessings of justice, peace, concord, abundance, and prosperity, his virtue ensures the well-being of the entire empire."[64] By the second century C.E. the association of the emperor with the virtues had become a cliché.[65]

In this context, the assertion by the followers of Jesus that they were the only group truly capable of virtue can be read as a pointed, if implicit, attack. Sexual slander is not only a tool of group self-definition, it can serve as a resistance strategy designed to undermine the legitimacy of ruler and empire alike.[66] By arguing that non-Christians are depraved, ruled by the passions, and guilty of incest and adultery, Christian authors from the New Testament period onward called the authority of their rulers into question, including, perhaps, the emperor himself. How can a "just" or "virtuous" emperor possibly allow, let alone practice, immorality? Those raised on a steady diet of the theory that only a good man can truly be king could offer only one answer: he cannot. Nevertheless, by employing sexual slander to define themselves and, possibly, undermine their rulers, Christian authors often simply repeated the very same power-laden, gendered categories of sexual virtue and vice that were more commonly used to support rather than undermine the empire. For example, the emperor Augustus was praised for taming the "unclean lust" that had plagued Rome prior to his ascension to power. Thanks to Augustus, the poet Horace claimed, "mothers are proud of legitimate children; punishment follows on the heels of guilt."[67] By contrast, Paul argued that faith in Jesus Christ is the sole guarantee of sexual self-control. As he put it in his letter to the Romans, though once "enslaved to sin," the followers of Jesus have become "slaves of Christ" whose bodily members serve God rather than desire.[68] Still, in both cases, it is one's ruler—be he Octavian Augustus or Jesus, the anointed son of God—who makes possible the proper sexual behavior of his subjects.

The "household codes" of later Pauline literature offer a further example. The author of 1 Timothy recommended that bishops be chosen on the basis of how well they manage their households: "if someone does not know how to manage his own household, how can he take care of God's church?"[69] Similarly, the Greek moralist Plutarch suggested that the control of women, children, and slaves offers an ideal test of the fitness of a man for leadership in the city: "A man must have harmony in his household to produce harmony in the city or in the agora or among his own friends."[70] Such similarities should not be surprising. Though early Christian authors adopted sexual slander to critique those who dominated them, resistance occurs "within power," that is, within a language shared by those we might identify as "the dominated" and those we might label "the dominators."[71] As Rosamond Rodman has noted, "In order for resistances to achieve their desired effect they must appropriate the cultural signs and symbols already in place."[72] As we shall see, the followers of Jesus appropriated a vituperative vocabulary they shared with their neighbors in such a way that moral categories were often simply rearticulated, but to the benefit of their own persuasive projects. Christian reversion or inversion of (sexualized) moralistic discourse may have been intended to corrode the power relations that they felt marginalized them, but such a move also restated and even amplified a shared moral status quo.

For early Christians, the strategy of justifying themselves by arguing that they alone were capable of moral action and attacking their enemies as moral degenerates can be read as a resistance intended, in part, to attack the authority of the governing elite. This may have been a particularly effective strategy in a world in which privilege was already justified in terms of virtue, however vacuous such references may have seemed to those who heard them. Christians who adopted sexual slander as a weapon entered a battle already waged, to varying degrees, in terms of sexual morality. Entering the fray, Christians frequently reinscribed a view of sexual morality that they shared with their neighbors, but they turned the tables of the argument by claiming virtue for themselves alone. Having staked their own claim to legitimacy on the basis of their (supposed) moral excellence, Christian authors could then use vituperative charges of sexual misbehavior against one another in a particularly effective way. Having constituted the category "true Christian" in terms of sexual purity, accusations of sexual vice from one Christian against another would have been received as an especially sharp critique.

To conclude, the early Christian authors under consideration here operated within their particular cultural and rhetorical contexts, employing tools of rhetoric they shared with their neighbors in ways that served their own persuasive projects. This book considers the discursive production of Christian "virtue" and "vice" within a matrix of power-laden, socially formulated categories that these authors both inherited and (re)fashioned to their advantage. Averil Cameron has observed that there is no one Christian discourse, but rather "a series of overlapping discourses always in a state of adaptation and adjustment, and always ready to absorb in a highly opportunistic manner whatever might be useful from secular rhetoric and vocabulary."[73] With this in mind, I have selected a set of Christian texts dating from the first through the third centuries for more careful study.[74] By examining sexual slander as a discursive practice implicated in competitive struggles for power and prestige, within the context of ancient polemics and within specific Christian texts, I seek to illuminate the functions of ancient sexual slander, especially as this slander participated in and enforced what Elizabeth Clark has called an early Christian "gendered disciplinary apparatus" designed to control insiders, shame outsiders, and, as I will argue, undermine anyone and everyone who would oppose their particular point of view.[75]

CHAPTER 1

Sexual Slander and Ancient Invective

There are perhaps few characters in Roman history as devious, greedy, and full of lust as Antony and Cleopatra, if we believe the representations of them found in ancient history and biography. Following the battle of Actium, Cassius Dio tells us, Cleopatra tricked Antony into taking his own life. Antony chose to enslave himself to her in life, and he remained her slave in death, demonstrating his servile nature (*douloprepeia*), even at the end (Cass. Dio 51.10–11, 15.2). Cleopatra, Cassius Dio concludes, had an insatiable appetite for pleasure and material wealth, an appetite that led, ultimately, to both her and Antony's demise (51.15.4). According to Plutarch, Cleopatra disarmed Antony and made sport of him (*Demetr.* .3; *Antony* 10.3; 25.1–28.1). From the perspective of many ancient authors, therefore, "Marcus Antonius was not merely a ruffian and a gladiator, a drunkard and a debauchee—he was effeminate and a coward"[1] and Cleopatra was "the Egyptian whore, a drunkard, and the mistress of eunuchs."[2] These representations have left their mark. According to Paul Zanker, Antony must have been utterly captivated by the infamous and beautiful Cleopatra, for how else could he have behaved like an "Oriental" instead of a "soldierly Roman"? "Antony had become totally corrupt, godless, and soft and was bewitched by Cleopatra. What else could explain why a Roman general would award conquered territory to the children of an Egyptian queen and even put in his will that he wanted to be buried in Alexandria beside Cleopatra?"[3] In the tradition of ancient biographers and historians before him, Zanker concluded that Antony was truly "a victim of the decadence and debauchery of the East."[4]

Whether or not Antony was a victim of decadence and debauchery, especially of the "Eastern" type, is for others to decide. Yet, it is worth noticing that the charges lodged against him by some modern and many ancient historians—decadence and debauchery—are standard fare in Roman political discourse. Cicero had accused Catiline of similar crimes:

> What mark of family scandal is there not branded upon your life? What deplorable episode in your personal affairs does not help form your reputation? What lust has never shone in your eyes, what crime has never stained your hands, what shameful deed has never fouled your entire body?
>
> (*Cat.* 1.13–16)[5]

Catiline's private life was so monstrous, his disgrace so complete, Cicero argues, that it scarcely needs to be mentioned, though Cicero spent a great deal of time doing so. What is one to make of all this? Shall we assume that Catiline was a degenerate, Antony a reprobate, and Cleopatra a conniving seductress?

Catherine Edwards has argued that the vilification of Antony must be placed in the context of the Roman invective tradition.[6] References to proper "morality" were offered to support claims of legitimacy in the competitive rivalries between elites.[7] Accusations of corrupt morals were intended to delegitimize these claims. The period between the assassination of Caesar and the battle of Actium was marked by relentless denunciations of Octavian by Antony and Antony by Octavian. Both were accused of adultery, bribery, and luxury. Similarly, in the war of words between Cicero and Piso, Cicero was also accused of indulging in the very things of which he so vociferously accused Piso.[8] Allegations of moral turpitude made by rival Roman nobles against one another can be read as part of a long rhetorical tradition. Ancient Greek rhetorical theorists emphasized the importance of morality to orators, especially the knowledge of the virtues and their opposites.[9] Roman rhetorical theorists acknowledged their debt to Greece in this regard, though they did endeavor to differentiate themselves from the Greek tradition.[10] During the Roman period, economic and political crises were represented as crises of morality.[11] The virtues were personified, worshiped, celebrated on coins, listed on inscriptions honoring the exemplary virtue of famous Romans from the past.[12] Historians explained historical events "not in terms of social and economic forces but almost entirely in terms of the moral attributes of the characters involved."[13] Cicero assumed that evaluations of character are standard subjects in history (*De or.* 2.63). Suetonius assessed each Caesar by means of a "minute examination of his record in certain areas of moral behavior."[14] The effects of these competitions in virtue and vice were felt not only in the small circle of the Roman senatorial class, but beyond: "All Romans and non-Romans living within the Empire's borders … were eventually exposed to the dissemination of the *virtutes Romanae*, even if only through the odd coin or family epitaph."[15] It is perhaps naive, therefore, to take at face value the lurid representations offered of Cleopatra, Antony, and others.[16] Nevertheless, these depictions do indicate something about what was considered "good" or "bad" behavior.

This chapter illustrates the importance of claims regarding virtue and vice to the discourse of the imperial period. Sexual slander, ancient and contemporary, is tied to power relations and to knowledge production. Assigning meaning to words, in this case words signaling virtue or vice, is a power-laden process, a site of conflict and contention within which the dynamics of power relations are negotiated. This was no less true for Greeks and Romans than for Christians. Literate Christians, those under consideration here, shared a great deal with other literate people in the ancient Mediterranean world.[17] They were trained in similar rhetorical techniques, informed by popular philosophical arguments, at least to some degree, and exposed to the same coins, inscriptions, legal pronouncements, building projects, and statuary as their neighbors. When Christians employed charges of sexual licentiousness to define themselves over and against others, they relied upon a long-standing discursive strategy that would have been familiar to everyone. Since definitions of sexual impropriety shift, it becomes important to explore the content and significance of these charges, both for Christians and those whom they attacked, to delve into the ancient fascination with virtue and its opposites in order to better situate Christian discourses discussed in later chapters.

SEX TALK AND ANCIENT RHETORICAL THEORY

Success as an orator, Aristotle observed, demands three capabilities: the capacity to reach logical conclusions, the ability to observe closely characters and virtues, and, thirdly, an understanding of the emotions (*Rh.* 1356a). Logical argument is only one element of an effective speech; sensitivity to the attitudes of the audience and familiarity with the virtues are equally important. This is the case for each of the three types of rhetoric that Aristotle identifies: deliberative (συμβουλευτικός), forensic (δικανικός), and epideictic (ἐπιδεικτικός). This threefold categorization was largely maintained in later Greek and Latin rhetorical theory. Virtue was said to be the primary topic of epideictic oratory, speeches that take as their subject praise (ἔπαινος) or blame (ψόγος), yet considerations of virtue and character are central to all three. In forensic oratory, rhetoric intended for the law courts, the ability of the orator to rouse the emotions of the jury by demonstrating that he is true (ἀληθής) and good (ἀγαθός) while the opponent is false (ψευδής) and bad (κακός) was understood to be an essential task (*Rh.* 1419b). So too, when offering a deliberative speech before the assembly, one must be cognizant of both virtue and emotion. Virtue, Aristotle insisted, is essential to happiness, and happiness is the aim of both city and citizen (*Rh.* 1360a).[18] Therefore, one needs to be familiar with the virtues when composing any speech, whatever the type of speech or its occasion. Furthermore, the moral character of the orator himself is fundamental to the ability of a given speaker to persuade. A good man makes a good orator (*Rh.* 1356a).[19]

Cicero, writing in Rome several centuries later, agreed in many respects with Aristotle's assessment of the importance of virtue and emotion to good oratory. The excellence of the orator is demonstrated by his ability to "rouse men's hearts to anger, hatred, or indignation" or to recall them from these passions, a task that is impossible without an understanding of the human character (*De or.* 1.12.53). Therefore, though philosophers claim that the discussion of the virtues is their exclusive domain, orators must be able to discuss them with an even greater eloquence (*De or.* 1.13.56). Additionally, successful persuasion requires that the audience approve of the character, principles, and lifestyle of both the orator and, in the case of forensic oratory, the person whom the orator is defending. Cicero offered advice on how to appear trustworthy and virtuous while describing the upright, modest character of one's client, if at all possible (*De or.* 2.43.182–87).

Quintilian went further, arguing that the positive formation of moral character is the most important accomplishment of a proper rhetorical education (*Inst.* 1.9–10).[20] As a result, Quintilian averred, his subject matter (oratory) demanded that he frequently speak of the virtues courage (*fortitudo*), justice (*iustitia*), and self-control (*temperantia*). "In fact," he wrote, "scarcely a case comes up in which some one of these virtues is not involved" (*Inst.* 1.12). An anonymous Greek contemporary agreed, claiming that the true purpose of good education (παιδεία) is moral excellence (ἀρετή) and happiness (εὐδαιμονία; [Plutarch] *Mor.* 5c), yet this author warned against paying attention to the "nonsense of ostentatious public discourse," the purview of many false orators who know only how to please audiences ([Plutarch], *Mor.* 6a–d). Rhetorical education has its place but must be given with caution. This advice echoes the earlier concerns of Plato, who persistently argued that the tools of rhetoric are dangerous when placed in the wrong hands (Plato *Prt.* 318E–319B; *Grg.* 451D. See also *Soph.*, esp. 232A).[21]

Even this brief survey of the "art of rhetoric" as presented by Aristotle, Cicero, and Quintilian reveals that a comprehensive understanding of virtue, morality, character, and the emotions was viewed as essential to the success of the orator. Orators took this advice to heart; appeals to emotion and character pervade the speeches that have been preserved from this period and beyond.[22] Rhetorical appeals to character were remarkably constant, including the terms and behaviors offered as examples of exemplary or reprehensible conduct; indeed, a rather fixed repertoire of virtues and vices said to reveal the good or bad man emerged. Perhaps the repetitive nature of moral categories was the result, in part, of the type of education students of rhetoric received. As part of their rhetorical training, students were expected to master sets of commonplaces designed to describe the character of the person or people they were discussing.[23]

COMMONPLACE VIRTUE AND VICE

Standard topics of praise (*epainos, laudatio*) or blame (*psogos, vituperatio*) were outlined in Greek rhetorical handbooks (*progymnasmata*) and in Latin oratorical treatises. In his handbook, Ap(h)thonius recommended that the following topics be addressed: family, nation, ancestors, livelihood, customs, prudence, beauty, manliness, and bodily strength, among other features (*Prog.* 8).[24] In his *De inventione rhetorica*, Cicero offered an almost identical list. (177–78).[25] An anonymous third-century C.E. teacher of rhetoric recommended that cities, emperors, and governors alike be praised, when possible, for their temperance (*sōphrosynē*), justice (*dikaiosynē*), and wisdom (*phronēsis*; Men. Rhet. 364, 375, 380, 384).[26] When praising or blaming cities, one should consider the amount of bad behavior (*hamartēmata*) evident there, especially whether or not citizens often commit adultery (364.1–2). When praising an emperor, one should note that, because of the emperor's good example, "marriages are chaste, fathers have legitimate offspring, spectacles, festivals and competitions are conducted with proper splendor and due moderation [*sōphrosynē*]" (376.5).

To Aristotle, a speech of blame (*psogos*) was intimately related to a speech of praise (*epainos*), and together they constitute the category epideictic oratory.[27] Since vice (*kakia*) is the opposite of virtue (*aretē*), when one knows the virtues, one can easily identify the vices.[28] Virtues and vices reveal states of character; we can judge character by the relative amount of virtue or vice displayed in the voluntary actions each person undertakes (*Eth. Nic.* 1106a17; 1110a10–1112a11). The rhetorical handbooks largely shared this view and, when discussing the sources of encomium (a speech of praise) or invective (a speech of blame), outlined standard categories, applicable for both. Thus, for example, when offering praise, one could refer to the noble origin of the subject's family. If, on the contrary, blame was appropriate, one could discuss the servile, lowly origin of the subject and his family.[29] According to the first-century C.E. rhetorician Theon, a student should consider the following categories when composing a speech of praise:

I. Exterior Excellences
   A. Noble birth (*eugeneia*)
   B. Environment
      1. native city
      2. fellow citizens
      3. excellence of the city's government
      4. ancestors and family
   C. Personal advantages
      1. education
      2. friends
      3. fame
      4. public service
      5. wealth
      6. number and beauty of children
      7. happy death

II. Bodily Excellences
    A. Health
    B. Strength
    C. Beauty
    D. Vitality

III. Spiritual Excellences
     A. Virtues
        1. wisdom
        2. moderation
        3. courage

    4. justice
    5. piety
    6. nobility
    7. liberality
B. Actions following from the virtues
    1. those following from their aims
      a. altruistic
      b. good
      c. acts in the public interest
      d. braves dangers
    2. the circumstances of the virtuous actions
      a. timely
      b. original
      c. performed alone
      d. surpassed others
      e. received little help from others
      f. acted with wisdom beyond his years
      g. persevered against all odds
      h. at great personal cost
      i. done promptly and efficiently[30]

A survey of classical and Hellenistic Greek sources yielded the following set of recommended categories for the successful composition of a speech of blame:

(1) former life as a slave or slave ancestry
(2) non-Greek origin
(3) having to work for a living
(4) being a thief or behaving like one
(5) engagement in reprehensible sexual acts
(6) hating one's family and friends (being a *misophilos*) or one's city (being a *misopolis*)
(7) having a gloomy nature
(8) improper appearance, dress, or behavior
(9) military desertion
(10) bankruptcy.[31]

Note how closely this list follows the recommended outline for a speech of praise, with each of the outlined sections assigned an opposite disadvantage or vice: noble birth or slave origin, association with a noble

(Greek) city or non-Greek origin, education and wealth or having to work in a degrading occupation, self-control or reprehensible sexual behavior, beauty and health or improper appearance and dress, courage or military desertion, vitality or gloominess. A summary of Latin invective terminology yielded similar categories, with lowly origin, degrading occupation, improper appearance, criminality, sexual vice, and gluttony emerging as central topics.[32]

Clearly, when learning to compose speeches, especially those of the epideictic type, students were offered detailed advice on appropriate commonplaces, including those pertaining to sexual behavior.[33] Accusations regarding improper sexual behavior were one of an arsenal of topics one could use to label an enemy as dangerous, incompetent, treasonous, or corrupt. By contrast, proper sexual behavior could demonstrate the praiseworthiness of a person or a city or even a king, at least according to ancient rhetorical theory. Furthermore, this repertoire of recommended topics was remarkably consistent across Greek and Latin rhetorical treatises, especially those concerning epideictic literature.[34] As we shall see, the speeches of Attic Greek orators such as Isocrates and Demosthenes contained many of the standard topics;[35] these speeches, in turn, became models for later orators who emulated many of the same themes. In this way, set commonplaces continued to inform moralizing discourse across several centuries.

MODEL ORATORY

Many of the topics and categories recommended by the later handbooks appear in Isocrates' *Panegyricus*.[36] This was Isocrates' "greatest speech,"[37] composed to convince the Greeks, including Sparta, to unite against the "barbarians" under the leadership of Athens.[38] According to Isocrates, the Athenians enjoyed a noble lineage, having sprung from the very soil they currently possess. Athens is characterized by justice, having established laws and a polity (*Paneg.* 39). She has given philosophy to the world. She remains brave in battle and never shrinks from duty (*Paneg.* 47, 75). When dealing with other states, the Athenians do not glory in their power but rather promoted self-control (*sōphrosynē, Paneg.* 81). The Persians, by contrast, are the opposite of these just, temperate, and courageous Athenians. They are excessively rich and therefore "pamper their bodies" (*Paneg.* 150).[39] They are faithless toward their friends and cowardly toward their foes (*Paneg.* 151). Their style of government produces a servile nature (*Paneg.* 152). Therefore, the Hellenes must not stand by while all of Hellas is being continually outraged (ὑβρίζομενης)[40] by these faithless, cowardly, and corrupt people (*Paneg.* 181). All of Greece was urged to revolt.

In this speech, the Athenians and the Persians were portrayed in predictable ways: The Athenians possess an exceptionally noble origin. They are wise, having given philosophy to the world. They are temperate (*sōphrosynē*), even when dealing with the people they have conquered. They are courageous and never shrink from battle. The barbarians, however, cannot be said to possess a noble origin. Whatever their origin, they display a servile nature (δουλοπρέπεια). They are extravagant, spending excessive amounts indulging themselves.[41] They are cowardly, faithless, and so on. Many of the standard categories appear.

A further example can be found in a forensic speech of Demosthenes, that "pillar" of classical education.[42] In his speech *De corona*, Demosthenes defended his private life and his public transactions in response to charges made by his accuser, Aeschines (*De cor.* 8). He did so by means of a series of attacks on the origin, education, occupation, and character of Aeschines: Aeschines was not properly educated; rather, he makes pretensions to the culture (*paideia*) that he is so obviously lacking (128).[43] His father was a slave. His mother engaged in indiscriminate sexual intercourse in a public latrine. He was brought up to excel in minor parts on the stage (129). His servile origin and lack of means led him to accept menial and degrading occupations (258). He possesses a spiteful temper, demonstrated by his mean-spirited attack on Demosthenes (252–53). He involves himself in suspect religious rituals involving exotic apparel and associations with old women (260). Demosthenes, on the other hand, was well educated and avoided turning to disreputable occupations to support himself (257).

A speech of Aeschines, Demosthenes' rival, given during the prosecution of Timarchus serves as a final example.[44] Timarchus was accused of prostituting himself in his youth and squandering his inheritance. A person who prostitutes himself (acting as either a πορνή or a ἑταῖρος), Aeschines argued, cannot be trusted to act in the best interest of the city: "One who had been a vendor of his own body for others to treat as they pleased would have no hesitation in selling the interests of the community as a whole" (*In Tim.* 32).[45] Demosthenes offered the speech for the defense. Aeschines prevailed and Timarchus was disenfranchised.

The speeches of Isocrates, Demosthenes, and Aeschines were standard fare in later Greek and Roman rhetorical education. About Isocrates, Cicero commented, "Then behold! There arose Isocrates, the master of all rhetoricians, from whose school, as from the Horse of Troy, none but leaders emerged" (*De or.* 22.94). Demosthenes and Aeschines were revered as experts at forensic oratory (*De or.* 23.94–95). Quintilian began his discussion of speeches of praise (*laudem*) and blame (*vituperationem*) with a discussion of Isocrates, remarking that Isocrates thought praise and blame had a place in every kind of oratory (*Inst.* 3.4.11). In two of his parallel *Lives*, Plutarch compared the Greek orator and politician Demosthenes with the Roman orator and politician Cicero. These two shared much in common, Plutarch stated, since both rose from obscurity to positions of influence by means of their remarkable oratorical skill (Plut. *Dem.* 2.3–4; Plutarch, *Comparatio Ciceronis cum Demosthene*): Demosthenes surpassed the eloquence and force of his rivals when delivering forensic speeches, and when offering deliberative speeches, his mastery of the art of rhetoric was clearly greater than that of other professional declaimers (*Comparatio Ciceronis cum Demosthene*, 1.1). Dio Chrysostom similarly asserted that Demosthenes was the best of the Attic orators. His style was the most vigorous, his thought the most impressive, and his vocabulary the most extensive of all the rhetoricians (*Or.* 18.11).

Clearly, literate people received a rhetorical training that included detailed instructions on how to offer praise or blame in a variety of contexts. As part of their education, young men during the imperial period would have become at least somewhat familiar with the speeches of select Attic orators—speeches that contained numerous examples of the commonplaces appropriate to praise or blame—and they were encouraged to refer to these commonplaces in their own speeches. This training provided its students with a stereotyped portrait of an ideal man: a man who could list illustrious ancestors, boast of his excellent city, and name his honorable friends. Such a man mastered both himself and his subordinates. He was brave in the face of danger but never rash. By contrast, his less honorable, less manly opposite failed to control his passions. His origins were humble and his circumstances unfortunate. He deserted his duty and hated his friends. These rhetorical commonplaces could be generalized to include entire groups, as Isocrates' speech to the Athenians demonstrates. Cities and their citizens could be described as brave, noble, just, and temperate or, alternatively, as servile, extravagant, disloyal, and cowardly. Good men, and the cities they ruled, displayed virtue. Bad men failed at ruling both themselves and their subjects. In other words, assertions regarding the control of self and others served to define and justify elite privilege. In this context, sexual propriety signified the "refinement and self-control that distinguished the well-born from their unruly inferiors."[46] An accusation of sexual impropriety, therefore, was a sharp rebuke designed to indicate that a man had become "like" the subordinates he was supposed to be ruling. Such accusations reiterated and reinforced cultural values regarding "natural" status and gender.

SEX, STATUS, AND "NATURAL" GENDER

The second-century humorist Lucian offered the following description of the dangers of Rome:

> Whoever loves wealth and is enchanted by gold, who by purple and power measures happiness, who has not tasted liberty or experienced free speech or contemplated truth, whose constant companions are flattery and servility; whoever has committed his entire soul to pleasure and resolved to serve pleasure alone, loving elaborate dining and wine and sexual pleasure, being full of trickery, treachery and falsehood; whoever enjoys hearing stringed instruments, whistling, and corrupt songs—'Such a one,' said he, 'ought to be suited to life here [in Rome], for every place and every agora is full of the things they love most, and they admit pleasure at every gate—this one by the eyes, that one by the ears or the nostrils, yet another by the throat and by sexual intercourse. By its ever-flowing, foul stream every street is widened; for it [Rome] brings in adultery, greed, false testimony and the whole family of the pleasures, and the soul, flooded from every side, is laid bare of modesty, virtue, and justice; and then the ground, having become a desert, forever burning with thirst, blooms with many a wild passion.
>
> (*Nigr.* 15–16)[47]

In this packed sketch of the vices of Rome, Lucian suggested that the city and its citizens were utterly enslaved to desire (ἐπιθυμία). According to Lucian, the person most suited to the depraved environment of the capital city had committed his soul to pleasure (ἡδονή); he devoted himself to elaborate dinner parties, wine, and sexual pleasure (ἀφροδίσια: what belongs to Aphrodite, i.e., sexual enjoyment).[48] Given his propensity for excess, this person can also be expected to deceive others, to act like a sycophant, and to offer false testimony.[49] Apparently, pleasure leads the city and its denizens to commit adultery (μοιχεία), together with everything else associated with illicit sex and community corruption.[50]

An anonymous contemporary of Lucian, offering his advice on how to educate young men properly, warned fathers that if they do not pay close attention to the education and rearing of their sons, they may end up be-having much like the dissolute Romans described by Lucian above:

> [They will] disdain the sane and orderly life, and throw themselves headlong into disorderly and slavish pleasures.... Some of them take up with flatterers and parasites,[51] men of obscure origin, corrupters and spoilers of youth, and others buy the freedom of courtesans [ηεταιρασ] and prostitutes [χηαμαιτψπασ], proud and sumptuous in expense; still others give themselves up to the pleasures of the table, while others come to wreck in dice and revels, and some finally engage in the wildest forms of vices, committing adultery and being decked with ivy,[52] ready to pay with life itself for a single pleasure.
>
> ([Plutarch] Mor. 5b–c)[53]

Musonius Rufus offered a similar warning, contrasting two young men, one "reared in luxury, his body effeminate, his spirit weakened by soft living, and having beside a dull and torpid disposition" and the other, unaccustomed to luxury, "practiced in self-restraint, and ready to listen to sound reasoning." The latter model was clearly to be preferred (Muson. 5–10).[54] According to Cicero, extravagant young men should not to be trusted, since revelry and a tendency toward treason often accompany one another (*Cat.* 2.10). A city—or a father—that fails to control its youth will come to ruin, or so these authors suggested.

Anxieties about the ill effects of luxury and overindulgence in plea-sure—lampooned by Lucian, warned against by Cicero, pseudo-Plutarch, and Musonius—abound in the moralizing discourse of this period. Sexual "crimes"—failure at self-mastery, enslavement to lust, whoring, effemi-nacy, adulteries, orgies, and so on—were imagined as signs of corruption and decay, a threat to a proper order that placed free, citizen men at the helm. In this way, sexualized invective participated in the naturalization of status norms. Ancient status positions—free, free noncitizen, citizen, freed, slave—were not based on inherent characteristics but discursively produced and maintained.[55] Greek and Roman "elites," and I use the term provisionally, may have discussed and legislated status as if it were a given, as if it was entirely obvious who may legitimately claim noble origin, free birth, and citizenship; a closer look reveals just how contested these cat-egories were. We have already noted that, according to ancient rhetorical theory, there were sets of attributes said to characterize "the good man," including noble origin, self-mastery, and courage. Bad men, then, were of servile or foreign origin, incapable of controlling themselves, and cowardly in battle. Legal and literary sources further promoted this view, suggesting that to be a slave or a foreigner necessarily implies that one is ignoble, incapable of true wisdom, and immoral, or simply exempt from morality altogether. The social-discursive production of "citizen" versus everyone else, especially "slave," served to constrain and constitute the definition of each.

Keith Bradley has argued that Roman slavery was "primarily a social, not an economic category." As a result, the Romans maintained "a stereotyped portrait of the slave as an unscrupulous, lazy, and criminous being, and while they thought of certain races, Asiatic Greeks, Syrians, and Jews, as being born for slavery, and while they thought certain punishments like crucifixion and burning alive were suitably servile, they never thought of any one form of work as being specifically appropriate just for slaves."[56] Bradley demonstrates that slaves fulfilled a dizzying array of economic roles during the early empire; some were very wealthy and owned slaves themselves. One is tempted to ask, then, what precisely was the distinction between slave and free? Perhaps "thinking" of slaves in a stereotyped way was a necessary prop to the rather slippery, uncertain boundary between slave and free. We know who is a citizen because he is not a slave. We know who is a slave because he is not a citizen. These knowledges reinforced and implied one another.

The theory that slaves are different from their masters "by nature" was infamously stated by Aristotle in the *Politics*. Aristotle argued that slaves have no faculty of deliberation but require their masters, those who have the capacity for moral goodness, to rule over them (*Pol.* 1260a4–1260b8). Freeborn women were said to be similarly incapacitated by the peculiarity of their gender—they do possess the faculty of deliberation but in them it lacks authority (*Pol.* 1260a4). Craftsmen and the like, those who labor for their living, free by birth or formerly slaves, can possess some virtue, though in a measure proportionate to the extent of servitude their profession requires of them (*Pol.* 1260a33). Therefore, slaves, laborers, and women cannot be citizens in the ideal polis since they lack the requisite capacity for virtue (1277b33–1278a40. Compare Plato *Leg.* 264e). Though Aristotle should not be viewed as representative of the entire ancient world, he was far from alone in his insistence that slaves, women, and, to a lesser extent, laborers (often thought to be former slaves, i.e., "freedmen") are deficient in virtue.[57] Nevertheless, slaves and freedmen could be "upwardly mobile,"[58] and an exceptional former slave could become a well-known philosopher.[59] The fact that such supposed anomalies could occur demonstrates that these categories were not impermeable but were, in fact, always dangerously subject to renegotiation.

The proposition that virtue has little or nothing to do with slaves was reiterated and enforced in legal sources. In both Athens and Rome, slaves were held to an entirely different sexual standard than were their masters.[60] According to Roman law, slaves could not legally marry (though at least some did "marry" anyway). [61] They were the sexual property of their masters and could not initiate sexual relations, even with other slaves, without their masters' permission.[62] Were they to do so, they could be punished or even, in the case of adultery with a free woman, executed.[63] In both the Greek and Roman case, prostitutes were often slaves, and a low sort of slave at that.[64] Freedmen and wage-laborers were often assimilated to the category "slave" as well, with Cicero asserting that anyone who works for wages lives in a state of slavery (*Off.* 1.150–1).[65]

Whether or not the author or the target of sexualized invective should be considered "an elite" in an economic or sociological sense is not my primary concern. Rather, I am interested in the various arguments marshaled to define what an "elite"—usually thought to be a freeborn, citizen male—is and what he does or does not do. In the introduction, I argued that power is social and discursive, not a thing that a person or group possesses. So too with "status."[66] Status is negotiated and produced and therefore vulnerable to change. Thus, those claiming to be elite, those who argue that they deserve special benefits or authority, must describe what it is that justifies their privileged status. In the words of Althusser, they must create an "ideological apparatus" capable of supporting their claims. Alternatively, knowledges must be produced and reproduced that enable "the elite" to constitute themselves as such.

In the ancient context, sexual behavior was an important component of the production and maintenance of status. The freeborn, citizen male was thought to be—told he should be, claimed he was—in control of his passions. He avoids excess. He is the active partner in sexual acts. To fail in these areas is to fail as both a man and as a citizen.[67] Charges of sexual vice, therefore, could serve to discount an individual's claim to status, just as praise of an individual's sexual virtue could justify his privilege. Those who (in theory) could not possibly be virtuous also could not possibly be "elite." Those who were supposed to be elite (they were, for example, freeborn) and yet failed to display virtue, especially sexual self-mastery, could not really deserve to be so. They were corrupt, depraved, unworthy. Sex was an essential ingredient to this discourse. Actual status (free, resident foreigner, freed, slave) was fundamental to whether or not a sexual act would be considered criminal in a legal sense. Furthermore, sexual acts dramatized status distinctions, reenacting a "natural" (i.e., entirely conventional) hierarchy along the lines of active partner or passive partner, dominant or submissive. The elite male was imagined as the actor and the dominator, at least in theory. Often, accusations of sexual misbehavior implied the violation of a prescribed role in this sexual drama, a drama imagined as the interplay between an active, citizen male partner and his various subordinates.

In the late 1970s, Kenneth Dover set out to describe the phenomena of homosexuality in ancient Greece. His "relentlessly empirical approach"[68] succeeded in countering the skepticism of several generations of classical scholars regarding the nature of "Greek love," and, in the process, he put forward a series of persuasive hypotheses regarding the attitudes of ancient Greeks toward homosexual behavior. Some of his main arguments include: (1) There was no moral censure against an adult male taking an adolescent boy as a lover. Indeed, men are expected to find both young males and females beautiful (καλός) and to desire them both. (2) Athenian law and custom did not disapprove of the sexual expression of this desire, as long as certain conventions were observed, including the preference for intercrural copulation and the view that the youth did not (or should not) seek sensual pleasure for himself from his lover.[69] (3) In light of the first two propositions, domination and submission were important organizing principles for what was considered proper sexuality for citizen Greek males. The adult citizen male must always be in the dominant position. He penetrates; he pursues. Women, slaves, young boys, and foreigners—the citizen male's "natural" subordinates—are pursued and penetrated; they are expected to be submissive. Near-adult citizen males, those who will soon assume the prerogatives of Greek manhood, can be loved and pursued by their adult counterparts, but they are expected to resist, at least partially, the advances of their adult lovers, refusing penetration in most cases.

Numerous scholars have made similar observations regarding the importance of dominance/submission and active/passive as organizing principles in ancient constructions of sexuality. To David Halperin, sex in Greek society "is conceived to center on, and to define itself around, an asymmetrical gesture, that of the penetration of one person by the body—and, specifically, by the phallus—of another."[70] Eva Cantarella agrees, noting that this view of Greek sexuality was "confirmed by Dover, maintained by Foucault in the volume on Greece in his *History of Sexuality* and extended by Veyne

to the Roman sexual ethic." She asserts: "The fundamental dichotomy between different types of sexual behavior, in antiquity, was not between het-
erosexuality and homosexuality, but between active and passive behavior.
Active behavior properly belonged to adult males, while women and *paides*
were supposed to practice passive behavior."[71] Regarding Roman sexual
theory, Amy Richlin notes, "clearly, what bothered the Romans most in
male homosexual behavior was assimilation to the female (i.e., receptive)
role, as witnessed by the definition of the pathic."[72] In his extended study of
Roman homoerotic (male) sex, Craig Williams recently concluded that "according to the prime directive of masculine sexual behavior, a Roman man
who wished to retain his claim to full masculinity must always be thought
to play the insertive role in penetrative acts, whether with males or females;
if he was thought to have sought the receptive role in such acts, he forfeited
his claim to masculinity and was liable to being mocked as effeminate."[73]

This active/passive paradigm was further supported by the complex of
charges present in ancient invective. Men who indulged in excessive luxury
were labeled "slavish." Like slaves, they had no control of their passions.
Their "slavishness" called into question their sexual habits, for slaves were
expected to be the passive partner in sexual acts with their masters, not the
other way around. If they were "slavish" in their personal habits, did they
also seek to be the passive partner in sexual acts? If so, then they must be
entirely depraved, like prostitutes who offer their bodies to anyone. These
accusations offer just a sampling of the manifold ways in which accusations regarding sexual acts—configured around active or passive roles—
were employed to attack an elite man for violating his status.

According to this paradigm, gender—and the sex appropriate to various genders—were presented as types rather than fixed identities. As
Maude Gleason has shown, in ancient medical texts, "masculinity" or
"femininity" were defined not in terms of anatomical sex but as a "type"
or a "style." A man could be like a woman, a woman like a man. "Masculinity" (ἀρσενικός) and "femininity" (θηλυκός) "function as physiog-
nomical categories for *both* male and female subjects."[74] Thus, Polemo,
a first-century native of Laodicea and author of *Physiognomy*, concluded,
"the male is in every way opposite to this description, and it is possible to
find masculine qualities also in women."[75] In this scheme, it becomes possible to malign an opponent for being womanish and effeminate not only
because he sought the passive role in sexual acts but because he proved
himself to be "feminine" in other ways. Furthermore, a woman's desire
to assert "masculine" prerogatives, especially by seeking to penetrate an-

other, was viewed as unnatural and monstrous, a "horror" described for comedic effect by Lucian.[76]

In his *Dialogi meretricii*, Lucian described the love of one woman, Megilla, for another, Leaina. Megilla was depicted "like a man" (ἀνδρική); she wore her hair closely shorn, invited Leaina to call her Megillos, and seduced Leaina into sexual acts which were hinted at but never fully described (*Dial. meret.* 5). Though Lucian did not reveal the specifics of how Megilla satisfied herself, he assumed that whatever she did was "unnatural," "shameful," and masculine in some way.[77] Similarly, Seneca decried women who rival men in their lusts, who "having devised so deviant a type of shamelessness, enter men" (*Ep.* 95.20);[78] these women may become subject to male diseases and male habits.[79] The active woman was thought to penetrate her partner in some way, "like a man." Therefore, she "must become phallic."[80] The phallic female who seeks to seduce and penetrate was deemed both "masculine" and monstrous.[81] Masculinity and femininity, therefore, were configured as modalities or styles with the superordinate, phallic, active position identified as "male" and the subordinate, receptive, passive position as "female," irrespective of the "sex" of the actor so engaged.[82]

Beliefs about status, sex and gender—described and constituted across a range of ancient medical, literary, and legal sources—served as mutually reenforcing cultural codes.[83] Ancient authors "knew" who the elite were because the elite were "virtuous" and, as such, were not slaves. Men were "male" because they were phallic, active, dominant, and superordinate, and women were "female" because they were nonphallic, passive, submissive, and subordinate. Men who violated these categories by desiring "female" sexual satisfaction were depraved and "slavish." Similarly, women who dared to desire "male" sexual satisfaction were viewed as monstrous deviants. These dichotomies—free/slave, dominant/submissive, active/passive, male/female—appear repeatedly. In a world where the male elite were supposed to be naturally "virtuous," therefore, sexual slander could prove to be a dangerous rhetorical weapon since, by violating status in a sexual act, such men also violated "nature."

DEVIANCE DEPLOYED

What, then, were the common charges of sexual weakness? How did they participate in the maintenance and policing of status? What beliefs about gender and sexuality are assumed? To what ends were these charges employed? As was suggested by the above reading of ancient rhetorical theory, charges of sexual vice tended to appear in lists rather than separately. If a man was condemned for his extravagance, he was also likely to be condemned for adultery, effeminacy, corruption of boys, or some other related charge. If a woman was accused of sexual licentiousness, she was also likely to be accused of excessive adornment and concern for her appearance.[84] For the sake of convenience, however, I will discuss some of the more prevalent charges separately.

EXTRAVAGANT EXCESS

Extravagant spending on pleasure was roundly condemned by many ancient authors. For example, in his *Lives*, Plutarch characteristically related the relative extravagance (τρυφή or πολυτέλεια) of his subjects and judged them accordingly: Crassus spent too much money on dinner parties (*Niciae cum Crasso comparatio*, 1.4). Lucullus was to be criticized for his luxurious style of living; he wasted his money on ostentatious building projects and costly dining (*Luc.* 39–41) and was "extravagant and like a Persian satrap" (*Niciae cum Crasso comparatio*, 1.5–6).[85] Plutarch offered Lysander as a contrast to these negative exemplars: Lysander rejected the lavish clothing and jewelry sent to his daughters since such extravagant presents would disgrace both his daughters and his family (*Lys.* 2; compare *Mor.* 151d). Here, Plutarch echoed the earlier opinion of Aeschines that extravagant dinner parties, flute-girls, courtesans (ἑταιρεία), and gambling ought to be avoided by honorable men (*In Tim.* 1.42). In his moral essays, Plutarch repeatedly recommended moderation (σωφροσύνη) over extravagance (τρυφή). For instance, husbands were warned to avoid "gilded drinking-cups, pictured walls, trappings for mules, and showy neckbands for horses," since their extravagant behavior may be imitated by their wives (*Mor.* 145b).[86] A husband who indulged in luxury, a father who attended wild banquets set a poor example for his wife and children.[87]

Setting *tryphē* (extravagance, luxuriousness) as an antithesis to *sōphrosynē* (moderation, temperance), Plutarch participated in an argument he shared with several Cynic and Stoic philosophers: moderation counteracts extravagance (*tryphē*), luxuriousness (*polyteleia*), and licentiousness (*akolasia*).[88] The Stoic philosopher Musonius Rufus stated it this way: "Gluttony, drunkenness, and other related vices, which are vices of excess and bring disgrace on those who cherish them, show that moderation is necessary for every person, male or female, for the only way to escape licentiousness is moderation; there is no other" (Muson. 4.20).[89] According to these moralists, extravagance frequently included overindulgence in sexual pleasure, especially with prostitutes or courtesans. Musonius advised those trained in philosophy, honorable men who pursue moderation, to avoid courtesans (*hetairai*) altogether, as well as intercourse with their female slaves. Still, Musonius recognized that his was the minority view (12.10–45).[90] Visits to brothels (to a *pornē*, male or female, or a *chamaitupē*),[91] the presence of courtesans[92] at dinner parties, or a man's sexual involvement with his own slaves were not condemned—brothels were legal and taxed, as were procurers and individual prostitutes;[93] that slaves were the sexual property of their owners was assumed[94]—yet overexpenditure on such luxuries was often frowned upon. Quoting Diogenes, pseudo-Plutarch summed it up: "Go into any brothel [*porneion*] to learn that there is no difference between what costs money and what costs nothing" ([Plutarch] *Mor.* 5c).[95] Corrupted sons squander their inheritance on excessive visits to brothels, expensive courtesans, or buying the freedom of the slaves they enjoy.[96]

Interestingly, some Roman authors claimed that wasting money on prostitutes and wild drinking parties was a Greek trait, a characteristic of "Greek leisure" (*otium*), something that had unfortunately infected Rome.[97] It is therefore striking that Plutarch usually condemned the Roman exemplar in his parallel *Lives* for indulgence in extravagant excesses. Furthermore, in the example from Lucian above, it was Rome that was described as rank with luxuries and therefore also with vice. Nevertheless, from the Roman point of view, luxury was a foreign vice[98] For example, Sallust condemned Sulla for allowing his soldiers to indulge in "luxury and license foreign to the ways of our ancestors" (Sall. *Cat.* 11.5).[99] The Roman version of a "Greek life of pleasure" involved "imported wine and perfume, leisure, feasting, love, and literature." This was a " 'soft' life, *mollis* … a life which was defined, at least partly, in opposition to the more authentically 'Roman' life of frugality and military virtue."[100]

A paradigmatic example of the connection between luxury, sexual indulgence, prostitutes, and supposed foreign influence can be found in representations, preserved in historiography and biography, of the infamous emperor Gaius Caligula. According to Suetonius, Gaius outdid all others in his reckless extravagance—baths in oil, unusual foods, extensive feasting, expensive perfume, drinks of pearls dissolved in vinegar, meals of loaves and meats of gold, lazy trips in huge boats adorned with jewels, villas of tremendous size—he squandered over 2,700,000,000 sesterces in less than a year (Suet. *Calig.* 37).[101] This same Caligula was frequently remembered as associating himself with prostitutes (Suet. *Calig.* 41.1; Cass. Dio 59.28.9; Tac. *Ann.* 15.71). He instituted a new tax on prostitutes (Suet. *Calig,* 40; Cass. Dio 59.28.8),[102] he treated freeborn, Roman matrons as if they were prostitutes (*Calig* 36), and he opened a brothel in his palace, which he apportioned lavishly (*Calig.* 41).[103] Caligula followed in the footsteps of his great-grandfather, Marc Antony, by seeking to introduce Eastern ways to Rome and by displaying a troubling interest in Egyptian religious cults, or so his critics alleged.[104] Nero, emperor from 54 through 68 C.E., was described along similar lines. According to Suetonius, Nero's defects first became apparent when, at an early age, he played pranks on unsuspecting old men and women under the cover of darkness (Suet. *Ner.* 26.1–2).[105] He soon graduated to long revels that lasted nearly all day, accompanied by prostitutes and dancing girls. Like Caligula, he recruited noble women to act like prostitutes and squandered his riches. He sought to emulate his uncle's extravagance for "nothing so excited his envy and admiration as the fact that he [Caligula] had in so short a time run through the vast wealth that Tiberius had left him" (Suet. *Ner.* 27.2–3; 30.1–2).[106] Gaius Caligula and Nero were accused of other depraved habits, to be discussed in more detail below.

Thus lavish expenditure on sexual pleasure was repeatedly condemned by both Greek and Roman authors. Prostitution was legal and taxed, the presence of courtesans at the dinner parties of well-heeled gentlemen was expected, and slaves were required to comply with their masters' wishes, sexual and otherwise. Still, a man could be accused of "slavish" extravagance were he to overindulge in such delights. Such a man had no self-control; he could not be trusted since he was insatiable and immoderate. Building on this tradition, elites accused their rivals of lavish sexual self-indulgence,[107] and Roman historians judged emperors on the basis of the relative extravagance each ruler displayed.[108] During the imperial period, authors who identified as "Greek" and authors who identified as "Roman" both attributed the vice of extravagance to one another and to others they sought to distinguish from themselves—the Romans characterizing luxury and indolence as "Greek," the Greeks suggesting that it was Rome and the Romans who wallow in lasciviousness and luxury. Persia and "the East" continued to signify sumptuary excess, with Plutarch comparing Lucullus to a Persian satrap,[109] Octavian implying that Antony was under the influence of "the East" (Cass. Dio 48.301), and Caligula remembered for his devotion to Oriental ways. Clearly, this complex of charges—extravagance, "foreignness," excessive indulgence in sex with prostitutes, lack of moderation—could work to denigrate a variety of opponents, be they a single individual in a law court or even an entire nation of people.

FAILED MEN

In the famous speech already mentioned above, Aeschines accused Timarchus of prostituting himself, a crime for which Timarchus lost his Athenian citizenship. Timarchus was accused of violating the following Athenian law: "*If* a man who has prostituted himself thereafter addresses the assembly, holds an administrative office, etc., *then* an indictment, entitled 'indictment of *hetairesis*,' may be brought against him, and if he is found guilty, he may be executed."[110] By law, therefore, citizen males should not prostitute themselves and then later seek to address the assembly. If they did so, they would incur a serious penalty, even execution. Those charged with sexual extravagance were frequently accused of lavish expenditure on prostitutes and courtesans. Another strategy was to accuse the target not only of associating with prostitutes but of acting as a prostitute himself. Demosthenes came close to charging Aeschines of the same crime in his speech *De Corona*: he accused Aeschines of resorting to menial and degrading occupations in order to support himself (Dem. *De cor.* 258); he alluded to Aeschines' slave origins, suggesting that his mother acted as if she were a prostitute, his father wore shackles, and Aeschines was brought up to excel at acting in minor parts on the stage. (*De cor.* 129–31, 262–63). Though Demosthenes did not go so far as to directly charge Aeschines with prostituting himself, targeting Aeschines' mother instead, the allusions to Aeschines' ignoble origins, the degrading occupations he was forced to perform, and his association with the stage implied the worst.[111]

Those charged with prostituting themselves were further maligned by accusations of pathic anal sex and "womanly" behavior.[112] Two terms are of importance here: κίναιδος and ἀνδρόγυνος. Both refer to an "effeminate" man, a man with feminine characteristics (as those were variously defined), but *kinaidos* implies full sexual deviance, defined in its strictest sense as a man who enjoys playing the receptive role.[113] Demosthenes and Aeschines associated one another with the *kinaidoi*. Aeschines asserted that Demosthenes was an example of "unmanliness" in dress and behavior, insinuating that Demosthenes assimilated himself to women and slaves by seeking phallic penetration (*In Tim.* 3).[114] There were several labels—

effeminate, weak, soft, womanish[115]—available to accuse a man of being "feminine," preference for the passive role being the most disturbing.[116] For example, one could be "soft" (i.e., effeminate) and therefore more likely to take bribes (too soft to resist money), a charge that rested on beliefs about gender, even if the main point was that this man takes bribes (Plut. *Them.* 4.1).

The accusation that a man had failed at being a "man"—or, worse, had intentionally revoked his male privileges by seeking sexual penetration—was repeated in later, Roman-era sources. For example, Apuleius compared his target Aemilianus to a brothel, calling him a "vile haunt and hideous habitation of lust and gluttony"; Aemilianus was a stage-dancer in his youth, Apuleius continued, yet he was "clumsy and inartistic in his very effeminacy" (Apul. *Apol.* 74).[117] According to Apuleius, then, Aemilianus had not only failed at being a "man," he had failed at being a "woman" as well. Often, as in the case of the charge of luxury, Greeks were blamed by their Roman counterparts. Plutarch complained that Romans typically characterized Greeks as soft (*malakia*) and slavish (*douleia*; *Mor. (Quaest. Rom).* 40.274d). Tacitus lamented the encroachment of Greek ways on Roman life, especially the new Roman habit of "indulging in the gymnasia and idleness and disgraceful love-affairs" (*Ann.* 14.20).[118] Cicero attacked Antony for turning his toga[119] into a whore's garment: Antony, Cicero alleged, was a common prostitute.[120] Cicero offered other less direct but equally suggestive insults to the "manhood" of other opponents. Catiline's "boys," Cicero argued, "loved to dance and sing, but also to brandish daggers and infuse poison" (*Cat.* 2.23). Could Cicero intend "daggers" to contain a double meaning here? Similarly, Suetonius criticized both Caligula and Nero for their effeminate tendencies. Not only did they desire to be penetrated, they adopted a feminine gait, wore women's clothing, and pampered themselves with perfumes.[121] Caligula had an insatiable desire for phallic penetration, Suetonius claimed (*Calig.* 36.1). He wore exotic, feminine garments, including a woman's robe and shoes (52.1). He fancied himself a singer or dancer, singing along with actors on the stage, and dancing in front of three consulars in a long cloak (54.1–2). He kissed an actor he particularly liked in public (55.1). Nero defiled every part of his body, enjoying the passive role in sexual acts with his freedmen (*Nero* 29.1), yet he also lusted after boys, and even went so far as to violate free-born youths (28.1).[122]

From Attic Greece to the Roman imperial era, therefore, rhetorical targets were maligned, rivals were eliminated, and rulers were denounced for failing to display and maintain "manliness." These men were said to be "effeminate" or "soft" and even to seek "feminine" sexual satisfaction, that is, oral or anal penetration by another man.[123] Revoking the (elite) male privilege of penetrating another was condemned as a shocking violation of maleness and status.[124] These charges were so dangerous that Roman youths were trained to shun "feminine" mannerisms (Quint. *Inst.* 11.3.76), and adult men carefully avoided walking in a "feminine" way (Sen. *Ep.* 52.12). Yet the twin charges "he seeks to be penetrated" (and therefore to be feminine) and "he seeks to penetrate those who are off-limits to him" regularly accompanied one another, as we saw in the example of Suetonius' representation of Caligula and Nero. Nero enjoyed being penetrated but he also sought to corrupt boys.[125] Caligula sought frequent penetration by one of his male slaves, but he also seduced Roman matrons (Suet. *Calig.* 36). In this way, sexual excess and the reception of a phallus were gendered feminine; both practices were described as a contrary to "manliness." Lurking behind these accusations of effeminacy was a stereotype of a good, citizen male, a master of his passions, who penetrates others designated "by nature" or station to be penetrated, male or female.[126] This active man shows courage (Greek: ἀνδρεία, a cognate of ἀνήρ, "man," this word could also be translated "manliness"; Latin: *virtus*) and shuns weakness.[127] By choosing to insult men by suggesting that they are like women, these charges implied an intimately related definition of femininity and the female.

WILD WOMEN

Like slaves, Aristotle argued, women are deficient by nature. Freeborn women possess virtues appropriate to women, but their gender incapacitates them (Arist. *Pol.* 1260a4). Many ancient authors accepted and promoted this view, asserting that women need special protection and surveillance.[128] A few second-century moralists did argue that women should be educated in the virtues, especially the virtue most appropriate to women, *sōphrosynē*. "It is necessary that a woman be chaste and self-controlled," Musonius Rufus stated (3.15).[129] *Sōphrosynē*, "moderation," when applied to a woman carried the primary meaning "chastity," that is, sexual fidelity to one's husband.[130] Musonius Rufus explained, "she must, I mean, be pure in respect to unlawful intercourse, pure in other improper pleasures, not be a slave to the passions [*mē doulevein epithymias*], or fond of strife, or extravagant, or excessive in adornment. These are the works of a female *sōphrōn*" (3.15).[131] A "good woman" stays at home, is quiet, beautiful, thrifty, and spins wool.[132] In his criticism of the corruption of his age, Juvenal harkened back to a time when Latin wives were kept chaste. In those days, poverty kept a woman busy with toil and her hands were chafed from spinning (6.285–90).[133] *Pudicitia* (chastity) has, unfortunately, fled and disappeared. This stereotype—a good woman stays at home, is chaste, and spins wool—prevailed even among the philosophers and moralists who supposedly took up the cause of women. Why should a woman be trained in virtue? Musonius Rufus concluded, "the teachings of philosophy exhort a woman to be content with her lot and to work with her own hands" (3.25).[134]

Given this definition of a "good woman," it is perhaps not surprising that when a woman was a target of abusive speech, she was regularly accused of violating *sōphrosynē/pudicitia* in some way. She was described as the opposite of the female *sōphrōn*:[135] she adorns herself with expensive, ostentatious clothing, perfumes and cosmetics; her passions are insatiable; she seeks unlawful intercourse with whomever she can, wherever she can; she is talkative or ugly or loud; she spreads rumors; she participates in reprehensible religious rituals; she, a freeborn woman, behaves like a prostitute, courtesan, actress, or musician.[136] So, Demosthenes associated Aeschines' mother with prostitution. She was not just a prostitute, Demosthenes claimed, she sought sexual gratification constantly, even in a public latrine (Dem. *De cor.* 129–30). Furthermore, she participated in suspect religious rites, bringing her enthusiastic son along (*De cor.* 258–60).[137] A Hellenistic epitaph accused an anonymous woman of playing the whore: "your sleepless, heavy eyes betray you, and the ribbon binding the crowns in your hair, and the ringlet shamelessly torn out, and your limbs shaking from unmixed wine. Go away, common whore, the party-loving lyre and the finger-rattling beat of castanets are calling you" (*Anth. Pal.* 31).[138] In this epitaph, the role of prostitute and musical performer were equated, a tendency in abusive rhetoric.[139] According to Suetonius, the one woman Caligula really loved, Caesonia, was known for her reckless extravagance and wanton behavior (*Calig.* 25.3). In his sixth satire, Juvenal offered a number of examples of good women gone bad. Eppia, a senator's wife, ran off with a gladiator (6.82–113). Emperor Claudius' wife Messalina, Juvenal asserted, crept out at night in a disguise to take her place in a brothel, taking on an assumed name, baring gilded nipples, receiving all comers for a fee, staying through until morning when, with her lust still unsatisfied, she returned to her imperial pillow (6.114–132; compare Cass. Dio 60.31.1).

Wives are having intercourse with slaves, Juvenal proclaimed. They lord it over their husbands; they attempt to fight in the arena like men; they think nothing of performing like a musician hired for a banquet; and they adorn themselves with costly jewelry and layers of cosmetics (6.345–50; 246–58; 384; 457–73).[140]

These attacks against women can be placed within a tradition of representation in which women could figure as signifiers in discussions about men and the larger society. The honor due a city, an emperor, or an individual man depended, in part, upon the chastity of the women they were expected to control. Conversely, corruption of city or empire was exemplified by the licentious behavior of these same women.[141] Particularly interesting examples of this phenomenon are found during the early empire, a period characterized by a "rhetoric of conjugal unity" and a new criminalization of sexual licentiousness, directed primarily at the adulteries and fornications of elite women.[142]

At the turn of the first century B.C.E., the emperor Augustus instituted a set of laws that changed legal considerations of marriage for several centuries, the *lex Julia de maritandis ordinibus* (18 B.C.E.), the *lex Julia de adulteriis coercendis* (17 B.C.E.), and the *lex Papia Poppaea* (9 C.E.). These laws, a striking innovation, set a precedent that was not lightly discarded.[143] The *Lex Julia* made adultery a crime, defining adultery as sex between a married citizen woman and a man other than her husband.[144] A father, a *paterfamilias* with a daughter in his "power" (*patria potestas*),[145] who caught this daughter in the act of adultery was entitled to kill the daughter and her lover at once (*D* 48.5.21.1, Papinian; *D* 48.5.24.1, Ulpian).[146] A husband could also kill the adulterer, but only if he discovered the pair in his own house or if the adulterer was a pimp, an actor, a freedman of the household, or a slave (*D* 48.5.25.1, Macer).[147] Deliberate adultery (*adulterium*) or fornication (*stuprum*) with a freeborn woman or man was criminalized for Roman men as well. All sex outside of marriage was a crime for free Roman women, though, whereas for men concubinage with a woman of lesser status, as well as sexual involvement with his own slaves, continued to be acceptable practices (*D* 24.7.1, Ulpian; *D* 24.7.5, Paul; *D* 32.49.4, Ulpian; *D* 48.5.35, Modestinus).[148] The preservation of status was also a concern of the legislation. Senators, their sons, grandsons, and great-grandsons were forbidden to marry freedwomen, actresses, or the daughters of actors and actresses (*D* 23.2.44, Paul). A senator's daughter who behaved like a prostitute or an actress could marry a freedman since she "has behaved so disgracefully" that she has no honor left (*D* 23.2.47).[149]

Several suggestions regarding Augustus' intentions in promulgating these laws have been offered. Garnsey understands them as social legislation designed to rehabilitate marriage and encourage the raising of freeborn children.[150] To Raditsa, the Augustan marriage laws sought to increase Italian stock and reaffirm a sense of Roman identity at a time when power was increasingly being consolidated into the figure of the emperor.[151] According to Rouselle, these provisions were designed to prevent Roman men from marrying beneath them.[152] McGinn argues that these laws attempted to reaffirm social status by setting up the Roman matron as the polar opposite of the *meretrix* (prostitute).[153] Augustus himself stated that he intended to revive exemplary ancestral customs (*RG* 8.5). Yet Augustus was "certainly far from the truth" when he claimed that he was reviving old customs. Censors, charged with the duty of preserving Roman mores, may have disapproved of men who seduced other men's women, "but the task of keeping women in order was mostly delegated to their husbands and menfolk."[154]

What could Augustus have meant to imply when he took on the duty of "keeping women in order"? One possibility is that he sought to make the following point: whereas Rome was in chaos prior to his ascension, a chaos exemplified by the poor state of (feminine) morals, he brought a new order based, in part, on the restoration of the old virtues. The criminalization of the vices *stuprum* and *adulterium* signaled his seriousness in this regard. Situating the Augustan marriage legislation within the tradition of rhetorical invective, Edwards offers this sort of interpretation. She notes the frequent mention of adulterous and extravagant women in descriptions of the corruption of Roman society.[155] Edwards also sites the Bacchanalian scandal, as characterized by Livy, as an instance where uncontrolled female sexuality became an emblem of both political and religious deterioration.[156] Thus, by promulgating his innovative marriage laws, Augustus "may be seen as making a claim, in accordance with the conventions of Roman invective, that the Roman republic failed because its governing class was composed of men who were not men enough to control their own wives."[157]

Further examples can be found to support Edwards's reading. As we have already seen, Cicero associated his enemies with licentious aristocratic women, indicating their corruption by describing the depravity of "their" women (e.g., Cic. *Cael.* 49). The satires of Juvenal, though written some one hundred years after the Augustan marriage legislation, continued the same theme. The deplorable condition of Rome was represented by the flight of *pudicitia* from the city, exemplified by the untamed, insatiable sexual exploits of Roman aristocratic matrons.[158] Horace makes the equation even more explicit, focusing on Rome's sexual immorality in his indictment of pre-Augustan Rome: "O most immoral age! First you tainted marriage, the house, and the family. Now from the same source flows pollution over fatherland and people" (Hor. *Carm.* 3.6). By contrast, Horace proclaimed, the Augustan moral revival has restored the city to its proper virtue. Thanks to Augustus, "the pure house is no longer sullied by adultery. Law and custom have tamed unclean lust. Mothers are proud of legitimate children. Punishment follows on the heels of guilt" (Hor. *Carm.* 4.5). The statement "punishment follows on the heels of guilt" probably refers explicitly to the marriage legislation.[159]

The behavior of daughters, mothers, and wives, therefore, could reflect on both men and city. The goodness of Rome was displayed by the purity of its freeborn women. A good husband or father was shown to be so by the proper behavior of his wife or daughters. Thus, men could be shamed by other men for neglecting to control the women in their lives or, conversely, men could derive honor by convincing others that they ruled over harmonious households.[160] Edwards is not the first scholar to argue that discussions, or, in this case, legislation, about women can often be directed, to some degree, at the men with whom these women were associated.[161] The mention of a woman's sexual licentiousness in the context of fourth-century Athenian discourse, for example, could bring shame upon her husband, son, or father. "To preserve honor, a man had the duty both to himself and to his kin to ensure seemly behavior on the part of the women in his *kyrieia.*"[162] Plutarch claimed that in the good old days of Athens, a daughter who failed to preserve her chastity could be sold into slavery by her father, for she would have violated both herself and her family (*Sol.* 23).[163] Similarly, Roman rhetorics that described the *concordia* of a household served "as a means by which aristocratic families could broadcast the moral character of their menfolk."[164] Propaganda associated with the empress Livia and her opposite, Cleopatra, offer a paradigmatic example of representations of women intended to shame or promote "their" men during early empire.

Antony, we have already noted, was depicted as being everything his enemy Octavian was not: effeminate, cowardly, haphazard in his application of justice, and unable to control his passions, his lusts so detestable that they were unmentionable by modest, respectable people.[165] Augustus, on the other hand, was depicted as the restorer of the *mores maiorum* and the greatest *exemplum*[166] of proper Roman self-control, simplicity, modesty, and courage.[167] Though Antony degraded himself with his Egyptian "wife,"[168] Augustus made the better choice. His wife Livia was a shining example of Roman female virtue, or so the coins and statuary produced in her honor suggested.[169] During Augustus' "moral revival," a revival accomplished not only through legislation but also by means of ambitious building projects,[170] Livia dedicated a sanctuary of Concordia containing portraits of the imperial family as a model of marital harmony.[171] Antony and Cleopatra, on the other hand, were remembered as emblematic of what happens when Rome is seduced by luxury and the corrupting influence of foreign ways.[172] Cleopatra was not a wife at all, but a royal whore. Augustus and his proper Roman wife were portrayed as models of traditional Roman values, Antony and Cleopatra as the horrific opposite.[173]

Representations of the behavior of a Livia or a Cleopatra can be intended to communicate information not only about their personal virtue or vice but also about the suitability of the men with whom they were associated. Livia, the proper Roman matron, illustrates the virtue of her husband, Augustus, an emperor who restored virtue to Rome and brought *concordia* to both his own household and the empire.[174] This is not to say that Livia did not work to promote her own political success as well as the success of her husband,[175] but rather to note that representations of her, whether put forward by her, her husband, or the Senate, which had voted to honor her, carried a message that went beyond her own personal honor and position. Prior to her defeat and suicide, Cleopatra had also been honored in coin issues and honorific statuary praising her wisdom, devotion, and conjugal love (Plut. *Ant.* 86.9; Sen. *Suas.* 1.6).[176] Yet after her downfall, she was not only dishonored, she became a symbol for the dishonor of Antony.[177]

Julia, the daughter of Augustus, offers another important example of female infamy during this period. Julia, together with her daughter, also named Julia, were "guilty of every form of vice," including adultery, and thus Augustus banished them (Suet. *Aug.* 65.1). Augustus, the very author of the legislation that demanded their punishment, was forced to relegate his own daughter and granddaughter to an island. Suetonius reports that he even contemplated putting his daughter to death (*Aug.* 65.2).[178] Seneca records this incident in the following way:

> The deified Augustus banished his daughter, who was shameless beyond indictment of shamelessness, and made public the scandals of the impe-

rial house—that she had been accessible to scores of paramours, that in nocturnal revels she had roamed about the city, that the very forum and the rostrum, from which her father had proposed a law against adultery, had been chosen by the daughter for her debaucheries, that she had daily resorted to the statue of Marsyas, and, laying aside the role of adulteress, there sold her favours, and sought the right to every indulgence with even an unknown paramour.

(*Ben.* 6.32.1)[179]

Whatever Julia's actual behavior may have been,[180] it is worth noting that Seneca's description of her was strikingly similar to Juvenal's description of the empress Messalina and even to Demosthenes' claims about Aeschines' mother. All three prostituted themselves, and still their lusts remained unsatisfied. Julia and Aeschines' mother did so in public, Julia at a statue[181] and Aeschines' mother in a public latrine. Julia and Messalina both wandered about at night seeking sexual satisfaction, or so their detractors claimed. Whatever we are to make of the behavior of the Julias, they, like Cleopatra, came to represent another female type: Roman royal femininity gone bad.[182]

Representations of Cleopatra, Livia, and the Julias were intended, at least in part, to send messages about men. Individual men could be evaluated according to their success at controlling women; cities could be evaluated in similar terms. We have already observed that pre-Augustan Rome was described by Horace as overrun with adulterous women. Following the rise of Augustus, Horace claimed, chastity was restored; Rome had finally mastered "her" women. Juvenal made the opposite claim; he satirized the corruption of Rome by describing the fornications of Rome's "good women" in exquisite detail, including those of the empress Messalina. Lucian, in his characterization of Rome as an ideal place for hedonists, remarked that the city was awash in its adulteries (*Nigr.* 15–16), an interesting contrast to Horace's assertions regarding the restoration of Roman chastity. According to the logic of this discourse, "good" cities are populated by "proper" women who preserve their chastity and defer to their husbands, but "bad" cities are overrun with adultery and fornication (e.g., Plut. *Cat.Mai.* 8.2–3).

Therefore, accusations of sexual misbehavior lodged against women are found in numerous sources and could serve a variety of purposes. Such accusations could malign not only the women so accused but also their men, who, according to the conventions of Greco-Roman gender relations, were expected to control them. As Plutarch put it, "a man must have harmony in his household to produce harmony in the city or in the *agora* or among his own friends" (*Mor.* 144c). Women, deficient by nature, required the protection and supervision of men. Without supervision, they may fall into vice, succumbing to their voracious sexual appetites and shaming their families in the process.[183] Women who were controlled and controlled themselves, exhibiting the *sōphrosynē/pudicitia* appropriate to their gender and their station, brought honor to themselves, their families, their cities, and their nation. Indeed, true heroines of *sōphrosynē* could even be described in "masculine" terms.[184] They were "like men" in virtue, but the virtue they displayed was a virtue particular to them, chastity.[185] "Bad" women shame their families, their city, and themselves by engaging in adultery and fornication; they adorn themselves with expensive perfumes and cosmetics; and they seek to satisfy their insatiable lusts at every opportunity.

MALE DALLIANCE

As we have seen, adultery committed by freeborn women was viewed as a horrific sign of the depravity of the accused woman, her family, and even her city. But what about the adulteries of men? In terms of Roman law, a man who had sexual intercourse with a freeborn youth, either male or female, was guilty of *stuprum* (D 48.5.35, Modestinus).[186] Intercourse with a widow or a divorcée who retained her rank as a matron was also *stuprum* (D 48.5.9, 11). Married citizen women were off-limits, though the jurists spent much more time worrying about the adulteress than the citizen adulterer.[187] In the Athenian case, a man could be charged with *moicheia* (adultery) if he had engaged in sexual acts with a respectable Athenian woman, whether or not she was married.[188]

Both men and women, therefore, could be charged with adultery (*moicheia, adulterium*) and fornication (*porneia, stuprum*), though for men such charges implied sexual activity with the women or youths prohibited to them, not extramarital sex. This double standard—elite women were expected to engage in sexual activity exclusively with their husbands while elite men could have relations with their slaves, with prostitutes, and with courtesans even while married—has often been noted.[189] Wives were encouraged to accept this standard, even to consider it a benefit. As Plutarch put it, if a husband indulges in an affair, his wife ought not to be angry, she should be grateful that he chose to share his drunken behavior, licentiousness, and violence with another (*Mor.* 140b).[190] Martial made a similar observation, urging wives to tolerate relations between their husbands and slave boys since such activity guarantees that they will be the only female sexual partner their husband enjoys (12.96).[191] In this way, the norm that elite men must be the penetrator of women and of men of lesser status was further reinforced. A man was guilty of adultery or fornication only if he dared to cross status or gender lines, that is, if he engaged in sexual intercourse with a free, citizen woman or girl not his wife or assimilated himself to the passive, "female" role. Sex with noncitizen women or men, male or female prostitutes, and male or female slaves was acceptable, so long as the active, "masculine" role was assumed.[192] In every instance, however, an adult citizen male who assumed the passive role was mocked as effeminate and perverse.

Though men were free to engage in sexual activity outside of marriage, within certain limits, at least one second-century philosopher, Musonius Rufus, encouraged elite men to restrict their sexual activity to intercourse with their wives (12.5–45). Musonius was in the minority.[193] Still, excessive sexual activity with slaves or prostitutes was taken as evidence for indolence and depravity. Furthermore, there are several examples in which adulteries, including those committed by men, indicated the debasement of a man or a city. Rome, a city seething with vice, "brings in adultery, greed, false testimony and the whole family of the pleasures" (Luc. *Nigr.* 16). Wicked sons, if they were not corrected, would certainly engage in adultery, together with other vices ([Plutarch] *Mor.* 5b–c). Among their many other crimes, Caligula and Nero were said to have forced freeborn women into adultery, acting as their procurers (Suet. *Calig.* 35, *Nero* 27).[194] Their adulteries, therefore, were made more monstrous by their willingness to corrupt proper matrons, even selling the favors of these women to others. The infamous Clodius was accused not only of committing adultery, but of doing so with his own sister, the wife of Lucullus (Plut. *Caes.* 6).[195]

The charges "he corrupts freeborn women and girls" and "he corrupts freeborn boys" often accompanied a charge of treason. A man who would seek to penetrate these special, protected groups could not be trusted to fulfill his duties as a citizen, for he chose to seek his own pleasure at the expense of the very social fabric, spoiling "our" youths, matrons, and virgins.[196] For example, the Athenian orator Dinarchus, in his speech against Philocles, stirred up the audience by reminding them that no one would dare trust their boys to Philocles; such a man must also take bribes, or so Dinarchus claimed (3.15–16).[197] Aeschines made a similar argument in his prosecution of Timarchus. He (mis)quoted the law in question to imply that anyone who sought to hire an Athenian to "use as he pleases" should be liable to punishment (*In Tim.* 87–88).[198] The term "*hubris*" and its cognates referred to a man with no control of his appetites who poses a threat to the "good" women, girls, and boys of the city.[199] Such a man must never be entrusted with the city or its lesser, protected members.[200] This sentiment was echoed several hundred years later by the Roman-era Stoic philosopher Epictetus; he argued that a man who commits adultery with the wife of another overthrows affection between neighbors, friendship, and even the city (Arr. *Epict. diss.* 2.4.3).

Character assassination by means of allusions to adultery were frequent in Roman-era invective; Antony, Pompey, Cicero, Caesar, Claudius, Titus, and Domitian were all accused of adulterous affairs.[201] Adultery could signify the decline of Rome, as we have seen in Horace's complaint that Rome, prior to Augustus, was filled with adultery. A further example can be found in Livy's famous retelling of the rape of Lucretia. In this story, the decline of pre-republican, monarchical Rome was epitomized by the forced adultery of a chaste Roman matron. Sextus Tarquinius, the son of the king, set out to have the matron Lucretia at any cost. He conceived of a devious plot designed to force Lucretia to comply with his wishes. He surprised Lucretia in her bedroom, threatened to murder her in such a way that it would appear she was involved in an adulterous liaison with a slave, and, in this way, overcame her resistance. He satisfied himself and her honor was lost. The next day, she called her husband and father to her, exacted an oath from them that she would be avenged, and committed suicide. As a result of Sextus' horrific act, the royal family was banished and the republic was established (Livy 1.57–59).[202]

Still, some accusations of adultery could be ambiguous in their intent. For instance, Suetonius reported that Augustus engaged in adultery repeatedly, yet for the sake of political gain: "That he was given to adultery not even his friends deny, although it is true that they excuse it as committed not from passion but from policy, the more readily to get track of his adversaries' designs through the women of their households" (*Aug.* 69).[203] Apparently, the motivation for the act was what distinguished the adulteries of Augustus from the adulteries of Caligula and Nero; Augustus sought political gain rather than sexual satisfaction, thereby maintaining his self-mastery, while Caligula and Nero allowed themselves to be overcome by their illicit, inextinguishable lust.[204] Men who succeeded at their seductions could be envied as well as condemned, depending on the circumstances. Such a man may render himself suspect, but, so long as he was the seducer and penetrator, he has also demonstrated his virility.[205] Moreover, as emperor, Augustus was in a superordinate position even to Roman senators. Hence, by sleeping with their wives, he was simply dramatizing his position as supreme actor, the most "male" man of all, to whom all were subordinate.

The problem with men who commit fornication and adultery, therefore, was that they allowed their passions to rule them to the detriment of their community. Suetonius's Augustus was the exception, or so Suetonius claimed, yet he pursued his adulterous liaisons rationally and for the sake of the political gain. Still, illicit intercourse with other men's wives threatened the "noble blood" of the "elite"[206] while calling into question the mastery of the husband and father of the adulteress since, as we have seen, they were supposed to guard and protect "their" women. Sexual involvement with freeborn boys intended, upon maturity, to enter the ranks of citizen men was also condemned (though permissible in the Greek context within certain constraints). Moreover, a man accused of rapacious sexual appetites was often accused of seeking sexual penetration with as much enthusiasm as he sought to violate others;[207] the immoderate man was described as both oversexed and effeminate since insatiable lust was commonly said to characterize women, not men. In this way, a man who could not control his passions was, by definition, "womanly."[208] Charges of adultery and fornication against men played a similar function to those of extravagance and effeminacy; they labeled the intended target as unsuitable, indicating that he lacks the requisite virtues of moderation and self-discipline.

CONCLUSION

This survey of charges of sexual depravity demonstrates that accusations of sexual licentiousness were important to a variety of ancient discourses. These charges depended upon and reinforced cultural codes about the characteristics appropriate to "the elite." "The elite" were here defined as those who are virtuous, and the nonelite as those deficient in virtue. The categories "man" and "woman" were constituted, in part, by these discourses. For elite men, virtue meant mastery of others (penetration, controlling the household, displaying military courage) but also self-mastery. The man who could not or did not control his passions was untrustworthy: if he could not master himself, how could he master others? He was depicted as enslaved to pleasure and unfit for his position. The man who reveled in luxuries—especially with prostitutes, courtesans, and expensive male slaves—corrupted both himself and his community. For elite women, virtue, by and large, meant chastity. Women who did not stay at home, who failed to remain loyal to their husbands, and who adorned themselves with luxurious clothing, cosmetics, or perfumes brought shame upon themselves, their families, and their community. According to this logic, when female *sōphrosynē* and *pudicitia* flee the city falters. When matrons, citizens, senators, or emperors fall prey to their lusts, they enslave themselves and the city. A man could be charged with being "like a woman"; citizens were accused of behaving "like slaves"; chaste matrons were represented as whores; and a nation could be evaluated in terms of the relative sexual virtue or vice displayed by its inhabitants. When hierarchical status and gender were overturned by illicit sex, the society crumbles and order falls away.[209]

This chapter has offered representative examples in sources stretching across several centuries, from fourth-century Athens to imperial Rome. By offering such disparate examples, I have sought to demonstrate the importance of sexualized invective across genres, eras, and regions while also establishing the prevalence of sexual slander as an ancient rhetorical strategy.[210] Certainly, fourth-century Athens and late-republican or early-imperial Rome were not "the same." What was specifically at stake when Aeschines accused Timarchus of prostituting himself or when Cicero accused Catiline of corrupting the youth of Rome was undoubtedly very different.[211] Yet both Aeschines and Cicero chose to disparage their targets by representing them as sexual deviants.

Perhaps the fact that Aeschines, Cicero, Plutarch, Suetonius and others attacked their opponents by accusing them of sexual vice could have been predicted, given the rhetorical tradition we noted earlier. Generations of Greek and, later, Roman schoolboys were trained in the repertoire of categories appropriate for praise or blame. Still, there is something larger than a stereotypical rehearsal of categories going on here. Both Aeschines and Cicero, not to mention Demosthenes, Plutarch, Seneca, and Suetonius, relied upon a legal and philosophical tradition that defined and defended privilege in terms of virtue. Aristotle suggested that slaves were (ideally) deficient "by nature" and, therefore, are better off being slaves.[212] Four hundred years later, Seneca raised the question again when he deliberated whether or not slaves could, in fact, cultivate virtue (*Ep.* 47). Furthermore, both Aeschines and Cicero, and many of the other authors cited above, understood "virtue" (ἀρετή, *virtus*) in gender-specific terms. A man is virtuous when he is in control of himself and his household, when he is courageous in battle, and when he is wise in his dealings with his subordinates. A woman is virtuous when she guards her chastity. Her courage lies in maintaining and displaying chastity in face of extraordinary threats. Thus, violations of virtue were equally gender specific. For a woman, any form sexual activity outside of marriage was improper and subject to censure. For a man, sexual acts with freeborn subordinates (boys, girls, women) were largely forbidden,[213] yet men were not expected to limit their sexual activity to their wives, though some philosophers may have encouraged them to do so. Since masculinity was defined as activity and dominance, voluntary renunciation of these prerogatives was considered to be depraved, a true indication of a man's corruption.

Behind these discussions of virtue and vice lay the further assumption that a man's character ought to be subject to scrutiny. "When a man went to court he threw his whole life, his family, and his friends into the balance against his opponent." He also did everything he could to vilify the family, friends, and person of his adversary.[214] Orators were expected to make this argument. Indeed, rousing the emotions of the jury, especially indignation or pity, was a key task of forensic oratory (Arist. *Rh* 1419b; Cic. *De or.* 1.12.53). Forensic orators could argue from the general behavior of a target to the particular instance. If a man corrupts boys, he would certainly not hesitate to take bribes (e.g., Cic. *Cat.* 2.10). If a man cannot be trusted to keep his women in line, then he should not be trusted with the well-being of the state (Plut. *Mor.* 144c). This logic extended beyond forensic oratory to all sorts of discourse. The Persians are slavish; they participate in every vice, but especially luxury. The Greeks are corrupt; they have no control over their passions. The sexual impropriety of a man, a nation, an emperor, and the women associated with them indicated social and political corruption, the degradation of the entire community.

In this discursive context, sexual slander could be a particularly compelling rhetorical strategy. Rival elites could use arguments about incapacity, effeminacy, luxury, and licentiousness to undermine one another's political aspirations. A satirist like Juvenal could mock the pretensions of his city by describing the decadence of effeminate senators and insatiable matrons. Humorists like Lucian could turn the tables on Rome, representing Rome not as a bastion of morality but as a vice-ridden den of orgiastic pleasure. Historians and moralists could evaluate infamous men almost entirely in terms of character, describing their sexual exploits in lurid detail. Representations of Octavian and Antony, Livia and Cleopatra served as a shorthand capable of summing up everything that was wrong or right with the early empire.

I have offered this selective survey in order to demonstrate the breadth and significance of vituperation in ancient discourses. In the process, I have broadened the rhetorical category "blame" (*psogos/ vituperatio*): ancient rhetorical commonplaces pervaded all sorts of discourses and were not limited to the formal practice of epideictic or forensic speech. Rather, the commonplaces of "blame"—slave ancestry, foreign origin, sexual misbehavior, improper appearance, and the like—were key to the telling of history, to the writing of law, to the promotion of the morality of the empire, and to the discrediting of other nations. In later chapters, I explore the participation of early Christians in this long-standing rhetorical technique. Christian arguments relied upon, critiqued, and appropriated aspects of the Greek and Roman sex- and gender-status discourse I have been exploring, as well as upon a rhetorical and philosophical training they shared with their neighbors, at least to some degree. They did so within the context of the empire.[215] What difference did the emperor make? How did he rule? What were the particular manifestations of his *auctoritas*?[216] Most of these questions are beyond the scope of my project. Nevertheless, I suggest that the emperor did make a difference to the particularities of virtue and vice during the era corresponding to the development of Christian discourse. Christians knew about and worked with traditions about the virtue (or vice) of the emperor.[217] Christians highlighted their own virtue against the vices of others, including Roman emperors, Roman citizens, and Roman governors. Rome was represented as an insatiable whore (Rev 17–19). "The world" was described as utterly corrupt, and sexual depravity was offered as proof (1 Thess 4:2–8; Rom 1:18–32; Eph 4:17–23, 5:3–5; 1 Jn 2:15–17). If "the elite" were supposedly "those who are virtuous," then Christian arguments about their own virtue, against the vice of everyone else, can be read as a direct challenge to the legitimacy of "the elite," including Rome and "her" emperor. This is the topic of the next two chapters.

CHAPTER 2

Paul, the Slaves of Desire, and the Saints of God

For this is the will of God, your sanctification, that you refrain from *porneia*, that each of you know to possess his own wife [*skeuos*, lit. "vessel"] in holiness and honor, not in the passion of lust like the gentiles who do not know God, that no one transgress and defraud his brother in the matter, because the Lord is an avenger concerning all these matters, just as we told you before, and we solemnly warned you. For God did not call us for impurity, but in holiness.

—1 Thess 4:3–7

In his letter to the Thessalonians, Paul warned the brothers in Christ to refrain from *porneia* ("fornication" or sexual immorality more generally), avoiding the passion of lust (*pathei epithymias*) exhibited by the gentiles (*ta ethnē*). Paul similarly exhorted the members of the Galatian church (*lit.* "assembly") to practice self-mastery (*enkrateia*), since they had "crucified the flesh with its passions and desires" (Gal 5:24). Writing about one hundred years later, Justin Martyr made comparable claims. First he decried the unreasonable passions of the Greeks and their gods (Justin *1 Apol* 5.9.2) then, remarking upon the transformation that occurs when one is devoted to the God of Israel, he concluded: "We who not long ago delighted in *porneia* now embrace *sōphrosynē* alone" (*1 Apol* 14). Ancient Christians from Paul onward frequently employed this basic argument: non-Christians are enslaved to desire, but Christians have gained control of their desires and rejected all impure, "unnatural" sexual behavior. Conflating a biblical polemic against gentile idolaters with Greco-Roman arguments that figured corruption in terms of sexual vice, authors such as Paul and Justin defined themselves against others by contrasting their exceptional virtue with the supposed vice of everyone else. The world is corrupt, they argued; it is infected with lust. Those who abandon themselves to this lust will be punished. By contrast, the followers of Christ are pure. They control their desires and will be saved.

Paul and later followers of Christ frequently defined the boundaries of their movement in sexual terms. Paul claimed that gentiles take their wives "in the passion of lust"; one of Paul's disciples added that gentiles "have given themselves up to licentiousness" (Eph 4:19). Justin suggested that gentiles are "driven by unreasonable passion and by the scourge of worthless demons" (*1 Apol* 5);[1] a later apologist added that they "have made a business of harlotry and established immoral houses of every base pleasure for their young" (Athenagoras *Leg* 34.2).[2] According to Paul, the followers of Christ must always be exceptionally chaste: They do not (or should not) visit brothels (Rom 6:15–20). They do not (or should not) tolerate *porneia* in their midst (1 Cor 5:1–13; cf. Eph. 5:5). His disciples insisted that Christian wives remain submissive and chaste (Col 3:18; Eph 5:22–4; 1 Tim 2:8–15; cf. 1 Pet 3:1–6) and that (male) leaders rule themselves and their households well (1 Tim 3:1–7).[3] Becoming "saints," they have "put to death" what is "earthly"—"*porneia*, impurity, wicked, lustful passion and greediness, which is idolatry"—or so one Pauline Christian asserted (Col 3:5).[4] Later Christian authors continued this theme, celebrating the fact that some Christians renounced sexual relations altogether for the sake of Christ.[5] Indeed, as one author boasted, "the world hates the Christians … for they resist the pleasures" (*Diogn.* 6.5).

Assertions about sexual morality pervade early Christian discourse. Paul worried about marriage practices, sexual renunciation, incest, adultery, intercourse with prostitutes, and other sexual practices he identified as *porneia*.[6] Later Christians discussed virgins, virginity, marriage, divorce, desire, *porneia*, and adultery at great length. Though followers of Christ did not always agree on the precise nature of the self-control required, there seems to have been universal agreement that desire (*epithymia*) and pleasure (*hēdonē*) would lead to sin. In contrast to all outsiders, the brothers and sisters in Christ were—or should have been—capable of keeping desire in check.[7] They were to be characterized by true righteousness and holiness. Turning away from idolatry, they no longer engaged in sexual excess of any kind, distinguishing themselves from the corrupt communities they left behind. Claims regarding the outstanding sexual virtue of "the saints" were accompanied by a corresponding depiction of "the world" as plagued by sexual vice. Sexualized invective became a key strategy for drawing boundaries between outsiders and insiders and also for enforcing insider sexual ethics. Who were the followers of Christ? They were not gentiles. Who were the gentiles? They are sexually immoral idolaters. In this way, Christian sexual ethics, and Christians as a group, were constituted as both different from and superior to others.

This chapter considers one aspect of this early Christian sex talk: charges of sexual licentiousness against gentile outsiders as lodged by the apostle Paul. My goals are twofold: to place Paul's arguments in the context of other ancient Mediterranean discourses and to offer an analysis of the function of these arguments. For Paul, drawing boundaries between the gentiles-in-Christ and gentile outsiders on the basis of sexual virtue (theirs) and vice (everyone else's) was an effective strategy during the early empire, a period in which claims about virtue, sexual and otherwise, were frequently deployed to justify status and difference. Despite his world-critical stance, Paul often relied upon the very categories of virtue and vice put forward in the philosophical and moralistic traditions of his targets, combining these categories with biblical assertions regarding the gentiles and illicit sex. On the whole, Paul upheld widely shared assumptions regarding sex, gender, and status. He may have been highly critical of outsiders, yet he reinscribed the gendered sexual norms he shared with many of those he criticized.

Trained to varying degrees in Greek or Latin rhetoric and living within the cultural environment of the Mediterranean, early Christian authors would have been well aware of the rhetorical commonplaces referencing virtue and vice discussed in the previous chapter. Paul utilized "all the subtleties of Greek logical argumentation," even if his rhetoric did not reach the heights of some of his more eloquent contemporaries.[8] The second-century Christian Justin called his *First Apology*, a *prosphōnēsis*, "an address," especially to a ruler, employing the technical term for the treatise he composed (*1 Apol.* 1.1).[9] By the second and third centuries, Christian authors like Justin demonstrated self-conscious attention to Greco-Roman rhetorical forms in the speeches, letters, and dialogues they composed;[10] Paul's letters also employed common Greek rhetorical tropes and devices.[11] Not surprisingly, then, Christian authors listed many of the same virtues and vices found in works by Greek moralists[12] and employed metaphors resembling those utilized by Stoic and Cynic philosophers.[13] Yet Paul and later Christians also built upon a familiar biblical argument: gentile idolaters engage in reprehensible sexual practices. "Idolatry"—itself a term of opprobrium meaning "worships other gods"—was figured as *znh* or *porneia*; one usually implied the other.[14] Paul adopted this rhetorical tactic as his own, reconfiguring "idolatry" to mean "does not worship God/Christ" while continuing to equate idolatry with sexual depravity. Later Christian writings adopted a similar point of view: so, for example, the author of the *Didache* warned against "murders, adulteries, lusts, *porneia*, thefts, idolatries, magic arts, sorceries, robberies, false witness," and "hypocrisy," among other behavior that leads to the "way of death" (*Did.* 5.1), and Polycarp cautioned that one who does not abstain from avarice "will be defiled by idolatry, and shall be judged as if he were among the gentiles who do not know the judgment of God" (Poly. *Phil.* 11.2). To the author of Colossians, "*porneia*, impurity, passion, evil desire and greediness" were a form of "idolatry" (Col 3:5). In this way, the followers of Christ incorporated Greco-Roman commonplaces—"blaming" others for immoral sexual behavior, ignoble family or national origin—into their own arguments and combined them with biblical and postbiblical Jewish[15] claims about the fornications of the gentiles.[16] The apostle Paul was the earliest follower of Jesus to put forward these sorts of arguments, so we begin with him. But first Paul's claims need to be placed within a larger tradition of anti-gentile sexualized invective.

CANAANITES, IDOLATERS, AND OTHER FORNICATORS

Speak to the children of Israel and say to them: I am the LORD your god. You shall not do as they do in the land of Egypt, where you lived, and you shall not do as they do in the land of Canaan, to which I am bringing you.

—Lev 18:2–3

The book of Leviticus prefaced prohibitions against incest, intercourse with a menstruating woman, child sacrifice, bestiality, and "lying with a man as with a woman" (LXX: *meta arsenos ou koimēthēsē koitēn gynaikos*) with a warning: the people of Israel are not to "do as they do in the land of Egypt" or "as they do in the land of Canaan." After listing the prohibited behaviors, Israel was warned once again: if they commit any of these abominations, they will defile the land just as the Canaanites had done and, as a result, "the land will vomit them up" (Lev. 18:24–30). By framing the commandments in this way, the book of Leviticus implied that certain sexual acts were non-Israelite practices. Furthermore, Leviticus cautioned, such acts lead to punishment by God no matter who commits them. In the process, God's true people were represented as sexually pure, and outsiders—be they Canaanites, Egyptians, or disobedient Israelites—were associated with abhorrent sexual and religious behavior.

This association between gentiles, apostate Israel, and (purportedly) depraved sexual behavior can be found in many other biblical and post-biblical writings. Throughout the Hebrew Bible, idolatry was described in sexual terms as "fornication" or "prostitution" (*znh* and cognates). Canaanites were said to "prostitute themselves to their gods"; they were guilty of both false religiosity and sexual licentiousness, or so these sources suggested (Exodus 34:15–16).[17] The prophet Ezekiel turned these accusations against Jerusalem. Jerusalem, by failing to live up to the covenant, acted just as one would expect idolaters to behave: as a whore. She "lavished her [Heb. "your"] whorings on any passer-by," betraying her faithful husband, God. Judgment, appropriately, was the result (Ezek 16:15).[18] As Hosea put it, Israel "plays the whore," and Ephraim, joined to idols, engages in sexual orgies, loving fornication more than glory (Hosea 4:15–19). As a consequence, God will punish Ephraim and Israel; Ephraim will become desolate and Israel will be put to shame (Hosea 5:9, 11, 14–15; 7:8–10, 12–13; 8:2–3; 9:1–3; 10:6).

These biblical commonplaces were extended to include Greeks and other gentiles by later Jews. To the Wisdom of Solomon, idolatry was the "beginning of fornication"; idolaters "kill children in their initiations," "hold frenzied revels," and "no longer keep either their lives or their marriages pure" (Wis. Sol.14.12). The Letter of Jeremiah accused gentile priests of stealing gold and silver from their gods, in part, to fund trips to a brothel (10–11).[19] The Book of Jubilees states that "all [the ways of the gentiles] are a pollution and an abomination and uncleanness" (22:20) and therefore a man who dared to give his daughter or sister in marriage to a gentile man ought to be stoned "because he has caused shame in Israel."[20] The *Testament of Levi* presented the patriarch Levi at his deathbed warning his sons to avoid behaving "like the gentiles" by eating the Lord's offerings with whores, committing adultery, having intercourse with prostitutes, taking gentile women for their wives, and becoming like Sodom and Gomorrah. If they do indulge in such abhorrent, "gentile" behavior, they will bring a curse upon Israel (*T. Levi* 14.1–8). The third Sibylline Oracle contrasted Judeans who "remember the hallowed marriage bed" with Phoenicians, Egyptians, Romans, Greeks, and others who (allegedly) commit adultery and "have impious intercourse with male children" (*Sib. Or.* 3.590–600).[21] According to Josephus, the Greeks follow the example of their depraved, incestuous gods, using the bad sexual behavior of their deities as an excuse "for the monstrous and unnatural pleasures in which they themselves indulged," "unnatural" pleasures that included incest, adultery, and male homoerotic sex (Joseph *Ap.* 2.275).[22] The sectarian Judeans of Qumran interpreted Hosea's earlier (sexualized) condemnation of Israel as a description of Judea during their own time: the (current) disregard of God's commands and the celebration of gentile festivals in Judea will soon leave these (new) apostates shamed and in mourning (4Q166–7).[23] The Alexandrian Jew Philo excoriated apostates for becoming "licentious, shameless, unjust, frivolous, small minded, quarrelsome, companions of falsehood and false testimony." Their impiety has led them to serve "the delights of the belly and the organs below it" (Philo *Virt.* 34.182).[24] In this way, gentiles and wayward Israelites were persistently identified with prostitutes, adultery, lust, fornication, idolatry, and homoerotic sex while "true" Judeans were identified with proper sexual and religious practices.

DANGEROUSLY STRANGE WOMEN

Arriving in Israel from exile, Ezra was profoundly disturbed to learn that Israelite men had married women associated with the "peoples of the lands [and] with their abominations," or so his ancient biographer suggested (Ezra 9:1).[25] "When I heard this, I rent my garments and my mantle, and pulled hair from my head and beard, and sat appalled" (Ezra 9:3). From Ezra's perspective, Israel had become dangerously polluted by intermarriage; the only solution was divorce. In this way, Ezra (or Ezra's biographer) reinterpreted and expanded earlier commandments forbidding Israelites to marry the descendants of certain, specified nations in favor of a general decree: endogamy was the only acceptable option; any and all mixing with "foreign" or "strange" women pollutes the land.[26] From Ezra's perspective, marriage to foreign women profaned "the holy seed" of Israel by combining it with the unclean (*lit.* "menstruous") people of the land (Ezra 9:2, 11–12).[27] Teachings in Leviticus had already asserted that Israelite men should beware of Canaanite women; Ezra took the argument a step further by offering a blanket condemnation of intermarriage. In the process, "the people of the land," whatever their ancestry, became "profane seed," permanently corrupt and corrupting.[28]

This emphasis on Israel as a "holy seed" has led some scholars to posit an intensification of anti-gentile sentiment in some post-exilic Judean literature. Jonathan Klawans explains:

> What is new in Ezra and Nehemiah is the view that the moral impurity of Gentiles is inherent. This view indeed contradicts the Holiness Code,

which extends to the Gentile populace of the land prohibitions that prevent moral impurity (e.g., Lev 18:25; Num 35:15). Obviously, the assumption of the Holiness Code is that the moral impurity of local Gentiles is not inherent: otherwise the code would not bother to obligate the stranger to follow these commands.[29]

From Klawans' perspective, there was a general escalation of concern about sexually defiling sins during Second Temple Judaism, as reflected in Ezra-Nehemiah, in popular Judean literature from the time, and, later, in the literature of Qumran.[30] This concern was often framed in terms of the sexual danger of outsiders. As the author of Ezra put it, strange or foreign women participated in practices that were "like" the gentiles. In this way, he proclaimed a crisis of sexual immorality—figured as a crisis involving sexually suspect women and the disobedient Jewish men who had married them—and then argued that Ezra had been uniquely designated to fix this crisis, thereby justifying Ezra's position as leader of the newly reconstituted Israel.[31] Claudia Camp observes that "Ezra in effect transforms a struggle over power and material interests into a struggle over the definition of Jewish identity at a cultural-symbolic level, a struggle that was definitively mounted in terms of divorce of 'foreign' wives—definitively, though perhaps only symbolically."[32] Whatever Ezra did or did not do in Israel upon his return, it is clear, from the perspective of his biographer, that the purity of Israel would be permanently marred if Israelite men dared marry foreign women. Foreign women were treacherous indeed.

An emphasis on the threat of foreign or strange women can be found in a variety of post-exilic sources. In the romance Tobit, the patriarch exhorted his son Tobias to marry only a fellow Israelite: "Keep yourself, son, from all *porneia*; first, take a wife from among the descendants (*lit.* "from the seeds") of your fathers and do not take a strange woman who is not from your father's tribe" (Tobit 4:12).[33] The "Letter of Aristeas," a pseudonymous work from Alexandria, suggested that Israel's God had erected a barrier around Israel so that there could be no (sexual) mixing between Israel and other nations, thereby keeping Israel pure in body and soul.[34] *The Book of Jubilees*, a retelling of Genesis dating from the second century B.C.E., asserted that the sexual union of gentile and Israelite was itself fornication. That author sought to prove his point by means of a creative reworking of biblical genealogy designed to demonstrate that successful patriarchs always married within the group.[35] Philo and Josephus asserted that Judean priests were forbidden to marry gentile women (Philo *Spec.*

3.29; Josephus *AJ.* 8.190–6). The danger of the foreign woman came to signify the allegedly insurmountable difference between Israel/Judea and her neighbors. From the juxtaposition of Wisdom and the Strange Woman in Proverbs—a passage that many scholars associate with the time of Ezra—to the reinterpretation of the rape of Dinah in *Jubilees* and the Qumran community's claim that outsiders are intrinsically defiling, foreign women were said to bring political, social, and sexual disaster upon any man of Israel foolish enough to succumb to their wiles.[36] Though multivocal and complex, the theme continued in rabbinic literature: intermarriage with gentiles mixes holy seed with profane seed, polluting all who engage in it and producing apostasy.[37]

MEN MOUNTING MEN: HOMOEROTIC SEX AS A DISORDER OF THE GENTILES

Leviticus had suggested that "lying with a man as with a woman" ought not to occur among the Israelites; it is a "moral impurity" punishable by death and the grounds for dismissal from the land.[38] The author of the Letter of Aristeas went further, suggesting that other nations defile themselves by procuring men and defiling mothers and daughters (152). Philo of Alexandria added that male homoerotic sex is "unnatural" (*para physin*) and "lawless" (*anomos*; see Philo *Abr.* 133–35; Philo *Contempl.* 59–62). His vivid description of the alleged sins of the people of Sodom offers a striking example of his claim: "The land of the Sodomites ... was entirely full of innumerable wrongs, especially those associated with gluttony and lasciviousness, made great and multiplied with every other pleasure" (*Abr.* 133). Sodom was so overfull with luxurious delights and so committed to lasciviousness, that the Sodomites "threw off the law of nature," eating and drinking and pursuing "lawless intercourse" (lit. "lawless impregnating"; *Abr.* 135). This "lawless intercourse" not only included adultery but also men mounting men. Even when the Sodomites discovered that their "lawless impregnating" of men could not result in the begetting of children, they continued with their unnatural and lawless behavior until the men became "accustomed to submitting to the things of women" (*Abr.* 136).[39] Whatever Genesis meant to suggest about the particular crimes of Sodom, according to Philo, "unnatural" sexual practices, combined with extravagant indulgence, led to that city's downfall.[40]

Philo elaborated on the identification of gentiles with male homoerotic sex to include concerns about the effeminate (read, "passive") male partner and the need for control of the passions.[41] For Philo, the final sign of the degradation of Sodom was male submission "to the things of women." A similar concern for male self-mastery is found in 4 Maccabees. There Joseph was praised for his refusal to become a victim of Potiphar's seductive Egyptian wife: "When he was young and in his prime for intercourse, by his reason he nullified the frenzied urge of the passions" (4 Macc 2.4). Sirach urged young men to avoid luxury, refrain from looking at whores, and keep a firm watch on their daughters and wives (37:29, 41:20–22, 42:11). To Josephus, the only "natural" sex was what occurred in the union of man and woman. Jews practice this "natural sex" for the sake of procreation only, and Jewish law forbids sex between men.[42] Among these authors, procreative sex was defined as best, the mastery of desire was viewed as making men "manly," and homoerotic sex was characterized as "against nature," a set of beliefs we have already encountered in works by Stoic philosophers from approximately the same period.[43] Moreover, as Michael Satlow has recently demonstrated, Palestinian rabbinic traditions were also influenced by Greco-Roman anxieties about the "passive" male.[44] Greco-Roman sources emphasized the importance of masculine self-mastery; so did Palestinian rabbinic sources. Greco-Roman sources expressed particular anxiety about the passive partner in a male homoerotic encounter; so did rabbinic sources. Greco-Roman sources equated "being a man" with self-control; so did rabbinic sources, although for the rabbis this control was to be gained through the study of Torah.[45] Still, however similar these sexual categories may be, gentiles continued to represent "the other," and the sexually suspect other at that.[46]

WHO IS THE "WOMAN" NOW? JUDEAN HEROINES AND THE REPROBATE POTENTATE

The reconstitution of Israel after the Babylonian exile was presented by the author of Ezra as requiring a reestablishment of male purity and control, figured as the rejection of foreign wives. Pure Israel, this story suggested, depends upon the pure seed of Judean men and the enforcement of "proper," endogamous marriage alliances for all Judean men and women. Men must deposit the "holy seed" in appropriate receptacles, the chaste women of Judah, and they must ensure that their sons do the same. Good Judean women were expected to play their part by remaining silent, modest, and sexually faithful to their husbands, a stereotype reiterated in several sources from this period. The heroic mother of seven brave sons martyred by the Greek Seleucid king Antiochus IV Epiphanes—a story recounted in both 2 and 4 Maccabees—offers a striking example. According to 2 Maccabees, this woman "reinforced her woman's reasoning with a man's courage" when she exhorted her sons to face death rather than break God's commands (2 Macc 7:21). The author of 4 Maccabees expanded the story, adding a speech (purportedly) given by the heroine after the death of her seventh and final son: "I was a pure virgin and did not go outside my father's house; but I guarded the rib from which woman was made. No seducer corrupted me on a desert plain, nor did the destroyer, the deceitful serpent, defile the purity of my virginity" (4 Macc 18.6–9). The narrator then commented that "the sons of Abraham with their victorious mother are gathered together into the chorus of the fathers, and have received pure and immortal souls from God" (4 Macc 18:22). In this way, the "manly" strength and virtue of the mother—she guarded her chastity from her youth and gladly saw her sons tortured rather than submit to a Greek tyrant and his gods—was contrasted with the decadence and bloodthirsty violence of Antiochus. Antiochus the Seleucid King was shamed by a "common" Judean woman.

The story of Judith offers an interesting parallel: Judith, a beautiful, upright Israelite widow, overcame the Assyrian general Holofernes by pretending to bring both information and sexual favors. Instead, she assassinated him, and victory over his army soon followed. Exhibiting Holofernes' head to her countrymen, she exclaimed, "The Lord has struck him down by the hand of a woman. As the Lord lives, I swear it was my face that seduced him to his destruction, and that he committed no sin with me, to defile and shame me" (Judith 13:15–16). Meanwhile, back at the Assyrian camp, a leader of the army proclaimed, "The slaves have tricked us! One Hebrew woman has brought disgrace on the house of King Nebuchadnezzar" (14:18). In other words, the powerful, cruel Assyrian men were no match for one brave, pure Hebrew woman who had married within her family, carefully administered her husband's estate, and managed to avoid sex with a foreigner, even though desperate circumstances had forced her to use her beauty to "unman" the tyrant. A Greek-speaking editor of the book of Esther described the similar attitude of his heroine. Before visiting the chamber of the Persian king, Esther prayed "you know I hate the splendor of the wicked and abhor the bed of the uncircumcised and of any alien … I abhor the sign of my proud position, which I wear on the days when I appear in public." This "sign"—her Persian crown—was to her "a menstruous rag."[47] In this version of the Esther story, as in the book of Judith, a chaste, beautiful Hebrew woman reversed the fortunes of her people by deploying her feminine wiles, yet she still managed to maintain her chastity, protect her Judean cultural identity, and guard her beauty.[48] These stories implied that it was the foreign king who has become "womanly"—he allowed himself to be overcome by desire—and the Hebrew woman who behaved "like a man" since she acted to save her people rather than to sate her desires.[49]

The "good" women of Israel deployed their sexuality in service of their community, and they guarded their chastity, even when forced to violate conventional moral norms in order to outsmart gentile tyrants.[50] By contrast, dangerous women—be they gentile women or fallen women of Israel—used their sexuality to lure Israelite men into apostasy and adultery. Famous biblical examples include Potiphar's wife, who sought to seduce the patriarch Joseph and then arranged for his arrest when he would not relent, and Jezebel, who so manipulated her husband King Ahab that she was able to arrange for the worship of Baal throughout the land.[51] Proverbs warned that such foreign or "strange" women wander the streets, looking for prey: "She is loud and wayward; her feet do not stay at home; now in the street, now in the squares, and at every corner she lies in wait" (Prov 7:11–12). Men were cautioned to keep away from such women and to keep a close eye on their daughters, preventing them from joining their ranks. Sirach warned, "Be ashamed of looking at a woman who is a harlot" and "keep strict watch over a headstrong daughter" (41:20, 42:11). According to the Letter of Jeremiah, gentile men have less success in this endeavor. Their women wait at the entrances to temples hoping for a tryst and competing with one another for the opportunity (43). The author of Susanna, an addition to Daniel written during the first century B.C.E., denounced two Judean elders for falsely accusing a chaste Judean woman of adultery: "You offspring of Canaan and not of Judah, beauty has deceived you and has perverted your heart. This is how you both have been dealing with the daughters of Israel, and they were intimate with you through fear, but a daughter of Judah would not tolerate your wickedness" (Susanna 56). In other words, Judean women do not submit to adultery, even when threatened, and Judean men who would dare to assume otherwise must actually be "Canaanites."

According to Amy-Jill Levine, "the women of the Apocrypha and Pseudepigrapha are the screen on which the fears of the (male) community—of impotence, assimilation, loss of structure—can be both displayed and, at least temporarily, allayed."[52] In biblical texts, Israel was figuratively described as a "woman," a faithful wife of God or an adulteress who dared deploy her sexuality elsewhere by "fornicating" with other gods. In later, Hellenistic Jewish tales, a "manly" Judean woman was often portrayed as overcoming the (supposedly) "manly" gentile king; Israel's purity was preserved and gentile degradation was exposed. Claims about illicit sex were employed to critique Israel's foreign rulers, associating these rulers with luxury and sexual excess and thereby gendering them as "female" and Israel as "male," and to reaffirm Israel's borders, even after these borders had been irrevocably shattered. Israel may be a "woman," at least in terms of "her" social position as a subject people, but it was the gentiles who are "womanly," or so these stories suggested.

THE DEPRAVITY OF THE GENTILES

The portrait of "man" and "woman" offered in these sources has much in common with the sources discussed in the previous chapter. Apocryphal literature such as Tobit and Sirach recommended that Judean men control their desires, be wary of seductive women, and keep careful watch over their households. The nation of Israel could be imagined as a woman and, therefore, the heroic deeds of one Judean or Israelite woman could stand for the prestige, and even the "manliness," of the entire community. Though we have seen such discursive strategies before, in the case of biblical and postbiblical Judean literature, the goal was the production of difference between Israel/Judah/Judea and the gentiles or, more simply, everyone else. Gentile tyrants, overcome by desire, could be conquered by "manly" Judean women. Judean men were repeatedly warned to keep away from seductive yet polluting gentile women. Homoerotic sex was characterized as a gentile, not Judean, "problem,"[53] as were adultery, rape, promiscuity, pimping, and bestiality.[54]

A crucial point in the holiness code of Leviticus seemed to be that incest, homoerotic sex, child sacrifice, intercourse with a menstruating woman, and bestiality cause impurity, an impurity then associated with the Canaanites. Though the contours of the argument changed over time, the basic strategy of defining insiders and outsiders according to sexual practice remained. The Sibyl objected to pederasty and adultery as foreign practices, opposing them to the pure marriage practices of Judeans, marriage practices that were affirmed again and again in such works as Tobit, *Jubilees*, and Sirach. To Josephus, Judean laws promoting endogamy and procreation and against male homoerotic sex demonstrated the exceedingly strict moral code of the Jews, a counter to accusations that the Jews are "full of lust." Furthermore, the "unnatural" sex of the Greek gods (adultery, incest, men lying with men) was offered as evidence for the superior moral position of the Judeans. As far as Leviticus, Exodus, Ezekiel, Hosea, Ezra, the Third Sibylline Oracle, Tobit, Judith, Susanna, *Jubilees*, the *Testament of Levi*, Pseudo-Aristeas, Philo, Josephus, and the rabbis were concerned, gentiles are corrupt, and that corruption is demonstrated by their degenerate sexual behavior. As we shall see, Paul, a Greek-speaking Judean from the Diaspora, both repeated and reconfigured this argument to defend his particular group of Judeans and gentiles-in-Christ, the followers of Jesus.

PAUL AND THE SLAVES OF LUST

According to Paul, transformation in Christ resulted in a decisive break with the depravity of the world. Gentiles were "enslaved to lust"; Christ-followers became "slaves of God" (Rom 6:13–23). Gentiles characteristically commit *porneia* (1 Thess 4:5; Gal 5:16–26; Rom 1:18–32); Christ followers glorify God in their bodies (1 Cor 6:15–20). Gentiles join their bodies to prostitutes (1 Cor 6:15); Christ followers exercise self-mastery, or they marry and thereby channel their passions appropriately (1 Cor 7:1–16, 25–40). In this way, Paul juxtaposed the brothers and sisters in Christ with the (allegedly) depraved gentile idolaters, condemning the "crooked and perverse generation" (Phil 2:15) for sexual corruption while setting the "saints" apart on the basis of their strict self-control. Sexual immorality on the part of Christ followers cannot be tolerated. For example, when Paul heard that a brother was guilty of *porneia* of a kind "not even found among the gentiles" (1 Cor 5:1), he instructed the Corinthians to hand him over (*paradidōmi*)[55] to Satan for the destruction of the flesh, "that the spirit may be saved in the day of the Lord" (1 Cor 5:5). No Corinthian Christ follower should associate with a "brother" (i.e., member of the community) who is a prostitute/fornicator (*pornos*), or who is greedy, or an idolater, reviler, drunkard or robber (1 Cor 5:11). Rather, "drive out the wicked from among you" (1 Cor 5:13).

This sexualized language had a two-fold purpose: to produce difference between the "saints" (*hagioi*) of God and those who would face God's wrath; and to persuade the audience to accept a kind of sexual morality that, Paul argued, belongs to Judeans and gentiles-in-Christ alone. Accusing gentiles of sexual depravity, Paul participated in a long-standing polemical strategy familiar to Greeks, Judeans, and Romans alike: vilifying outsiders and defining insiders on the basis of sexual virtue and vice. Furthermore, he adopted the conventions of both Greek rhetoric and Judean anti-gentile polemics to do so. Paul's example was imitated by later Christian authors who also condemned outsiders for depravity and celebrated the exceptional virtues displayed by their own community.[56] According to Paul, rejection of God is the problem, sexual depravity is the symptom, and Christ is the cure. Those who continued in sexual sin were promised a divinely initiated punishment. Those who suppressed the truth necessarily engage in "unnatural" lust, Paul argued, a direct result of their rejection of God (Rom 1:18–32). Those involved in *porneia*, idolatry, homoerotic sex, and adultery, among other vices, will not inherit the kingdom of God (1 Cor 6:9–11; compare Gal 5:16–26). The Lord will punish those gentile Christ followers who dare to continue in the lustful passions that characterized their former idolatrous lifestyle. In other words, they must accept Paul's particular definition of sexual self-control or face eternal destruction (1 Thess 4:3–6; 1 Cor 10:7–22). This is clear from an exegesis of Paul's letters to the Romans and to the Corinthians, as well as from the anti-gentile argumentation he employs throughout his letters.

THE LETTER TO THE ROMANS AND THE DEPRAVITY OF THE WORLD

Romans was the only letter written by Paul to a community of Jesus followers that he had not visited (Rom 1:8–12; 15:22–29). He wrote to the "saints" in Rome in preparation for a visit, possibly to deflect criticisms of him and his views prior to his arrival, with the hope of making a favorable impression upon a church from which he sought support for his further missionary work (Rom 15:22–23).[57] Romans follows some of the conventions of Greek letters—the body of the letter is framed with an initial greeting and thanksgiving and concluded with a final greeting and blessings[58]—but it is much longer than a common letter. It has been called a "letter essay" that combines several genres,[59] an extended Cynic-Stoic diatribe with an epistolary frame,[60] or a προτρεπτικὸς λόγος (a speech intended to attract students) in letter form.[61] The issue of genre is far from settled. Still, Paul's familiarity with the basics of Greek rhetoric is clear.[62] I do not propose to solve the issue of rhetorical genre here. For my purposes, it is enough to note that Romans offers a coherent argument containing motifs, figures, and stylistic devices found in Greek rhetoric, techniques that Paul employed for his own purposes.[63]

Romans is among the more logical and carefully constructed of Paul's letters. Paul offered a careful presentation of his mission, a mission that seems to have included the following points: (a) gentiles are under the indictment of sin (1:18–3:20); (b) Christ provided the solution to the problem of gentile sin (3:21–8:38); (c) even though the Judean law did not solve the problem, at least for gentiles, God's promises to Israel were not negated but rather fulfilled in Christ (9:1–11:36); (d) gentiles, now transformed by Christ, should live moral lives in harmony with one another as they wait for the "the hour" when Christ will return and God's final judgment will be revealed (12:1–15:13).[64] Sexual morality was clearly not the, or even a, central concern of Romans. Nevertheless, significant portions of Paul's larger arguments were presented in sexual terms. His argument may not have been *about* sex or gender or status per se, yet he repeatedly used sex, gender, and status to think with.[65]

Claims about sexual behavior, the body, slaveries, and the flesh are essential to the persuasive force of much of the letter. For example, in order to demonstrate the depravity of the idolatrous gentiles, a primary task of 1:18–3:20, Paul describes the "unnatural" and "dishonorable" lusts of those who have rejected God. In his discussion of the transformed lives of the faithful (4:1–8:38), Paul compares the pre-Christ life of Jesus' followers with their postbaptismal transformation in Christ. To do so, he suggests that there are two types of slavery, slavery to sin or slavery to God. Slavery to sin is portrayed as the condition of every gentile who does not follow Christ. Slavery to God refers to the new, purified state of believers. Both are represented as bodily conditions, exhibited in the "members" (μέλη, i.e, bodily parts). Paul goes on to contrast "flesh" and "those who live according to the flesh" with "spirit" and those who obey the spirit's directives. His description of the "works of the flesh" implies that living "according to the flesh" means living in a state of uncontrolled desire. Living "in the spirit" means controlling one's body and one's desire. In his concluding ethical exhortations, Paul suggests that believers ought to conduct themselves "becomingly" (*euschēmonōs*), not in licentiousness (*aselgeias*), while they remain subject (*hypotassō*) and wait for the day (i.e., the final judgment of God). Thus, whether or not Romans was *about* sex, Paul often puts forth his arguments in terms of sex, flesh, body, and slavery. When Paul was interested in drawing boundaries between insiders and outsiders, when Paul discusses the nature of sin or overcoming it, when Paul offers a diagnosis of the condition of gentiles prior to their incorporation into the "body of Christ," he does so by talking about sexual depravity.[66]

THE UNNATURAL LUSTS OF THOSE WHO
SUPPRESS THE TRUTH

Following a brief greeting and thanksgiving, Paul describes the punishment that God has reserved for those who suppress the truth: they have been "given up in the lusts of their hearts to impurity, to the degrading of their bodies among themselves, because they exchanged the truth of God for a lie and worshipped and served the creature rather than the Creator, who is blessed forever" (Rom 1:24). Three times Paul states that they were "given up" (*paradidōmi*) by God to lust. God "gave them up in the lusts of their hearts to impurity," "gave them up to dishonorable passions" (Rom 1:26), and "gave them up to a base mind" and "to do the things which are improper" (Rom 1:28). Their first mistake was refusing to recognize and honor God, resulting in futile thinking and foolishness, for they chose to worship "images resembling a mortal human being, or birds, or animals, or reptiles" rather than the immortal God (Rom 1:23). Therefore, God abandoned them to their desires, they have become consumed with dishonorable passions, they engage in "unnatural" sex,[67] and they are filled with "all manner of injustice, wickedness, greediness and vice" (ἀδικία, πονηρία, πλεονεξία, κακία). The wrath of God has already been revealed, they are already experiencing the consequences of their idolatry, and those consequences are largely sexual: abandonment by God leads to "unnatural" sex and uncontrolled desire.[68]

The affinities between this description of corruption and traditional representations of the vices of the gentile idolaters are obvious.[69] Gentiles were commonly associated with *porneia*, lust, adultery, incest, homoerotic sex, and bestiality. Paul never actually identified the target of his condemnation as "the gentiles," yet the stereotypical character of the accusations—especially the claim that they "exchanged the glory of the immortal God for images resembling mortal man or birds or animals or reptiles" (Rom 1:23)[70]—suggests that Paul expected his audience to think of gentiles here.[71] Paul did not need to identify the targets of this invective because his audience would readily recognize the typical list of accusations against gentile idolaters. Judean authors frequently condemned the Egyptians for their worship of animals.[72] As already noted, idolatry was persistently linked to fornication in Jewish literature from the Hebrew Bible to the Talmud.[73] Paul reconfigured this common polemic—gentile idolaters are enslaved to lust—in order to further his argument that gentiles without Christ could not attain either salvation or self-mastery. The corrective Paul recommended for the pandemic state of gentile corruption was Christ, that is, joining the movement he supported.[74] Paul began his letter to the saints in Rome by describing the degradation of the world in sexual terms, with desire (ἐπιθυμία), dishonorable passions (πάθη ἀτιμίας), and "unnatural" intercourse constituting the symptoms of the perverse world and God's just abandonment of it. By contrast, he identified those "in Christ" with purity and self-control, ascribing impurity and out-of-control lust to gentiles as a group. This tendency to formulate the break between Christ followers and the world in sexual terms can be found throughout the letter.

THE SLAVES OF SIN AND THE SLAVES OF GOD

Following the general indictment of (gentile) humanity in the early chapters of Romans, Paul argues that "the righteousness of God through faith in Jesus Christ" is the best available cure for the problem of sin (*hamartia*), a problem that ought no longer to trouble the saints (Rom 3:22; compare 1:16–17). What were the contents of this category, "sin"? A primary attribute of "sin" as described in Romans is lack of control of one's body. In baptism, Paul asserts, "the sinful body" (*to sōma tēs hamartias*) is destroyed so that "we might no longer be enslaved to sin" (*doulevein hēmas tē hamartia*; Rom 6:6). Sin causes the sinner to "obey the appetites" (*to hupokovein tais epithymias*) and to yield his "members" (*ta melē*, i.e., bodily parts)[75] to impurity (*akatharsia*; Rom 6:19). Sin is linked to death—sin "leads to death," the end (*telos*) of "the things of which you are now ashamed" is death, and "the wages of sin is death" (Rom 6:16, 21, 23)—just as those guilty of idolatry, homoerotic sex, dishonorable passions, and other offenses were said by Paul to "deserve to die" at the conclusion of Rom 1:18–32.[76] He imagines sin, therefore, as a bodily condition, as was righteousness, with sin resulting in death and righteousness in life.[77] Sin "reigns in your mortal bodies so that you obey its desires" (Rom 6:12). Righteousness (*dikaiosynē*) involves yielding your "members" to God. The body ought to become an obedient instrument of God as opposed to an obedient instrument of desire (Rom 6:13, 17–18, 19). In this way, Paul suggests that two types of slavery are possible: slavery to desire and impurity or slavery to God and righteousness. Christ followers who do not control desire join gentile idolaters in a dishonorable, debased sort of "slavery."

Paul was not the first ancient author to connect slavery and desire. As noted in the first chapter, slaves in the ancient world were often represented as morally suspect or exempt. They were morally deficient and less capable of self-control than their masters; they were supposedly "unscrupulous, lazy, and criminous,"[78] different "by nature," and lacking the requisite faculty of deliberation.[79] Tied to this negative evaluation of slaves was the accusation that a free citizen could become a "slave" to luxury and desire,[80] and "free" or "slave" could be differentiated on the basis of self-mastery. Masters mastered both their own bodies and the bodies of their slaves, at least in theory, but slaves were incapable of mastering their own bodies, both literally and figuratively.[81] This confusion between the material circumstances of slaves—who could not control their bodies because their bodies were owned by others—and slavery to desire as a problem that could trouble masters is evident in the writings of a Roman contemporary of Paul, Seneca the Younger. Seneca recommended that Roman masters occasionally invite deserving slaves to dine with them since, "if there is any slavish quality in them as a result of their low associations, it will be shaken off by keeping company with men of gentler breeding" (Sen. *Ep.* 47.16). In other words, slavish slaves could be improved by the company of noble noblemen. This argument only becomes possible if one presupposes the moral failings of slaves and the moral superiority of masters. Seneca then went on to argue that even masters can become "slaves," one to lust, another to greed, another to ambition, and all to fear. He concluded, "No slavery is more disgraceful than that which is voluntary" (Sen. *Ep.* 47.17). Thus, Seneca proposed that slavish slaves can benefit from the example of their honorable masters. At the same time, he sought to shame citizen men into rejecting "slavishness," that is, indulgence in lust, greed, and excessive ambition, once again linking slaves with dishonorable behavior.[82]

Paul may have had this traditional association between "slavishness" and desire in mind when he composed Romans. The "sin" that the "slaves to sin" engaged in was largely sexualized. Sin and the passions (*ta pathēmata*) were linked, and the body, prior to baptism, is said to be inherently sinful (*to sōma tēs hamartias*). Without faith in Christ, bodily parts were said to be obedient to impurity (*ta melē humon doula tē akatharsia*), lawlessness, and shame.[83] Like Seneca, Paul suggested that all were in danger of becoming "slaves" to the appetites[84] and warned against "yielding one's members" to sin, impurity, and lawlessness (Rom 6:13, 19). Still, unlike Seneca, Paul suggested that the cure for slavery to lust was slavery to God rather than moral improvement through the study of philosophy.[85] To Paul, all of the brothers and sisters in Christ must choose "slavery to sin" or "slavery to God," whether they were slave or free.[86] All will yield their members; the question was to what, God or lust? Anyone who rejected

Christ was portrayed as essentially incapable of virtue, whether slave, freed, or free. One can sell oneself to impurity, lawlessness, and desire, or one can sell oneself to God.

Juxtaposing the slaves to sin with the slaves of God in Romans, Paul emphasized the significant break between the brothers and sisters in Christ and everyone else. He did so in bodily, sexual terms, with negative slavery conforming to the Greco-Roman trope "enslavement to lust" and positive slavery defined as slavery to (his) God. Slavery to God, Paul argued, leads to a kind of bodily discipline in which one's body becomes an instrument of *dikaiosynē* (righteousness). By placing these two slaveries in opposition to one another, making a very real institution—slavery—stand for devotion to God or devotion to desire, Paul subverted traditional status conceptions to some degree, even as he built upon the commonplace association of slavery and desire. Instead of simply reinscribing the traditional relationship among enslavement, lust, and shame, Paul asserted that slavery to God is advantageous, demanding that all the believers become the right kind of slave.[87] Still, he continued to play upon ancient assumptions about "slavishness," even as he asserted that all gentiles in Christ, regardless of status, must become God's "slaves."[88] The link between slavery and sexual immorality was both preserved and contrasted with a positive, righteous slavery—slavery to God.

By employing slavery as a positive as well as a negative metaphor, Paul partially undermined ideological apparatuses that supported slavery. In Paul's schema, slaves were not necessarily morally deficient, for they shared the status "slaves of God" or, even better, "freedmen of the Lord" (1 Cor 7:22), and "sons of God" (Gal 3:25–29) with their free brothers and sisters in Christ. "Slavery to God," especially for actual slaves and other low-status people, could be understood as especially salvific since, as Dale Martin points out, "to raise one's status by becoming the slave of a good and powerful master was to be saved from a harsher or less honorable fate."[89] Paul utilized status language to elevate the lower-status, slave Christ follower even above the higher-status free person. Both became, metaphorically, members of Christ's household, but within that "household" the slave was granted the higher relative position. The slave became Christ's "freedman," but the free person became Christ's "slave." Both free and slave became members of the most prestigious household of all, the household of God. In return, people of higher status had to "give up their own interests" and "identify themselves with the interests of those Christians of lower status," while people of lower status gain status enhancement by joining the household of God, even though they remained enslaved. Thus, while Paul did not advocate the abolition of slavery, he challenged the presuppositions that made this hierarchical structure possible.[90] Paul continued to build on the theme of metaphorical slavery later in the letter, distinguishing those who live "according to the flesh" from those who live "according to the spirit." There he asserted that, in the spirit, the "slaves of God" have become something even better, the "sons of God."

FROM FLESH TO SPIRIT

Later in Romans, Paul furthers the theme of gentile sexual depravity, this time by arguing from the hierarchical dualisms flesh (*sarx*) and spirit (*pneuma*), a theme he broaches more directly in his letter to the Galatians.[91] In Romans, Paul states, "those who live according to the flesh set their minds on the things of the flesh, but those who live according to the spirit set their minds on the things of the spirit" (Rom 8:5). Paul puts it this way in Galatians: "what the flesh desires is against the spirit, and the spirit is against the flesh" (Gal 5:17). The flesh and its desires lead to death, just as slavery to sin was said to be death dealing to the idolaters of Romans 1 and 6 (Rom 8:6). The "works of the flesh" include: "*porneia*, impurity, licentiousness, idolatry, sorcery, enmities, strife, jealousy, anger, quarrels, dissensions, factions, envy, drunkenness, carousing, and things like these" (Gal 5:19–21). According to this argument, those who are "in the flesh" cannot submit to or please God, for they are utterly opposed to God and the things of God (Rom 8:7–8). They are enslaved by their desires and their vices. Those "in the spirit," on the other hand, have put to death the deeds of the flesh and will live. Indeed, they received "the spirit of sonship" instead of a "spirit of slavery" (Rom 8:13–15).[92] They are not only "slaves of God," they are God's children and heirs. In this passage the slaves of God have become sons of God who live according to the spirit and are free from the works of the flesh and the slavishness of desire.[93]

Arguing for the corruption of "the world" and describing the decisive transformation that occurs "in Christ," Paul offered the following representation of gentiles: Idolaters, they have been given up to lust, impurity, the dishonoring of their bodies, their dishonorable passions, and homoerotic sex; they possess base minds, exhibit improper conduct, and are fornicators and slaves of sin. They deserve to and will die. Living according to the flesh, they are lawless, hostile, and cannot please God (Rom 1:18–32; 2:8–9, 21–24; 6:12–13, 19; 7:14–15; 8:5–8, 12–13; 12:2; 13:12–14). The brothers and sisters in Christ, by contrast, are represented quite differently: United with Christ, they have destroyed their sinful bodies and gained bodies that are instruments of righteousness. They are now slaves of God and sons of God, living according to the spirit whether they are slave or free. They have been sanctified, set free from sin, and they bear the fruits of the spirit, having "crucified the flesh with its passions and desires" (Gal 5:24).[94] The distinction between these two groups could not be more plain. Those who were not "in Christ" were expected to engage in πορνεία. By contrast, gentiles-in-Christ control their bodies and themselves. Paul staked his claim of purity and righteousness in Christ on sexual self-mastery. In the process, he called into question gentile assertions about their own self-mastery, a hostile rhetorical move in the first-century Mediterranean world. Writing a letter to Rome, the capital of the empire, did Paul dared to suggest that the empire and "her" emperor were illegitimate? Or was Paul willing to grant an exception for these gentile rulers, masters of the world, at least for the time being?

BE SUBJECT TO RULING AUTHORITIES

Toward the end of his letter to the Romans, Paul offers a series of instructions regarding appropriate Christian behavior. Christians ought not to be "conformed to this age" but "transformed," demonstrating the good (*agathos*), acceptable (*euarestos*), and perfect (*teleios*) will of God (Rom 12:2). This good behavior involved, for example, loving one another, serving the Lord, rejoicing in hope, practicing hospitality, living in harmony, and "giving place to the wrath" (*dote topon tē orgē*), probably a reference to the coming eschaton (Rom 12:10, 12, 16, 19). In this context, Paul exhorted his readers to "be subject to the governing authorities [ἐξουσίαι], for there is no authority [*exousia*] except by means of God" (Rom 13:1).

Given Paul's indictment of the depravity of gentiles-without-Christ earlier in this letter, these instructions seem oddly out of place. In other letters, Paul had suggested that Christ followers should remain subordinate to those who possess authority over them, at least for now.[95] Still, having repeatedly referenced the depravity of these gentiles, the view that the *exousia* (authority) of idolatrous rulers (*archontes*) is given by God is striking. Yet, Paul specifically instructed Christians to submit to *archontes*:

For rulers are not a fear to good work, but to bad. You do not want not to have fear of authority? Do what is good, and you will have its approval. For it is God's servant for you, for good. But if you should do wrong, be afraid, for it [authority] does not carry the sword in vain. For it is a servant of God to execute wrath against those who do wrong.

(Rom 13:3–4)

Having argued that those who do wrong are condemned to the wrath of God,[96] Paul now places rulers in the position of those who, knowingly or unknowingly, carry out God's wrath against those who commit evil. Still, he prefaces these comments by noting that the beloved (i.e., the Christ followers) ought not to avenge themselves but "give place to the wrath"; in other words, God will take care of them. He further reminds his audience that "the hour" is near (Rom 12:19, 13:11). Since "the day is at hand," believers ought to conduct themselves in a presentable manner (*euschē-monōs*), not in "reveling, drunkenness, beds [*koitais*, euphemistic for sexual indulgence], licentiousness [*aselgeiais*], quarreling and jealousy." Rather, they ought to "put on the Lord Jesus Christ" and avoid the flesh and its desires (Rom 13:13–14). The saints ought to submit to the rulers, since, as doers of good rather than doers of evil, they should have no reason to fear them. Paul characteristically defined "good" (*agathos*) here as rejection of desire and "bad" (*kakos*) as overindulgence in activities related to desire, especially sexual intercourse. Paul then recommended obedience to proper "authority" (*exousia*), in this case "the authorities" that collect taxes, wield a sword, demand fear, and seek honor (Rom 13:6–7). But did Paul believe that his rulers were "good"?

By stating that one ought to have nothing to fear from the rulers as long as one is doing good, Paul may have referenced the view that good rulers reward good, virtuous behavior but punish vice. In theory, good kings, good rulers, and good emperors are pious, beneficent, brave, just, moderate, and wise. Consequently, they encourage bravery, moderation, justice, piety, and wisdom among their subjects.[97] Horace makes precisely this point when praising Augustus. Thanks to the Augustus, adulteries have ceased, mothers bear legitimate children, lust has been tamed, and punishment follows guilt.[98] Similarly, Pliny praises Trajan's exceptional virtues and their marvelous, empirewide effects. Thanks to Trajan, all the subjects of the empire, even the poorest, raise legitimate children who will grow into adulthood. Slaves obey their masters and masters care for their slaves (Plin. *Pan.* 26–7, 42). Across the empire, emperors were represented as universal benefactors, saviors, sons of a god, fulfillments of divinely ordained providence, and the guarantors of peace, security, and piety.[99] Even Philo linked the exceptional virtue and piety of Augustus and Tiberius with the peace and prosperity of the empire during their reigns. According to Philo, Augustus's every virtue "outshone human nature" (Philo *Leg.* 143).[100] He brought peace to the entire empire, rid the sea of pirates, and set every city at liberty (*Leg.* 145–47). He was "the first and universal benefactor," and thus the whole world voted him honors equal to those of the gods (149). Similarly, Tiberius, possessing noble ancestry, wisdom and eloquence, preserved the peace across the empire throughout his reign (142). These two noble emperors were contrasted with Gaius Caligula, whom Philo represents as a deranged, impious murderer. Gaius greedily stole from every inhabitant of the empire and brought sickness to the healthy and premature death to the living, while transforming the peace his predecessors had established to uproar. Augustus and Tiberius, Philo notes, had been favorably compared with the gods; however, Gaius—profligate, greedy and mad—indulged in a previously unheard of pretension, declaring himself to be a god (74–114). Building upon traditional categories of virtue and vice, Philo sought to win favor from Emperor Claudius for the redress of the grievances of the Alexandrian Jews. To that end, he extolled the virtue of two exemplary emperors and condemned the wickedness of the previous emperor.[101] The decadence, inconsistency, and greed of Gaius led to disorder, sickness, and misery of emperor, empire, and subjects. The good ruler embodied virtue; therefore, he ought to establish virtue among his subjects and grant peace in his kingdom. The good *princeps*, according to this theory, was firmly in control of himself and responsible for a moral climate in which the virtues flourish and vices are punished.[102]

Paul's argument that (good) rulers are not a terror to good behavior but to bad was therefore quite typical. What is missing, however, is the qualifier "good" (*agathos*), for as everyone knew, rulers could also be "bad" (*kakos*), a character flaw that would bring misery upon ruler and subject alike. Did Paul think that every ruler, good or bad, was a servant of God whose responsibilities included the execution of God's wrath against those who do wrong? Certainly, Paul has been interpreted in this way.[103] Yet Paul's other arguments suggest that he believed that his rulers were already indicted by God's wrath, for they, like every gentile, had been handed over in the lusts of their hearts to impurity and to the dishonoring of their bodies among themselves. They live according to the flesh, are idolaters, possess base minds, are slaves to lust and incapable of sound judgment, and can only continue to corrupt an already corrupt world. Where Philo, Suetonius, and Plutarch singled out particular rulers as licentious, in contrast to those good rulers who kept their desires in check, Paul implied that such a good gentile ruler could not possibly exist. How could he if the only virtuous gentile, let alone ruler, is a Christ follower?

Paul does not advocate a forceful overthrow of the current gentile regime. On the contrary, he warns the brothers and sisters in Christ to submit to the authorities, no matter how corrupt. Perhaps, by leaving out the qualifier "good," however, Paul means to suggest that the gentiles-in-Christ must submit for the time being, even to a bad ruler who behaves in a way contrary to his station, punishing the good rather than the bad and promoting vice rather than virtue. After all, "the day is at hand" and so the Christ followers in Rome ought to "live peaceably with all," if possible (Rom 12:18). God will soon take care of the bad rulers; indeed, God already has. Their corruption is revealed by their unwillingness to "put on the Lord Jesus Christ," and, in consequence, God has already abandoned them to dishonorable lust. Given Paul's representation of the corrupt world, how are we to read the injunction to "pay all of them their dues; taxes to whom taxes are due, revenue to whom revenue is due, respect to whom respect is due and honor to whom honor is due" (Rom 13:7)? If all the gentiles-not-in-Christ are prone to vice and enslaved to their passions, can they ever deserve honor and respect? No, but God's devastating judgment will soon be revealed. In fact, the wrath is apparent even now, so live peaceably and wait.[104]

ILLICIT SEX AND THE CORINTHIAN SAINTS

Paul offers more specific instructions regarding the content of in-Christ sexual purity in his letters to the Corinthian church. These letters contain Paul's responses to questions raised by the Corinthian community—a church he had founded—as well as Paul's reactions to news he had received about their activities. Evidence for the conversational nature of 1 and 2 Corinthians includes possible quotations of phrases used by the Corinthians themselves[105] and references to letters received by Paul and to reports given to him by others.[106] Paul had heard that there were schisms (1:11, 11:18). He had heard that they were tolerating *porneia* (5:1). He had received a letter with questions about proper behavior in the churches (7:1). He referred to the issues they raised on several occasions, introducing his arguments with the phrase "now concerning" (*peri de*).[107] This evidence has led some scholars to seek to reconstruct the positions and behaviors of the Corinthians with whom Paul was in dialogue. For example, some have argued on the basis of Paul's discussion of women and marriage that a group of independent, charismatic women were causing trouble in the Corinthian church, at least from Paul's perspective.[108] Others have sought to ascertain the identity of the "super apostles" whom Paul denounces in 2 Corinthians.[109] Many have supposed that the Corinthian church was a particularly enthusiastic, charismatic group. These gentiles-in-Christ emphasized spiritual gifts, questioned the value of status, gender, and sexual norms, and, in Paul's opinion anyway, were in need of a great deal of guidance.[110] Since I am primarily interested in the contours of Paul's rhetoric, I will not attempt to reconstruct the views of his "opponents," if such a title is warranted for them. Rather, I seek to understand the specifics of the sexual morality that Paul recommends.

In Romans, Paul relies upon sexualized language to describe the depravity of the world, articulating difference in sexual terms. In his letters to the Corinthians, he offers more explicit advice about the sort of sexual morality he envisioned. As he does in Romans, Paul contrasts gentile idolaters with the brothers and sisters in Christ. He shames the Corinthians for tolerating a type of fornication that not even gentiles allow (1 Cor 5:1). He reminds them that before Christ, they had been idolaters, adulterers, effeminates (*malakoi*) and fornicators/prostitutes (*pornoi*; 1 Cor 6:9–11). He warns them not to be mismated (*heterozygountes*) with nonbelievers, since righteousness and lawlessness can have no fellowship (*koinōnia*; 2 Cor 6:14–7:1).[111] In Romans, Paul exhorts believers to commit their bodily parts to the service of God rather than desire; in 1 Corinthians, he describes more fully the specifics of the sort of bodily control required. My discussion of Paul's advice to the Corinthian Christians is limited to the extensive discussion of sexual morality found in 1 Corinthians 5–7 and to his presentation of "natural" gender in 1 Corinthians 11. These instructions are contained within the series of responses and rejoinders that make up Paul's first letter to the Corinthians.[112]

DRIVE OUT THE WICKED ONE FROM AMONG YOU

Following a pointed reminder that he was their "father" (1 Cor 4:14–21),[113] Paul relayed his disgust for what he had heard about the lax morals of the Corinthian church: "It is actually reported to me that there is *porneia* among you, and of a kind that is not found even among gentiles; for a man is living with [*lit.* "has"] his father's woman" (1 Cor 5:1). Here Paul turns his anti-gentile invective against a specific man and against those who welcomed him. According to Paul, by accepting this man the Corinthians had dared to tolerate behavior that even their neighbors would condemn, thereby shaming them on the basis (presumably) of a shared disdain for gentile sexual morals. Yet Paul offered few specifics regarding the actual circumstances of this man's *porneia*. Was the man living with his father's current wife, his father's widow, a (current or former) concubine, a former wife, or a (current or former) slave? Paul did not say, and the Greek is entirely ambiguous.[114] Marriage to one's stepmother was illegal from the perspective of both biblical and Roman law.[115] Still, some in the church did not regard the man's actions as sinful, though they had embraced Paul's message about Christ. As we shall see, some of these same Corinthians had also adopted the saying "it is well for a man not to touch a woman" (1 Cor 7:1) as their own. It seems curious, therefore, that they would knowingly welcome a man living in some sort of incestuous relationship. Paul may be exaggerating for effect.

Earlier scholars sought to resolve this dilemma by positing that there were two (false) positions circulating in the Corinthian church, one suggesting that "freedom in Christ" implies freedom from moral constraints, another asserting that believers must avoid sex altogether.[116] According to these readings, the man and his sympathizers belonged to a "freedom in Christ" party that had either rejected or misunderstood Paul's (and Christ's) teachings in favor of a theology that overturned common moral strictures. Yet these interpretations fail to take the polemical context of Paul's comments into account. Paul did not provide specific information about the man's circumstances because he was not interested in doing so; shaming the Corinthians was his primary goal. It is at least possible that a case for the legitimacy of the relationship between the man and his partner could be made, even among those who had embraced what they understood to be a strict moral code. After all, Paul could not hope to shame them for tolerating an action that "even" gentiles avoid if they had not already come to understand themselves as morally superior to their gentile neighbors. Perhaps the woman was quite young, a widow after a brief marriage, or a slave of the father whom the man had inherited at his father's death, and freed for the purposes of marriage.[117] Since the focus of Paul's rebuke was the community in Corinth, not the man or, even less so, the woman (whom he scarcely mentions), we simply cannot determine the specifics of their behavior.[118] Instead, Paul's comments were designed to reestablish his authority over his "children" (the Corinthians) in moral matters while enforcing his preferred definition of moral purity.

A few verses earlier, Paul accuses the Corinthians of being "arrogant," warning them that as their "father" he could legitimately "come with a stick" to discipline them (1 Cor 4:18, 21). What better way to admonish them, proving their need for his watchful guidance than to accuse them of (re)assimilating themselves to the category "gentile" by means of *porneia*? Chapter 1 observed that honorable men were expected to master both themselves and their subordinates. This theory was extended to include male rulers, who, ideally, promoted (and enforced) mastery among their subjects. Thus, the emperor (purportedly) preserved—and, in the case of Augustus, legislated—the sexual morality of the empire. Paul seems to be operating under a similar set of presuppositions. As the "father" of the Corinthian community, it was his responsibility to preserve and define the sexual purity expected of the church in Corinth. Calling the community to expel the man, Paul provided his own version of sex legislation:

> I wrote to you in my letter not to associate with the *pornoi* [male prostitutes/sexually immoral persons]—not at all meaning the *pornoi* of this world, or the greedy and the robbers and the idolaters, since you would then need to go out of the world. But now I am writing to you not to associate with anyone of the name of brother who is a *pornos* [male prostitute/fornicator], greedy, an idolater, reviler, drunkard or robber. Do not even eat with such a one. For what have I to do with judging those outside? Is it not those who are inside that you are to judge? God will judge those outside, "Drive out the wicked person from among you."
>
> (1 Cor 5:9–13)

Thomas McGinn has observed that the Augustan marriage legislation was designed, in part, to preserve elite privilege, especially elite male privilege, and to validate Augustus' own status as the (appropriate) codifier of the *regimen morum*.[119] Paul was obviously not a member of the Roman senatorial aristocracy; nevertheless, his "legislation" could be read in a similar way. He mentioned his previous instructions, sent in a letter (note that laws were often promulgated in letters),[120] he provided clarification regarding the true intent of his instructions, and he drove his authority home by quoting existing law. "Drive out the wicked from among you" may well be a direct quotation of Deuteronomy 17:7 (LXX), a passage that recommends the death penalty for idolaters; it is certainly reminiscent of biblical prescriptions against sexual sinners.[121] Whatever the behavior of the man in question, Paul's own message was clear: he was the moral arbiter of the community, and the community must enforce Paul's (Christ's) moral dictates.

YOUR BODY IS NOT YOUR OWN

All things are permissible to me, but all things are not useful. All things are permissible to me, but I will not be mastered by anything. Food is for the belly and the belly for food, but God will destroy both one and the other. And the body is not for *porneia* but for the Lord and the Lord for the body.

(1 Cor 6:12–13)

In this introduction to his discussion of the requisite holiness of Christian bodies, Paul quotes two sayings—"all things are permissible to me" and "food is for the belly and the belly for food"[122]—which he then attempts to overturn with the phrase "I will not be mastered by anything." One can be under the authority of food and *porneia* or of "the Lord," but not all three. Again, Paul contrasts being under the authority to desire with being in the power of God. Gluttony and sexual excess often appear together as evidence of corruption and "slavishness" in Greco-Roman discourses.[123] Allowing oneself to be mastered by either food or *porneia* was to fail in one's duties as a master of oneself and others.[124] One cannot be a ruler of others if one cannot rule one's own belly and body.[125] Paul also connected these two related problems, food and sex, reiterating in this passage the view that saintly bodies must be mastered by "the Lord" rather than by the belly or by sexual desire. He then went on to assert that the bodies of Christians together make up the body (*sōma*) of Christ: "Do you not know that your bodies are members of Christ?" (1 Cor 6:15; compare 1 Cor 12:12–31; Rom 12:3–8). Thus, the metaphor of bodily enslavement to God or to sin was taken a step further: the believer's body is not only mastered by the Lord, it is a part of the body of the Lord. Together with the other "members," the follower's bodily parts make up Christ's bodily parts. Since this is the case, "members" of the community and the "members" of each body must not engage in sexual immorality.

Having claimed that each person's body is a member of Christ's body and that the body of the community is Christ's body, Paul then argues that *porneia*, especially *porneia* involving a prostitute (*pornos*), must not occur: "Taking the parts [*ta melē*] of Christ, shall I make parts of a prostitute? Certainly not!" (1 Cor 6:15b). Paul added that the one who employs a prostitute "sins against his own body,"[126] as well as against the body of Christ, since his body is a "temple of the holy spirit" (6:19). By piling up metaphors—ownership by the Lord versus ownership by food and sex, the believer's bodily parts as Christ's bodily parts, the believer's body as a temple of the holy spirit (1 Cor 6:19–20, 10:14–22, 12:12–31)—Paul made the purity of the church dependent upon the sexual purity of the believers.[127] Bodies must be kept "pure" because they signify the social, as well as the individual body. Keeping body and community "pure" in Corinth meant avoiding intercourse with prostitutes (1 Cor 6:15–16).[128] It also meant refusing to tolerate sexual immorality of any kind among (1 Cor 5:1–13), holding fast to hierarchical "natural" sex,[129] exercising self-control (1 Cor 7:9), and engaging in intercourse only within the context of marriage (1 Cor 7:1–9, 36–38).

THERE SHALL BE NO *PORNEIA* AMONG THE SAINTS

First Corinthians 7 addressed sexual intercourse within marriage, widows, divorce, marriage to unbelievers, virgins, the unmarried, and the importance of remaining in the state in which one was called (slave/free; male/female; married/unmarried).[130] An overarching theme of this complicated passage is the problem of desire:

It is well for a man not to touch a woman.

(1 Cor 7:1)[131]

Because of *porneia*, each man should have his own wife and each woman her own husband.

(1 Cor 7:2)

Do not refuse one another, except perhaps by agreement for a season, in order that you might devote yourselves to prayer, and come together again, so that Satan might not test you through lack of self-control.

(*akrasia*; 1 Cor 7:5)

If they cannot exercise authority over themselves [*enkrateuomai*], they should marry, for it is better to marry than to burn.

(1 Cor 7:9)[132]

Whoever is firmly established in his heart, not being under pressure, but having authority [*exousia*] over his own desire [*thelēma*] and having deliberated in his own heart to maintain his own virgin [*parthenos*], he will do well.

(1 Cor 7:37)

Paul recommends marriage for those who cannot keep desire in check.[133] For those capable of self-control, celibacy was the better choice.[134] Paul was so anxious about out-of-control desire that he settled for marriage as a caution against *porneia*. He suggests that those who had married should remain as they are (i.e., they should stay married) but offers practical and eschatological reasons for his counsel, not an endorsement of sexual intercourse.[135] To Paul, it is preferable for virgins (*parthenoi*) to remain virgins since "the unmarried woman or virgin is anxious about the things of the Lord, that she be holy in body and spirit" (1 Cor 7:34). Still, he further advocated that a man overcome by strong passion for his *parthenos* should marry her. Again, Paul raised the concept of "authority" (*exousia*) over desire, in this case described as authority over one's will (*thelēma*).[136] Better that his own virgin relinquish her virginity, granting him a proper target for the lack of authority (*exousia*) he has over his desire, than that he fall into *porneia*. The holiness of her body and spirit pale in comparison to the danger of his lust.[137]

By endorsing marriage as a counter to *porneia*, even while favoring sexual abstinence, Paul suggested that two types of Christ followers were to be welcomed: the believer strong enough to overcome desire altogether and the believer, incapable of full self-mastery, who ought to marry.[138] In chapters 5 and 6 of this letter, Paul expressed outrage at the idea that believers would tolerate sexual immorality. Paul pointedly argued that such practices must not be permitted since "even the gentiles" know this behavior is wrong. In this chapter, he urged married couples to engage in intercourse as a caution against *porneia*, though he recommended that unmarried believers remain unmarried so long as they can also control their desires. Marriage was to be preferred to *porneia*, for it is better to marry than to be aflame with desire: "I wish all people to be as I myself am [i.e., sexually abstinent] but each has one's own gift from God" (1 Cor 7:7).[139] In this way, Paul constructed two types of Jesus followers, those who were able to imitate him—overcoming their desires and thereby making marriage unnecessary—and those who remained susceptible to lust and so continued to engage in sexual intercourse in the context of marriage. In either case, however, believers must always maintain strict control of their desires.[140]

First Corinthians 7, when read against Paul's representation of the despicable sexual behavior of gentiles, offers further evidence of the importance of sex as a sign of saintly purity and righteousness against the impurity and immorality imputed to everyone else. To Paul, *porneia* and *epithymia* were such a threat that marriage was warranted, though celibacy was represented as the better option. The power of desire was so dangerous that virgins, though better employed in full-time concern for Christ, should submit to their lustful fiancés. Perhaps, after arguing so vehemently that believers were to be distinguished from outsiders on the basis of the way they utilize their bodily parts, Paul had no choice but to describe exactly when and under what conditions the shameful parts may be employed.[141] Having been told that their bodies are "temples," and "members of Christ," with their bodily parts described as slaves of God, under the authority of the Lord, and meant for purity and righteousness, the Corinthian believers may have been confused as to what, precisely, constituted this proposed purity. Paul's response indicates that marriage was the only proper venue for the expression of desire, though sexual renunciation was to be preferred.

LET WOMEN BE WOMEN AND MEN BE MEN

Another example of Paul's concern for the sexual propriety of "the saints" can be found in his instructions regarding the veiling of women during worship.[142] Paul's insistence that women veil themselves—no other practice can be recognized among the churches of God (1 Cor 11:16)—was tied to his anxiety about the dangers of desire and his worries about "unnatural" sex. Men must be men and women must be women, even (or especially) while praying and prophesying, Paul argues. Hence, women should wear veils and men should not. Proper women should continue to wear their hair long and remain covered. Honorable men should wear their hair short and should not cover their heads. Paul argues from the order of creation, from nature, and from custom that women should be veiled and covered but men need not be. Paul prefaces his insistence that women wear veils with the following general principle: "I want you to know that the head of every man is Christ, the head of a woman is her husband and the head of Christ is God" (1 Cor 11:3).[143] Paul seems to be playing on a double meaning of "head" (*kephalē*) here: head as source and head as ruler.[144] Paul goes on to argue that man is "the image and glory of God; but woman is the glory of man" (1 Cor 11:7). Alluding to the order of creation in Genesis, Paul asserts that man was not made from woman but woman from man. She was created for and from him (1 Cor 11:8). Man is also the image and glory (*doxa*) of God, whereas she is the glory of man.[145] "In such a context, 'head' as 'source' does not exclude 'head' as 'ruler' but justifies it."[146] As "source," man must be "head." Paul later softens this hierarchical gender arrangement by noting "just as woman was made from man so man is now born of woman" (1 Cor 11:12),[147] yet he continued to insist that woman and man are qualitatively different, with man at the "head" of the pair. This difference, a difference in kind and degree, was symbolized by head coverings and hairstyles.

A woman who prays or prophesies with her head uncovered "shames her head," Paul argues. If she refuses to veil, then she should cut off her hair. But shaving her hair is not really an option, since "it is shameful [aischros] for a woman to be shorn or shaven" (1 Cor 11:5–6). "Nature itself" [hē physis autē] teaches that a woman's hair is her pride, whereas long hair for a man is degrading. A woman's hair is her "natural" covering (1 Cor 11:14). Her veil is therefore nature's helpful assistant. What are we to make of this concern for male and female hairstyles and female covering? Paul's primary concern in this passage seems to be the reinstitution of veiling for women. Nevertheless, he built his argument, in part, on hairstyles. A woman's long hair is her glory but long hair for a man is shameful. If a woman uncovers her hair, then she should cut off her hair, but for her to do so is shameful.

What is dishonorable about long hair for men and short hair for women? According to the elder Seneca, the effeminati braid their hair and thin their voices to compete with women in softness and finery.[148] Similarly, according to Dio Chrysostom a man who violates "nature's laws" in secret is discovered when one observes his voice, glance, posture, and hairstyle.[149] The Sentences of Pseudo-Phokylides cautions against allowing young boys to wear their hair long and braided, for long hair is reserved for voluptuous women.[150] According to these authors, long, carefully coifed hair symbolized an abandonment of masculinity. Plucking the beard was thought to be an even clearer indication of gender deviance, but long hair also cast suspicion on a man's manliness.[151] By the same token, women's short hair also indicated gender deviance. For example, Megilla, the woman lover of Leaena in Lucian's "Dialogues of the Courtesans," wears a wig to conceal her short hair:

> Eventually Megilla, being now rather heated, pulled off her wig, which was very realistic and fitted very closely, and revealed the skin of her head which was shaved close, just as on the most energetic of athletes. This sight gave me a shock, but she said, "Leaena, have you ever seen such a good-looking young fellow?"
>
> (Lucian Dial. meret. 5.3)[152]

Paul's concern for hairstyles and his appeals to nature, honor, and shame, when read in light of ancient associations between hairstyle and gender, are reminiscent of his description of the corrupt world in Romans 1:18–32. In that passage, Paul condemns the idolaters for unnatural intercourse and dishonorable passions:

> For this reason, God handed them over to their dishonorable passions. Their women exchanged natural intercourse [*lit.* "use"] for unnatural, and, in the same way, the men, forsaking natural intercourse with women [*lit.* "the natural use of women"], were consumed by desire for one another, men in men, accomplishing shameless and dishonorable acts and receiving in their own persons the due penalty for their error.
>
> (1:26–27)[153]

Elsewhere, Paul asserts that the fornicators/male prostitutes (πόρνοι can mean either) and effeminates (*malakoi*) will not inherit the kingdom of God. Male prostitutes were penetrated by other men for a living or, if enslaved, for the profit of their owners. Thus, as noted in chapter 1, for a man to be called a "prostitute" was a particularly sharp insult. Such men were especially "slavish," having abandoned manhood (i.e., the active, penetrative role) for profit.

Violations of "nature" for Paul involved violations of gender.[154] Men should desire the "natural use" (*physikē chrēsis*) of women, not penetration by other men. Paul's comment that the unnatural men receive "in their own persons the due penalty for their error" may be a euphemistic reference to the supposed injury that the passive partner receives.[155] Similarly, "honor" (*timē*) requires gender conformity. An honorable man should look like a man. His bare head is his "glory" (*doxa*). A woman's covering (hair or veil) is her *doxa*. Short, uncovered hair is her shame (*aischros*). Furthermore, if a woman desires at all, it should be for her "natural use" (*physikē chrēsis*). "'Natural use of the female' means that a male penetrates a female in an act that signified the subordination of the woman and control by the man over her."[156] Having chosen to describe the downfall of sinful humanity in terms of unnatural use and dishonorable desire, is it any wonder that Paul could not tolerate any gender deviancy in Corinth, signified by hairstyles and by veiling?

Paul offers yet another reason why a woman ought to wear a veil. She ought to do so "on account of the angels." This verse is particularly enigmatic: "For this reason woman ought to have a veil/authority over her head, on account of the angels" (1 Cor 11:10). Instead of repeating his previous terminology for veiling, Paul states that a woman ought to have an "authority" over her head. Why would Paul use the term "*exousia*" here? He may be purposefully countering the claims of some women that they have the authority (*exousia*) to prophesy without the veil, since they have overcome their gender "in the spirit" and "in Christ," thereby attaining "male" self-mastery.[157] Such an argument may have been made possible by the baptismal formula now preserved in Galatians 3:28: "There is neither Jew nor Greek, neither slave nor free, not male or female."[158] No, Paul argues, a veil, the symbol of female "authority" over her own desire as well as over the male desire she may attract, are both necessary. Ultimate gender equivalence "in Christ" did not result in the abolishment of "natural" gender in the community of the saints.

Paul's use of "*exousia*" earlier in this letter suggests that he may have chosen to employ a play on words here to raise, once again, the problem of desire. In 1 Cor 5:1–5, Paul implies that having chosen to ignore his authority as their "father," the Corinthians had become worse than gentiles, tolerating a *pornos* in their midst. In 1 Cor 6:12, Paul remarks that one could not place oneself under the authority (*exousia*) of food, *porneia*, and also "the Lord." In 1 Cor 7:37, Paul recommends celibacy for men who have gained authority (*exousia*) over their desire. "Authority," or lack of it, was embodied in sexual self-mastery or the opposite, sexual license. Thus, by claiming that women must have a veil/authority over their heads, Paul may have sought to remind them that their desire needs to be kept in check and by a proper "authority." Desire must be covered, just as the "shameful parts" (i.e., the genitals) of the body are also covered (1 Cor 12:23–24).[159] The next portion of this verse offers further support for this interpretation.

The reason Paul gives for the veil/authority—"on account of the angels"—is puzzling, yet it may also refer to the problem of desire and temptation. There was a tradition stemming from Genesis 6:1–4, expanded in 1 Enoch and other postbiblical literature, in which the "sons of God" desired and had intercourse with "the daughters of men," leading to wickedness and immorality.[160] Tertullian reads the Pauline injunction to veil as a precautionary measure against these fallen angels/"sons of God." These angels, viewing the beauty of the "daughters of men," lusted after them and transgressed. Therefore, virgins must be veiled to protect angels, men, and boys from similar temptation (*Virg.* 7.2–4).[161] If Tertullian's interpretation was correct, Paul, ordering women to put on the veil/authority "on account of the angels," was concerned with the sexual temptation of an unveiled woman. Therefore, for Paul veils may have offered a "prophylactic" capable of protecting women from the male gaze and men from sexual temptation.[162] Women must have an "authority" (veil) over their heads because they must keep their desire in control while, at the same time, providing assistance to the men and angels who also endeavor to keep desire in check.[163] Indeed, the entire community needs to submit to the proper "authorities"—including Paul—to avoid sexual temptation.[164]

Paul's argument regarding veiling renders desire problematic while insisting that gender deviance must not be tolerated. Women remain secondary to men by nature and creation, even if men are born through women. Therefore, it was considered disgraceful and unnatural for men to adopt the hairstyles of women, a practice that would mark them as effeminate and "unnatural," as *malakoi* and *arsenokoitai*. Likewise, it was shameful for women to shave their heads in a vain attempt to be like men. Such women may even be mistaken for the "unnatural" women Paul described in Rom 1:26–27. Taking off the veil, therefore, placed the entire community in danger, or so Paul suggests. Women may lose control over their own desire. Men, viewing women, may become tempted and lose their self-mastery. Veiling for Paul signifies everything he claims for the followers of Christ: sexual purity, self-control, and "natural" gender. Unveiling, in this context, was risky indeed.

SEX AND PAULINE ELITISMS

If, in a Greco-Roman context, an "elite" was one who avoids excess, masters desire, conforms to "natural" gender, and displays virtue, then Paul's condemnation of gentiles—they are incapable of mastering desire—suggests that only the followers of Christ were truly "elite." The category "elite"—when understood as not only, or even primarily, a socioeconomic designation but as a discursive production—is subject to constant renegotiation. In Paul's world, the "elite" purportedly included only virtuous, wealthy men of impeccable ancestry and the chaste women they controlled. Ideally, the elite exhibited mastery over themselves, their households and their subordinates. They took the dominant position in all matters, including sexual intercourse. Their women were modest and sexually loyal to the men who controlled them, bearing only legitimate children. The emperors, as the archetypal elite male in this paradigm, ought to embody the piety, self-control, and munificence expected of all who were truly noble. Hence imperial virtue, however fallacious, was proclaimed throughout the empire, with emperors honored for their exceptional, even divine, virtue and piety. At the opposite end of this ideological spectrum were slaves. Morally suspect or exempt, they possessed no legal control over their own bodies, were vulnerable to bodily penetration and violation by their superiors, and were thought to be low "by nature."

To Paul, however, the only men truly capable of mastering desire were those "in Christ." These men, like the "elite" of the empire, would never allow themselves to be penetrated. In a true exhibition of self-mastery, they also avoided intercourse with prostitutes and had sexual intercourse with appropriate subordinates so as to avoid *porneia.* Some "saints," men and women both, were able to control desire so completely that they did not need to marry to avoid *porneia* but rather remained sexually continent. Still, married or not, "sisters in Christ" were properly subordinate. They veiled themselves and their desires. They submitted to their husbands, even as their husbands submitted to them. These men and women, overcoming desire through Christ, kept themselves pure. At the opposite end of this Pauline elite were idolaters (including, by implication, the emperor and his representatives). They were not pious; rather, they were hostile to God and could not possibly control themselves. They were "naturally" morally suspect. For now the followers of Christ must be subordinate to the rulers, those *archontes* who masquerade as the "elite," but the day is at hand, the wrath is already being revealed, God's swift judgment will be merciless. Paul's alternative elitism claimed righteousness for his group alone.

In his letters to the churches of Rome and Corinth, Paul builds upon Greek and Roman cultural norms to claim elite status for all Christ followers, slave and free alike, while adopting a traditional biblical and post-biblical argument that the gentiles are enslaved to lust. Paul does not really challenge the terms of the argument—sexual virtue and sexual vice are preserved as important, if not the most important, signs of "the elite"— rather, he reconfigures this cultural logic in order to claim elite status for his group exclusively. Slaves are not necessarily "slavish." Instead, those who suppress the truth, the idolaters, the gentiles, the perverse generation, the slaves of sin, and those who gratify the flesh were the true "slaves." The theory that the citizen men and their women are sexually virtuous but the slaves are morally suspect is displaced by a system in which Christ followers are elite but everyone else is "slavish." All who reject God are portrayed as incapable of virtue, since the rejection of God leads to sexual depravity by definition and Christ provides the sole solution to the problem of vice. Insider sexual ethics were also at stake. Having depicted outsiders as sexually corrupt, Paul could shame his audience for tolerating a sexual misdeed that "even the gentiles" would denounce. Suggesting that gentiles had been perverted by "unnatural" lust, Paul could then insist that the Corinthian church conform to his version of "natural" gender. Suggesting that "the saints" were freed from desire, having enslaved their "members" to God, Paul could further claim that gentiles are necessarily slaves to desire. Sexualized othering and community definition went hand and hand, a tradition that continued in later Christian discourse.

CHAPTER 3

Sexual Vice and Christian *Apologia*

During the second century, there arose a defensive sort of Christian writing designed to address new, pointed criticisms of the movement. Christian authors composed defenses of the faith that reassured their non-Christian audiences by registering a commitment to a number of the central values of the larger culture and by claiming that, of all people, they were the most friendly toward the emperor and "his" empire. Though they did "not completely identify themselves with the broader society," these authors were also not "advocates of confrontation or revolution"; rather, they hoped to persuade educated elites familiar with Greek philosophy to adopt a more sympathetic view towards the Christians, explaining their movement in terms that outsiders could both understand and appreciate.[1] A few of these treatises were addressed specifically to the emperors, perhaps reflecting a sincere hope that the emperor could be converted the to their cause. After all, the emperors they addressed were more reasonable than most: Antoninus Pius was "broad-minded," and his son Marcus Aurelius had adopted Stoic philosophy, ending the persecutions suffered by Stoic philosophers under previous emperors.[2] In this way, second-century Christian authors took it upon themselves to argue that Christianity "was the embodiment of the noblest conceptions of Greek philosophy,"[3] defending their religion as decent, law abiding, and loyal to Rome.

This is a summary of one standard line of interpretation applied to a set of second-century Greek Christian writers identified as "apologists." This chapter presents a different reading of this same material by offering a reconsideration of the "apologies" of Justin Martyr. Justin addressed writings to the emperor, the emperor's heirs, and the Roman Senate. In an address he identified as a "προσφώνησις," a term employed to label speeches of praise addressed to rulers,[4] and a "ἔντευξις," or petition, he claims that the Christians obey the emperor "joyfully" (Justin *1 Apol.* 17). But the critical edge of Justin's prose is apparent even here: in the same sentence, he notes that though Christians acknowledge "you [the emperor and the Senate] as kings and rulers of men," they do so "praying you may be found to have, besides royal power, sound judgment" (*1 Apol.* 17). He goes on to argue that those who abuse the Christians are enslaved by demonic, profligate, bloodthirsty gods (*1 Apol.* 4; *2 Apol.* 5); that, by persecuting the Christians, they behave like public executioners rather than rulers (*1 Apol.* 12); and, furthermore, that they fail to obey—let alone promote—their own laws (*1 Apol.* 24–25, 27; *2 Apol.* 2). In other words, Justin consistently maintains that the emperor and the Senate utterly failed at sound judgment; their religious and moral practices prove it. Justin did not compose an accommodationist defense of Christian loyalty, his petition reads much more like a speech of blame.

Later "apologists" presented equally paradoxical arguments. According to Theophilus of Antioch, Christians happily pay their taxes and acknowledge "you" as the kings and rulers; they also love their enemies and bless those who persecute them (Theophilus *Ad Auto.* 3.14, citing Rom 13:7–8). Their God instructs them to be subordinate to the rulers and powers (*archais* and *exousiais*) and to "pay all things to all, honor to whom honor is due, fear to whom fear is due, tax to whom taxes are due; to owe no one anything but to love all" (*Ad Auto.* 3.14). Nevertheless, Theophilus accused Autolychus—the (hypothetical?) Greek critic to whom he addressed his three-volume book—of being an adulterer, a fornicator, and a thief by virtue of his disgusting devotion to the gods (*Ad Auto.* 1.2). Autolychus, and others like him, worship gods like Zeus, a demon guilty of incest, adultery, and uncontrolled lust (*Ad Auto.* 1.9; 3.8), building temples and crafting idols in their honor (*Ad Auto.* 1.10; 2.2). Therefore, Theophilus insisted, they will be punished (*Ad Auto.* 1.14).

Athenagoras wrote an "embassy" (a formal petition) to the "philosopher" emperors Marcus Aurelius and Lucius Verus pleading the Christian cause (Athenagoras *Leg.* 1.1).[5] Athenagoras insists that the Christians confirmed their goodness with good deeds and the affection that they hold toward their neighbors (*Leg.* 11.3). Therefore, those who truly condemn bad behavior ought not to hate them; rather, they should hate Zeus, who begot children by his mother and daughter (*Leg.* 20).[6] The gods of the Greeks and Romans—gods "you" worship—were guilty of the worst sorts of offenses (*Leg.* 18–22). By contrast, Christians are not even permitted to look at a woman with lust (*epithymia*), Athenagoras asserts, let alone contemplate incest or adultery (*Leg.* 32). Christian men seek intercourse only with their wives and then engage in it solely for the sake of procreation, not to indulge their desire (*epithymia*); in fact, many Christians grow old without marrying at all (*Leg.* 33). "You," however, have intercourse with prostitutes, male and female: "Men work their frightful deeds with men; they violate in every way those whose bodies are especially noble or comely" (*Leg.* 34).[7] The opponents of the Christians are all adulterers (*moichoi*) and pederasts (*paiderastai*) though they perversely abuse those who married only once or abstained from intercourse altogether (i.e., the Christians, *Leg.* 34). Athenagoras portrays the Romans as hypocrites—as well as sexual and religious deviants—of the worst kind.

Tatian, a student of Justin's, composed a speech against the Greeks as a people, setting out to prove that what they considered honorable was never actually practiced by them.[8] Honorable behavior, Tatian claims, is the property of Christians alone. Christians preserve their chastity (*sōphrosynē*), but the behavior of the Greeks "borders on madness" (Tatian *Or.* 33).[9] Sappho the courtesan (i.e., the famous Attic poet) "sang her own lewdness" (*Or.* 33). By contrast, chaste Christian women spin at their distaffs while they discuss godly things (*Or.* 33). Tatian expressed particular disdain for actors and those who would watch them, offering the following description of one (supposedly) depraved thespian:

> [He appeared] very affected and putting on all sorts of delicate airs, now with flashing eyes, now wringing his hands and expressing madness with clay make up ... being in one man an accuser of all the gods, epitome of superstition, slanderer of heroism, actor of murders, interpreter of adultery, repository of madness, teacher of *kinaidoi*,[10] instigator of condemned criminals—and such a one is applauded by them all!
>
> (*Or.* 22).[11]

From Tatian's perspective, then, the utter depravity of the Greeks can be summed up by the effeminate, licentious, and false behavior of this actor whom they boldly revere.

Recent interpreters, noting the oppositional tone of the rhetoric these authors employed, have come to regard the opening address to the emperor or other rulers—when it occurs—as a literary fiction. "In practice," Mary Beard, John North, and Simon Price observe, "the Apologies seem not be have been much read by non-Christians, their importance lying in their internal consumption within the church."[12] Frances Young agrees, arguing that these writings were probably in-group documents designed to justify the decision by Christian elites to reject the literature and customs of their ancestral community in favor of a religion that was "regarded by most people ... as a suspiciously alien culture."[13] The "apologies," then, were not directed at the emperor or even at interested outsiders but at fellow Christians who had already converted but were having second thoughts. According to this reading, Justin's and Athenagoras's ironic appeals to "philosopher-kings" were designed, at least in part, to allay the concerns of educated Christians like themselves, not to persuade the emperor. To do so, they had to address non-Christian philosophy in some way, and so they argued that true philosophers recognize truth, Christianity is true, and "any really committed philosopher would see this."[14]

The apologists did engage philosophy in their writings, comparing Christianity to philosophy and noting that philosophers were occasionally persecuted. Justin declared himself to be a philosopher and a Christian, or, more accurately, a Christian philosopher (Justin *Dial.* 2, 8).[15] Tatian celebrated the "true, barbarian philosophy" of the Christians, comparing his superior philosophy to the corrupt, degraded philosophies of the Greeks (*Or.* 1–3).[16] Theophilus observed that Plato, like the Christians, also believed in an uncreated God, though, Theophilus argued, this important insight was lost once Plato and his followers posited that uncreated matter is also God (Theophilus *Ad Auto.* 2.4).[17] Athenagoras noted several points of convergence between Christian theology and the theology of Plato's *Timaeus*, though he went on to assert that Plato did not fully comprehend the truth of his arguments (*Leg.* 6, 16, 19, 23).[18] Justin granted that a few philosophers spoke some measure of truth (Socrates, Heraclitus, Musonius Rufus), but he further claimed that whatever truths they obtained had been given to them by the Logos (i.e., by Christ, *1* Apol. 5, *2 Apol.* 10). Indeed, many of the truths Plato mentioned were drawn from Moses (*1 Apol.* 10),[19] and the Logos in its fullness is available to Christians alone (*2 Apol.* 10).[20]

Perhaps Christians trained to value a philosophical upbringing were (re)convinced by these descriptions of philosophy as an incomplete, deformed precursor to the fullness of Christian truth. Certainly, fellow Christian philosophers would have been powerfully reminded of the allegedly great chasm between them—reasonable, pure, chaste, obedient, fully in possession of truth—and the imperfect philosophies they had left behind. But the need to justify Christian abandonment of traditional piety to wavering Greek or Roman Christians cannot fully account for the vehemence of this rhetoric. Moreover, as Rebecca Lyman has pointed out, engagement with philosophers and philosophical argument did not imply that these writers were working to *reconcile* Christian and Greek ideals. Indeed, such an approach presupposes a false distinction between "Christian" and "Greek"; these were not distinct categories that needed to be, or could be, reconciled but identity positions in constant flux and negotiation.[21] Therefore, a defense of *Christian* philosophy as uniquely "safe and profitable" on the part of Justin and other Christian authors included both a "resistance to and negotiation of existing [philosophical] authorities."[22] Justin reconfigured the philosophical "truths" current among his contemporaries in order to argue that all truth, since it must come from (his) God, was in fact Christian truth.[23]

As Justin understood it, the problem was not that there is no truth outside of Christianity but that truth had been constantly distorted by evil demons and evil desire prior to the advent of Christ (*1 Apol.* 10).[24] A limited appreciation of philosophy, such as is found in Justin's writings, did not reconcile Christianity with broader cultural ideals—Christian authors could not and did not stand outside the larger culture in which they operated—but described Christianity as the fulfillment of all truth, wherever it might be found. In other words, even when these writers discussed philosophy, they did so to lend further credence to beliefs they identified as "Christian," not to recommend central (non-Christian) values. Indeed, they made the opposite argument, repeatedly insisting that, without Christ, outsiders were doomed to resemble their depraved gods. They were arguing that Christians were different, and better. Moreover, Justin's principal argument regarding the philosophers—those who managed to reach some semblance of truth were often persecuted—served to emphasize the tremendous and unjustified wrong Christians were suffering at the hands of their rulers, an attempt to vindicate his own cause rather than a defense of the heroic philosophers of old.[25] The apologists did not seek to harmonize Christianity and Platonism or Christianity and Stoicism; they employed the heroes of Platonism and Stoicism to demonstrate the cruelty and foolishness of their neighbors.

Paul had defined the boundaries demarcating the brothers and sisters in Christ from others in sexual terms. Justin adopted a similar strategy and with similar results: the empire and "her" emperor are repeatedly associated with sexual licentiousness and thereby accused of failure at mastery.[26]

In this case, however, the charges are explicit. Justin addresses his appeals to emperors and the Senate, not to local churches. Did he imagine that the emperor would read them? Did he want him to? Earlier scholars believed that he did, though more recent scholars are unconvinced. By the second century, Christians were facing direct challenges to their movement in the form of verbal abuse and, in some (probably rare) cases, public execution. Under these circumstances, a defense of some sort was needed. Yet, as we shall see, this defense did not placate the emperor or "reconcile" Christianity with philosophy; rather, Justin launched a forceful attack upon the manhood and mastery of his rulers, adopting terms and rhetorical strategies that he shared with the authors of the *Martyrdom of Polycarp*, *The Letter of the Churches of Lyons and Vienne*, and other writings that celebrated the heroic, "manly" suffering of Christian martyrs. Before discussing Justin's arguments, however, we need to further explore second-generation Christian proposals regarding the nature of the sexual self-mastery required of those "in Christ." Justin's description of Christian "chastity" (*sōphrosynē*) included both married Christians and those who had renounced sexual intercourse (*1 Apol.* 15). In the last chapter, we observed that Paul had recommended that the brothers and sisters in Christ marry because of the danger of *porneia* or remain continent if they could control desire. This ambiguous position left plenty of room for disagreement, even among those who claimed Paul's own authority to validate their moral norms.

SHOULD ONE MARRY? PAUL, THE HOUSEHOLD CODES, AND CHRISTIAN SEXUAL DIFFERENCE

Second-generation Christians, writing in Paul's name or claiming his authority in other ways, continued to argue that πορνεία characterized outsiders but never insiders.[27] For example, the "Paul" who wrote Colossians reminded his audience that they had put to death *porneia*, impurity, the passion of lust, wickedness and greed: that is, the "earthly parts" within them. Formerly, their lives were characterized by vice, but now they have become something new (Col 3:5–11). According to the "Paul" of Ephesians, gentiles without Christ are estranged from God and have been abandoned to licentiousness (ἀσέλγεια; Eph 4:18–19). By contrast, the brothers-in-Christ overcome their former way of life, put aside their old humanity (*palaios anthrōpos*), and reject deceptive desire (*epithymia thēs apathēs*; Eph 4:22). The author of Titus, taking on the guise of Paul writing to a trusted disciple,[28] argues that although "we" were once "foolish, disobedient, deceived, slaves to various desires and pleasures, leading our lives in wickedness and envy, hateful, and hating one another" (Titus 3:3),[29] now God has trained (*paideuō*) us to renounce godlessness (*asebeia*) and worldly desires (*hai kosmikai epithymiai*); we ("Paul," "Titus," and their followers) live moderately (*sōphronōs*), justly (*dikaiōs*), and piously (*eusebōs*) while waiting patiently for Christ to appear again in glory (Titus 2:12).

According to these Pauline authors, an orderly household was the appropriate venue for displaying (supposedly unique) Christian sexual virtue. In Colossians and Ephesians, harmonious household hierarchy was said to be grounded in "love"(*agapē*) and sanctified by Christ. Wives were instructed to remain subject to their husbands "as is fitting in the Lord" or "as to the Lord" (Col 3:18; Eph 5:22). Husbands were encouraged to love their wives "as Christ loved the church" (Col 3:19; Eph 5:25). Children were reminded to obey their parents (Col 3:20; Eph 6:1), fathers to discipline and instruct their children (Eph 6:4), slaves to obey their masters "in singleness of heart, fearing the Lord," and masters to treat their slaves fairly, remembering that they too have a master—in heaven (Col 3:22; Eph 6:5–9).[30] In this way, hierarchical household arrangements were represented as God-given requirements, characteristic of all those who truly dwell "in Christ."[31] The author of the Pastoral Epistles (1 Timothy, 2 Tiimothy, Titus) adopted a similar position. Young women, this author claims, must be trained in *sōphrosynē* at home, learning to love their husbands and children (Titus 2:4–5). Women are saved by childbearing, so long as they continue in faith, love, and holiness, with *sōphrosynē* (1 Tim 2:15). Community leaders were to be selected on the basis of their well-ordered households. After all, "if a man does not know how to manage his own household, how can he care for God's church?" (1 Tim 3:5; compare Poly. *Phil.* 11.2). Believers were expected to marry, unless they happened to be widowers and older widows. A widow older than sixty could be "enrolled"—presumably, supported by the church—so long as her good deeds were well known, she married only once, and she had brought up her children (1 Tim 5:9–10).[32] Younger widows, however, must remarry, or they will run amok and embarrass the church (1 Tim 5:11–14). From this author's perspective, marriage and household enable believers to master "the potentially unruly passions of the soul" so that they might command themselves, their households, and the church appropriately.[33]

Similar celebrations of the well-ordered, harmonious household, governed by a master who masters himself, may be found in all sorts of Greco-Roman moralizing literature.[34] When "Paul" asks the rhetorical question,

"If a man does not know how to manage his own household, how can he care for God's church?" he knows what the answer should be: he cannot. His contemporaries agreed. Plutarch offers strikingly similar advice: "A man therefore ought to have his household well harmonized who is going to harmonize city, agora, and friends."[35] In other words, a man must command obedience among his "subjects" at home if he hopes to obtain subjects in the marketplace or polis.[36] To Plutarch, Christ was irrelevant to the project of keeping women, children, and slaves in line. For those writing as Paul, however, Christ alone made this idealized harmony possible. Christ blesses and demands the submission of woman, child, and slave—they are "saved" by their subjugation. Masterful command of self and subordinate ought to characterize those Christian free men designated to lead household and church; judgment awaits those who fail to adopt their proper position in this rigidly hierarchical, divinely authorized scheme (Col 2:23, 3:10; Eph 4:23–24; 1 Tim 2:8–15, 3:6–7, 3:11, 5:5, 5:11–14; 2 Tim 3:1–9; Titus 1:5–16).

The orderliness of the harmonious Christian household is contrasted in these letters with the alleged decadence and disorderliness of outsiders. Outsiders—the "sons of disobedience"—hide their shameful deeds in secret (Eph 5:6–14). Without Christ, these people are enslaved to various desires and delights (*douleuontes epithymiais kai hēdonais poikilais*, Tit 3:3). Thus, these authors reiterate Paul's own argument regarding the followers of Christ—only they are capable of virtue—yet shift the argument in such a way that a familiar sex-gender-status system was further maintained: a masterful free man rules the house, the most virtuous free man rules the community, and all are ruled by a (the) beneficent god(s). Still, good household management was represented as something that only Christians could do well. As Paul argued earlier and as these authors reaffirm, gentiles without Christ are slaves of desire, victims of every sort of vice, and utterly incapable of *enkrateia* or *sōphrosynē*.

The anonymous second-century author of the *Acts of Paul and Thecla* offered an alternative reading of Pauline sexual values. According to this author, Paul instructed Christians to avoid marriage and sexual intercourse if at all possible; perpetual virginity was the preferred option.[37] "Blessed are the continent, for God shall speak with them… . blessed are those who have wives as if not having them, for they shall experience God… . Blessed are the bodies of the virgins, for they shall be well pleasing to God and shall not lose the reward for their chastity," or so this author taught (5–6).[38] The *Acts of Paul and Thecla* present a heroine who, upon hearing the gospel of Paul, betrays her household and family in favor of a life of continence and virginity. She rejects her earthly "masters" (her mother and her fiancé) in favor of her heavenly "master," Christ, and, in the process, she achieves full mastery over her desires, avoiding human marriage altogether.[39] This story, and others like it, seem to have been intended as Christian inversions of popular Greek romance narratives. In the romance, the goal was a proper match between a beautiful virgin and a brave elite young man in marriage.[40] In the Christian version, earthly marriage is rejected in favor of valiant sexual renunciation. Kate Cooper suggests that this alternative Christian "romance" was designed to offer a direct challenge to received social conventions:

> In the Apocryphal Acts we find continuity and subversion: continuity, in that the heroine established in the ancient romance appears again in relatively unchanged form; subversion in that the traditional hero's position is insecure, and he eventually loses the heroine to a man who is clearly superior but whose goals are not those of the social order. Thus we move from a celebration of sexuality in the service of social continuity to a denigration of sexuality in service of a challenge to the establishment.[41]

Cooper understands the *Acts of Paul and Thecla* and other Christian stories regarding the heroic sexual renunciation of apostles and virgins as discursive weapons in a battle waged between elite Christian men and their non-Christian rivals.[42] The *Acts* broadcasts the immunity of the apostles to the temptations of desire and the unexpected self-mastery that women gain under their tutelage, a direct claim of moral superiority in an ancient context and also a pointed challenge to the status quo.[43] This moral superiority is gained at the expense of traditional marriage, even as the chastity of women—in this case, the sexual renunciation of women—is once again used to broadcast the moral fitness of the men (apostle, Christ) to whom they submitted. The call to sexual renunciation in the *Acts of Paul and Thecla* extends and intensifies Paul's own us/them language by narrating a dramatic clash between the ascetic apostle and his non-Christian competitors, Greek nobles determined to marry off their daughters.

Perhaps those Pauline Christians who preferred sexual abstinence to marriage did offer a sharper critique of the surrounding culture—even while upholding a rhetoric of self-mastery that they shared with that culture. Still, the Pauline Christians who preferred that Christian virtue be worked out in a "proper" Christian household were also critical of the larger society, as already observed. Pauline Christians, whatever position they took on sexual renunciation, continued to represent difference in terms of sexual virtue and vice. Whether marriage or abstinence was favored, these authors agreed: sexual self-control belongs to the Christians alone. Checking the indulgence of the flesh, avoiding *porneia*, maintaining proper order, these authors represented their movement as entirely unique, even as they adopted aspects of a moral code they shared with their neighbors. As Lewis Donelson has commented in his analysis of the Pastorals, "the author is co-opting for his own system the highest ethical ideals of his culture. In so doing he pronounces an apology for his community, since he is asserting that the ideal ethical life to which the majority of his culture aspires is available only within the doors of the Christian church."[44]

Donelson has argued that the Pastorals embraced and enforced a traditional order of the household within the churches, in part, to offer an "apology" to the surrounding community. By living up to a strict version of the hierarchical household, Christians sought to appear honorable to outsiders, to make their movement more attractive to others, and to deflect criticism against them. What is missing in this analysis, however, is anticipated by Donelson's comment "the ideal ethical life" is "available only within the doors of the Christian church." Christians may have quarreled about the content of the "ideal ethical life"—for some it meant sexual abstinence, for others, marriage[45]—yet the literature surveyed thus far is universal in the conviction that true believers are alone capable of achieving virtue, however virtue is defined. As Cooper has argued, there was a sharp edge to the Christian rhetoric of sexual self-control: if Christians were better at self-mastery than everyone else, surely they also deserved to be accorded the most prestige, the most honor, the highest status. Could the elites of the city, elites who dared contest the superior moral fitness of their far more masterful Christian rivals, possibly deserve the honor they demanded? The thesis Donelson recommends, while persuasive, cannot easily account for the force of the emerging Christian rhetoric of sexual virtue and vice, even among the Pastorals. Christians did not simply insist upon sexual self-mastery for their ranks, they denied the possibility of true mastery for outsiders. This strategy is not "apologetic" in an obvious sense, even in cases where household hierarchy was embraced as "Christian." Christian authors may have sought to defend their movement, but they also clearly, and pointedly, characterized outsiders as immoral lovers of vice.

JUSTIN'S OFFENSIVE DEFENSE OF THE CHRISTIANS

Addressing the Emperor Antoninus Pius, his adopted sons Marcus Aurelius and Lucius Verus, and the Roman Senate, Justin Martyr urges his rulers to judge Christians not by passion (*pathos*) but in accordance with piety (*eusebeia*) and philosophy (*philosophia*, Justin *1 Apol.* 1). He then proceeds to describe the beliefs and practices of these rulers in opposite terms: The Romans bestow rewards and honors on those who worship Zeus and follow his incestuous example (*1 Apol.* 4). The Greeks and the Romans are led by unreasonable passion (*alogos pathos*) and wicked demons to persecute those who speak the truth (*1 Apol.* 5). The artisans who build temples and form statuary to honor the gods are as licentious as the gods they seek to commend (*1 Apol.* 9). Unlike the Christians, "you"—the rulers, Romans, and Greeks more generally—expose infants, producing a steady supply of children to be reared for the purposes of prostitution. Hence, the father of an exposed child may unknowingly visit his own scion to sate his promiscuous lusts, thereby committing incest and *porneia* at once (*1 Apol.* 27; compare Tatian *Or.* 28).[46] "Indeed," Justin laments, "the things openly done and honored by you [i.e., emperor, sons, and Senate], as if the light of God were overturned and not present, you charge against us. This, in truth, does no harm to us who depart from such things, but rather [it does do harm] to those who do them and then falsely accuse us" (*1 Apol.* 27).[47]

Justin further contrasts "you" and "your" gods with the exceedingly chaste (σώφρων) Christians. True Christians would never commit adultery, marry only once, and never look at a woman for the purpose of lusting after her (*1 Apol.* 15). Indeed, Justin boasted, some Christians remain pure (*aphthoros*, in this case, sexually abstinent) even to the age of sixty or seventy (*1 Apol.* 15). In fact, people who once reveled in fornications (*porneiai*) have finally adopted chastity (*sōphrosynē*) under the influence of Christ (*1 Apol.* 14). Justin makes a similar point in a supplementary appeal written, ostensibly, to the Roman Senate. There he recounts the story of a Christian woman in Rome who, prior to her conversion, had engaged in every sort of licentious, adulterous pleasure with the full approval of her lascivious husband. After conversion, she adopted a temperate lifestyle and tried to convince her husband to do the same. When, after several attempts at persuasion, her efforts failed, she was forced to divorce him. Her dissolute husband, instead of rejoicing that she had given up sex acts with household slaves—an outrageous and illegal practice from the perspective of Justin and his contemporaries[48]—sought to have her punished by accusing her of being a Christian. When she managed to escape punishment, her husband directed his ire against one of her Christian brethren, arranging to have him arrested and punished (2 *Apol.* 2). At the end of the episode, Justin sums up the injustice by presenting a spontaneous protest, allegedly offered by a Christian named Lucius to Urbicus, the prefect of the city of Rome: "What is the accusation? Why do you punish this man, not as an adulterer (*moichos*), nor as a *pornos* (prostitute/fornicator), nor murderer, nor thief, nor robber, nor convicted of any crime whatsoever, but as one who has only professed that he is called by the name Christian?" (2 *Apol* 2.16).[49] In theory, the husband of the woman ought to have divorced her for committing adultery with slaves, yet he not only tolerated her behavior, he encouraged it.[50] Could Justin be suggesting that the husband was the true criminal since he had behaved as his wife's procurer? His criminality was further attested by the "unnatural" pleasures he pursued. According to Justin, the man sought pleasures "contrary to the law of nature" (*para ton tēs physeōs nomon*) in addition to chasing after various female paramours.[51] Like the infamous Emperor Gaius, the husband's sexual excess included a preference for anal penetration, a shocking violation of gender and status conventions.[52] As anyone aware of Roman law would have realized, the husband should have been punished for tolerating adultery, for prostituting his wife, and for prostituting himself; he certainly should have never been granted a favorable hearing from the prefect of Rome. Justin's argument suggests that the Christians—the only moral people in this tale—should have been set free.

JUSTIN'S SPEECH OF BLAME

Justin's assertions regarding Christian obedience and his alleged openness to both philosophy and empire are further contradicted by the apocalyptic undercurrent that runs throughout his address. Justin proclaims Christian innocence and notes the perfection of philosophical truth in Christian teaching. He also threatens the emperor and the Senate with hellfire and eternal punishment. He describes the purity and propriety required by the Christian God. He also suggests that the gods of the emperor and the Senate are profligate and bloodthirsty. In enslaving themselves to these gods, the imperial court was in danger of following their example, or so Justin suggests. Over the course of his appeal, Justin offers a series of contrasts between "you" (emperor, imperial heirs, and Senate) and the Christians, contrasts that left no doubt regarding who will ultimately be punished for wrongdoing:

> You surrender to irrational passions and are led by a scourge of worthless demons to punish us; we reject these wicked and impious demons as unworthy of all people who pursue virtue [*aretē*].
>
> (*1 Apol.*5)

> You condemn us on the basis of precedent alone, without investigating our conduct; we are eager for you to investigate us. If you discover those among us who are evildoers, we ask that you would punish them.
>
> (7)

> You appoint people as guardians of temples of idols made by debauched craftsmen, "not recognizing that it is unlawful even to think or to say that people are the guardians of gods;" we do not honor these lifeless idols or visit these temples to evil demons.
>
> (9)

> You hear that we look for a kingdom and assume that we mean a human one; we do not want a human kingdom, a fact that is demonstrated by our willingness to be executed.
>
> (11)

> You seem to be anxious that everyone will become righteous and you will no longer have anyone to punish, behaving like public executioners, not good rulers [*archonton agathon*]; by contrast the Logos is a kingly and just ruler [*basilikotaton kai dikaiotaton arhconta*].
>
> (12)

> You are forewarned: the demons strive to have you as their slaves and assistants, luring you into porneia and greed; we renounce these gods, follow the Logos, maintain chastity, share our wealth, and pray for our enemies.
>
> (14)

> We are unjustly hated above all others though you honor philosophers who make some of the same points.
>
> (20)

> The sole accusation you bring against us is that we do not worship the same gods as you, yet your gods are monstrous, profligate demons.
>
> (24–25)

You levy taxes on prostitution, raising boys to become *kinaidoi* and tolerating those who should be executed for their sexual perversions; we never even expose children.

(27)

You yourselves do openly the terrible things of which you accuse us.

(27)

The wicked demons [i.e., your gods] persuade "those who live contrary to reason, and are subject to passions and wicked customs and are deluded" to kill and hate us.

(57)

We forewarn you that you will not escape the coming judgment of God if you continue to abuse us; our cause is just.

(68)

Thus, Justin's appeal to his rulers asserts that "you"—rulers unwilling to listen to reason—are in fact enslaved by the passions and by demons; promote despicable, immoral behavior; behave like violent tyrants; and, therefore, are the very opposite of the good rulers "you" purport to be. Justin repeatedly warned "you" that punishment from the true king and heir—God and his son Jesus—would soon follow.

The radical nature of this argument is actually quite striking. The emperors and the Senate proclaimed that Roman privilege and ascendancy were upheld by the gods. By contrast, Justin argues that the divinities sustaining imperial rule were part of a demonic, not a divine, pantheon. Elaine Pagels explains that "Christians share in common with pagans the conviction that invisible networks of superhuman beings energize human activity, and above all, empower the emperor and his subordinates to dominate the world. But there agreement ends. What pagans revere as assuring divine protection, Christians abhor as demonic tyranny."[53] Despite his protests of Christian fidelity, Justin's appeal to the emperor may be interpreted as a forceful attack designed to call into question Roman imperial hegemony. Could Justin possibly have believed that the emperor was capable of sound judgment? After persistently and vehemently arguing that those who persecute the Christians are demonically inspired and perverse, earlier protestations of Christian loyalty and friendliness are rendered hollow. The edge to Justin's attack is obvious, especially in light of imperial propaganda regarding the virtue and the piety promoted by the emperor.[54] The emperors and the rulers are not virtuous, Justin argued. They do not exhibit the reason, moderation, justice, or piety that is supposed to characterize good rulers. Instead, they enslave themselves to demons and desire, tolerating—indeed, promoting—sexual promiscuity, homoerotic sex, and prostitution even in the city of Rome.[55]

Justin's appeal to the emperor, therefore, resembles a speech of blame much more closely than it does a conventional appeal to the emperor's reason, despite his decision to identify his work as a *prosphōnēsis* and a *enteuxis*. Initially, Justin followed convention; he began his treatise with an appeal to the reason, justice, and piety of the emperor, his sons, and the Senate: "Reason [*logos*] dictates that those who are truly pious and philosophers should honor and love only the truth.... . Since you are called pious and philosophers and guardians of justice and lovers of culture [*paideia*], listen in every way; and it will be shown if you are" (*1 Apol.* 2).[56] This initial appeal to the reason of the emperor and his associates was soon abandoned, however, in favor of a series of proofs of their tyrannical behavior. As promised, Justin showed what the emperor is not. From Justin's perspective, so long as the emperor, his heirs, and the Senate refused to listen to his petition on behalf of the Christians, they would continue to expose themselves as governed by passion rather than reason; they were represented as mere pawns in the wicked machinations of deceptive, promiscuous demons. Such men cannot be called pious, philosophers, guardians of justice, or lovers of *paideia* (culture, learning, or good breeding).

Justin's characterization of the imperial court built upon traditions of vituperation he shared with his predecessors. As in the Wisdom of Solomon, Justin proposes a direct connection between idolatry and *porneia*.[57] Like Paul, he suggests that gentiles—in this case, the Roman emperors and Senate—will soon be judged by the truly kingly rulers, God and Christ. As in the *Acts of Paul and Thecla*, Justin offers Christian virgins as a proof of Christian moral superiority. His denunciation of anthropomorphic representations of the gods resonates with critiques offered by Greek philosophers. [58] Yet, where Paul is general—outsiders and idolaters are enslaved to lust but gentiles-in-Christ are masters at self-mastery—Justin is specific. Antoninus Pius, his heirs, the Roman Senate, and Urbicus, prefect of Rome, are enslaved by demons and overcome by passion. They honor promiscuity. They listen to the false accusations of demon-inspired madmen. They prefer perversion to justice. Hadrian, Antoninus Pius' illustrious predecessor, remembered by others for his munificence, his wonderful public building projects, including his magnificent temple of Venus and Rome, and his pious devotion to the gods[59] is ridiculed by Justin for his devotion to his youthful male lover Antinous (*1 Apol.* 29).[60] Antoninus Pius, divinized after his death, honored with a temple in the Roman forum, and known for his strict defense of traditional piety,[61] is chastised by Justin for approving of prostitution and raising boys for the purpose of sodomy (*1 Apol.* 29). Marcus Aurelius, commemorated by Cassius Dio as the father of a Golden Age and known for his professed Stoic principles,[62] is labeled a "philosopher" by Justin at the start of his address but then shown to be as depraved as his father.[63] "You" may promote yourselves as virtuous, just, and wise philosophers, Justin implies, but you practice violence and tyranny.

In the end, Justin did not compose an address honoring the wisdom of the emperor or celebrating the truth of philosophy; over the course of his appeal, he sets out to demonstrate imperial folly and uses philosophy to make that argument. His representation of gentile folly involves repeated references to sexual immorality and failed self-mastery. His decision to expand and elaborate what was by then a Christian critique of non-Christian morality and his audacity in naming names—purportedly, he was writing to Antoninus, Lucius, Marcus, and the Roman Senate—requires further explanation.

JUSTIN, THE MARTYRS, AND THE PROBLEM OF CHRISTIAN "MANLINESS"

By the early second century, accusations of Christian sexual misbehavior had begun to circulate in some quarters. Orgies, incest, and adultery were said to characterize clandestine Christian meetings, the very same behavior that Justin had associated with his non-Christian neighbors. For example, the second-century philosopher Celsus describes Christianity as an illegal, immoral, and secret society: Their founder Jesus was a magician, as are his followers (Origen, *Contra Celsum*, 1.6). Mary was no virgin, she was convicted of adultery with a Roman soldier (1.28). Jesus gathered wicked men and tax collectors around him, and together they sought their livelihood "in a disgraceful and importunate way" (1.62). Christian teachers attracted and targeted only ignorant, illiterate people, especially women, children, and slaves (2.50; 3.44). Christians are in constant disagreement, both among themselves and with the Jews (2.27; 3.1). The Christian story of Jesus' resurrection is based on the ranting of a hysterical female (2.55), and their rituals are "more iniquitous and impure than ... the revelers of Antinous in Egypt" (3.63).[64]

Many of Celsus' arguments, or something like them, were probably standard fare at the time.[65] Accusations similar to those put forward by Celsus were repeated for the purpose of refutation in a variety of works composed by second-century Christians. Justin tried to deflect the charges onto his Christian rivals: "And whether they [the false Christians] commit the shameful deeds about which stories are told—the upsetting of the lamp, promiscuous intercourse, and eating human flesh—we do not know; but we do know that they are neither persecuted nor put to death by you [the emperor], at least for their opinions" (*1 Apol.* 26). Athenagoras declared that the opponents of the Christians "bring three charges against us: atheism, Thyestean banquets, and Oedipean unions" (*Leg.* 3.1).[66] The Letter of the Churches of Lyons and Vienne offered an identical list: "[they] falsely accused us of Thyestan banquets and Oedipal intercourse and things about which we should neither speak nor think"(Eusebius *Hist. Eccl.* 5.1.14). According to Minucius Felix, the Roman aristocrat M. Cornelius Fronto denounced Christians, in part, for their orgiastic, incestuous feasts, their ritualized cannibalism, and their veneration of male genitalia (9.1–7).[67] The stereotypical nature of these accusations is readily apparent. Celsus' critique is a very model of ancient vituperation: the Christians and their founder are of disreputable origin; the disciples had to work for a living and, to make it worse, they chose disgraceful occupations; their beliefs are attractive only to ignorant people and to women; they cannot agree; they engage in reprehensible sexual behavior; and so on. Nevertheless, the commonplace nature of the charges does not suggest that they were not seriously intended. Indeed, as Rives and McGowan have demonstrated, the stereotypical charge of human sacrifice in particular—believable or not—served to indicate an (allegedly) immense difference between "good" citizens and the misanthropic, depraved Christians.[68] These charges, attacking as they did the sexual self-mastery of the Christians and implying that Christian men could not or would not control "their" women or themselves, can be read as an assault on the "manliness" and the status of the brothers and sisters in Christ.

In a letter to the Emperor Trajan regarding his investigation into Christian misbehavior, Pliny the Younger reports that, though Christianity certainly was a "depraved and excessive superstition [*superstitionem pravam et immodicam*]," the food served at community meals probably was "innocent [*innoxius*]." Still, Christians deserve to be punished for their crimes.[69] Tacitus, a contemporary of Pliny, offers a similar critique: Christians are engaged in a "deadly superstition." The presence of the followers of an executed Jew in Rome, Tacitus argues, offers further evidence that "all de-graded and shameful practices collect and flourish in the capital."[70] The Roman historian Suetonius agreed: Christianity was a superstition, and Christians deserved what they got.[71] Lucian of Samosata—a Syrian Greek satirist—was more tolerant. He merely depicts the Christians as silly reli-gious enthusiasts, easily duped by any charlatan who comes along.[72] The extent of anti-Christian polemic, therefore, should not be overestimat-ed. The charges against the Christians preserved in these non-Christian sources—Pliny, Suetonius, Tacitus, Lucian—are decidedly less inflam-matory than those found in writings by Christians themselves. Indeed, Christian authors may have amplified the critique in order to emphasize the gravity of the injustices they faced. Justin and Athenagoras leave the impression that Christians were relentlessly charged with crimes so outra-geous that only the most impious, immoral non-Christian could dream them up. In response, Keith Hopkins observes, "As I see it, the image of persistent persecution which Christians manufactured for themselves was more a mode of self-representation, or a tactic of self-unification than an objective description of reality."[73]

Still, there can be no doubt that Christians were occasionally verbally abused, arrested, and, in some cases, executed. Pliny the Younger referred to his particular investigatory technique: he tortured some Christian slaves to determine the truth of the matter, and, after asking those charged to curse Christ, he put to death any who would not offer a small sacrifice to the gods.[74] From the Christian perspective, the torture of Christian slaves and the death of even one "martyr" may have been enough to convince them that they were under constant threat. Elizabeth Castelli offers the following helpful reminder:

> Indeed, one might argue that the capriciousness of state violence—the mere presence of the imperial judicial apparatus with its omnipresent threat of violence, whether or not it was actually carried out—performed a critical kind of psychological work for all manner of subjected peoples, Christians included. It may be precisely because of the unpredictability of persecution as a practice that it came to loom even more largely in the Christian imagination.[75]

From the point of view of those entrusted with ruling provinces or main-taining order in the city, therefore, the Christians may have been no more than a minor annoyance, an irritating fly in the ointment of Roman impe-rial hegemony. Perhaps these superstitious haters of humanity simply provided a useful supply of prisoners whose executions could be offered up as public entertainment—Justin suggested as much in his address to the emperor (*1 Apol.* 12).[76] Christians may have been perceived as no more or less threatening than other rebellious slaves or provincials. Nevertheless, the public degradation of even a few Christians presented an important problem for Justin and his Christian contemporaries, no matter how sporadic the persecution and irrespective of the intentions of the persecutors. Accused of superstition, sexual depravity, and hatred of humanity, associated with orgiastic ritual and anthropophagy, occasionally tortured and even executed, Christian "manliness" was under attack. Justin and the authors of the second-century martyrologies sought to provide a solution.

PLAYING THE MAN

According to many Roman sources, to be a victim of corporal punishment was to be humiliated, degraded, and, in a sense, "feminized," since elite male bodies were inviolate.[77] Corporal punishment was considered to be so dishonorable, so devastating to one's status and gender, that a large fine was preferred to even a slight beating. The Roman jurist Macer explained, "one single stroke of the rods is more serious than condemnation to a fine."[78] In theory at least, corporal punishment was reserved for people of debased status whose bodies were already vulnerable to the beatings (and penetrations) of masters, that is, slaves and poor freedmen.[79] The worst punishments—*damnatio ad bestias,* immolation, and crucifixion, all of which involved prolonged, agonizing public exposure and death—were reserved for people of low status found guilty of heinous crimes, especially crimes against the *maiestas* of Rome.[80] Public, degrading executions were designed to be humiliating, offering an example for the consumption and approval of the broadest possible audience. Thus, a brigand, slave, or murderer was shamed in the city square or in the arena so that spectators could enjoy the opportunity to reaffirm the public order and be reminded of the price of infamy.[81]

I have already indicated the close intertwining of discourses involving status and gender during this period. Ideally, elites ought not to be displayed for public view in the amphitheater, the city square, or anywhere else; elites view others.[82] To be viewed publicly was to lose one's claim to status and "masculinity," an ideology reflected in the stereotype of the bad ruler. For example, Suetonius reported with shock that Emperor Nero went to Achaia for the express purpose of the public display of his own person. He sang in public at a musical competition, participated in wrestling matches, and drove chariots in the races. Nero was so determined to show off for an audience, Suetonius claimed, that he forbid anyone to leave the theater when he was singing, including pregnant women who were forced to give birth during an extraordinarily long performance (Suet. *Ner.* 23). Suetonius linked Nero's (supposedly appalling) enthusiasm for the violation of his imperial status in the amphitheater to his sexual appetites: according to Suetonius, Nero also arranged for noble women to behave as harlots, seduced Roman matrons and debauched a vestal virgin, castrated a freeborn boy for the sake of his sexual enjoyment, had intercourse with his own mother, and cried out like a deflowered virgin while being penetrated by his freedman Doryphorus (Suet. *Ner.* 27–29). In other words, from Suetonius' perspective, Nero's "femininity," his "slavishness" to his appetites, and his failure as an emperor were demonstrated by his need for public adulation, his excessive sexual desire, and by the pleasure he gained through submission to the phallus of his freedman. Contrast this portrayal of Nero with Marcus Aurelius' depiction of his "father," Antoninus Pius. Antoninus Pius taught Marcus by example to suppress all passion for boys, to refuse to pander to the desires of the mob, to organize measured performances in the arena (he certainly did not perform in the arena himself), and to think nothing of the beauty of his slaves (M. Aur. *Med.* 1.16). To be publicly viewed was to be degraded; to be ripped apart by beasts or to otherwise "perform" for the benefit of an audience was humiliating and feminizing, at least to some degree.[83]

By the second century, therefore, Christians had been feminized and debased in at least two ways: they had been accused of out-of-control sexual behavior—an allegedly "feminine" or "slavish" trait—and some had been publicly executed. Christian authors were aware of this problem and, as Castelli has demonstrated, they sought to reclaim both masculine gender and elite status for themselves by emphasizing the "manliness" of the martyrs. Thus, legendary accounts of martyrdom made frequent reference to the "nobility" and "manliness" of the victim, be he an old honorable man or a "weak" young slave woman. For example, in the *Martyrdom of Polycarp* the narrator tells us that a voice from heaven exhorted the aged bishop to "be strong" and "play the man."[84] The narrator takes care to make Polycarp's elite status explicit: during his ordeal, he was forced to untie his own sandals, a task he had never had to perform before since his slaves usually provided this service (*Martyrdom of Polycarp*, 13). Blandina, another martyr, is described by her hagiographer as a "blessed noble athlete" who exhausted her persecutors with her endurance in face of torture.[85] The martyr Blandina, though a slave, is described as "putting on Christ," inspiring her brothers, and winning "the crown of immortality" (*Martyrs of Lyons*, 17, 42). In her diary, the martyr Perpetua, a daughter of a family of decurial rank and the mother of a healthy young son, envisions herself as a male wrestler, capable of defeating a huge Egyptian rival.[86] In other words, she "became a man," at least in a dream. Still, the editor of her story is careful to note that she behaved like a proper matron throughout her gruesome death, noting that she pulled up her tunic when it was ripped (*Martyrdom of Perpetua and Felicitas*, 20).

Justin Martyr also describes the Christians as "athletes" who prefer the hard life of virtue to the deceptive beauty of vice; their athletic manliness, he declared, leads them to be both unafraid and undeterred by death (*2 Apol.* 11–12). Like the authors of the martyr legends, Justin is keen to point out that Christians behaved in a noble and manly fashion at all times, regardless of their sex or status.[87] Describing manliness and nobility in these terms, Justin and other second-century Christian authors portray themselves as "elite" and "manly" despite—because of?—the (obvious) femininity and lowliness that had been attributed to them by others. They also turn the tables on their accusers, feminizing them by means of sexualized invective and, further, by the accusation that they singled out Christians for punishment not because they had reasonably pursued justice but because they had given into an irrational, violent anger.

THE ANGRY TYRANT

"Whenever you get angry, Caesar, do not say or do anything before repeating to yourself the twenty-four letters of the alphabet" (Plut. *Mor.* 207c).[88] According to Plutarch, Augustus was so thrilled with this valuable advice that he refused to allow the elderly resident philosopher who offered it to retire from court service. The Roman stereotype of a "good king"—and, as usual, Augustus set the standard—included the belief that the king ought not to lose his temper. As William Harris observes, "tales about imperial anger and *clementia* were used to set up a general standard to which emperors ought to aspire," with the good emperor represented as steadily in control of his anger and the bad emperor depicted as a victim of uncontrolled rage.[89] Marcus Aurelius seems to have taken this advice to heart; in his "Meditations" he reminded himself "how much harder to bear are the consequences of our anger and vexation at actions than the actions themselves" (*Med.* 11.18).[90] Irascibility (ὀργιλότης), Plutarch explained, is evidence of a weak, unmanly soul:

For the actions and the motions and the whole demeanor of angry persons declare their utter littleness and weakness.... . Their meanness of
soul is apparent in their cruelty and their perverted state in their action.
[Their anger] is like the bites of vipers, which, when thoroughly inflamed with rage and pain, eject their excessive fiery passion upon those
who have hurt them.   (Plut. *Mor.* 457a)[91]

Since irascibility was supposed to be a vice of the weak, women were said
to be more prone to anger then men, sick people more likely to lose their
temper than men in their prime, and old men less capable of anger management than their younger counterparts, or so Plutarch asserted.[92] Tyrants, not good kings, display an irrational, anger-prone disposition, sur-
rendering themselves to rage—as well as desire.

Marcus Aurelius may have asserted that he could control his anger, but
Justin and Athenagoras implied otherwise. According to Justin, the gods
worshipped by the empire demanded that their devotees engage in both
porneia and in blood sacrifice to satisfy their insatiable lust for violence
and sex (*2 Apol.* 5).[93] From Justin's perspective, it was the gods, the rulers
who worshipped them, and their subjects that demanded bloody sacrificial victims, including the bodies of Christians. Christians, by contrast,
displayed peace and good will toward all (Justin *1 Apol.* 17).[94] Justin offers accusations about sacrifice, illicit sex, violence, and irrational anger to
prove that the rulers had failed as both rulers and "men."[95] By going after
the Christians and by enslaving themselves to demons, the rulers forsook
their "manhood," their elevated status, and their claims to virtue, a theme
that was repeated in martyr legends from the same period.[96]

According to the author of the *Martyrdom of Polycarp,* Polycarp's tor-
mentors were thirsty for blood, a thirst willingly sated by the extreme injustice of their governor: The governor determined to burn Polycarp alive;
the mob sought to have him killed by beasts. Since the time for *damnatio
ad bestias* had ended, the governor stood by his original plan and had
Polycarp burned. When the fire failed to consume him, the lawless men
(*hoi anomoi*) demanded that Polycarp be stabbed to death (*Martyrdom of
Polycarp,* 10–16). Similarly, the *Letter to the Churches of Lyons and Vienne*
equates crowd and governor, attributing a bloodthirsty hatred to them
both: "these wild and barbarous people once stirred by the wild beast were
difficult to satisfy ... both the governor and the populace showed towards
us the same undeserved hatred" (*Martyrs of Lyons,* 57–58).[97] A dramatic

retelling of the trial and death of Carpus depicts him declaring, "I venerate Christ … it is impossible for me to sacrifice to these demons with their deceptive appearances. For those who sacrifice to them are like them."[98] In this way, Justin and the authors of these martyr acts associated their opponents, ruler and ruled alike, with a perverse, "dandyish" violence, calling into question the regularized, predictable, and "masculine" violence employed by a "philosopher king."[99]

JUSTIN AND CHRISTIAN MANHOOD

Justin's petition to the emperor represents the Christians as innocent victims of an out-of-control, unjust, and bloodthirsty regime, a project he shared with other second-century Christian apologists and with the authors of the acts of the martyrs. The choice to employ sexualized language to clinch his argument may have been entirely predictable—after all, charging Christians with nearly identical "bad" behavior and sexualized invective was standard in ancient polemic—yet the vivid depiction of the sexual immorality of the gods and their devotees, accompanied by the juxtaposition of reason (the rulers refuse to follow it) and passion (the rulers are enslaved by it) accomplished something else as well: these arguments regendered the Christian as "male" and insisted that Christians, men and women alike, were the very opposite of the "slavish" idolaters. Challenges to Christian status and gender in the arena and in the vituperative arguments of their critics may partially account for this turn to the commonplaces of sexualized invective. An emphasis on the chastity of the Christians, contrasted with dramatic descriptions of the depravity of outsiders, also imitated the rhetorical strategies of earlier Christian authors, including Paul and his later interpreters. Still, by addressing the emperor and the imperial court, Justin added something new: his "appeal to the emperor" demonstrated the injustice of specific "tyrants," the current imperial regime. Those who dared to accuse the Christians were portrayed as licentious, irascible, and effeminate.

Though questions of audience can never be entirely settled, I fully agree with those recent scholars who view the "apologies," including Justin's *prosphōnēsis* to the emperor, as in-group documents. These apologies "were another means by which Christianity represented itself as a community of the persecuted and suffering,"[100] they offered a justification of an increasingly unpopular position to those who viewed themselves as under attack,[101] and, I would add, they helped to maintain group boundaries by enforcing a sexualized definition of "Christian virtue." According to Justin, "true Christians" are characterized by *sōphrosynē*, and they worship a God who demands full self-mastery. Homoerotic sex was forbidden, as was prostitution, adultery, incest, and all sexual intercourse outside of marriage. According to these writers, Christians never look with lust at another, and they marry only once or not at all. Christian self-mastery is offered as a proof of Christian "manliness," and the failed self-mastery of the "demons" and their "slaves" denied manliness to pagan targets. "Apologetic" argument depicts Christians as innocent sufferers; it also suggests that Christian "virtue" necessarily included sexual self-control.

Having defined Christian belief and practice in these terms, Justin turns briefly to Christians he deemed false. These Christians, Justin claims, probably are guilty of the sort of gross sexual misconduct associated with all the followers of Christ by some of their critics. Justin exhorted "you" to investigate the bad behavior of these traitors and to put them to death (*1 Apol.* 27). Apparently, Justin's anti-imperial rhetoric—his resistance to imperial claims regarding the virtue of the current rulers and their gods— could also be employed against fellow Christians, real or imagined. Once again, sexualized invective serves several purposes at once: outsiders are pushed further away, insiders are policed, and morality is both constituted and defined as "Christian." The next two chapters address in-group, anti-Christian rhetoric such as is briefly found in Justin's *First Apology.* If sexual vice is the problem and Christ is the cure, what better way to eliminate a claimant to the title "Christian" than to accuse him or her of sexual misbehavior? Moreover, by associating outsiders with desire, demons, and sexual license, insiders can be efficiently disciplined—banned or warned that they will be banned—if they fail to conform to the superior standard this discourse recommends. Claims about superior Christian morals may have provided a needed defense of Christian legitimacy. They made possible a Christian resistance to social conventions and the exigencies of Roman imperial power, even as Christian authors relied upon shared beliefs about masculine self-mastery to make their arguments. As we shall see, these claims also provided an excellent weapon for attacking an enemy within.

CHAPTER 4

The False Teachers of the End Time

In the Book of Revelation, Rome is represented as a great whore "with whom the kings of the earth have fornicated"(Rev 17:2).[1] At the end of times, the author of Revelation promised, Rome and the kings who copulated with her, together with the merchants who have grown rich from her luxury, will be destroyed. The kings and merchants will weep and mourn as they watch her and all her great wealth laid to waste, burned and burning for eternity following the true and just judgment of God (Rev 18:1–19:4; cf. Rev 14:18–11, 21:8). In this way, Revelation offered one of the more explicit Christian critiques of Rome and "her" coconspirators while declaring Christians to be the ultimate winners in a battle with cosmic and universal significance.[2] "We"—the 144,000 sealed virgins (*parthenoi*) of the sons of Israel (Rev 7:1–8, 14:1–5),[3] the great multitude from every nation who have washed their robes in the blood of the Lamb (i.e., Christ; Rev 7:9–17, 14:1–5), the "saints" (*hagioi*) who endure and keep the commandments of God and the faith of Jesus, (Rev 14:12) refusing to worship "the beast or its image"(Rev 20:4–6)—will receive an eternal reward, worshipping God and the Lamb forever.

Revelation offers an early example of a Christian "apocalypse"—a written account describing the details of a final, divine, end-time judgment[4]—recording the vision of John of Patmos. John envisions an end in which Rome gets "her" due and "the saints" receive their just reward.[5] But it is not only Rome that will burn, for evil men (*kakoi*), that is, men who call themselves apostles but are not, have crept in and tested the churches (Rev 2:2). Some who say they are Jews are not but are a "synagogue of Satan" and act as instruments of evil and revile the Christians; such persons will face "the second death"(Rev 2:9–11; cf. Rev 3:9). Another threat takes the form of a (Christian) prophetess, "Jezebel," who teaches fornication and apostasy. She and those who join themselves to her, learning "the deep things of Satan," will face terrible tribulations if they do not repent (Rev 2:20–24). According to the author of Revelation, therefore, dangerous delegates of evil threaten the church from within as well as without. The enemy within is a malignancy that may well destroy the "saints," tempting them away from the true path. Still, the author assures his readers, Rome the great whore will be punished by God; Jews who reject Christ will be punished with a "second death"; and insidious insiders like "Jezebel" with her false teachings, secret fornications, and adulterous liaisons will receive a just penalty.

This chapter considers charges of sexual licentiousness lodged by brothers and sisters in Christ against one another. As we have seen, Christian authors frequently defined themselves against outsiders in sexual terms: outsiders are sexually promiscuous; they have been handed over to "unnatural" lust; they follow the example of their incestuous and adulterous gods and listen to the corrupt teaching of their degenerate philosophers. These authors claimed sexual purity for themselves with *sōphrosynē* and *enkrateia* described as uniquely Christian traits. Outsiders who rejected Christ were then represented as incapable of virtue, especially self-mastery. They lack the essential prerequisite: faith. Sexual immorality and faith in Christ were supposed to be utterly incompatible. Paraphrasing Paul, can a Christian be a Christian and fornicate? Never! (1 Cor 6:15). Christians put aside every kind of vice, but especially *porneia* (fornication/prostitution), *moicheia* (adultery), *aselgeia* (licentiousness), *arsenokoitēs* (lit. "bedding men"), and the like (see, for example, 1 Cor 6:9; 1 Tim 1:10; Poly. *Phil.* 5.3; 1 Clem 30.1, 35.2; Herm. *Mand.* 8.). "True" Christians can never and must never fornicate. Transformed by Christ, these "brothers and sisters" have finally attained the otherwise elusive goal of controlling their desires.

Similarly, when the followers of Christ sought to denounce one another they often did so in sexual terms. "False" brothers were identified as licentious corrupters of the true faith. Illegitimate teachers were said to chase after the things of the flesh: they loved pleasure more than God; they seduced weak women (e.g., Phil 4:18–19; Eph 5:6–18; 2 Tim 3:1–9; Heb 6:4–8; 2 Peter 1:4–9, 2:1–22, 3:3–4; 1 John 2:18–19, 4:1–6; Jude 3–18; Rev 2:14, 20; Ign. *Eph.* 7.1, 16.1; Ign. *Trall.* 6.1–7.1, 11.1; Ign. *Phil.* 2.2–3.1; Ign. *Smyr.* 4.1, 5.1, 6.2; Poly. *Phil.* 7.1–2; Justin *1 Apol.* 26.). But these authors did not simply charge one another with sexual corruption and apostasy; as apostates and fornicators, false believers were said to be on the side of evil and evil's master, Satan.[6] These authors warned their readers to be on their guard against false teachers, antichrists, children of Satan and the sons of darkness who sneak into the churches, seeking to seduce the faithful to faithlessness (e.g., 1 John 4:1–6; 2 John 7; Poly. *Phil.* 7.1; *Did.* 16; *Barn.* 4.1–14; *Apoc. Pet.* 1–4 [Ethiopic]). Polycarp, for example, offers this denunciation of the Christians he opposed:

> For anyone who does not confess that Jesus Christ has come in the flesh is an antichrist; and whoever does not confess the witness of the cross is from the devil, and whoever distorts the words of the Lord for his own passions [*epithymiai*], saying that there is neither resurrection nor judgment—this one is the first born of Satan.
>
> (Poly. *Phil.* 7.1; Ehrman's translation)[7]

The mistakes of these "anti-Christs," as Polycarp describes them, are doctrinal and practical. Such people have an improper understanding of the significance of Christ, he suggests, for they deny his resurrection and the coming judgment. They are inspired to present these false teachings by their uncontrolled desires. Therefore, true Christians ought to turn from their false teachings and return to the word (*logos*) that was given to them in the beginning (Poly. *Phil.* 7.2). Irenaeus remembered this passage fondly, attributing the "first-born of Satan" phrase to an interaction between Polycarp and Marcion, the "heretic": "And when Polycarp himself once met Marcion, who ran to him and said, 'Recognize us,' he answered, 'I do recognize you, firstborn of Satan'" (Iren. *Adv. Haer.* 3.3.4).[8] To Polycarp and Irenaeus, Christians who offered a doctrine or teaching different from their own were properly understood as emissaries of Satan who are ruled by desire (*epithymia*) rather than God.[9]

The false brothers denounced by the "Paul" of 2 Timothy were also represented as sexually depraved, generally wicked, and signs of the coming judgment:

> You must understand this, that in the last days distressing times will come. For people will be lovers of themselves, lovers of money, boasters, arrogant, abusive, disobedient to their parents, ungrateful, unholy, inhuman, implacable, slanderers, profligates, brutes, haters of good, treacherous, reckless, swollen with conceit, lovers of pleasure rather than lovers of God, holding to the outward form of godliness but denying its power. Avoid them! For among them are those who make their way into households and captivate silly women, overwhelmed by their sins

and swayed by all kinds of desires, who are always being instructed and
can never arrive at a knowledge of the truth.

(2 Tim 3:1–7).

These devious brothers—characterized by a whole host of traditional vices
and allegedly dangerous to "weak" women[10]—are offered as an indication
of the approaching final judgment.[11] So, the author warns, Timothy must
be vigilant. He must teach and preach the word to the faithful, for the time
is soon coming when such teachers will find an audience among those who
formerly listened to "the truth" (2 Tim 4:3–5).

Why was the vilification of Christians by other Christians for supposedly loving pleasure, seducing the faithful, and following after their base
desires—often accompanied by apocalyptic warnings of doom—such a
recurring theme in ancient Christian literature? By far the most endur-
ing answer to this question has been to assert that some of the "heretical" Christian opponents of "orthodox" Christianity actually did encourage orgiastic or other unusual sexual behavior. In his now classic work
Orthodoxy and Heresy in Earliest Christianity, Walter Bauer argues that
"heretical" forms of Christianity may have actually been more prevalent
than those forms now associated with "orthodoxy."[12] Region by region,
he demonstrates that Christian "heresy" was early and widespread. Indeed,
the "heresies" may not have been viewed as "heretical" at all during the
earliest stages of Christianity. Rather, "at least here and there, [they] were
the only form of the new religion—that is, for those regions they were
simply 'Christianity.'"[13] The alternate view—that "orthodoxy" preceded
"heresy," since "heresy" involves a perversion of a preexisting, authentic,
and apostolic tradition—is, he proposes, an artifact of later ecclesiastical argument rather than an accurate portrayal of the situation in most
of the primitive churches.[14] Still, Bauer suggests that Paul's opponents
may well have indulged in the "unhesitating satisfaction of sexual desires"
and, further, that this behavior was probably characteristic of the heretical
Christians of Pergamum, of the followers of the "heretic" Basilides, and,
possibly, of "the gnostics in general."[15]

Bauer's portrayal of the pneumatics in Corinth,[16] the "heretics" addressed by the author of Revelation, the Basilidians, and the Gnostics re-
peats ancient charges made against them. Paul cautions the Corinthians
not to tolerate incest or intercourse with prostitutes; Bauer assumes that
Paul's rivals promoted such behavior. Revelation compared some in the
church of Pergamum to Balaam—a villain who attempted to persuade
Israel to eat food sacrificed to idols and to commit *porneia*; Bauer assumes

that Pergamum had been similarly influenced. Irenaeus suggests that the Basilidians promoted the indiscriminate indulgence of lust; Bauer accepts this assessment and, on the basis of evidence from Justin, extends Irenaeus' complaint to include Gnostics in general. Defining "orthodoxy" as "adhering to the teachings of the apostles" and "heresy" as "promoting a teaching other than that of the apostles," Bauer directly adopts criteria developed by second-century "church fathers" to differentiate the type of Christianity they promoted from that of the "heretics."[17] Tertullian explains, "We have the example of the apostles of the Lord who chose not to introduce any doctrine on their own authority but faithfully dispensed to the world the body of doctrines received from Christ" (*Praesc. haeret.* 6.2–4). Heretics, Christian authors claim, pervert the authentic teaching given by Christ to the apostles and then preserved by the legitimate disciples of these apostles. "Heretics" are innovators, developing their doctrines independently.[18]

Such a stereotyped portrait of heresy and orthodoxy is no longer accepted, though Bauer's compelling hypothesis regarding the diversity of early Christianities remains justly influential. As Marcel Simon pointed out, the term *hairesis* can simply mean "choice," especially the choice to embrace a school of thought. The term developed in later Christian use, coming to mean "whatever diverges from the authentic position of the church," but this very definition suggests the contested nature of the term.[19] As is now recognized, the authors of texts identified with the Gnostics saw themselves as Christians not as heretics, often claiming apostolic teaching as their own.[20] The label "heretic" is, like other labels I have been exploring, a contested category that signals conflict between Christians, not a fixed or obvious category indicating "right" or "wrong" belief.[21] Bauer, ever insightful, prefigured this problem in his analysis of Eusebius's portrayal of the Montanist "heresy." Eusebius, Bauer argues, offered nothing more than abusive caricatures of Montanists, attributing illegitimate motives to practices that, when promoted by Montanists, were said to have gluttony and perversion at their root. These same practices when performed "in the context of orthodoxy," however, earned the highest praise.[22]

Despite several persuasive studies that have called into question stereotypical reconstructions of heresy and the Gnostics,[23] the opponents of the apostles are still portrayed as sensualist libertines on occasion, especially in the context of studies of the New Testament. So, for example, members of the Corinthian church, the opponents of the author of Jude and 2 Peter, and the false teachers excoriated in the Pastoral Epistles continue to be represented as licentious, antinomian, and libertine.[24] From the accounts of second- and third-century heresiologists and from various New Testament books, "modern scholarship has inherited the stereotype of two types of 'gnostic' attitudes toward sex: libertinism and asceticism."[25] The authors of Jude, 2 Peter, the Pastorals, and Revelation and the second-century authors Justin Martyr and Irenaeus, together with a few contemporary scholars, suggest that false believers were guilty of the sexual crimes that were attributed to Christians in general by their non-Christian critics.[26]

I will not attempt to decide whether Gnostics or other "false" believers actually did promote libertinism or incorporate ritualized sexual intercourse into their cultic practices, though I do call into question the historical reliability of such charges.[27] My interest in accusations of sexual immorality lies elsewhere. As in the rest of this book, I am interested in the types of charges that are made, the definition of sexual propriety that these charges presuppose, and the power relationships they seek to establish or undermine. That is, I seek to understand how charges of sexual deviance promoted a particular view of what a Christian *is* while serving as a tool of legitimization or delegitimization of rival Christian perspectives. Having asserted that "the saints" are *essentially* (in every sense of the term) sexually pure, charges of sexual corruption were especially effective at maligning fellow believers. Since what a Christian possesses is faith (*pistis*) in Christ and since, from this faith, sexual virtue must follow, sexual vice among true Christians is logically impossible. No one can "be" Christian and also "be" a sexual deviant. Moreover, accusing believers of sexual licentiousness offered a counterpoint to positive arguments about what a true Christian is or should be. Christians are virtuous, self-controlled, holy members of God's army. They are not vice-ridden lovers of luxury ruled by their desires or by Satan. These are attributes of false Christians only. Defining "the other"—in this case "the other (false) Christian"—reinforces definitions of what the true Christian must be like. In the process, the boundaries between "us" (true Christians) and "them" (false Christians) are drawn in stark terms: We are the righteous of God. They are the emissaries of Satan. We are destined for eternal life. They are singled out for destruction. The true, blessed, holy brothers in Christ are distinguished from the false, seductive brothers in Christ who are actually enemies of God.

In the previous chapters, I observed that Christians' claims about their own sexual virtue can be read, in part, as a resistance strategy—Paul and Justin reconfigure ancient constructions of "the elite" and of "manliness" in their favor, suggesting that they and their followers alone possess virtue, whatever imperial propaganda may have proclaimed about the emperor or the empire. Yet slander can also serve as a policing tactic, a way of controlling insiders and eliminating rivals. Charges of sexual vice could be effective in-group weapons in the ancient world. Rival elites employed accusations of incapacity, effeminacy, luxury, and licentiousness to undermine one another's political aspirations, all while defining "the elite" as "one who is virtuous." In the case of Christian polemics, charges of wicked desire and demonic influence can be read in a similar light.

I begin my analysis of Christian accusations against other Christians with a close reading of the epistle of Jude. This letter, though brief, is wholly focused on the character and significance of the "ungodly"—"false" teachers who, the author asserts, will attempt to corrupt the faithful during the end time. By means of biblical examples and prophetic oracle, the author of Jude portrays these Christians as destined for destruction and motivated by desire (*epithymia*); their existence is interpreted as a sign of the imminent end. This argument was reiterated by the author of 2 Peter.28 Like Jude, 2 Peter emphasizes the licentiousness of the false teachers, the swift punishment that awaits them, and the quick advance of the day of judgment. These two epistles illustrate the manner in which biblical arguments about the illicit desires of apostates were combined with traditional rhetorical commonplaces denouncing the licentiousness of an opponent to describe the typical false brother or sister in Christ. Next, I discuss the theory that "evil spirits" or the devil are the animating force behind false, licentious teachers by considering instructions on the testing of the spirits given to Hermas in the *Shepherd*.29 I explore the implications of the twin charges licentiousness and demonic influence, suggesting that, for Christians, these two charges came to constitute and define the model heretic.

JUDE, 2 PETER, AND THE LICENTIOUSNESS OF FALSE PROPHETS

The brief New Testament letter of Jude contains a sustained indictment of false teachers who enter the community secretly to "pervert the grace of our God into licentiousness." Jude is dominated by a carefully constructed series of denunciations grounded in biblical and pseudepigraphical traditions about the swift punishment that awaits those who would disobey God.30 Though biblical examples predominate, the author demonstrates a close familiarity with Greek rhetorical style,31 and the letter possesses one of the more complex vocabularies in the New Testament.[32] Many exegetes suggest that Jude was written to respond to a group of treacherous trouble-makers whose false teachings threatened a fledgling church. Still, the specific occasion, date, and circumstances surrounding the letter cannot easily be determined.[33] Some suggest that Jude was written to oppose a group of Gnostics or proto-Gnostics who, spreading their licentiousness, "revile what they do not understand" (Jude 10a).[34] Adopting a more cautious approach, others assert that the author sought to denounce a group of bold libertines, though they need not be Gnostic in type.[35] The majority, however, believe that the targets of Jude's polemic taught antinomianism, rejected moral authority, and indulged in sexual misconduct.[36]

Whether or not the author of Jude's opponents were sexual deviants or simply alleged to be so, the false Christians he denounces are represented in a manner that remained popular among later polemicists. As far as this letter is concerned, all false Christians are licentious perverters of the truth who stand in a long line of biblical examples of disobedience, rebellion, and lust. Drawing boundaries between true and false Christians, Jude repeatedly contrasts "you" (ὑμεῖς, the beloved, the saints) with "these" (οὗτοι, the ungodly, the licentious ones). "You" must remain faithful and keep the love of God if you hope to avoid the punishment endured by past examples of men such as "these" ("these," Jude 7, 8, 10, 12, 16, 19; "you," Jude 3.17, 18, 20).[37] "These" deny the Lord Jesus Christ, are unfaithful, commit *porneia*, are revilers and revelers, and will be harshly judged. Jude goes on to identify "these" with "those"—biblical characters from the past who were associated with crimes of varying types, but especially with fornication and lust. Alleged sexual depravity served as one of the most important indicators of a false teacher throughout this brief letter.

JUDE AND THE UNGODLY CHRISTIANS

The discussion of the end-time false Christians begins with a programmatic statement describing the licentiousness of "these," the (contemporary) ungodly who crept into the community of the "saints" (Jude 4) and concludes with a saying of the "apostles"[38] predicting the coming of "these" licentious end-time teachers. This final apocalyptic warning cautions the church to watch out for the "mockers" of the last-days who follow their own "ungodly desires" (Jude 18). Thus, the charge of licentiousness—repeated in a variety of forms throughout the letter—both frames the letter and provides the focus for the critique. What emerges is a stereotypical portrait of the licentious false Christian, enflamed with lust and incapable of controlling himself.

Following his opening statement about the "ungodly" (ἀσεβεῖς) who pervert the grace of God and deny "our Lord Jesus Christ," Jude offers three biblical models as evidence for the fearful punishment that awaits the disobedient: the destruction of the unfaithful members of Israel's wilderness generation (Jude 5; see Num 11:33; 14:11–12, 20–24, 26–35; 25:1–5; 26:65), the condemnation of the Watchers (angels who lusted after women; Jude 6; see Gen 6:1–4; *1 Enoch* 6–19; 1 Cor 11:10; 1 Pet 3:19–20; 1 Tim 2:9), and the punishment of eternal fire unleashed against the men of Sodom and Gomorrah (Jude 7; see Gen 19:4–11; *T. Naph.* 3:4–5). Following this triad of examples, the presumption of the false teachers is contrasted with the respectful approach adopted by the archangel Michael when contending with the devil for the body of Moses (Jude 9).[39] The letter then offers another triad of examples comparing the false teachers to three models of sin and disobedience, Cain (Gen 4:1–25; also see *T. Benj.* 7.5; Joseph *Ant.* 1.52–66; Philo *Post.* 38–39), Balaam (Num 22:18, 24:13; also see Philo *Mos.* 1.266–68),[40] and Korah (Num 16:1–35, 26:9–10; also see Joseph *Ant.* 4.12–21; Ps.-Philo. 16; 1 Clem 51.1–4). The letter closes by citing two prophecies that (purportedly) foretold the coming of the ungodly: a prophecy from the pseudepigraphical book *1 Enoch* (Jude 14)[41] and a saying of the apostles regarding the "mockers" who follow after their desires (Jude 17–18). Though disobedience and the resulting judgment is the key theme throughout, several of the examples of disobedience supplied have sexual overtones.

JUDE 5–8: THE GENEALOGICAL LINE OF THE UNGODLY

In the first of three grouped illustrations of God's wrath, Jude reminds his readers of the destruction of unfaithful Israel in the wilderness: "I wish to remind you, though you have been informed of all things once for all, that the Lord[42] who saved the people from the land of Egypt, afterwards [lit. "the second time"][43] destroyed those who were not faithful." According to biblical tradition, Israel in the wilderness complained against God and was unfaithful, despite a miraculous rescue from slavery in Egypt. These various acts of faithlessness, as told in Numbers, include the "lusting" after flesh (i.e., meat), the attempt to return to Egypt after an initial sighting of the Canaanites, and sexual intercourse with Moabite women (Num

11:1–34, 14:1–35, 25:1–18). In all three of these examples, Israel's inconstancy was linked to illicit desire. In the first example, the Israelites were said to lust after (ἐπιθυμέω) the rich food they had left behind in Egypt. God sent quails to satisfy their complaint even as his wrath burned against them (Num 11:1–34, LXX). God then sent a terrible plague to smite the complainers. The people named the place where their unfaithful comrades died "Graves of Lust," for there the people lusted (Num 11:34, LXX).

In the second example, the people sought to return to Egypt after receiving a false report about the strength and size of the Canaanites. Joshua and Caleb, however, pleaded with Israel to trust in God. With divine anger kindled against the rest, the Lord promised that the unfaithful generation would die in the wilderness: "And your sons will be fed the wilderness for forty years and will bear your *porneia* until your corpses are wasted in the wilderness" (Num 14:33, LXX; compare Deut. 1:34). Thus, the righteous generation, after putting up with the fornications of their ancestors, will finally be allowed to enter the promised land. The corpses (lit. "limbs") of unfaithful Israel, on the other hand, will be left to rot. Only Joshua and Caleb, the two faithful Israelites, will join the younger generation and escape the wanderings in the wilderness. In yet another example of Israel's faithlessness, the men of Israel are depicted as fornicating (*ekporneuō*) with the daughters of Moab and, at the request of their Moabite wives, bowing down to Baal (Num 25:1, LXX). Worshipping the god of the Moabites is presented as yet another type of *porneia*. These unfaithful Israelites were also destroyed, for God ordered Moses to behead every man who participated in these despicable infidelities (Num 25:4–5).

As a second illustration of the destruction that comes upon those who disobey God, the author referred to the tradition of the Watchers—recalcitrant angels who lusted after the daughters of men: "And the angels who did not keep their own ἀρχή [rule, domain] but deserted their own dwelling place, [God] has kept [them] under darkness in eternal bonds until the judgment of the great day" (Jude 6). According to this legend, the angels (called "watchers" in *1 Enoch*) desired the daughters of men and, copulating with them, produced giants who committed even further abominations.[44] As a result, God bound these angels and threw them into darkness until the Day of Judgment (*1 Enoch* 10). Christian authors referred to this tradition on numerous occasions. Justin, for example, argued that the *porneia* of these angels resulted in the birth of the "demons" (δαίμονες, i.e., the gods of the Greeks and Romans; *2 Apol.* 5; *1 Apol.* 5), a view repeated by Athenagoras in his *Legatio* (*Leg.* 25.1; compare Tertullian

Apol. 22). This story was referred to by Tertullian to exhort virgins to veil themselves "for the sake of the angels" (*Virg.* 7.2.4; citing 1 Cor 11:10). The author of Jude certainly knew some version of this story, possibly even the version now preserved in *1 Enoch*.[45] His regard for Enoch is evident later when he cites a passage from the "Book of Watchers" explicitly (now chapters six through eleven in *1 Enoch*; citing *1 Enoch* 1.9).[46]

Though the author of Jude did not explicitly describe the angels' sin—beyond the fact that they "did not keep their own *archē* [domain?]"—his next example in this triad of disobedience suggests that familiarity with the forbidden sexual desires of the angels was presupposed: "As Sodom and Gommorah and the cities around them, which practiced fornication in the same way as these [angels] and went after different flesh, serve as an example by undergoing the punishment of eternal fire" (Jude 7). "These" may refer to the angels and, possibly, to unfaithful Israel, since, as cities, Sodom and Gommorah are referred to in the feminine gender (αἱ πόλεις) earlier in this verse. "Angels" and "people" (*laos*, i.e., unfaithful Israel), however, are referred to in the masculine. In this way, the *porneia* of Sodom and Gommorah serves as a summary description of all three biblical examples. Unfaithful Israel went after strange gods and strange women when they fornicated with the Moabites and bowed down to Baal. The disobedient angels desired the daughters of men and actually copulated with them (*1 Enoch* 15.2–12).[47] The men of Sodom and Gommorah, seeking intercourse with angels, were guilty of a similar crime—whereas the Watchers desired the daughters of men, the men of Sodom desired angels. Therefore, both Watchers and Sodomites desired "different flesh" (i.e., flesh of a kind different from their own). Though the author of Jude does not offer any specifics regarding the unfaithfulness of the wilderness generation, he may have included them in this summary description as well.[48] Alluding to the terrible punishments meted out against wayward Israel, the author may have intended his readers to supply the (sexualized) content of these stories.[49] All three groups (Israel, angels, and Sodomites) desired what was (or should be) "different" (*heteros*)—foreign gods and foreign women, the daughters of men, or angels.[50] All three types were sexual sinners who lusted after what was forbidden to them.[51] All three, the letter points out, received a severe punishment: unfaithful Israel was destroyed, the angels are now chained in darkness, and Sodom and Gommorah have been punished with eternal fire.[52]

In the next verse, Jude equates these biblical paradigms of disobedience with the current false teachers whom Jude disparagingly refers to as "these" (οὗτοι). In this verse, he explicitly connects the "ungodly" of today with disobedient and licentious biblical figures of the past: "But in the same way also these men, dreaming, defile the flesh, reject authority, and revile the glories" (Jude 8). The "dreaming" that "these" participate in probably refers to (false) revelatory visions.[53] False "dreaming," the letter asserts, leads to three interrelated errors: defiling or polluting the flesh, rejecting the Lord, and reviling the angels. "Dreaming," then, leads to a refusal to recognize the sovereignty of the Lord.[54] In their "dreaming," they insult the "glories," probably a class of angelic beings.[55] Thus, "these," in their false prophecies, not only refuse to recognize the authority of the Lord, they revile the angels, perhaps raising the example of Sodom once again since the Sodomites insulted the angels by seeking to engage in intercourse with them.[56] The first error, defiling the flesh is even more opaque. In what sense does "dreaming" defile? One possibility is that sexual immorality was again implied.

The word here translated "defile" (μιαίνω) was frequently connected to sexual misconduct. According to *1 Enoch*, when the angels engaged in sexual relations with women, they defiled themselves (*miainō*); according to the author of *Jubilees*, the men of Sodom defiled themselves when they committed fornication in their flesh (*1 Enoch* 7.1; 9.8; 12.4; 15.3. *Jubilees*, 16.5.).[57] Moreover, when Israel committed *porneia*, she "defiled" herself with other gods.[58] Thus, when the author stated that "these" behave "in the same way" (ὁμοίως) as those negative examples from the past—defiling the flesh and dreaming—the (contemporary) false prophets were implicitly charged with both sexual and religious violations.[59] The current false teachers were numbered among the infamous fornicators, dreamers, defilers, and models of disobedience of the old days. The punishment these former villains received could then serve as a warning of the severe punishment God reserves for such people.[60]

JUDE 8–19: THE DEPRAVITY OF "THESE" LICENTIOUS TEACHERS

Verse 8 begins a series of more direct denunciations of the (current) false teachers, repetitiously referring to them as "these" (*houtoi*):

> These men, dreaming, defile the flesh, reject authority, and slander the glories.
>
> (Jude 8)

These men revile what they do not understand.

(10)

[What "these" do know, they understand] naturally, like irrational animals.

(10)

These are blemishes on your love-feasts.

(12)

These are grumblers and malcontents; they follow after their own desires.

(16)

These are the ones who cause division, worldly men, who do not have the spirit.

(19)

Claiming to have superior knowledge, the author argues, these false dreamers "are in fact following the sexual instincts which they share with the animals."[61] Furthermore, they "follow the way of Cain, abandon themselves to the error of Balaam for payment, and perish in Korah's controversy"(Jude 11). Cain, the first murderer, was considered by Josephus to have introduced both violence and luxury (i.e., sexual indulgence) to humanity.[62] Balaam, offering false prophecy in search of gain, seduced Israel into sinning with other gods and with foreign women.[63] Korah led a rebellion against Moses and was remembered in later Jewish tradition as an envious, greedy schismatic.[64] "These," by analogy with three additional biblical antiheroes, were further labeled as greedy and self-indulgent men who corrupt the faithful. "Woe to them," for like Cain, Balaam, and Korah, destruction will surely come upon them (11).[65]

The author concludes his denunciation with a torrent of opprobrium:

These, feasting together boldly, are blemishes[66] on your love feasts,[67] shepherding themselves, waterless clouds carried away by winds, trees in late autumn without fruit, twice dead, uprooted, wild waves of the sea casting up their own shameless deeds like foam, wandering stars for whom the gloom of darkness has been kept forever.

Here "these" are charged with caring only for themselves, rejecting all authority, and wandering aimlessly while failing to produce "rain" or "fruit." Moreover, their feasting pollutes community meals, and they, like the "stars" (i.e., the disobedient angels mentioned in verse 6) will be judged, uprooted, and destroyed. Though they now glory in their shameless deeds, soon they will be judged and convicted, a conclusion that Jude confirms by offering two apocalyptic punch lines at the close of his critique, a prophecy of Enoch and a saying of the apostles.

Enoch, Jude states, prophesied that God would come to judge the ungodly for all their deeds of ungodliness. As Jude understands it, this prophecy pertains to the current ungodly who are the "mumblers, those who find fault, following their own desires, and their mouths speak haughty [words], showing partiality for the sake of advantage" (Jude 14–16).[68] In addition to "following after their own desires," the "ungodly" grumble against God, speak ostentatiously, and take bribes. The appearance of such people was foretold by Enoch and is now taking place. The time of the final judgment—the "great day" referred to in verse 7—is near and the prophecies are being fulfilled. The "apostles" also prophesied that this day would come, Jude reminds his readers. They said, "in the last time there will be mockers, following their own ungodly desires" (18). The ungodly of today are the last-time mockers predicted by both Enoch and the apostles. Just as "those"—the infamous sinners of Biblical times—earned for themselves a swift and severe punishment, so too "these" will be punished, and soon. The last days can be discerned by the appearance of ungodly, licentious, depraved, and faithless false teachers who pervert the grace of God.

THE APOSTATES

Throughout this letter, therefore, the allegedly "ungodly" Christians are classified among biblical antitypes whose misbehavior was motivated by misplaced desire: Israel lusting after the gods, angels lusting after women, men seeking to rape angels. Jude repeatedly accused the "ungodly" of uncontrolled desire (*epithymia*). If, as Jude suggests, false teachers are a sign of the end times, then so is licentiousness among the faithful, something that cannot and must not occur. When believers with false teachings and ungodly desires successfully sneak into the congregation of the faithful, the last-time prophecies are fulfilled. In this way, apocalyptic warning was combined with parenesis to denounce any believer who might disagree with Jude. At the same time, the author's polemic constructs a familiar version of what makes someone a true "saint" and reemphasizes the metonymic equivalence of idolatry and *porneia* discussed in the chapter 2. The saints cannot follow after desire. They must not reject authority or revile the angels. They do not go after strange flesh. If they do, they are numbered among the false prophets of old and promised that their punishment will be severe. The principal error of the apostates—be they ancient biblical enemies or those foretold by the apostles—is misplaced, unchecked desire, desire that leads to disobedience and faithlessness.

The author of 2 Peter, writing sometime after Jude, also accused the targets of his reproach with an inability to control desire. He expanded upon Jude's argument about the licentiousness of the end-time false teachers, borrowing some of Jude's language and polemical technique.[69] Jude compares false Christians to infamous Biblical antitypes. Second Peter adopts the same strategy, comparing the "ungodly" he opposed to the wicked generation before the flood, the disobedient angels, and the men of Sodom (2 Pet 2:4–10). Jude links false teaching with ungodly desire (4, 8, 12, 16, 18). Second Peter also suggests that phony Christians are plagued by insatiable desire (2:13–14, 18–20). Second Peter, however, offers more explicit information about the character of the true Christians. Summing up his version of Peter's teaching, he maintains that Christians can escape the corrupting influence of desire altogether through faith (1:3–9).

SECOND PETER, FALSE TEACHERS, AND WICKED DESIRE

Second Peter—part testament and part epistle—offers ethical exhortation, apocalyptic warnings, and, most prominently, an extended denunciation of false Christian prophets and teachers.[70] The author's chief aim is to exhort the faithful to virtue while refuting false teaching. The importance of virtue and the control of desire to this author are evident from the introductory statement onward:

> All things pertaining to life and godliness are given to us by his divine power, through the knowledge of the one who has called us by his own glory and virtue, through which he gave us the valuable and excellent promises, in order that through these things you might become participants in the divine nature and escape the corruption that is in the world by means of desire.
>
> (1:3–4)

In this opening summary of the theme of the letter, we are told that God, through Christ, gives life, piety, and promises while protecting the faithful from destruction and corruption. This destruction is brought on by desire. "Peter" then asserts that faith must be supported by virtue (ἀρετή), knowledge (γνῶσις), self-control (ἐγκράτεια), endurance (ὑπομονή), piety (εὐσέβεια), love of the brothers and sisters (φιλαδελφία), and love (ἀγαπή) more generally (1:5–7). Those who do not possess these qualities have forgotten that their sins (ἁμαρτία) were cleansed (1:9).

A few verses later, the author introduces a major theme—the denunciation of false prophets and their licentiousness (2:1–3). The remainder of the document contains an extended refutation of their teachings and practices. Clues to the content of the "false teaching" of concern to the author are distributed throughout the document. Peter reminds his audience that "we" (i.e., the apostles) were eyewitnesses to the life and activity of Jesus, suggesting that apostolic authority has been challenged (1:17–18). Pseudo-teachers, Peter submits, have turned from faith and denied the authority of Christ. Consequently, the true Christians are reminded of the confirmation of Christ given by God and heard by the apostles (2:1). Some wayward Christians have questioned the impending judgment, asking, "Where is the promise of his coming?"(3:3–4). Judgment will come, Peter assures the faithful, but in God's time, not human time (3:8–13). Condemning their misguided views, Peter also denounces the character of his opponents. Reasserting the importance of the approaching judgment, Peter promises that false prophets will be destroyed. Reminding the faithful of the centrality of virtue, he characterizes his targets as utterly depraved. Faithfulness, he argues, is indicated by self-control and obedience. Faithlessness and disobedience occur when desire is left unchecked.

In his introductory remarks, the author of 2 Peter asserts that God, through Christ, has given "us" his own glory and virtue, enabling "us" to "escape from the destruction in the world," a destruction brought "by means of desire" (1:4). In this, "Peter" sounds much like Paul. Will your "members" be slaves of sin or slaves of God? Paul asks (Rom 6:15–23). According to Paul, yielding to sin leads to death. Becoming "slaves of God" leads to eternal life (6:21–23). "Unnatural lust" is said to be a direct result of the rejection of God (1:18–32). Yet, in Paul's writings, "unnatural" and uncontrolled lust is (or should be) a problem that tempts others; Christians control their desire. Paul distinguishes between the "saints" or the "brothers and sisters" and morally corrupt gentiles by referencing sexual virtue. The author of 2 Peter, however, contends that the principal threat comes from within. Pseudo-teachers, motivated by licentiousness, have secretly brought destructive opinions into the community, threatening the purity of the saints. The charges brought against them include:

They will secretly bring in destructive opinions.

(2:1)

With greed, by false words, they will exploit [ἐμπορεύσονται, lit. "traffic in" or "sell"] you.

(2:3)

They [like the Biblical villains of old] follow after flesh, desiring defilement.

(2:10)71

They despise ruling powers.

(2:10)

Bold and arrogant, they are revilers and do not tremble at the glories.

(2:10)

They are like irrational animals.

(2:12)

They consider reveling [τρυφή] during the day a pleasure.

(2:13)

Their eyes are full of adultery and look incessantly for sin.

(2:14)

Their hearts are trained in greed.

(2:14)

They have gone astray.

(2:18)

They lure by means of the licentious desires of the flesh those who have only just escaped.

(2:18)

They are slaves of corruption.

(2: 19)

Escaping the defilements of the world by the knowledge of the lord... they are entangled in them again.

(2:20)

They are the end-time scoffers who follow after their own desires.

(3:3)

Uncontrolled desire provides the overarching theme of these numerous charges. Desire is labeled as a defilement (*miasma*) and identified with the world (*kosmos*). Desire is something that apostates follow after;[72] their eyes are full of adultery.[73] They seduce, they entice, they operate in secret. They pretend to offer freedom but are actually enslaved, presumably to desire and sin.[74] In short, they are everything a true believer cannot be. They do not possess virtue or knowledge or self-control or godliness or love. Therefore, they can have no part in salvation.

These charges reiterate points found elsewhere in early Christian literature. For example, Paul, the "Paul" of Ephesians, and the author of 1 John agreed that the corruption of the world is made plain by illicit desire.[75] Like the author of 2 Peter, Ignatius compared his opponents to beasts who secretly bite their prey[76] and, in a manner similar to the author of 2 Timothy, Peter worried that his rivals would use desire to lead weak Christians away from the faith (2 Tim 3:6–8; 2 Pet 2:18). Peter, like Paul, identified flesh with desire, suggesting that *sarx* (flesh) and *epithymia* (desire) can lead to defilement (Gal 5:24; Rom 6:13, 17–18, 19.). Peter, like Paul, suggested that believers can sell themselves to desire, in this case by listening to treacherous false Christians who have enslaved themselves to corruption (Rom 7:5).[77] Moreover, 2 Peter repeated the frequent Christian claim that true faith (*pistis*), virtue (*aretē*), knowledge (*gnōsis*), piety (*eusebeia*), steadfastness (*hupomonē*), and self-mastery (*enkrateia*) belong to the brothers and sisters in Christ. Licentiousness (*aselgeia*), corrupting desire (*epithymia*), adultery (*moicheia*, even of the eyes), and reveling (*truphē*, lit. "luxury") is an attribute of "the world" and of apostate Christians, both of which will be destroyed on the coming, end-time day of God: "The day of the lord will come like a thief, and then the heavens will pass away with a loud noise, and the elements will be dissolved with fire, and the earth and the works that are done on it will be revealed" (3:10).

THE LIBERTINE OPPONENTS OF JUDE AND 2 PETER?

Reading 2 Peter and Jude along similar lines, a majority of exegetes take "Peter" and "Jude" at their word, suggesting that these letters sought to counter the immorality promoted by groups of misguided Christians. For example, Richard Bauckham described 2 Peter's opponents in the following manner:

> "Freedom" was their catchword, and evidently they felt free to indulge in sexual immorality, drunkenness and sensual excesses generally (2:2, 10a, 13–14, 18). No doubt the easy compromise with pagan moral standards which their teaching allowed was one source of their popularity.[78]

To Bauckham, the opponents of Jude and 2 Peter shared one prominent characteristic—ethical and practical libertinism.[79] Bauckham further assumes that this libertinism led to their popularity and mirrored "pagan" morality. J. N. D. Kelly offers a similar analysis, suggesting that 2 Peter's opponents were "professed antinomians."[80] Donald Senior agrees: "These same teachers also led lives of promiscuity, claiming to be 'free' of ordinary moral restraints."[81]

Certainly, Jude and 2 Peter do accuse their targets of ethical and practical antinomianism. Jude suggests that the "ungodly" are characterized by "licentiousness" and that they "follow after their own lusts." The author of 2 Peter then reconfigures some of these same charges for his own purposes. According to "Peter," false, formerly Christian prophets and teachers are licentious—they indulge in defiling lusts; they revel in the daytime; they have eyes full of adultery; they lure others by means of the licentious passions of the flesh; they are entangled in and overpowered by the defilements of the world (2:2). As such, false believers are revealed to be the end-time mockers whose coming was predicted by the apostles (3:3). They will be severely punished, even as they deny that the judgment will come (3:4; compare 2:1, 11, 19).

Still, rather than describing their misdeeds in detail, sexual or otherwise, the letters of Jude and 2 Peter offer blanket and stereotypical accusations. The false prophets are licentious. They are greedy. They despise authority. Targets of ancient invective were regularly denounced in these terms.[82] So, for example, defending orators, Aelius Aristides found that he had to counter the charge that rhetoricians are slaves of desire and pleasure.[83] Repeating a familiar triplicate, Plutarch warned that vice (*kakia*) arouses every desire (*epithymia*), awakens intemperance (*akolostos*), and enjoys lawlessness (*paranomos*; Plut. *Mor.* 101a). Describing typical tyrants, Dio Chrysostom stated that they are invariably licentious, arrogant, and inconstant; that is, they are ruled by every kind of desire and take delight in lawlessness.[84]

Though the charges lodged by Jude and 2 Peter against their opponents are not identical to these non-Christian examples, they are suspiciously similar. Antony is represented as a licentious slave of desire. So, too, are the "ungodly" of Jude and "pseudo-teachers" of 2 Peter. Rhetoricians, Aristides suggests, were frequently charged with serving the desires and pleasures of their audiences for the sake of their own, illicit gain. The targets of Jude and 2 Peter faced nearly identical charges: they "follow their own desires" and flatter people "for their own gain" (Jude 16, 18); in their greed they exploit (lit. "sell") the faithful, enticing them by means of "fleshy desire" (2 Peter 2:3, 18). Moreover, charges of greed, licentiousness, and depraved sexual practices almost always accompanied charges of apostasy in the biblical examples surveyed in chapter 2. Apostates were always fornicators, and apostasy was always motivated by illegitimate desire, at least in theory. Finally, when read against the nearly universal claim on the part of Christian authors that believers always control themselves and their desires, the argument that false prophets are motivated by desire rather than faith becomes particularly suspect.

The interesting question, as far as I am concerned, is not whether or not "Peter" or "Jude" sought to combat a (real) tendency toward "pagan moral standards" but how the control of desire functioned as the mark of the true Christian against the false Christian or non-Christian. At least three factors suggest that such reconstructions of "the opponents" are fallacious: the prevalence of similar charges in Greek invective; the metonymic equivalence of sexual depravity and apostasy in biblical and early Jewish writings; and the insistence that Christian faith is marked, above all, by the control of desire. Indeed, it is possible to wonder if there were "real" opponents at all. The insistence of the letters of Jude and 2 Peter that false Christians do not and will not control desire may have had more to do with their attempts to make self-mastery the hallmark of their own movement than with any depraved behavior on the part of the targets of their invective. On the other hand, should there be Christian "opponents" to combat, the charge of wicked desire would have been a particularly effective weapon, especially if these Christians had also adopted the position that faith in Christ necessarily leads to sexual self-mastery. In either case, the choice of weapon does not necessarily provide any real evidence of the practices of the other side.

Identifying Peter's opponents with "pagan moral standards," Bauckham and others uncritically repeat what was an ancient and incessant Christian claim—authentic, proper morality is the property of true Christians alone. Remarkably, it is Bauckham, not "Peter," who paganizes the opponents. Whereas Paul frequently cautions Christians not to become "like the gentiles," and numerous Christian authors contrast the profligate pre-Christian lives of believers with the virtuous lifestyle that now characterizes them, the author of 2 Peter does not adopt this particular rhetorical strategy.[85] If anything, "Peter" relies upon "pagan moral standards" to shame the false teachers, worrying that "because of them the way of truth will be reviled" (2:2). "The way of truth" can only be reviled for the licentiousness of the false prophets if non-Christians hold higher moral standards than the false Christians. The behavior of these pseudo-Christians, 2 Peter implies, is so deplorable that even non-Christians will recognize it and be appalled. In sum, the contention of Bauckham, Kelly, Senior, and others that a group of antinomian Christians inspired the authors of Jude and 2 Peter is highly suspect.

DESIRE DENOUNCED

In the letters of Jude and 2 Peter, uncontrolled desire, frequently described as "licentiousness" (*aselgeia*), emerges as the principal charge against false Christians. Classifying Christians according to their control of desire, Jude and 2 Peter imply that improper desire is enough to indict a fellow Christian. According to Paul, the threat of *porneia* necessitates the control of desire by means of marriage for those who cannot maintain authority over themselves. In these two epistles, however, desire itself serves as a mark of defilement. The authors of Jude and 2 Peter do not charge ungodly Christians with *porneia*, "unnatural" sexual relations, or incest. Rather, it is enough to accuse them of desiring falsely and of a propensity toward "licentiousness." The content of this licentiousness (*aselgeia*) is never named. Was the intended audience of these letters expected to guess that false Christians violate Pauline or some other Christian sexual ethic? Or was the charge that they "follow after desire" sufficient? As noted in the previous chapters, Christians frequently claimed that *sōphrosynē* and *enkrateia*—usually described as the control of desire—were their exclusive property. Without faith in Christ, these virtues can never be fully attained.[86] It was but a small step, perhaps, to argue that the primary distinguishing characteristic of false, faithless, and sneaky Christians was desire itself.

This sort of problematization of desire has already been observed in Paul's letter to the Corinthians. A little over a century later, Clement of Alexandria claimed that total freedom from desire can be one of the great benefits of Christian faith. As he puts it,

> The human ideal of continence, I mean that which is set forth by Greek philosophers, teaches that one should fight desire and not be subservient to it so as to bring it to practical effect. But our ideal is not to experience desire at all. Our aim is not that while a man feels desire he should get the better of it, but that he should be continent even respecting desire itself. This chastity cannot be attained in any other way except by God's grace.
>
> (Clement *Strom*. 3.7.57)[87]

True Christians, according to a authors from Paul to Clement and beyond, control desire. The best Christians overcome desire altogether.

Desire in general, and sexual desire in particular, has been rendered problematic by these texts. As I noted in chapter 2, Paul suggests that desire is a dangerous threat that can lead to *porneia*. Thus, marriage is the only choice for weak Christians: it serves as a "prophylaxis" against desire, though sexual renunciation and the concomitant control of desire is the better option.[88] Directing their arguments against a (potential?) enemy within, Jude and 2 Peter imply that desire is dangerous not only because of *porneia* but also because of the threat of apostasy. Disobedience against God is always motivated by illicit desire, or so it would seem, given the traditional examples of disobedience listed by Jude and 2 Peter. The consequences of illicit desire/apostasy are devastating: absolute destruction in the day of God.[89] Desire, therefore, is not only a threat to the purity of the faithful, it is death dealing. Wicked desire and disobedience among "the saints," these two letters suggest, will bring on the cataclysmic end-time judgment. The gentiles without Christ may be abandoned to their lusts (or so Paul suggests), but the lusts of false believers, Jude and 2 Peter warn, will produce the end of the world.

The imputation of wicked desire, though prominent, was not the only charge available to Christian polemicists. The accusation that a fellow Christian is proven false by his wicked desires was often accompanied by the suggestion that he is animated by the devil, a demon, or by some evil spirit. Thus, the author of 1 John explains, "The one who sins is from the devil because the devil has sinned from the beginning" (1 John 3:7–8). To Polycarp, Christians who do not accept that Christ came in the flesh but offer some alternative explanation of the incarnation are the "first born of Satan" (Poly. *Phil.* 7.1). Justin Martyr suggests that Simon, a Samaritan "magician," was influenced by demons to perform mighty acts. So, too, was Marcion who, though called a Christian, was actually controlled by demons (Justin *1 Apol.* 26). Jude and 2 Peter impy that, motivated by lust, false Christians deliberately lead the "saints" astray and therefore God's consuming judgment must be at hand. Other Christian authors suggest that illicit desire and disobedience among Christians is the direct result of demonic influence. These two charges—illicit desire and animation by the devil—were central to representations of Chrisitan deviance.

In his analysis of Jude and 2 Peter as early "heresiologies," Frederik Wisse suggests that the versions of the ungodly (*asebeis*) offered by Jude and of the pseudo-teachers (*pseudodidaskaloi*) in 2 Peter provided later Christian authors with a model of the ideal heretic that was frequently imitated. This model includes the following characteristics: heretical sects are said to originate outside of authentic Christianity in the line of biblical villains; the heretics are supposedly libertines, with false teaching inevitably leading to sexual and sumptuary excess; the teaching of the heretics is represented as a deliberate or demonic distortion of the truth; the motivation of the heretics is to blaspheme God and lead the faithful astray; and they are said to be singled out by God for condemnation and must therefore be categorically rejected by the true church.[90] I would agree with Wisse that something approaching an ideal type of the false Christian does emerge in the context of these letters—the false Christian as a sexually promiscuous religious deviant.[91] The ungodly in Jude and the pseudo-teachers in 2 Peter have all the characteristics associated with "heretics" by later Christians.[92] Misplaced, unchecked desire, logically speaking, should only present a problem for misguided, disobedient Christians, a point made by virtually every heresiologist from earliest Christianity onward. In this paradigm, false religion and corrupt, insatiable desire always imply each other.[93] Wisse's suggestion that the charge of antinomianism was stereotypical is further supported by the representation of false prophets in *The Shepherd of Hermas*. Few would argue that *The Shepherd* was written with genuine "false prophets" in mind, yet the description of them is remarkably similar to that found in Jude and 2 Peter, with the added charge that their prophecy was derived directly from the devil.[94]

DESIRE, THE DEVIL, AND THE MODEL HERETIC IN THE SHEPHERD OF HERMAS

The Shepherd of Hermas,[95] a late-first- or early-second-century[96] Christian apocalypse,[97] offers an extended moral exhortation presented to one "Hermas."[98] Hermas is initially guided through a series of visions by a woman who is revealed to represent the church. For most of the text, however, he is guided by a shepherd/angel.[99] *The Shepherd* is divided into three sections, ὁράσεις, ἐντολαί, and παραβολαί, usually referred to in English as *Visions*, *Mandates*, and *Similitudes*. There is evidence that portions of this rather long text circulated separately.[100] This, together with what has seemed to some scholars to be a disjointed, uneven text, has suggested to some that *The Shepherd* had more than one author.[101] Nevertheless, the majority of contemporary interpreters view *The Shepherd* as the work of a single author. Awkward transitions and disjunctures between books are usually explained by theories of multiple redactions or multiple sources. Following a survey of the arguments for multiple or single authorship, Carolyn Osiek concludes, "a theory of sequential composition in the order in which the parts are now arranged is the simplest solution."[102] For my purposes, I assume that *The Shepherd* was written by a single author and, at some point in the early to mid-second century, included all three books.[103] *The*

Shepherd is dominated by a series of interrelated themes: the urgent need for repentance among the saints,[104] the danger of "double-mindedness," and the importance of self-control. The necessity for immediate repentance or conversion among Christians (μετάνοια and cognates) is stressed in every book. So, for example, Hermas is told by the elderly lady/church that he must lead his sinning family to repentance, no longer tolerating their iniquity (Herm. *Vis.* 1.3.1–2). Hermas then asks if a woman who commits adultery may be taken back by her husband if she repents. She should be taken back, his Shepherd replies, but not often since "the slaves of God have but one repentance" (Herm. *Mand.* 4.7–8). Wayward Christians are divided into those who may repent before the last day and those for whom repentance is scarcely possible (Herm. *Vis.* 3.5–6; Herm. *Sim.* 6.1.3–4, 3.6, 8.3.5–8, 6.1–10.4, 9.14.1–2, 18.1–4, 19.1–20, 23.5, 26.1–8, 33.1–3).[105]

A second theme in *The Shepherd* is the problem of διψυχία (double-mindedness). Double-mindedness is the "daughter of the devil" and does wickedness to the slaves of God (Herm. *Mand.* 9.9). The slaves of God ought to have strong faith, thereby keeping away from doubt and loving God with their whole heart.[106] A third theme is the importance of self-control (*enkrateia*). *The Shepherd* begins with the protagonist unable to control the desire he experiences in his heart and incapable of understanding just how dangerous a wicked thought can be.[107]

I will not attempt to comment on every episode in this long, complex document. I am interested, rather, in the depiction of the prototypical false prophet and apostate Christian the work produced. How is a false prophet to be recognized? *The Shepherd* offers a detailed description of the expected characteristics: deceitfulness, arrogance, luxury, greed, desire, and animation by the devil. What would lead a faithful Christian to rebel against God? *The Shepherd* identifies the culprits: desire and the devil. The taxonomy of the false prophet found in the Mandate 11 and the discussion of apostate and weak Christians in the Similitude 9 encapsulate these arguments.[108] *The Shepherd* may not contain any explicit attack against specific false Christians. Nevertheless, the typical false prophets of Mandate 11 look very much like the (actual?) false prophets and teachers of Jude, 2 Peter, and other early Christian texts.

THE ELEVENTH MANDATE: DISCERNING THE SPIRITS

Mandate 11 suggests that the source of false prophecy is the devil, the motivation for the prophecy is desire, and the message offered seduces double-minded Christians by pandering to their lusts.[109] Though desire and a concomitant tendency to engage in illicit sex are not the only "problems" exhibited by the false prophets, as expected, these two characteristics emerge as important features of their corruption. The following criteria emerge:

FALSE PROPHET	TRUE PROPHET
filled with the spirit of the devil	filled with the spirit of God
earthly, empty, powerless, stupid	powerful
exalts himself, is bold, shameless, talkative	meek, tranquil, humble
lives in much luxury of this age	refrains from all evil and futile desire
accepts payment	poor, does not accept payment
prophesies to the double-minded (*dipsychia*)	does not answer when consulted
speaks at the request of the double-minded	speaks only when God wants it
tells them what will fulfill their desires	speaks what the Lord wishes
flees the assembly of the just	speaks only in a gathering of just men

False Christians, illicit desire, evil spirits, the devil, and the vices become inextricably linked in this passage.[110] Pseudo-prophets are animated by the devil. They lead Christians to idolatry and to becoming "like the gentiles." In this way, those who listen to false Christian prophets are no better than idolaters: they consult oracles "like the gentiles" and "bring upon themselves greater sin by becoming idolaters."[111] They tempt people by offering to fulfill wicked desires. They live in riotous luxury, seeking payment to maintain their decrepit lifestyle. Mandate 11 offers a taxonomy of the typical false prophet, a taxonomy of charges that appears elsewhere in denunciations of "false" Christians.

Paul claims that his rivals in Corinth were in league with the devil: "For such men are pseudo-apostles, deceitful workers, disguised as apostles of Christ. And no wonder, for Satan disguises himself as an angel of light. It is not a great thing, therefore, if his servants disguise themselves as servants of justice" (2 Cor 11:13–15). The author of 1 Timothy warns that in the last days some (Christians) will listen to deceitful spirits and the teachings of demons (4:1). The typical false prophet in *The Shepherd* "exalts himself." So, too, do the false prophets denounced by the author of James, 1 Peter, the *Didache,* and the *Epistle of Barnabas* (Jas 4:10; 1 Pet 5:6; *Did.* 3.9; *Barn.* 19.3. Compare Matt 23:1–12). The model false prophet pursues "luxury" (*tryphē*).[112] So, too, do the false teachers in 2 Peter (2:13).[113] False prophets are said to pander to the desires of their audience, telling people what they want to hear. Justin accuses Crescens, a Cynic philosopher, of a similar crime.[114] In short, the description of the prototypical false Christian prophet in the *Shepherd* turns out to be virtually identical to the representation of supposedly real, antinomian false prophets or teachers in numerous other Christian texts.

Jude and 2 Peter do not make an explicit connection between "wicked desire" and the devil, preferring instead to propose that desire brings about the end time. *The Shepherd*, however, combines the suggestion that bad Christians are in league with the devil with the view that desire is a dangerous threat to faithfulness. Hermas is told that false Christians are to be identified both by their lusts and by the true source of their (illegitimate) prophecies: the devil. In this way, wicked desire and the machinations of the devil are explicitly connected. False prophets are not only contaminated and ruled by desire, they are filled with evil spirits who, in turn, use them as instruments to deceive others. The best and only protection against them (prophets and evil spirits), *The Shepherd* insists, is single-minded devotion to God.[115] Anything less leaves the faithful open to the seductive powers of the evil spirits. A similar point is made later in the document when disobedient Christians are said to fall into rebelliousness after allowing themselves to be tempted by evil spirits. A detailed description of this process is found in the Similitude 9.

THE NINTH SIMILITUDE: THE TEMPTATIONS OF PERSONIFIED VICE

The Ninth Similitude recapitulates and extends a vision of the church first given to Hermas in the Vision 3. In the earlier vision, Hermas is shown a tower by the lady/church and told that the stones that are either being placed in the tower or thrown away represent Christians of different types. The stones that easily fit into the tower are church leaders who have lived in purity and remained at peace with one another, those who have suffered for the name of the Lord, and those who are righteous and have obeyed God's commandments (Herm. *Vis.* 3.3–5). The rest of the stones, as yet unfit for the tower, are rejected for various failings, including having given themselves up to depraved licentiousness (Herm. *Vis.* 3.6–7). In the Similitude 9, Hermas revisits this vision, this time with the Shepherd as his guide. Though the vision of the tower is similar in the Vision and the Similitude versions, there are some elaborations and new elements were added.[116] One of the new elements is a juxtaposition of twelve virgin virtues with twelve personified vices.[117] The virgins (*parthenoi*) carry the stones/Christians to the tower. The twelve vices carry defective stones away.

The virgins, Hermas is told, are "holy spirits" and the very "powers of the Son of God" (Herm. *Sim.* 9.13.2). Without them a man cannot enter the kingdom of God. They are Faith, Self-Mastery, Power, Patience, Simplicity, Innocence, Holiness, Cheerfulness, Truth, Understanding, Harmony, and Love, with Faith, Self-Mastery, Power, and Patience said to be the principal four (Herm. *Sim.* 9.15.2). These are matched by twelve vices, also revealed to be "spirits" and depicted as women in black: Faithlessness, Lack of Self-Control, Disobedience, Deceit, Sorrow, Wickedness, Licentiousness, Quick Temper, Lying, Foolishness, Slander, and Hatred, with Faithlessness, Lack of Self-Control, Disobedience, and Deceitfulness designated as the chief four (Herm. *Sim.* 9.15.3).[118] These spirits, Hermas is told, play a key role in the rejection or acceptance of the "stones":

> "All of these," he said, "received the name of the Son of God and the power of these virgins. And so, they were empowered by receiving these spirits and they accompanied the slaves of God, sharing one spirit, one body, and one clothing. For they were harmonious with one another and did what was righteous. And then, after some time, they were seduced by the women you saw wearing black garments, with uncovered shoulders, loose hair, and beautiful figures. When these men saw them they desired them and clothed themselves in their power, taking off the clothing and power of the virgins. And so they were cast out from the house of God and handed over to those women."
>
> (Herm. *Sim.* 9.13.7–9; Ehrman's translation)

In other words, the source of their apostasy was evil desire and evil spirits: they desired the wicked but beautiful spirits/vices. When they proved unable to resist desire and the seductive power of the vices/women, God gave them over (*paradidōmi*) to evil.[119] If they repent, clothing themselves with the virtues once again, they may still be placed in the tower. Their time is running short, however, for those who know God and yet do wrong will be doubly punished, dying forever (Herm. *Sim.* 9.18.3).[120]

DESIRE, SEXUAL SIN, AND THE DEVIL IN *THE SHEPHERD OF HERMAS* AND BEYOND

What is the significance of the assertion in *The Shepherd* and elsewhere that the source of apostasy, wicked desire, and false prophecy is "the devil" or "evil spirits"? In her discussion of the origin of Satan, Elaine Pagels suggests that sectarian Jews began to invoke Satan to characterize their

Jewish opponents when the dichotomy "Israel" against "the nations" was no longer satisfactory. Identification of rival Jews with "Satan"—once simply God's adversarial angel but later the leading evil angel, the Evil One—was a way of indicating which Jews are "really on God's side."[121] Christians adopted this strategy, Pagels argues, demonizing outsiders ("the nations," Rome, "pagans") but, even more, fellow Christians, "the most intimate enemies of all."[122] Bernard McGinn has also suggested that Satan or the devil—together with his peculiarly Christian extension, the "Antichrist"—are especially useful characters when the object of concern is one's "intimate enemy." The myth of the Antichrist, McGinn suggests, asks the believer to consider the possibility that the ultimate evil and the most dangerous threat may come "from within the righteous themselves, or even from within the believer's own heart."[123]

Be that as it may, identifying one's opponent with personified evil—all the while claiming direct access to the divine for oneself and those one hopes to persuade—is a potent rhetorical move, a move that was popular among such diverse early Christians as Paul, Polycarp, the author of the Johannine epistles, and the author of *The Shepherd*. As is clear from *The Shepherd*, an actual opponent was not necessary, for this document can hardly be read as an attack against any "real" false prophets. *The Shepherd* offers a description of the typical false prophet in an attempt ensure that "the slaves of God" will recognize a bad Christian when they see one. In a world populated with "others" who are condemned to a final death, true Christians who were figured as the representatives of God, and (allegedly) false Christians who were cast as Satan's representatives, staying true to the faith—as the author conceived of it—was granted absolute importance. Christians who remained obedient, who practiced self-mastery and who demonstrated that they experienced the requisite transformation in Christ gained eternal life for themselves, were granted mastery over their desires, and avoided becoming aligned with evil. In this way, the true, manly Christians were not only rewarded in the world to come, they were promised an escape from the horrific punishment that God has specially reserved for Satan and his collaborators at the end of time.[124]

Later Christian authors followed the example of Jude, 2 Peter, and *The Shepherd*, accusing their opponents of demonic inspiration and wicked desire, often in prurient detail. Not only do the alleged "heretics" succumb to their desires, these authors asserted, they engage in orgies,[125] seduce women with promises of spiritual fulfillment,[126] and attempt to cover their debaucheries with the name of Christ.[127] A new charge was added,

however: some heretics take sexual renunciation too far, rejecting marriage as Satanic and declaring all flesh to be corrupt.[128] Yet the very same
authors who labeled the "heretics" in this way also insisted that Christians
must maintain sexual purity or face the wrath of God, boasting that the
"gift" of sexual abstinence offers the best sort of Christian life.[129] Perhaps
charges of sexual licentiousness, outlined in increasingly prurient detail in
such writers as Justin and Irenaeus are linked to these ever more strident
claims about the heroic sexual renunciations of the followers of Christ.

CHAPTER 5

Illicit Sex, Wicked Desire, and the
Demonized Heretic

Charges of demonic influence and slavery to desire, found throughout late-first- and early-second-century Christian literature, built upon the traditional association of illicit sex, idolatry, and apostasy; upon well-known categories of Greek invective; and upon moralistic writings that made *sōphrosynē* and its opposites (*akolastos, aselgeia, tryphē*) the distinguishing characteristics of a "good" (*agathos*) or "bad" (*kakia*) person. These charges, directed at real or imagined opponents, could serve at least three functions simultaneously: to eliminate rivals who, if the charge stuck, would be viewed as anything but Christian; to persuade insiders to adopt and display a strict sexual virtue or face demonization and labeling as an "idolater," "gentile," or worse; and to suggest to an audience that the author embodies the in-Christ-ness that he has been promoting, lending legitimacy to his argument and granting him the authority to make it. Sexualized vituperation, therefore, can be read as a rhetorical tactic designed to enforce a sexualized Christian identity—Christians *are* sexually pure or they are not Christians at all—and to enhance the prestige of the authors who promoted this view. Therefore, when Justin and Irenaeus define, list, and categorize false Christians they call the "heretics," they adopt what was already a familiar strategy, associating their targets with sexual misbehavior and gender deviance. Justin describes Christian heretics as demon-inspired sex fiends (*1 Apol.* 26; *Dial.* 35). Irenaeus defines the error of the heretics according to the two, equally reprehensible practices they purportedly recommended: either they promoted idolatrous slavery to desire or they perversely overcommitted themselves to *enkrateia* (i.e., self-mastery or self-restraint; Iren. *Adv. Haer.* 1.6.2, 1.13.2–7, 1.24.5, 1.25.3–4, 1.26.3, 1.28.2, 2.32.2, 5.8.4, 1.24.2; 1.28.1). In both cases, Irenaeus claims, they advanced erroneous, ungodly doctrines and exhibited blameworthy practices. False religion and illicit sexual habits were linked once again.

This chapter explores charges of sexual vice as they appear in the anti-heretical writings of Justin Martyr and Irenaeus of Lyons.[1] Composing a work (lit., a σύνταγμα) "against all the heresies," Justin Martyr began a trend that was imitated by Irenaeus approximately twenty-five years later. Though Justin's contribution is now lost, his procedure in identifying and classifying "heresies" (lit. "choices" or "schools of thought") can be detected in a series of asides found in his extant works.[2] Listing the false teachings and the shocking sexual exploits of his rivals, Justin blames them for bringing negative attention to his movement. Since Justin's "true Christians" must always be chaste, self-disciplined models of sexual virtue, only false Christians could be capable of "the overturning of the lamp stand and promiscuous intercourse and devouring human flesh" (Justin 1 Apol. 26.7). These not-Christians, Justin asserts, teach ridiculous opinions, associate with prostitutes, and engage in the sort of wicked behavior of which all the Christians stand accused: that is, free intercourse under the cover of darkness after dining upon human flesh. If these imposters are guilty of such crimes, Justin contends, then they should be punished severely by the Romans (and by God) for their wicked behavior but not for their "Christianity." According to Justin's logic, they could not possibly be "Christian"; they forfeited any claim they had to the title by partaking in such practices.

Following Justin's lead, Irenaeus composed a comprehensive work against Christian "falsely so-called knowledge," listing each alleged heresy in turn and cataloging each group by founder, erroneous teaching, and illegitimate practice. According to Ireanaeus' system, the "Simonians" were the first heretics; all other heresies originated with them. As descendants of the Simonians, the heretics "naturally" followed the example of their "father," living licentious lives, practicing magic, worshipping statues, and teaching impious doctrines (Iren. Adv. Haer. 1.23.4). The Valentinians, Irenaeus' principle target, "are insatiably enslaved to the pleasures of the flesh" and "treacherously corrupt those women who are being taught this teaching by them" (Adv. Haer. 1.6.3).[3] According to Irenaeus, the Valentinian Marcus seeks out women to seduce and tempts them with the hope that they might prophesy; then, after luring them in, he takes all they have, body and soul: "And she endeavors to repay him, not only by the gift of [her] possessions, by which he has amassed a great fortune, but also by intercourse of the body, being eager to unite in every way with him, in

order that she might join together with him into one" (*Adv. Haer.* 1.13.3).[4]
The Carpocratians are similarly accused of performing "deeds which it
is not only wrong for us to speak of and listen to, but which we may not
even think or believe that such things are done among people who live in
our cities" (*Adv. Haer.* 1.25.4).[5] The Nicolaitans are charged with asserting
that "there is no difference between committing fornication and eating
food sacrificed to idols," both of which they were supposedly eager to
do (*Adv. Haer.* 1.26.3).[6] To this list, Irenaeus adds another heretical type:
the radical renunciant. According to Irenaeus, the followers of Saturninus,
Marcion, and the so-called Encratites declared that marriage is from Satan,
displaying a despicable hatred of the flesh (*Adv. Haer.* 1.24.2, 1.28.1). So,
for example, the disciples of Saturninus refrained from meat altogether,
"misleading many by this pretense of *enkrateia*" (*Adv. Haer.* 1.24.2).[7] Still,
when summarizing the alleged faults of the heretics, Irenaeus seems to
have forgotten about the (heretical) renunciants, remembering only those
who gave themselves up to every kind of reprehensible sexual and religious
act (*Adv. Haer.* 5.8.2–4). To Justin and Irenaeus, promiscuous thinking—
that is, thinking that they disagree with—inevitably results in promiscuous behavior.

These sorts of arguments are by now familiar; Justin and Irenaeus
joined in the denunciations of "false prophets," this time by condemning illegitimate Christian "schools of thought." Recent interpreters have
pointed to the formulaic character of heresiological representation, arguing that the antiheretical writings offer scant evidence of the actual beliefs
or practices of the groups they purport to describe.[8] According to this
view, the heresiologies of Justin, Irenaeus, and later Christian authors are
better understood as evidence of conflict, rhetorical grandstanding, Christian identity production, and the effort to deflect outsider criticism away
from one Christian group and onto another; these writings do not provide evidence of antinomian heresies.[9] As Elizabeth Clark has shown, late
antique "church fathers" attempted to place charges of Christian hatred
of the body—lodged by outsiders against Christians in general—squarely
on the shoulders of alleged "heretics."[10] By associating the "Simonians"
with orgiastic love-feasts and anthropophagy, Justin makes a similar move,
blaming them for rumors circulating about illicit Christian rituals. As le
Boulluec has argued, heresiological writing was central to the contentious
project of early Christian identity formation and formulation, a project
that sought to create purity by exclusion.[11] Heresiology, therefore, including that of Justin and Irenaeus, lists, names, describes, and constrains,

defining what true Christianity is not; in the process, Christianity is elaborated, defended, and constructed.[12] By representing the beliefs and practices of Christian "falsely so-called knowledge" and other (allegedly) false Christian positions, Justin and Irenaeus were engaged in powerful epistemological and cultural work that did not necessarily require "real" hedonistic heretics at all.

In addition to employing standard charges of sexualized invective to characterize their targets as corrupt, Justin and Irenaeus adopted another common vituperative practice: they contrast the legitimate origins of their group with the allegedly illegitimate lineage of their rivals. Justin refuses to grant Christian heretics the name "Christian," insisting that they ought to be labeled according to the founders of their groups; they were not the descendants of Christ, they were "Simonians," "Marcionites," "Valentinians," or "Basilidians" (Justin *Dial.* 35.6; *1 Apol.* 26). Irenaeus juxtaposes the supposedly pure genealogy of the church with the suspect lineage of the heretics throughout his polemic against them, contending that they were all derived from Simon, their true "father," though they had since grown appallingly diverse, splintering into "Marcionites," "Valentinians," "Nicolaitans," "Carpocratians," "Basilidians," and other groups (Iren. *Adv. Haer.* 1.16.3, 3.3.2, 3.4.1–2, 5.20.2).[13] The authors of Jude and 2 Peter also place false teachers in a disgraceful genealogical line; in their case, that line extends back to the biblical villains of old.[14] In Justin's and Irenaeus' schemes, the heretics were "born" after Christ's ascension; hence, they traced their opponents' origins not to biblical villains but to demonically inspired pseudo-Christians.[15]

Asserting Christian difference on the basis of genealogical metaphors, Justin and Irenaeus circumscribe their group's borders while positing an elite, divine lineage for those who accept their authority and opinion.[16] Heretics are removed from the *genos* (a group descended from common ancestors) of Christ and God, as are non-Christian Jews and gentiles.[17] Christians were not "Jews," they argue, since the Judeans had largely rejected Christ and were therefore cut off from divine favor.[18] Christians, though derived "from every *genos*," were a new *genos* that refused to worship or imitate the demon-gods honored by their ancestors (Justin *1 Apol.* 25; Justin *Dial.* 138.2; Iren. *Adv. Haer.* 4.24.2, 4.33.1). In this system, true Christians—the not-Judeans, not-gentiles—become the only legitimate heirs of Christ and, therefore, of God. Justin explains: "For all the Gentiles [*ta ethnē*] were desolate of the true God, serving the works of [their] hands; but Jews and Samaritans, having the word [*logos*] from God delivered to them through the prophets and constantly expecting the Christ, did not recognize him when he came" (*1 Apol.* 53; compare *Dial.* 43.4–5, 67.5, 119.5, 120.5; Iren. *Adv. Haer.* 4.15.2–2).[19] Therefore, "knowing the truth that is contained in his words and those of his prophets," the Christians are confident that they will "inherit the incorruptible things of eternity"(Justin *Dial.* 139.5; compare Iren. *Adv. Haer.* 4.33.1–9, 5.33.3).

Rhetorically assimilated into the category "idolatrous gentiles," members of illegitimate pseudo-Christian "schools" are promised a share in eternal punishment even as Christians are reminded of their share in eternal bliss. "Too gentile," they cannot inherit God's blessings, but, like unrepentant Jews, they will be condemned. Indeed, unlike the Jews, the heretics are never actually included by Justin and Irenaeus in the privileged *genos* at all; their demon-inspired origin precluded them from salvation. Damned they would remain, whatever they might choose to call themselves. Justin's and Irenaeus' accusations regarding illicit sex and illegitimate birth denies heretics a place in a noble Christian lineage that originated, ultimately, with God.[20]

JUSTIN AND THE PURE PEOPLE OF GOD

Listing, sorting, and defining various heresies (αἱρέσεις) for the sake of comparison or refutation was an established tradition by the time Justin made the task his own.[21] Epictetus, for example, offered the following advice to his students: "Observe yourselves thus in your actions and you will find out to what sect [*hairesis*] of the philosophers you belong. You will find that most of you are Epicureans, some few Peripatetics, but these without any backbone.... But as for a Stoic, show me one if you can!"[22] Epictetus, a Stoic, challenges his students to live up to the "heresy" Stoicism, belittling the Epicurean and Peripatetic "heresies" as schools for the weak. Justin also mentions Epicurean, Pythagorean, Platonic, Stoic, Cynic, and Peripatetic philosophical "heresies"; to this list he adds Jewish "heresies," including the Pharisees, the Sadducees, and the Galileans, among others.[23] To Justin, however, the existence of heresies indicates an adulteration of an original truth and, therefore, heresies could only have been a negative development. Justin therefore interprets the presence of diverse opinions—philosophical, Jewish, or Christian—as proof of others' error. Christian philosophy was not construed as the best "school" among comparatively less vigorous competitors but as the only philosophy that had achieved the fullness of truth.

All true philosophical insight has been given by God in the form of a "seed of the Logos," Justin claims in his apologies, but the philosophers preserved only an adulterated form of this divine "seed," if they managed to preserve truth at all (*1 Apol.* 56; *2 Apol.* 8, 13). He explains: "For whatever either lawgivers or philosophers uttered well, they elaborated according to their share of Logos by invention and contemplation. But since they did not know all that concerns Logos, who is Christ, they often contradicted themselves" (*2 Apol.* 10.2–3; see also *2 Apol.* 13).[24] In other words, partial revelation led to contradictions and to the development of many schools of thought, transforming philosophy into a monstrous "hydra of many heads" as Justin put it elsewhere (*Dial.* 2.1–2). Christians, by contrast, received the entirety of the Logos, the "whole rational principle," which became Christ (*2 Apol.* 10.1); that is, they possessed "the thing itself" (*2 Apol.* 3).[25] Hence, Christians are the best philosophers of all.[26]

Justin's argument regarding Jewish heresies is similar: anyone who "examines the matter rightly" recognizes that there can only be one Judaism; those who identify with various Jewish heresies are not properly Jews at all, but something else (*Dial.* 80.4). Justin goes on to assert that the Christians have become the "true Israel" since the Jews failed at being the "seed of Abraham," an argument he presented in great detail in his *Dialogue with Trypho.*[27] The Jews, the "seed of Abraham," preserved the divine truth about Christ in their Scriptures, a "fact" they should have recognized. [28] Consequently, Justin declares, "we are the true, spiritual Israel, the *genos* of Judah, Jacob, Isaac and Abraham" (*Dial.* 11:4–5; see also *1 Apol.* 63):

> Some of your *genos* will be found children of Abraham, seeing as they are found in the portion of Christ. But others, though children of Abraham, are as the sand on the sea-shore which is unproductive and unfruitful, though great and innumerable, not producing any fruit at all but only drinking the water from the sea; of this the majority of your *genos* are accused, for you drink doctrines of bitterness and godlessness while you spurn the word (*logos*) of God.
>
> (*Dial.* 120.2)[29]

According to Justin, then, the Christians, by recognizing and embracing the "true" meaning of the Jewish scriptures, had become the "children of Abraham," the chosen *genos*, and the heirs to God's favor. The vast majority of Jews, however, had been cut off because by rejecting Christ, they "did not bear fruit." Justin then deploys familiar biblical tropes involving the sexual and religious misadventures of Israel in the wilderness to claim that the Jews had always been enslaved to desire, hard of heart, and prone to idolatry.[30] In this way, Justin describes Christians and Jews as distinct peoples and offers biblical examples of Israel's apostasies as proof of Jewish intransigence.

As we have seen, the authors of Jude and 2 Peter employ biblical examples of the misbehavior of Israel in the wilderness, but they do so to characterize false insiders rather than a group of outsiders they then labeled "Jews." In these earlier writings, insider followers of Christ are warned to conform to particular definitions of in-Christ-ness or face the sort of punishment reserved for apostate Israel, fallen angels, and Sodom and Gomorrah. By contrast, Justin employs biblical tales of Israel's *porneiai* (sexual misbehavior/apostasy) to distance Jews from the new and supposedly pure Christian *genos*. The Jews, he claims, "spurn the *logos* of God," investing the charge with a double meaning: they spurn Christ, who is the Logos, and the word of God contained in their own Scriptures since they misunderstand everything God had intended to teach them when they deny that Jesus was the Christ. In this way, Justin claims Jewish scriptures and even Jewish genealogy for the Christians—"we" are the spiritual *genos* of Judah, "we" are the house of Jacob—while simultaneously excising the Jews from God's community. [31] Justin no longer construes himself or his group as "Jewish" per se, therefore the misadventures of Israel apply neither to him nor to other Christians but to sinful Israel alone.[32]

Justin's method of eliminating Christian heresies from the family tree is slightly different. They never gained a share of God's "seed" at all, he argues, but were fashioned by demons to torment the church after Christ ascended into heaven.[33] Simon "through the art of the demons" performed magic; Marcion, "with the aid of demons," caused people of every *genos* to speak blasphemy; heretics in general were animated by "spirits of error" to say and do things that are godless and blasphemous, or so Justin claims (*1 Apol.* 26; *Dial.* 35.1). Animated by "demons," they actually remained gentiles all along:

And they say that they are Christians, just as they who are among the Gentiles inscribe the name of God upon their idols made by hands and take part in lawless and godless rites. And some of them are called Marcionites, and some Valentinians, and some Basilidians, and some Saturnilians, and others by other names, each being named from the originator of the opinion, just as each of those who think

they are philosophers ... think it is right to bear the name of the father of that system.

(*Dial.* 35.5–6)[34]

In other words, they, like the founders of philosophical schools, adulterated truth. Like the gentiles, they worshiped demons. As such, they have
kept "those from every *genos*" who were invited to join the new Christian
genos locked in a dark, degenerate world of "being gentile," even as they
pretended to be Christian. Justin's message is clear: the Christian heretics
and their followers could have no share in divine patrimony.

Justin's genealogical scheme, therefore, implies two points of exit or
entry, both of which pivoted on Christ. The gentiles, though at a disadvantage because of their demonic gods, were invited by Christ to receive
the full Logos and become "spiritual Israel." The Jews, advantaged by
their ancestry and the God-given prophecies that were preserved by the
Scriptures, were also invited but had largely rejected the invitation. The
heretics never entered the family at all, but remained gentiles, and an
especially pernicious sort of gentile at that. The Christians, by contrast,
constituted God's own *genos*, the one pure race, and the true heirs to
God's glory. Justin employed a variety of metaphors to make this argument: "The Christians are the one vine, planted by God" (*Dial.* 60.4).
The Christians "as one person believe on God the Maker of the universe,"
and "are now the true high priestly *genos* of God" (*Dial.* 66.3). "Christians
are a holy people [*laos*], chosen by God" (*Dial.* 69.3). Christians are the
heirs to God's blessings, having been "begotten" (*gennēsantos*) into God
by Christ (*Dial.* 123.9). The Christians are "quarried from the bowels of
Christ" (*Dial.* 135.3). Christ is "the head of another *genos*" that was begotten "by water and faith and wood [.e., the cross]" (*Dial.* 138.2). Whether
because of their relationship to the "vine," their election as the "high
priestly *genos*," their formation in the "bowels of Christ" (*ek tēs koilias tou
Christou*), their designation as a holy people, or their "birth" through baptism, faith, and the crucifixion, Christians had become a distinct people,
destined to remain God's legitimate heirs.[35]

In contrast to the dispossessed Jews and the demon-inspired gentiles or
heretics, the new Christian *genos* is described as pure in every way. Remarkably chaste, they avoided lust and married once if at all (*1 Apol.*15). Free
from anger, they never quarreled and regarded everyone with patience and
gentleness (*1 Apol.* 16). In fact, Justin claims, the Christians live in perfect
harmony with one another and with the rest of the world:

And we who were filled full of war and slaughter one of another, and every kind of evil, have from out of the whole earth each changed our weapons of war, our swords into ploughshares and our spears into farming tools, and we farm piety, righteousness, the love of humanity, faith, and hope, which comes from the Father himself through him who was crucified.

(*Dial.* 110.3; see also *1 Apol.* 67; *Dial.* 14.2)[36]

The empire claimed to promote *concordial/homonoia* ("harmony"), but to Justin it was the Christians who had actually achieved this goal, thanks to the intervention of Christ.[37]

Throughout the *Dialogue*, then, Justin presents his Christians as a distinct and holy people, separate from Jews and pre- or non-Christian gentiles. The Jews were the conduit of God's prophecies, but they had been largely cut off from divine guidance in punishment for their misbehavior and their rejection of Christ.[38] The gentiles, people from every *genos*, could be included, but first they were required to transfer their loyalty from the demons to the one true God who then became their "father." Once they did, they were fully incorporated into a privileged group described as a *genos*, a *laos* (a people), or a household, a group of people with a common descent and shared expectations regarding hereditary privileges. Justin's language for this process was quite literal: the Christians received a "new inheritance" (διαθήκη; *Dial.* 11.2, 119.5); they were "children of Abraham" because of their faith (*Dial.* 119.5); they had become the "seed of Judah" and the "house of Jacob" born of faith and spirit (*Dial.* 135.6).[39] In this way, Justin places Christians within an ethnoracial hierarchy, linking his Christians, whatever their original *genos*, to the ancestors of the Jews while eliminating Jews, gentiles and heretics from the group.[40] Alienation from Justin's God, however, had universal symptoms and universal consequences: he charges Jews with *porneiai* (illicit sex/apostasies), bloodthirstiness, demon worship, and child sacrifice (*Dial.* 16.2, 17.1, 19.9–22.11, 46.1–47.1, 110.5, 131.2–134.1, 151.4);[41] he accuses gentiles of prostitution, incest, demon worship, bloodthirstiness, and human sacrifice (*1 Apol.* 9, 21, 25, 54, 64; *2 Apol.* 5, 12; *Dial.* 30.1, 34.7); he associates heretics with demon worship, error, cannibalism, and promiscuous sex (*1 Apol.* 26; *Dial.* 35.4, 80.3). All of these outsiders will be destroyed by God if they do not repent (*1 Apol.* 5; *Dial.* 35.7, 141.2). Those Justin wishes to denigrate and exclude—Jew, gentile, or heretic—are said to be guilty of almost identical forms of misbehavior and promised the same horrific "inheritance":

eternal punishment. In Justin's genealogical and moral scheme, therefore, Christians who adopt his authority and perspective are the only *genos* that can boast a proper lineage as well as the concomitant moral and religious purity. Everyone else is genetically, religiously, and morally corrupt.

IRENAEUS' ENDLESS GENEALOGIES

Alluding to 1 Timothy 1:4, Irenaeus begins his refutation of Christian heresies by proposing that some Christians "reject the truth and introduce false narratives [*pseudeis logous*]," by developing "endless genealogies, seeking after questions" rather than preserving truth (Iren. *Adv. Haer.* Pr.1). He then proceeds to ridicule their "endless genealogies," distancing himself from the origin myths of the heretics while claiming that his own group preserved the truth about God and origins. To make the latter argument, Irenaeus is quite willing to engage in his own genealogical speculation: Christ Jesus is the one son of God; God is the Father who created all things; the prophets of the Jews received teachings about Christ from the holy spirit before he came; the apostles received the one faith and the one tradition from God through Christ; the church, though dispersed throughout the whole world, guards this true tradition and true faith "as [those] living in one house" (*Adv. Haer.* 1.10.1–2, 3.3.1–4.2). Father God, divine son, holy spirit, prophet, apostle, bishop, and church were said to form a legitimate chain of command: Christ appointed apostles, who appointed bishops, who in turn appointed (honorable male) successors, thereby safely guarding tradition and truth (*Adv. Haer.* 3.Pr–3.3.1). Irenaeus places himself within this privileged patrilineage by way of the blessed martyr and bishop Polycarp, a true Christian who had been taught by the apostles: "We ourselves saw him in our early youth, for he lived long and was in extreme old age when he left this life in a most glorious and most noble martyrdom" (*Adv. Haer.* 3.3.1–4).[42] Those who accepted Irenaeus' authority, therefore, could count themselves as members of the one true church and heirs to the divine patrimony (*Adv. Haer.* 5.28.4–29.1, 5.33.3–35.1). They were "mingled" with the Logos and had become God's own adopted sons (*Adv. Haer.* 3.19.1). Thus Irenaeus, like Justin before him, contrasted the legitimate genealogical line of Christians with the purportedly illegitimate line of the heretics. Refining Justin's theory of multiple heresies and multiple origins, Irenaeus further suggests that all the heresies had one "father" and therefore one origin: the heresies began with Simon the Samaritan.

SIMON, ORIGINATOR OF THE HERESIES

Simon the Samaritan, the father of the heresies, was first mentioned by the author of Acts: "Now a certain man named Simon had previously practiced magic in the city and amazed the people of Samaria, saying that he was someone great. All of them, from the least to the greatest, listened to him eagerly, saying, 'This man is the power of God that is called Great'" (Acts 8:9–11, NRSV). Despite his propensity for magic, Simon heard the preaching of the apostle Philip and was convinced, becoming baptized in the name of Jesus Christ. Still, after his baptism he sought to buy the power of the holy spirit, provoking a swift rebuke from Peter for his wickedness (Acts 8:14–23). The Simon of Acts, therefore, is accused of greed, but there is no mention of demonic inspiration, prostitutes, continuing magical practices, or a group founded in his name. Simon was next mentioned by Justin: "One certain Simon, a Samaritan from the village called Gitta, during the reign of Claudius Caesar, through the art of the demons who worked in him, did mighty works of magic in your imperial city of Rome and was thought to be a god" (Justin *1 Apol.* 26). Justin adds a series of provocative details to the Simon story: Simon traveled with "a certain Helena" who had been a prostitute (*proteron epi tegous statheisan*), declaring that this former prostitute was his "first thought" and claiming that he and Helena were a god and goddess of sorts. Simon attracted a disciple named Menander who was also animated by demons, who performed magic tricks in Antioch, and who sought to lead the faithful astray (*1 Apol.* 26). Irenaeus further diverges from the text of Acts: Helena served as Mother of All in Simon's disgraceful creation myth, the members of his heresy venerated the images of their founders in the guise of Zeus (Jupiter) and Athena (Minerva), and their priests engaged in further debauchery and magic (Iren. *Adv. Haer.* 23.1–5):

> The mystic priests of these people live licentious lives and practice magic, each one in whatever way he can. They make use of exorcisms and incantations, love-potions too and philters, and the so-called familiars, and dream-senders. They also have a statue of Simon patterned after Jupiter, and one of Helen patterned after Minerva. They worship these statues. They also have a name for themselves, the "Simonians" derived from Simon the author of this most impious doctrine, from whom the falsely so-called knowledge took its origin, as one can learn from their assertions.[43]

Thus, in Irenaeus' rewriting, the greedy Simon of Acts becomes the founder of a full-fledged libertine heresy.[44]

HERETICAL EMBELLISHMENT AND
GENEALOGICAL SPECULATION

Justin considerably expanded the tale of Simon the Samaritan; Irenaeus adds still more details. The author of Acts accused someone named Simon of engaging in magic prior to his acceptance of Christ. Justin accuses Simon of continuing magical practices after baptism for the express purpose of leading the faithful astray. Irenaeus spells out the type of magic the Simonians preferred.[45] Justin suggests that Simon presented himself and Helena as a god and goddess. Irenaeus reports that their followers made idols of their founders in the form of demon-gods. Justin implies that the Simonians were licentious. Irenaeus informed his readers that the Simonians were, in fact, led by "mystic priests" who actively promoted licentiousness and pursued debauchery at every opportunity. The horror of the "Simonians" was described in increasingly lurid terms.[46] A similar process can be observed in Irenaeus' treatment of the Nicolaitans. The Nicolaitans were first mentioned by John of Patmos in the book of Revelation; they were a group of Christ followers with whom the author disagreed, perhaps because they permitted the consumption of food that had been sacrificed to the gods (Rev 2:6, 14–15). Justin does not mention them, but Irenaeus includes them among other miscellaneous heresies, connecting them to Nicolaus, a proselyte from Antioch mentioned in Acts 6:5. John of Patmos implies that their error involved idolatry, labeling this idolatry "fornication" (*porneia*). Irenaeus goes a step further, explicitly accusing them of teaching that *porneia* and the consumption of sacrificial meat "are matters of indifference" (Iren. *Adv. Haer.* 1.26.3).[47] In other words, Irenaeus actively embellishes tales of earlier "heretics" in order to provide the Valentinians with an appropriate family tree.[48]

Justin argued that the philosophical heresies were a "hydra of many heads"; their degraded condition was made evident by their diverse opinions and their many schools. Irenaeus applies a similar image to the Valentinians, asserting that their doctrines were generated "like a Lernaean hydra" out of the Valentinian school (Iren. *Adv. Haer.* 1.30.14). Irenaeus and Justin share the opinion that diversity implies error and unity implies truth; hence, the more numerous the heresies the more obvious their error. Irenaeus then produces an impression of diversity and multiplicity by comparing rival Valentinian origin myths—even the Valentinians cannot agree on their doctrines, Irenaeus argues—and by listing other heresies for comparison. The Valentinians were the principle target of the refutation, as Irenaeus explains in the preface to the first book: having read some of their commentaries, he resolved to demonstrate that their propositions were "absurd, inconsistent, and discordant with the truth" (*Adv. Haer.* Pr. 2). He begins the first book with a lengthy, decidedly prejudiced narration of their creation myth, designed to make their beliefs appear to be as ridiculous as possible (*Adv. Haer.* 1.1–7.5).[49] After mocking their beliefs, he sets out to challenge their exegesis of Scripture: "They disregard the order and the connection of the scriptures and, as much as in them lies, they disjoint the members of the truth" (*Adv. Haer.* 1.8.1). He then accuses them of contradictions and fragmentation, presenting alternative versions of their myths (*Adv. Haer.* 1.11.1–5).[50] Finally, he announces his intention to overthrow all the heresies by exposing their "root," Simon, and by demonstrating that all of the heretics are ultimately related to one another through him (*Adv. Haer.* 1.22.2). He then introduces Simon's spawn—that is, the heresies—one by one, developing a suitably repugnant genealogy for the Valentinians in the process.

By cataloging Christian heresies, highlighting their diversity, and comparing their opinions and practices, Irenaeus places the Valentinians within a genealogical line of Christian corruption that can be contrasted with the line of faithful and apostolic Christians. By beginning with Simon, Irenaeus places the origin of the heresies within the apostolic age, adopting the perspective that Christian heresies began only after Christ's ascension, a belief he shared with Justin (*1 Apol.* 26.1). By enumerating the diversity of Valentinian and other Christian myths, he diversifies their doctrines even as he unifies their origins and their basic characteristics. They were unified in their failure at consistency: the Valentinians "do not say the same things about the same subject, but contradict themselves in regard to things and names" (Iren. *Adv. Haer.* 1.11.1); each heresy had its own nonsensical spin on the "endless [divine] genealogies" these heretics love.[51] They were unified by the demonic source of their teachings: inspired by demons, they had Satan as their divine "father" and could not be counted either among the Jews or among the Christians.[52] They were unified by their disguised demon worship: though they pretended to be Christians, they remained demon-worshipping gentiles. Finally, they were united by their (alleged) promotion of *porneia*: even when they pursued *enkrateia* (self-mastery) they did so out of slavery to lust. Contradictory, demon-inspired, and enslaved to desire, the heretics remained "gentiles" even when they pretended to be "Jews."

IRENAEUS AGAINST THE JEWS, THE PSEUDO-JEWS, AND THE (GENTILE) HERETICS

According to Irenaeus, the Jews of his time read their scriptures "like a fable" since they did not accept the true meaning of what they had been told (*Adv. Haer.* 4.26.1). "Tradition" demonstrated there was one God, identical with the God of Israel, and this God had chosen the followers of Christ as his people.[53] The patriarchs and the prophets "prefigured our faith and sowed on earth the coming of the Son of God, announcing who and what he would be" (*Adv. Haer.* 4.23.1), yet the Jews misunderstood and, therefore, they will be judged (*Adv. Haer.* 4.33.1). With the Jews placed outside of salvation, Irenaeus can further disparage his opponents by accusing them of adopting pseudo-Jewish practices and procedures: they might be demon-inspired gentiles, but they foolishly acted like "Jews." The Valentinians, for example, pronounced phony Hebrew words during worship to impress their initiates (*Adv. Haer.* 1.21.3), and the Ebionites foolishly practiced circumcision, maintained Jewish legal customs, and prayed while facing toward Jerusalem (*Adv. Haer.* 1.26.2).[54] Marcion, though he identified the creator God as a demon, "circumcise[d] the scriptures" when he chose to adopt only the Gospel of Luke and portions of the writings of Paul (*Adv. Haer.* 1.27.2–4). In other words, Irenaeus accuses him of behaving like a Jew even as he rejects any continuity between Judaism and Christianity.[55] The heretics could attempt to "be Jewish," but they always failed, remaining gentile through and through.

Irenaeus repeatedly likens heretics to gentiles, depicting them as gentile in type if not in name.[56] He compares Valentinian, Marcosian, and other Christian narratives of divine origins to the tales of Homer and Hesiod, suggesting that the heretics drew their beliefs from the poets rather than from the apostles. The Valentinians, for example, devised "false fabrications" that were invented in imitation of those who misquote Homer for their own self-aggrandizement (*Adv. Haer.* 1.9.2–4). Moreover, their narratives included sexual unions between divine beings, an aspect of gentile myth that the apologists had previously derided;[57] these ideas could not have originated with Christ but only with demons (*Adv. Haer.* 2.14.1–5).[58] The Valentinians also displayed their inner gentile by deriving doctrines from Cynic contrariness, Pythagorean numerology, and Aristotelian argument, developing "subtle investigations" in their efforts to attack the true faith (*Adv. Haer.* 2.14.5–6). Not only were their origin myths gentile in type, their practices were equally idolatrous. The Valentinians were "the first to meet during the festivals of the gentiles," eager to honor idols and attend "the murderous spectacles"(*Adv. Haer.* 1.6.3). Valentinians, Simonians, Carpocratians, and Nicolaitans went so far as to venerate idols in the name of Christ (*Adv. Haer.* 1.15.4, 1.23.4, 1.25.6, 1.26.3). Some Christian schools recommended ritual orgies (*Adv. Haer.* 1.6.3, 1.13.2–7, 1.23.2, 1.25.4–5, 1.31.2), others declared that marriage was from Satan (*Adv. Haer.* 1.24.2, 1.28.1), but all were "slaves of lust" (*Adv. Haer.* 5.8.4). In other words, these people remained gentiles even as they posed as Christians or adopted the errors of the Jews.

SEX AND CHRISTIAN ORIGINS

Placing their rivals, real or imaginary, within diverse "schools" with multiple founders and one inspiration (Satan), Justin and Irenaeus developed a classificatory scheme that produced Christianity as a distinct, legitimate, and restricted *genos*. These legitimate Christians were not Jews; therefore Israel's misdeeds did not apply (Justin) and heretics could be condemned for behaving "like Jews" (Irenaeus). Biblical language regarding "seed," discussed in chapter 2, had been transformed; whereas previously this language was designed to protect and enforce a certain Judean identity, now it was employed to remove Israel from the *genos* of God altogether. Israel was now described as the unproductive "seed of Abraham"; the Christians had become the spiritually productive "seed," "race," and "household."[59] Having been expelled from the family tree, Jews were condemned en masse for idolatry, polygamy, *porneia*, and uncontrolled lust. Even so, Justin and Irenaeus presupposed and preserved their own versions of a rhetoric they shared with "the Jews," including Paul: they lumped gentiles into one indistinguishable group of impious sexual sinners. They also repeated and revised the earlier, biblical strategy of describing target insiders as fornicators, apostates, and idolaters; that is, as gentiles. Their principal charge against the heretics—they were inspired and fathered by demons—identified them as unrepentant gentiles, all the more reprehensible because they called themselves Christian.

By labeling heresies, presenting them for examination, and describing their attributes, Justin and Irenaeus constitute the Christians as not-heretics, not-Jews, and not-gentiles, policing insiders even as they work to eliminate specific rivals.[60] To achieve the status of Christian, as Justin and Irenaeus describe it, one had to accept the authority of certain male leaders, including themselves,[61] recognize the legitimacy of certain books and certain interpretations,[62] adopt particular ideas about god, humanity and the world,[63] and display "good morals," especially *sōphrosynē* (self-control) and *eusebeia* (piety). Otherwise, one failed at "being Christian" and remained a "gentile" or a "Jew." By classifying the beliefs and practices of outsiders as illegitimate, Justin and Irenaeus delimited the legitimate beliefs and practices of insiders, drawing boundaries with a customary "language of disqualification" involving charges of impiety, illegitimacy, and sexual misbehavior.[64] Yet in this case "Jews" were disqualified as well, a departure from earlier forms of Christian argumentation.

In chapter 2, I noted that gentiles were regularly accused of sexual perversion by biblical authors; in-group targets were said to be "like the gentiles," that is, idolatrous and sexually wicked. "Bad" Israelites were the exception that proved the rule: good Israelites simply did not engage in such behavior. By and large, Paul and the authors of Jude and 2 Peter adopted this assumption as their own, presumably because they viewed themselves as within the category "Judean." For example, Paul warned his gentile-in-Christ audience to refrain from *porneia,* thereby avoiding the lust that regularly and characteristically troubled gentiles (1 Thess 4:3–7). By contrast, he never accused Judeans of *porneia,* even when he lamented the failure of some the members of his *genos* to conclude that Jesus was the Christ.[65] Like biblical authors before him, the author of Jude also described the behavior of Israel in the wilderness as an exception, warning his audience not to become like them or face similar punishment (Jude 5, 17–19); the author of 2 Peter adopted a similar perspective, exhorting his readers to be wary of the false prophets of their own time just as the righteous in Israel had refused to listen to the unrighteous during their time, implicitly comparing the righteous followers of Christ to righteous Israel (2 Pet 2:1, 3, 7–10). Among these writers, Israel was presumed to be a holy people with a few bad apples rather than rotten to the core. Justin adopted a different perspective: the "bad" Israelites were not the exception, they were the rule. Indeed, God had given Israel the law to control their innately wicked disposition, yet even then they committed idolatry, fell prey to their lusts, and practiced child sacrifice (Justin *Dial.* 16.2–22.11, 92.1–93.4, 131.2–134.1). Justin identifies the Jews as an "other" that can be summarily—and stereotypically—attacked. Irenaeus then built on this argument, likening the heretics to pseudo-Jews and warning that the Jews will be punished (Iren. *Adv. Haer.* 5.33.1). To these authors, Christians were no longer "Jews"; they were a new, privileged *genos* of God.[66]

Of course, Justin and Irenaeus were not alone in their effort to assert purity, status, or privilege by enumerating the elite lineage of their group. As observed in the first chapter, status was often defended and justified by referencing virtue; free men were said to be more reasonable, more self-disciplined, and more courageous than their enslaved counterparts. Status distinctions were further validated in terms of kinship and patrimony.[67] The emperors advertised their descent from the gods and other famous ancestors, including the illustrious, deified emperors.[68] Ancient genealogies linked fathers to sons and families to peoplehood by means of tropes about "seed," adoption, shared customs, beliefs, or geographic origin.[69] As observed in the second chapter, Judean authors also validated their community by references to God's "holy seed," a strategy that sought to establish Israel's (genetic) sexual and religious superiority.[70] Thus, when Justin and Irenaeus claimed to be representatives of the "true *genos* of Israel," descended from the apostles, recipients of the implanted Logos, keepers of the ancient traditions, members of one harmonious household, and heirs to God's eternal kingdom, they were constructing a system of noble descent that competed for privilege in recognizable ways. They mapped Christian unity onto a dynastic scheme whereby truth was guarded by a chain of legitimate male heirs from God to Logos to prophet to apostle to Christian.

In this way, the effort to police insiders remained an outsider-focused strategy as well. According to Justin and Irenaeus, the Christians were a righteous *genos* and an honorable family, the sons and heirs of God.[71] Their righteousness could be, and was, compared with the depravity of their rulers. In the third chapter I considered Justin's repeated insistence that the emperor and his heirs were ruled by demons and lust. Likewise, Irenaeus warned that rulers "will perish for everything they do to harm the just, iniquitously and illegally and in tyrannical fashion" (*Av. Haer.* 5.24.2). Irenaeus leaves open the possibility that they could turn to his God, control their lust, and properly discipline unruly humanity with their law and their sword (*Adv. Haer.* 5.24.2), yet he is equally confident that the Christians would rule in the end, a theory he supported by citing Daniel and Revelation in particular (*Adv. Haer.* 5.26.1–36.3). Justin's and Irenaeus' Christians, then, were not simply one *genos* among many; they were the best *genos* of all. They were not simply one school of thought among many possible options; they were the only "heresy" that taught the truth. Sexualized invective served as a resistance strategy as well as a policing tactic.

SEXUAL SLANDER AND CHRISTIAN IDENTITY

From biblical tradition, to Greek invective, to early Christian polemics, "the opponents"—be they gentiles or slaves or barbarians or heretics—were universally said to devote themselves to sexual excess. Though there may have been licentious gentiles, slaves, rulers, philosophers, barbarians, heretics, or Christians, the sources I have been exploring will not help us find them. Instead, these sources indicate a widespread attempt to employ moralizing claims regarding sexual behavior and gender deviance to validate authority. Still, there is a sense in which all this sex talk was actually about sex: by strategically claiming superiority on the basis of a strict sexual morality, early Christians were under tremendous pressure to display the *sōphrosynē* they had defined for themselves.[72] Therefore, all of this highly charged sex talk was necessary. Christians had to be convinced to live up to *sōphrosynē*, displaying it for all to see. Moreover, the content of in-Christ self-discipline required frequent renegotiation and reiteration in light of the changing circumstances of the first Christians. Charges against the heretics provide further clues regarding the contested nature of Christian *sōphrosynē* as well as the imagined constitution of the group.

Justin does not charge his heretics with an overactive commitment to *enkrateia* (self-mastery) in his extant writings; instead, he describes them as universally prone to lust. Yet, a few years later, Irenaeus condemned Tatian and other "heretics" for preaching abstinence from marriage thereby "[making] void God's pristine creation" and indirectly reproving God himself "who made male and female for generating the human race" (Iren. *Adv. Haer.* 1.28.1). Irenaeus gives a name to their "school"; they were the "Encratites." Could it be that the overly ascetic heretic was invented, in part, to define what "good sexual asceticism" might look like? In her analysis of some of the antiheretical writings, Elizabeth Clark notes that the church fathers were forced to defend themselves against accusations that they promoted a hatred of marriage and the body.[73] Their views on ascetic discipline, especially on sexual renunciation, were read by their enemies as a disparagement of the Creator and creation. The fathers responded to this criticism by deflecting it onto their rivals.[74] Clement of Alexandria refers to the problem: "There are some who say outright that marriage is fornication and teach that it was introduced by the devil. They proudly say that they are imitating the Lord who neither married nor had any possession in this world, boasting that they understand the gospel better than anyone else" (*Strom.* 3.6.49; compare 3.12.81).[75] Because of Christians like this, Clement laments, the Christian name was blasphemed. Yet Irenaeus, Clement, and the other fathers also recommended sexual renunciation to the faithful. As noted in chapter 4, Clement of Alexandria taught that Christians ought to overcome desire altogether, though it is *porneia*, not marriage, that is a sin (*Strom.* 3.11.90). Irenaeus, like Hermas, asserts that God punishes sins of thought as well as deed; God was offended not only by adultery but by the thought of adultery (Iren. *Adv. Haer.* 2.32.1; 4.15.5; 4.28.2). Jerome offers another, particularly striking example. He argues, on the one hand, that all sexual intercourse was unclean but, on the other, that only heretics would deny the goodness of marriage.[76] The dividing line between the "heretical" renunciative practices of, for example, Tatian and Saturninus, and those recommended by Irenaeus, Clement of Alexandria, or Jerome may have been rather more blurred than their writings initially suggest.[77]

Clark argues that charges of excessive ascetic rigor against the heretics can be read as a diversionary tactic, designed to privilege one Christian group at the expense of another. I have made a similar suggestion regarding Justin's attempt to associate promiscuous intercourse and the eating of human flesh with the followers of Simon, Menander, and Marcion. But such accusations were not only diversionary tactics since, as Clark rightly notes, the church fathers were intensely interested in developing a program of sexual renunciation that would meet the standards of orthodoxy as they defined it.[78] Christians of all sorts sought to promote sexual renunciation.[79] Irenaeus' contention that false Christians can only be of two types—radical ascetics or libertine sensualists—can be read as part of this intense discussion about the importance of sexual renunciation. Charges of sexual license against the heretics reflected an attempt on the part of early Christian authors to develop a sexualized disciplinary discourse that could be effective at eliminating their opponents, protect them from their non-Christian critics, and enhance their own status as the authentic bearers of Christian tradition. The alleged sexual practices of the heretics, then, point to the internal debates of Justin's and Irenaeus' respective communities, debates that were partially framed in response to pressures from without.

The impact of outsider critique on insider-directed heresiology can be observed in other areas as well. As observed in the chapter 3, by the second century Christians were being accused of ritual orgies, incest, and cannibalism, the very same charges that Justin and Irenaeus lodged against heretics, Jews, and gentiles. There are still further parallels: Irenaeus accused the heretics of playing at being Jews; Celsus asserted that the Christians tie their antiquity to the Jews and foolishly adopt Jewish customs although they are not Jews at all (Origen, *Contra Celsum*, 1.16, 5.41). Irenaeus suggested that the heretics developed numerous nonsensical and contradictory doctrines; Celsus argued that the Christians disagreed about everything and repeated a ridiculous myth involving an earth creature and a woman formed from his side (Origen, *Contra Celsum*, 3.1–10, 4.36, 4.63). If Celsus was repeating standard arguments against the Christians, as some scholars have argued, these parallels may not be coincidental.[80] In other words, the sorts of charges lodged against heretical insiders shifted in concert with the sorts of charges Christians as a group were facing, reflecting the unstable terrain of insider-outsider controversies and group definition.

Disagreements over the content of Christian *sōphrosynē* provide further evidence of this phenomenon. As observed in the chapter 2, Paul presupposed that women were "naturally" more prone to desire than men and therefore they "naturally" required surveillance by men; he was anxious to ensure that the brothers and sisters in Christ remained "real men" and "real women." Still, he presupposed that women would prophesy during church meetings and contribute to the churches as patrons, deacons, and even apostles.[81] Within a generation, however, women's (limited) authority was reinterpreted as improper and shameful by many Christian authors,[82] a position that was reinforced by Irenaeus' critique of the heresies. Irenaeus depicted women's leadership as an indication of heretical sexual deviance, implying that such behavior could not be imagined among apostolic Christians.[83] His patrilineal theory of apostolic succession also eliminated women from the divine genealogy, with the exception of Mary whose purpose was to undo the sin of Eve (Iren. *Adv. Haer.* 3.22.4–23.5). Irenaeus' exclusively patrilineal notion of descent together with his accusations against the heretics may have been designed to silence women within his Christian community as well as to deflect charges—lodged against Christians in general—that they attracted "silly women."[84] Arguments regarding the strict control of good Christian women could serve an additional purpose: Christian male authors advertised their own "manly" self-control by broadcasting the firm hold they maintained over "their" women, a particularly pressing need given the feminization of Christians by critical outsiders.

Claims about Christian manliness and self-discipline and about heretical, gentile, and Jewish slavishness and decadence involved cultural production and the performance of power relationships. As such, the implied content of sexual immorality was subject to constant reinterpretation and renegotiation by those who attempted to define and constitute them for the sake of their own persuasive projects. When the early Christian authors I have been discussing suggest that sexual licentiousness is a sign of God's rejection—non-Christian gentiles are abandoned by God to lust, false Christians are motivated by their lusts, Jews were slaves to lust all along—they are not describing what immorality *is*, they were creating a definition of immorality that suited their interests. Accusations regarding immorality characterize and constitute "the other" by describing what "they" are and what "we" are not, just as "slavishness" was supposed to be a characteristic of slaves, not of free citizens. By accusing enemies of sexual immorality, Christians such as Justin and Irenaeus not only challenged the claims and pretensions of those they opposed—insiders or outsiders—they defined their own movement in sexual terms. Nevertheless, the very terms of the argument remained (and remain) inherently unstable.

NOTES

INTRODUCTION. WHO'S ON TOP?
SEX TALK, POWER, AND RESISTANCE

1. Peter Baker, *The Breach: Inside the Impeachment and Trial of William Jefferson Clinton* (New York: Berkley, 2000), 18. Though scandal mongering regarding "presidential peccadilloes" was on the wane prior to the Clinton impeachment trial, the assumption that respectable sexual behavior ought be a characteristic of the president and other political leaders continued, the same assumption that fueled accusations about illegitimate children, adulterous liaisons, and seductions of vulnerable young women against such earlier figures as Thomas Jefferson, Andrew Jackson, Grover Cleveland, and William Henry Harrison. See John H. Summers, "What Happened to Sex Scandals? Politics and Peccadilloes, Jefferson to Kennedy," *The Journal of American History* 87, no. 3 (December 2000): 825–54.

2. Seth Mydans, "Top Opposition Leader in Malaysia Is Jailed in Sex Case," *New York Times*, 21 September 1998; Mydans, "Malaysian Police Break Up Protests on Arrest," *New York Times*, 22 September 1998; Mydans, "Using a Sexual Slur, Malaysian Calls Ex-Deputy Unacceptable," *New York Times*, 23 September 1998. For further discussion on the case, from the perspective of those who support Anwar Ibrahim, the former deputy prime minister, who remains imprisoned today, see the articles and links at www.freeanwar.com. Human Rights Watch issued a press release regarding the case in August 2000. See www.hrw.org/press/200/08/anwar0808.htm.

3. See Bruce Lincoln, *Discourse and the Construction of Society: Comparative Studies of Myth, Ritual, and Classification* (Oxford: Oxford University Press, 1989), 71–79.

4. Father Pierre Baird, S.J. (1611), in *New American World*, ed. D. B. Quinn (New York: Arno Press and Hector Bye, 1979), 4:392.

5. Juan Ginés de Sepúlveda, *Democrates secundus*, in *Demócrates segundo. Apolgía en favor del libro sobre las justas causas de la guerra*, ed. Jamie Brafau Prats with Spanish translation by A. Coroleu Lletget (Pozoblanco, Spain: Excmo. Ayuntamiento de Pozoblanco, 1997). For a helpful discussion of Spanish imperialism and the use of pietistic and moralizing discourse to support this imperialism, see Anthony Pagden, *Lords of All the World: Ideologies of Empire in Spain, Britain, and France, c. 1500–1800* (New Haven, Conn.: Yale University Press, 1995), esp. chapter 2; on Sepúlveda, see 99–102.

6. Peter Brown, *Authority and the Sacred: Aspects of the Christianisation of the Roman World* (Cambridge: Cambridge University Press, 1995), 11. Brown is interested here in the "Christianisation" of the empire of the fourth century, where the governing elite "presented themselves to themselves" by means of "symbolic forms" that "owed little or nothing to Christianity." See also Virginia Burrus, " 'In the Theater of this Life': The Performance of Orthodoxy in Ancient Christianity," in *Essays on Late Antique Thought and Culture in Honor of R. A. Markus*, ed. William E. Klingshirn and Mark Vessey (Ann Arbor: University of Michigan Press, 1999), 80–96.

Burrus notes that late ancient Christian orthodoxy also sought to represent itself to itself as legitimate, often by referencing the absolute unanimity that all orthodox Christians allegedly (and impossibly) shared.

7. See John H. Kautsky, *The Politics of Aristocratic Empires* (Chapel Hill: University of North Carolina Press, 1982), 169–210; and Bruce Lincoln, *Authority: Construction and Corrosion* (Chicago: University of Chicago Press), esp. chapter 1.

8. Vine Deloria Jr., *Custer Died for Your Sins: An Indian Manifesto* (New York: Macmillan, 1969), 153–54. For an interesting comparative example, see Ana María Alonso, "Gender, Power, and Historical Memory: Discourses of *Serrano* Resistance," in *Feminists Theorize the Political,* ed. Judith Butler and Joan W. Scott (New York: Routledge, 1992), 404–25.

9. On the dynamics of parody, joke telling, trickster tales, and other "hidden transcripts" designed to undermine the "public transcript" of a dominant group, see James C. Scott, *Domination and the Arts of Resistance: Hidden Transcripts* (New Haven, Conn.: Yale University Press, 1990); Lincoln, *Authority,* 74–89; Robert M. Adams, *Bad Mouth: Fugitive Papers on the Dark Side* (Berkeley: University of California Press, 1977); F. G. Bailey, *Gifts and Poison* (New York: Schocken, 1971). Adams comments, "Men have been killed with leather swords, and insult and invective, even after we've surrounded them with all the cotton wool at our disposal, are still felt to provide the potential for dangerous fun" (42).

10. I use the word "slander" to indicate that the accusations made were intended to malign and defame. I do not mean to suggest that such charges have no basis in fact—I leave that question to others. Rather, I am exploring the content and implications of these charges, the "slander."

11. Famously argued by Oswald Spengler, *The Decline of the West,* trans. Charles Francis Atkinson, 2 vols. (New York: Knopf, 1976; originally published in 1922–23 as *Der Untergang des Abendlandes*).

12. On Caligula's sexual exploits, see Suet. *Calig.* 36–41; Cass. Dio 59.28, taken as clear-cut evidence of Caligula's "private pursuits" by Anthony A. Barrett, *Caligula: The Corruption of Power* (New Haven, Conn.: Yale University Press, 1989), esp. 42–49. Arther Ferrill mocks those historians who seek to "whitewash" Caligula, agreeing with the ancient historians before him that Caligula probably did engage in incest; see his *Caligula: Emperor of Rome* (London: Thames and Hudson, 1991). For a fictionalized yet influential rendering of Caligula, the monstrous and insane pervert, see Robert Graves, *I, Claudius* (New York: R. Smith and R. Haas, 1934).

13. Stephen Benko, *Pagan Rome and the Early Christians* (Bloomington: Indiana University Press, 1986), 71–73; Hans Jonas, *Gnosis und spätaniker Geist,* vol. 1 (Göttingen: Vandenhoeck und Ruprect, 1934), 170; Stephen Gero, "With Walter Bauer on the Tigris: Encratite Orthodoxy and Libertine Heresy in Syro-Mesopotamian Christianity," in *Nag Hammadi, Gnosticism, and Early Christianity,* ed. Charles W. Hedrick and Robert Hodgson Jr. (Peabody, Mass.: Hendrickson, 1986), 287–307. Though skeptical of the evidence, Kurt Rudolph suggested that behind the polemic there probably were some set of innovative sexual rites and an ethic of spiritual and psychic freedom, *Gnosis: The Nature and History of an Ancient Religion,* trans. Robert McL. Wilson (Edinburgh: T. & T. Clark, 1983), 248–57. Peter Brown speculated that heretical Christians probably did experiment with "free love"; see *Body and Society: Men, Women, and Sexual Renunciation in Early Christianity* (New York: Columbia University Press, 1988), 61, 61 n. 133: "It is not altogether surprising that, at just this time, we hear shocked rumors that esoteric Christian groups had turned to free love. Their enemies claimed that these explored, through promiscuity, the nature of 'true communion.' ... One cannot rule out the existence of such groups within second-century Christianity: they were not merely figments of a polemist's imagination."

14. For a different interpretation of the representation of Caligula by Suetonius, see Donna W. Hurley, *A Historical and Historiographical Commentary on Suetonius' Life of Caligula* (Atlanta: Scholars Press, 1993). On the Simonians, see Iren. *Adv. Haer.* 1.22.2–23.4 and Epiph. *Pan.* 21.2–7. The suggestion that the Simonians collect seminal emissions and menstrual blood is found in Epiph. *Pan.* 21.4.1–2 Epiphanius' representation of the Simonians is generally understood to be

unreliable. See Aline Pourkier, *L'Hérésiologie chez Épiphane de Salamine*, Christinisme Antique 4 (Paris: Beauchesne, 1992), 164–65. Still, many scholars do accept the view that the Simonians included some sort of sexual experimentation among their worship practices. See, for example, Riemer Roukema, *Gnosis and Faith in Early Christianity: An Introduction to Gnosticism*, trans. John Bowden (Harrisburg: Trinity Press International, 1999), 22; and Karlmann Beyschlag, *Simon Magus und die christliche Gnosis*, Wissenschaftliche Untersuchungen zum Neuen Testament 16 (Tübingen: Mohr [Siebeck], 1975), 193–201.

15. See Judith Butler, *Gender Trouble: Feminism and the Subversion of Identity* (New York: Routledge, 1990); and "Contingent Foundations: Feminism and the Question of 'Postmodernism,'" in *Feminists Theorize the Political*, ed. Judith Butler and Joan Wallach Scott (New York: Routledge, 1992), 15–16; Joan Wallach Scott, *Gender and the Politics of History* (New York: Columbia University Press, 1988), 49; Philippe Ariès and André Béjin, *Western Sexuality: Practice and Precept in Past and Present Times*, trans. Anthony Forster (Oxford: Basil Blackwell, 1985); Nancy C.M. Hartsock, *Money, Sex, and Power* (Boston: Northeastern University Press, 1983), 156; Michel Foucault, *The History of Sexuality*, vol. 1, *An Introduction*, trans. Robert Hurley (New York: Random House, 1978); Simone de Beauvoir, *The Second Sex*, ed. and trans. H.M. Parshley (New York: Vintage Books, 1952). The implications of this approach for the study of ancient history has been a topic of considerable debate. See especially David M. Halperin, *One Hundred Years of Homosexuality and Other Essays on Greek Love* (New York: Routledge, 1990); and *How to Do the History of Homosexuality* (Chicago: University of Chicago Press, 2002); Eve Cantarella, *Bisexuality in the Ancient World*, trans. Cormac Ó Cuilleanain (New Haven, Conn.: Yale University Press, 1992); John J. Winkler, *Constraints of Desire* (New York: Routledge, 1990); and "Laying Down the Law: The Oversight of Men's Sexual Behavior in Classical Athens," in *Before Sexuality: The Construction of Erotic Experience in the Ancient Greek World*, ed. David M. Halperin, John J. Winkler, and Froma I. Zeitlin (Princeton, N.J.: Princeton University Press, 1990), 171–209; Michel Foucault, *The History of Sexuality*, vols. 2 and 3, *The Use of Pleasure* and *The Care of the Self*, trans. Robert Hurley (New York: Vintage Books, 1985); Eva Keuls, *The Reign of the Phallus: Sexual Politics in Ancient Athens* (Berkeley: University of California Press, 1985). But also see Bruce Thornton, *Eros: The Myth of Ancient Greek Sexuality* (Boulder, Colo.: Westview Press, 1997); and the responses to Foucault found in David H.J. Larmour, Paul Allen Miller, and Charles Platter, eds., *Rethinking Sexuality: Foucault and Classical Antiquity* (Princeton, N.J.: Princeton University Press, 1998); and by David Cohen and Richard Saller, "Foucault on Sexuality in Greco-Roman Antiquity," in *Foucault and the Writing of History*, ed. Jan Goldstein (Oxford: Blackwell, 1994), 35–59. Ruth Mazo Karras offers an excellent overview of the topic and the issues involved; see her "Active/Passive, Acts/Passions: Greek and Roman Sexualities," *The American Historical Review* 105, no. 4 (2000): 1–42.

16. My thinking here has been informed by the work of philosophers, historians, and feminists who regard discourse as constitutive of social worlds and even of "the self," especially Michel Foucault. There is, I would argue, a reciprocal and generative relationship between power, knowledge, and discourse. As a discursive practice, Christian sexual slander is implicated in social formation, power relations, and constructions of communal and personal identity. In other words, discourses "constitute the truths they claim to discover and transmit," including truths about the virtue or vice of Christians, pagans, heretics, Jews, Greeks, Romans, and so on. See Michel Foucault, *Discipline and Punish*, trans. Alan Sheridan (New York: Vintage Books, 1979); "The Subject and Power," in *Michel Foucault: Beyond Structuralism and Hermeneutics*, ed. Herbert Dreyfus and Paul Rabinow (Chicago: University of Chicago Press, 1982); *The Essential Words of Michel Foucault*, ed. Paul Rabinow, vol. 1, *Ethics, Subjectivity, and Truth* (New York: The New Press, 1994); Irene Diamond and Lee Quinby, eds., *Feminism and Foucault: Reflections on Resistance* (Boston: Northeastern University Press, 1988); and Susan J. Hekman, *Feminist Interpretations of Michel Foucault* (University Park: Pennsylvania University Press, 1996); Jana Sawicki, *Disciplining Foucault: Feminism, Power, and the Body* (New York: Routledge, 1991). Quotation from Paul A. Bové, *Mastering Discourse: The Politics of Intellectual Culture* (Durham, N.C.: Duke University Press, 1992), 8.

17. Athenagoras *Leg* 3; Minucius Felix *Oct*.x 9.2; Theophilus *Ad Auto*. 3.4–5; Tertullian *Ad. nat.* 1.15. For an overview of accusations of Christian *flagitia*, see Albert Henrichs, "Pagan Ritual and the Alleged Crimes of the Early Christians: A Reconsideration," in *Kyriakon: Festschrift Johannes Quasten*, vol. 1, ed. Patrick Granfield and Josef A. Jangmann (Münster: Verlag Aschendorff, 1970), 18–35. Henrichs argues that such practices did occur among some groups, but not among the Christians. The Christians had the misfortune to be identified with these practices through a process of guilt by association. For a discussion of the association between Christians and hysterical women in particular, see the excellent treatment by Margaret Y. MacDonald in her *Early Christian Women and Pagan Opinion: The Power of the Hysterical Woman* (Cambridge: Cambridge University Press, 1996).

18. Minucius Felix *Oct.* 9.6–7. For a helpful introduction to Latin Christian apologetics, see Simon Price, "Latin Christian Apologetics: Minucius Felix, Tertullian, and Cyprian," in *Apologetics in the Roman Empire: Pagans, Jews, and Christians*, ed. Mark Edwards, Martin Goodman, and Simon Price (New York: Oxford University Press, 1999), 105–29.

19. Joseph *Ap.* 2.89–102; Tac. *Hist.* 5.4–5: "They sit apart at meals, and they sleep apart, and although as a race, they are prone to lust, they abstain from intercourse with foreign women; yet among themselves nothing is unlawful." On the charge that Jews worship the head of an ass, see esp. Louis H. Feldman and John R. Levison, eds. "An Ass in the Jerusalem Temple: The Origins and Development of the Slander," in *Josephus' Contra Apionem: Studies in its Character and Context with a Latin Concordance to the Portion Missing in Greek*, ed. Louis H. Feldman and John R. Levison, Arbeiten zur Geschichte des antiken Judentums und des Urchristentums 34 (Leiden: E. J. Brill, 1996), 310–26. For a discussion of the polemics against the Jews, see Louis H. Feldman, *Jew and Gentile in the Ancient World* (Princeton, N.J.: Princeton University Press, 1993), esp. 123–76.

20. Wis 14:12; *T. Levi* 14.1–8; Joseph *Ap.* 2.197, 273–5; *Sib. Or.* 3.590–600; Philo *Virt.* 34.182. For discussion, see Maurice Gilbert, *La Critique des dieux dans le Livre de la Sagesse*, Analecta Biblica 53 (Rome: Biblical Institute Press, 1973); Aryeh Kasher, "Polemic and Apologetic Methods of Writing in *Contra Apionem*," in *Josephus' Contra Apionem: Studies in its Character and Context with a Latin Concordance to the Portion Missing in Greek*, ed. Louis H. Feldman and John R. Levison, Arbeiten zur Geschichte des antiken Judentums und des Urchristentums 34 (Leiden: E. J. Brill, 1996), 147–50; Erich S. Gruen, "Jews, Greeks, and Romans in the Third Sibylline Oracle," in *Jews in a Graeco-Roman World*, ed. Martin Goodman (Oxford: Clarendon Press, 1998), 15–36; Martin Goodman, "Josephus' Treatise *Against Apion*," in *Apologetics in the Roman Empire: Pagans, Jews, and Christians*, ed. Mark Edwards, Martin Goodman, and Simon Price (New York: Oxford University Press, 1999), 45–58.

21. The view that Persians were slavish due to their extreme wealth and the tyrannical form of government they preferred is at least as old as the Persian wars. Aeschylus argued that the Greeks are free but the Persians are slaves (1.242); Herodotus records the Spartans telling the Persians that they know how to be slaves and have never tasted freedom (7.135); Euripides has Helen state that all barbarians (i.e., Persians) are slaves, with the exception of their king (1.276). See discussion in Yvon Garlan, *Slavery in Ancient Greece*, trans. Janet Lloyd (Ithaca, N.Y.: Cornell University Press, 1988), 120.

22. For example, Sall. *Cat.* 11.5. See discussion of this charge in Craig A. Williams, *Roman Homosexuality: Ideologies of Masculinity in Classical Antiquity* (Oxford: Oxford University Press, 1999), 40–42; Paul Zanker, *The Power of Images in the Age of Augustus*, trans. Alan Shapiro (Ann Arbor: University of Michigan Press, 1988), 52; Catharine Edwards, *The Politics of Immorality in Ancient Rome* (Cambridge: Cambridge University Press, 1993), 93; Ronald Syme, *The Roman Revolution* (Oxford: Oxford University Press, 1939), 270–77.

23. Justin *1 Apol.* 5.9,18; *2 Apol.* 12; Tatian *Or.* 22, 33; Theophilus *Ad Auto.* 1.2, 9–10; 3.3, 5, 6, 8; Athenagoras *Leg.* 20.3–21.4; 32.1; Tertullian *Apol.* 9.16–16; 13.9; 15.1–3, 7; 35.2–5; Minucius Felix *Oct.* 28–31.

24. As we shall see, in Christian usage, "heresy" became a label with pejorative content meaning something like "whatever diverges from the 'true' doctrine." By using such terms I do

not mean to imply—with the Christian authors who employed these labels—that the group or doctrine under consideration was not in fact "Christian." For further discussion, see Marcel Simon, "From Greek Hairesis to Christian Heresy," in *Early Christian Literature and the Classical Intellectual Tradition: In Honorem Robert M. Grant*, ed. William R. Schoedel and Robert L. Wilken, Théologie Historique 53 (Paris: Éditions Beuchesne, 1979), 101–16.

25. Iren. *Adv. Haer.* 1.25.3. Unger's translation, 88.

26. All too often, conclusions about the sexual practices of the ancients have been drawn from these sources without adequate consideration of the rhetorical function of slander. For example, charges of depravity lodged by Christians against gentiles have led to the conclusion that the Christians were especially pure and their neighbors especially promiscuous, yet many "pagan" authors consistently argued that it was they who were distinctively virtuous. So, for example, New Testament scholars sometimes mention the (allegedly) depraved morals of non- or pre-Christian Corinthians, arguing that Paul had no choice but to spend so much of his first letter to that city dealing with problems of sexual immorality, especially since these practices continued to be promoted by Paul's Christian opponents. For recent examples of this view, see Amos Jones Jr., *Paul's Message of Freedom: What Does It Mean to the Black Church?* (Valley Forge: Judson Press, 1992), 29–30; and Allen Verhey, *Remembering Jesus: Christian Community, Scripture, and the Moral Life* (Grand Rapids, Mich.: William B. Eerdmans, 2002), 220–28. In an analogous argument regarding the epistle of Jude, Richard Bauckham observed that "pagan morality" often involved the promotion of hedonism and, hence, the author of Jude properly identified idolatry with sexual immorality; see his *Jude, 2 Peter*, Word Biblical Commentaries 50 (Waco, Tex.: Word Books, 1983), 155. See also Benjamin Fiore, "Passion in Paul and Plutarch: 1 Corinthians 5–6 and the Polemic Against Epicureans," in *Greeks, Romans, and Christians*, ed. E. Ferguson, D. L. Balch, and W. A. Meeks (Minneapolis: Fortress Press, 1990), 124. On pagan claims about their own virtue, see James A. Francis, *Subversive Virtue: Asceticism and Authority in the Second-Century Pagan World* (University Park: Pennsylvania State University Press, 1995); Averil Cameron, "Redrawing the Map: Early Christian Territory After Foucault," *JRS* 76 (1986): 266–71; Judith Evans Grubbs, "Constantine and Imperial Legislation on the Family," in *The Theodosian Code*, ed. Jill Harries and Ian Wood (Ithaca, N.Y.: Cornell University Press, 1993), 120–42. All of these studies note the continuity between pagan claims about their own virtue and the claims of Christian authors about the unique moral excellence of the followers of Christ. Another common argument presupposes that, while "true," "orthodox" Christians were sexually self-controlled, the "heretics" probably were guilty of antinomian sexual ethics, or worse. In recent years, several influential monographs have called this particular argument into question, noting that the evidence for "bad" behavior on the part of the "heretics" or "gnostics" is highly suspect. See esp. Karen King, *What Is Gnosticism?* (Cambridge, Mass.: Harvard University Press, 2003); Michael Allen Williams, *Rethinking "Gnosticism": An Argument for Dismantling a Dubious Category* (Oxford: Oxford University Press, 1996); Anne McGuire, "Women, Gender, and Gnosis in Gnostic Texts and Traditions," in *Women and Christian Origins*, ed. Ross Shepard Kraemer and Mary Rose D'Angelo (Oxford: Oxford University Press, 1999), 257–60; Frederick Wisse, "The Epistle of Jude in the History of Heresiology," in *Essays on the Nag Hammadi Texts in Honour of Alexander Böhlig*, ed Martin Krause, Nag Hammadi Studies 3 (Leiden: E. J. Brill, 1972), 133–43. See also the helpful and succinct comments of Bart D. Ehrman, *The Orthodox Corruption of Scripture: The Effect of Early Christological Controversies on the Text of the New Testament* (New York: Oxford University Press, 1993), 15–17. I am sympathetic with these studies. Nevertheless, I have bracketed questions of what Christians, pagans, heretics and others were doing in favor of a close examination of what Christians were saying about their rivals, about outsiders, and about themselves.

27. Dem. *De cor.* 129, 260. Similarly, Aeschines attacked the target of one of his forensic speeches by claiming that he had prostituted himself in his youth and squandered his inheritance: Aeschin. *In Tim.*

28. Cic. *Cat.* 1.13–16. R. M. Nisbet offers a thorough survey of the sorts of charges commonly employed by Cicero in "The *in Pisonem* as an invective," appendix 6 to *Cicero: In L. Campur-*

nium Pisonem (Oxford: Clarendon Press, 1961), 192–97. Cicero specifically commended the rhetorical methods of his Athenian predecessors in *De or.* 22.94, 23.94–95. Plutarch compared Cicero to Demosthenes in his *Parallel Lives*, noting that they share much in common. See Plut. *Dem.* 2.3–4, and Plutarch, *Comparatio Ciceronis cum Demosthene.*

29. See Jacqueline Flint Long, *Claudian's In Eutropium: Or, How, When, and Why to Slander a Eunuch* (Chapel Hill: University of North Carolina Press, 1996), 65–146; Severin Koster, *Die Invektive in der griechischen und römischen Literatur*, Beiträge zur Klassichen Philologie 99 (Meisenheim am Glan: Verlag Anton Hain, 1980); James Rives, "Human Sacrifice Among Pagans and Christians," *JRS* 85 (1995): 65–85.

30. Luke Timothy Johnson, "The New Testament's Anti-Jewish Slander and the Conventions of Ancient Polemic," *JBL* 108 (1989): 433, emphasis in the original.

31. Andrew McGowan, "Eating People: Accusations of Cannibalism Against Christians in the Second Century," *JECS* 2 (1994): 413–42; and Rives, "Human Sacrifice," 65–85. See also Henrichs, "Pagan Ritual," esp. 24–29.

32. Rives, "Human Sacrifice," 70.

33. Rives, "Human Sacrifice," 74; McGowan, 434: "To be a 'cannibal' meant to be lawless, primitive, foreign, immoral, secretive, and violent."

34. Edwards, *Politics of Immorality*, 11.

35. Virginia J. Hunter, *Policing Athens: Social Control in the Attic Lawsuits, 420–320 B.C.* (Princeton, N.J.: Princeton University Press, 1994), esp. 102–5. Indeed, that the charges were stereotypical reemphasizes how closely they were linked to a standard definition of proper behavior. See also Winkler, *Constraints*, 46: "The *kinaidos* is a scare-image standing behind the more concrete charges of shaming one's integrity as a male citizen by hiring out one's body to another man's use." In other words, according to Winkler, the most devastating charge that could be made against an Athenian male citizen was that he sought sexual penetration by another, the "feminine" role. Such a charge could have serious social consequences. For further discussion, see chapter 1 below.

36. Exod 34:15–16; see also Lev 17:7, 20:1–9; Deut 31:16; Judg 2:17, 8:27; 1 Chr 5:25; Ezek 6:9, 20:30; 2 Kgs 9:22. See Phyllis A. Bird, "'To Play the Harlot': An Inquiry Into an Old Testament Metaphor," in *Gender Difference in Ancient Israel*, ed. P. Day (Minneapolis: Fortress Press, 1989), 75–94. See also Bird, "The Harlot as Heroine: Narrative Art and Social Presupposition in Three Old Testament Texts," in *Missing Persons and Mistaken Identities* (Minneapolis: Fortress Press, 1997), 197–218; Fokkelien van Dijk-Hemmes, "The Metaphorization of Women in Prophetic Speech: An Analysis of Ezekiel 23," in *On Gendering Texts: Female and Male Voices in the Hebrew Bible*, ed. Athalya Brenner and F. Van Dijk-Hemmes, Biblical Interpretation Series 1 (Leiden: E. J. Brill, 1993), 167–76; Howard Eilberg-Schwartz, *God's Phallus and Other Problems for Men and Monotheism* (Boston: Beacon Press, 1994), 97–105; Yvonne Sherwood, *The Prostitute and the Prophet: Hosea's Marriage in Literary and Theoretical Perspective*, JSOT Supplement Series 212 (Sheffield: Sheffield Academic Press, 1996), 19–20; Tikva Freymer-Kensky, "Law and Philosophy: The Case of Sex in the Bible," in *Women in the Hebrew Bible: A Reader*, ed. Alice Bach (New York: Routledge, 1999), 293–304.

37. Matt 19:12, Rev. 14:4.

38. 1 Cor 5:1–13; Eph 5:3, 5, 22–32; Col 3:5–7, 18–25; 1 Tim 2:8–15; 3:2–7, 12; 5:11–16; 2 Tim 3:2–9; Titus 2:3–7; Ign. *Pol.* 5.1–2; Poly. *Phil.* 4:2–3, 5.3.

39. Arist. *Apol.* 15; Athenagoras *Leg.* 32.2–5, 33.1, 4–5; Justin 1 *Apol.* 15; Tatian *Or.* 33; Theophilus *Ad Auto.* 13; Tertullian *Apol.* 39.

40. *Acta Pauli et Theclae*, in *Acta apostolorum apocrypha*, ed. R.A. Lipsius, vol. 1 (Leipzig: Mendelssohn, 1898; repr., Hildesheim: Olms, 1972), 235–271; *Acta Joannis*, in *Acta apostolorum apocrypha*, ed. M. Bonnet, vol. 2.1 (Leipzig: Mendelssohn, 1898; repr., Hildesheim: Olms, 1972), 151–215; *Acta Thomae*, in *Acta apostolorum apocrypha*, ed. M. Bonnet, vol. 2.2 (Leipzig: Mendelssohn, 1903; repr., Hildesheim: Olms, 1972), 99–288.

41. The bibliography on early and late ancient Christian discourses of sexuality, virginity, masculinity, and femininity is immense. A few important examples include: Peter Brown, *The*

Body and Society; Virginia Burrus, *Chastity as Autonomy: Women in the Stories of the Apocryphal Acts*, Studies in Women and Religion 23 (Lewiston, N.Y.: Edwin Mellen Press, 1987); Elizabeth Castelli, "Virginity and Its Meaning for Women's Sexuality in Early Christianity, *Journal of Feminist Studies in Religions* 2 (1986): 61–88; Elizabeth A. Clark, *Reading Renunciation: Asceticism and Scripture in Early Christianity* (Princeton, N.J.: Princeton University Press, 1999); Kate Cooper, *The Virgin and the Bride: Idealized Womanhood in Late Antiquity* (Cambridge, Mass.: Harvard University Press, 1996); Susanna Elm, *Virgins of God: The Making of Asceticism in Late Antiquity* (Oxford: Clarendon Press, 1994); Kathy L. Gaca, *The Making of Fornication: Eros, Ethics, and Political Reform in Greek Philosophy and Early Christianity*, Hellenistic Culture and Society 40 (Berkeley and Los Angeles: University of California Press, 2003); Bernhard Lohse, *Askese und Mönchtum in der Antike und der alten Kirche*, Religion und Kultur der alten Mittelmeerwelt in Parallelforschungen 1 (Munich: R. Oldenbourg, 1969); Aline Rousselle, *Porneia: On Desire and the Body in Antiquity*, trans. Felicia Pheasant (London: Basil Blackwell, 1988); Elisabeth Schüssler Fiorenza, *In Memory of Her: A Feminist Theological Reconstruction of Christian Origins* (New York: Crossroad, 1983); Vincent Wimbush and Richard Valantasis, eds., *Asceticism* (New York: Oxford University Press, 1995). See also the broad yet detailed survey of medieval legislation regarding sexual conduct by James A. Brundage, *Law, Sex, and Christian Society in Medieval Europe* (Chicago: University of Chicago Press, 1987). Brundage notes that a widespread Christian disdain for sex and veneration of sexual abstinence, rooted in the writings of the earliest Christians, transformed thinking about sex in the West and continues to inform the Western cultural landscape today.

42. Brown, *Body and Society*. Following an exhaustive survey of various Christian approaches to the topic, Brown remarks, "The Early Church was so creative largely because its most vocal members so frequently disagreed with each other" (429).

43. Tatian *On Perfection* fr. 5 = Clement *Strom.* 3.12, 17, in *Tatian: Oratio ad Graecos and Fragments*, ed. and trans. Molly Whittaker (xford: Clarendon Press, 1982), 79–80. For further discussion, see Gaca, *Making of Fornication*, 221–46; see also Brown, *Body and Society*, 90–93.

44. Iren. *Adv. Haer.* 1.28.1.

45. See esp. Tatian *Or.* 22, 33 and Iren. *Adv. Haer.* 1.6.3, 1.13.3, 5.8.2–4. These differences in approach to the question of sexual renunciation have led Kathy Gaca to posit that there were three "very different sectors of patristic thought—the sexually encratite, the proto-orthodox, and the more libertine positions," which she then discusses in detail (see *Making of Fornication*, esp. part 3; quotation from page 15 of the introduction).

46. For example, Matt 6:32; Rom 1:18–32; Eph 4:17; 1 Thes 4:5; 1 Peter 4:3–5.

47. For example, Phil 4:18–19; Eph 5:6–18; 2 Tim 3:1–9; Heb 6:4–8; 2 Peter 1:4–9, 2:1–22, 3:3–4; 1 John 2:18–19, 4:1–6; Jude 3–18; Rev. 2:14, 20; Ign. *Eph.* 7.1; 16.1; Ign. *Trall.* 6.1–7.1; 11.1; Ign. *Phld.* 2.2–3.1; Ign. *Smyr.* 4.1; 5.1; 6.2; Poly. *Phil.* 7.1–2; Herm. *Mand.* 4; 6; 11; Herm. *Sim.* 6.2; 7.5; 9.19; Justin *1 Apol.* 26.

48. Justin *1 Apol.* 26; Justin *Dial.* 35; Iren. *Adv. Haer.* 1.6.2; 1.13.2–7; 1.22.2–23.4; 1.24.5; 1.25.3–4; 1.26.3; 1.28.2; 2.32.2; 5.8.4; Clement *Strom.* 3.2.5, 1,11; 4.28; 5.42–3; 6.46, 54; 11.78; Epiph. *Pan.* 21.2.2–3.

49. Caroline Johnson Hodge, "'If Sons, Then Heirs': A Study of Kinship and Ethnicity in Paul's Letters" (Ph.D. diss., Brown University, 2001), states the problem succinctly: "There is no ethnically neutral 'Christianity' in Paul; there is no 'Christianity' in Paul at all. The term 'Christians' is an anachronistic designation for Christ-followers in Paul's letters" (3).

50. On "ethnic reasoning" as an important aspect of Christian self-definition, see Denise Kimber Buell, "Rethinking the Relevance of Race for Early Christian Self-Definition," *Harvard Theological Review* 94, no. 4 (2001): 449–76.

51. James B. Rives, "Roman Religion Revisited," *Phoenix* 52 (1998): 353. See the excellent set of essays in Simon Goldhill, ed., *Being Greek Under Rome: Cultural Identity, the Second Sophistic, and the Development of Empire* (Cambridge: Cambridge University Press, 2001); the helpful treatment of Greek identity by Simon Swain, *Hellenism and Empire: Language, Classicism, and*

Power in the Greek World, A.D. 50–250 (Oxford: Clarendon Press, 1996); and the important work by Jonathan M. Hall, *Ethnic Identity in Greek Antiquity* (Cambridge: Cambridge University Press, 1997); and *Hellenicity: Between Ethnicity and Culture* (Chicago: University of Chicago Press, 2002).

52. See esp. Tim Whitmarsh, *Greek Literature and the Roman Empire: The Politics of Imitation* (New York: Oxford University Press, 2001).

53. See Shaye J. D. Cohen, *The Beginnings of Jewishness: Boundaries, Varieties, Uncertainties* (Berkeley and Los Angeles: University of California Press, 1999); and Seth Schwartz, *Imperialism and Jewish Society, 200 B.C.E to 640 C.E.* (Princeton, N.J.: Princeton University Press, 2001). Hence, as Seth Schwartz has shown, one could investigate just what sort of category "Jew" has been, asking whether "the Jews constituted a group in antiquity and, if they did, of the character of that group." The limitations of the evidence make such an inquiry difficult, Schwartz acknowledges, but the alternative—simply assuming the "groupness" or nationhood of the Jews—is unacceptable (5).

54. Pierre Bourdieu, *Language and Symbolic Power*, ed. J. B. Thompson, trans. Gino Raymond and Matthew Adamson (Cambridge: Cambridge University Press, 1991), 105.

55. Plato *Rep.* 427c–434d, 543c–580a.

56. Dio Chrys. *Or.* 1.14.

57. For example, Diodorus Siculus described the Egyptian kings of old as illustrative of the sort of virtue expected from good rulers, especially self-control, justice, and magnanimity Dio. Sic. 1.70.6–12. Elsewhere, Diodorus records with approval their exceedingly strict laws regarding women, 78.4–5. Stylianou observes, "moralizing judgements on individuals in the form of set *epainoi* or *psogoi* are characteristic" of much of Diodorus' lengthy history, a practice he took over from his sources. See P. J. Stylianou, *A Historical Commentary on Diodorus Siculus Book 15*, Oxford Classical Monographs (Oxford: Clarendon Press, 1998), 3–8. Similarly, Arrian related the (supposedly) exceptional *sophrosyne* of Alexander who chose not to violate the wife or daughters of the kings he defeated, though as the victor he had the opportunity to do so, Arr. *Anab.* 4.19.4–6, 20.1–3. In response, Darius, king of Persia, stretched his hands to heaven and prayed that his empire would be restored to him but, if not, then that both he and Persia would be ruled by the moderate, just Alexander (20.3). According to Arrian, Alexander was a model of physical stamina, liberality, fearlessness, piety, and sexual temperance. See discussion in A. B. Bosworth, *From Arrian to Alexander: Studies in Historical Interpretation* (Oxford: Clarendon Press, 1988), 135–56. Plutarch also praised Alexander's exceptional σωφροσύνη, a characteristic evident from his youth. Though Alexander may have been "impetuous and violent in other matters, the pleasures of the body had little hold upon him, and he indulged in them with great moderation," Plut. *Alex.* 4.4–5.

58. See, for example, the descriptions of Nero found in Suetonius, Tacitus, and Dio and discussed in Jaś Elsner and Jamie Masters, ed. *Reflections of Nero: Culture, History, and Representation* (Chapel Hill: University of North Carolina Press, 1994).

59. On the significance of the title "Augustus," see Mary Beard, John North, and Simon Price, *Religions of Rome*, vol. 1, *A History* (Cambridge: Cambridge University Press, 1998), 182–84.

60. Zanker, *The Power of Images*, 101–39; Syme, *Roman Revolution*, 150. On the religious reforms of Augustus, see Beard, North, and Price, *Religions of Rome*, 186–210; on actions against foreign cults, see 228–35.

61. *RG* 34.2: "For this service of mine I was named Augustus by decree of the senate, and the door-posts of my house were publicly wreathed with bay leaves and a civic crown was fixed over my door and a golden shield was set in the Curia Julia, which, as attested by the inscription thereon, was given me by the senate and people of Rome on account of my courage, clemency, justice, and piety." For discussion, see J. Rufus Fears, "The Cult of the Virtues and Roman Imperial Ideology," *ANRW* 2.17.2 (1981), 885–6; Brian Bosworth, "Augustus, the *Res Gestae*, and the Hellenistic Theories of Apotheosis," *JRS* 89 (1999): 1–18. Bosworth argues that Augustus purposefully adopted the language of Hellenistic kingship to describe his accomplishments.

62. See Helen North, "Canons and Hierarchies of the Cardinal Virtues in Greek and Latin Literature," in *The Classical Tradition: Literary and Historical Studies in Honor of Harry Caplan*, ed. Luitpold Wallach (Ithaca, N.Y.: Cornell University Press, 1966), 177–78. For one interesting example, see Philo *Leg.* 143–61.

63. On Nero, see Sen. *Clem.* 1.1.6. On Trajan, see Plin. *Pan.* 22–28, 42.

64. Fears, "The Cult of the Virtues," 938.

65. Andrew Wallace-Hadrill, *Suetonius: The Scholar and His Caesars* (London: Duckworth, 1983), 147.

66. Compare Lincoln, *Authority*, 6, 45, 48, 71, 78–79, 93. Lincoln challenges the notion that any one person or group can be said to be "in authority" where authority is conceived as "authority over." To Lincoln, authority is "not so much an entity as it is 1) an effect; 2) the capacity for producing that effect; and 3) the commonly shared opinion that a given actor has the capacity for producing that effect" (10). This effect is produced, in part, by hiding the individual behind the office and the ideals associated with that office. Attacking the individual behind the office by means of "corrosive discourse" (slander, invective, insult, gossip, curses, mockery, heckling, jokes, rumor) challenges the "fig leaf of legitimacy" worn by those "in authority" by restoring "to the level of the human those frail and fallible individuals who would prefer to represent themselves as the embodiment of some incontestable office or some transcendent ideal." The Christians, I argue, go further, implying that the office itself is corrupt, even demonic, so long as the officeholder refuses to embrace Christ.

67. Hor. *Carm.* 4.5. Along similar lines, a third-century treatise on rhetoric recommends that emperors be praised for setting a good example. Thanks to the emperor, "marriages are chaste, fathers have legitimate offspring, spectacles, festival and competitions are conducted with proper splendor and due moderation" (Men. Rhet. 376.5).

68. Romans 6:15–23. For further discussion, see chapter 2.

69. 1 Tim 3:1–7. The similarities between the "household codes" found in the Deutero-Pauline and Pastoral Epistles and Greco-Roman moralistic discourse is well-known. See esp. Margaret Y. MacDonald, *The Pauline Churches: A Socio-Historical Study of Institutionalization in the Pauline and Deutero-Pauline Churches*, SNTS Monograph Series 60 (Cambridge: Cambridge University Press, 1988).

70. Plut. *Mor.* 144c.

71. See Bourdieu, *Language*, 94–105; Foucault, *History of Sexuality*, 1:101. Foucault suggests that nineteenth-century discourses that defined "homosexuality" as a domain susceptible to social control allowed demands for legitimacy to be framed in the very terms that had been invented to control it. Thus, "perversity" could be said to be "natural" and therefore legitimate. Similarly, Bourdieu has noted that the transgression of discursive, linguistic norms (esp. "slang") is based upon the very existence of such norms. Therefore, resistance occurs within the language and symbology that has already defined what tack the transgression will take. A transgression of the status quo in the name of resistance does not necessarily imply that the status quo has been challenged. Rather, the status quo suggests the very form of the resistance and, whatever its intention, the resistance works to partially reinscribe the status quo.

72. Rosamond C. Rodman, "Who's On Third? Reading *Acts of Andrew* as a Rhetoric of Resistance," in "Rhetorics of Resistance: A Colloquy on Early Christianity as Rhetorical Formation," ed. Vincent L. Wimbush, *Semeia* 79 (1997), 43.

73. Averil Cameron, *Christianity and the Rhetoric of Empire*, Sather Classical Lectures 55 (Berkeley: University of California Press, 1991), 5.

74. For the sake of clarity, I have organized this book according to a basic but problematic scheme of background (chapter 1), critique of outsiders (chapters 2 and 3), and insider debate (chapters 4 and 5). Such an organizational strategy could, I fear, serve to obfuscate the complex interrelationships of culture and rhetoric I am exploring. For example, treating Greek and Roman invective in one chapter and biblical sources in another could serve to blur one of my basic premises: that Christian rhetoric could be "Greek," "Roman," and "Jewish" too. Still, I do not

intend to treat the material discussed in the first chapter as simply "background" to what follows. Indeed, I would argue that those discourses labeled "Greek," "Roman," "biblical," "Hellenistic," "Jewish," and "Christian" with some inaccuracy ought to be read as deeply interconnected. The Christian sources I discuss in later chapters could potentially be read as "background" to many of the non-Christian sources I discuss earlier in the book. Moreover, many of the texts I have chosen to include under a rubric of outsider-focused Christian resistance literature could also be read as insider-focused polemic and vice versa. For example, Paul's warning to the Cornithian Christians that they ought to avoid sexual immorality, discussed in chapter 2, can be read as an attempt to establish an insider ethic capable of excluding or eliminating fellow Christians, the topic of chapter 4. Still, I placed my consideration of Paul's warning among other examples of his denunciations of (alleged) gentile depravity. Sexual slander, as we shall see, cuts both ways. It can never be wholly insider or outsider directed. It is always both. I have divided the sources I examine according to emphasis only, signaling insider/outsider dynamics throughout this project.

75. Elizabeth Clark, "Sex, Shame, and Rhetoric: Engendering Early Christian Ethics," *JAAR* 59, no. 2 (1991): 221. See also Virginia Burrus, "Reading Agnes: the Rhetoric of Gender in Ambrose and Prudentius," *JECS* 3 (1995): 25–46. On the totalizing aspects of Christian discourse (indeed, of all the "world religions"), see Robert W. Hefner, "The Rationality of Conversion," in *Conversion to Christianity: Historical and Anthropological Perspectives on a Great Transformation,* ed. Robert W. Hefner (Berkeley: University of California Press, 1993), 3–44, esp. 29: "Whatever their relationship to official power, the world religions arrive with the most remarkable of appeals. They proclaim a Truth that stands above others and assert that its recognition is essential for a meaningful life.... The message may be used to justify attacks on received social values and their elite custodians.... In so doing the message may also create new opportunities for social mobility and prestige." Thus, according to Hefner, marginalized groups find new sources of prestige through the claim that they, and they alone, possess access to the Truth that stands above all others. Christian assertions of moral superiority—we alone possess self-control—may be read along these lines.

1. SEXUAL SLANDER AND ANCIENT INVECTIVE

1. Syme, *Roman Revolution,* 150.

2. Maria Wyke, "Augustan Cleopatras: Female Power and Poetic Authority," in *Roman Poetry and Propaganda in the Age of Augustus,* ed. Anton Powell (London: Bristol Classical Press, 1992), 98. See also Lucy Hughes-Hallett, *Cleopatra: Histories, Dreams, and Distortions* (New York: Harper & Row, 1990).

3. Zanker, *Power of Images,* 57; following Cass. Dio 48.301.

4. Zanker, *Power of Images,* 65. On the view that Antony was Cleopatra's dupe, bewitched into her Asiatic ways, and swept away by her monstrous ambition, see Syme, *Roman Revolution,* 270–77. Syme argues that Cleopatra the '*fatale monstrum*' (Hor. *Carm.* 1.37.10) was an invention of Octavian and the victors, designed to secure popular Roman support for Actium.

5. MacDonald's translation. See further, Nisbet, "The *in Pisonem* as an Invective," 192–97.

6. Edwards, *Politics of Immorality,* 256.

7. Edwards, *Politics of Immorality,* 26–68.

8. See Nisbet, "The *in Pisonem* as an invective," 193. Compare Cass. Dio 46.18.3–6 (Dio reports that Cicero was accused of adultery). Nisbet rejects the *Invectiva in Ciceronem* as an actual invective of Piso against Cicero; see his "Piso and the *Invectiva in Ciceronem,*" appendix 7 to *Cicero: In L. Campurnium Pisonem* (Oxford: Clarendon Press, 1961), 197–98. The theory that the invective is the work of Sallust is also rejected.

9. See discussion in Kenneth J. Dover, *Greek Popular Morality in the Time of Plato and Aristotle* (Oxford: Basil Blackwell, 1974).

10. See M. Winterbottom, "Quintilian and Rhetoric," in *Empire and Aftermath*, ed. T. A. Dorey (London: Routledge and Kegan Paul, 1975), 83; and D. A. Russell, "Greek and Latin in Antonine Literature," in *Antonine Literature* (Oxford: Clarendon Press, 1990), 10.

11. Donald Earl, *The Moral and Political Tradition of Rome* (London: Thames and Hudson, 1967), 11–42.

12. Elizabeth Forbis, *Municipal Virtues in the Roman Empire* (Stuttgart and Leipzig: B. G. Teubner, 1996).

13. M. J. Wheeldon, "'True Stories': The Reception of Historiography in Antiquity," in *History as Text*, ed. Averil Cameron (Chapel Hill: University of North Carolina Press, 1989), 38.

14. Wallace-Hadrill, *Suetonius*, 142.

15. Forbis, *Municipal Virtues*, 1.

16. Noted by Syme, *Roman Revolution*, 271: "The version of the victors is palpably fraudulent; the truth cannot be disinterred, for it has been doubly buried, in erotic romance as well as in political mythology.... A fabricated concatenation of unrealized intentions may be logical, artistic and persuasive, but it is not history."

17. On the lack of widespread literacy in the ancient world, see William V. Harris, *Ancient Literacy* (Cambridge, Mass.: Harvard University Press, 1989), 3–25, 139–46, 248–84. For a critique of Harris, see the articles in J. H. Humphrey, ed., *Literacy in the Roman World*, Journal of Roman Archaelogy Supplementary Series 3 (Ann Arbor, Mich.: Journal of Roman Archaeology, 1991). On the importance of Greek intellectual culture to the early Christians, see Werner Jaeger, *Early Christianity and Greek Paideia* (Cambridge, Mass.: Harvard University Press, 1961). On literacy and early Christianity, see esp. Harry Y. Gamble, *Books and Readers in the Early Church: A History of Early Christian Texts* (New Haven, Conn.: Yale University Press, 1995).

18. Happiness is "well-being combined with virtue, or independence of life" and the things compatible with these three; see also 1362b.

19. Though, Aristotle argues elsewhere, a good orator is not always a good man.

20. A position taken by the Attic Greek teacher of rhetoric, Isocrates, in *Contra Sophistas*. On Isocrates' concern with the formation of moral character in the training of rhetoric, see George A. Kennedy, *Classical Rhetoric and Its Christian and Secular Traditions from Ancient to Modern Times* (Chapel Hill: University of North Carolina Press, 1987), 32.

21. Plato worries that orators, especially those he calls "sophists," were able, with their clever words, to represent matters as true that, in fact, were not true at all.

22. Contemporary scholars seem shocked by this phenomenon. For example, Carey and Reid comment: "The point is that they [accusations of 'private' vice] are, in our eyes, irrelevant to the matter at hand," yet they can be found in every one of Demosthenes' speeches. D. Carey and R. A. Reid, eds., *Demosthenes: Selected Private Speeches* (Cambridge: Cambridge University Press, 1985), 9. It may be inappropriate, however, to view the "surprising" presence of accusations of vice or praise of virtue as "irrelevant" on the basis of contemporary expectations regarding what is or is not appropriate in public speeches.

23. Koster, *Invektive*, 13–21. H. I. Marrou also considers the practice of copying the speeches of one's teacher and on the influence of "commonplaces" (κοινοί τόποι) on Greek and Latin literature: *A History of Education in Antiquity*, trans. George Lamb (Madison: University of Wisconsin Press, 1956), 51–54.

24. See the summary of typical categories in Koster, *Invektive*, 16–17. This list includes: γένος (ἔθνος, πατρίς, πρόγονοι, πατέρες), ἀνατροφή (ἐπιτηδεύματα, τέχνη, νόμοι), πράξεις (ψυχή—ἀνδρεία, φρόνησις, σῶμα—κάλλος, τάχος, ῥώμη, τύχη—δυνάστεια, πλοῦτος, φίοι).

25. The list is as follows: *nomen, natura, victus, fortuna, habitus, affectio, studia, consilia, facta, casus, orationes.*

26. The tradition that individuals and cities correspond to one another, possessing similar virtues (or vices), characters and temperaments is at least as old as Plato (see Plato *Rep.* 434d–449a; 543a–592b).

27. Arist. *Rh.* 1358b: "the subject of epideictic is praise or blame."

28. Arist. *Eth. Nic.* 1105b28. "Blame is derived from the contrary things ," Arist. *Rh.* 1368a; compare Arist. *Eth. Nic.* 1107a25–b17.

29. Koster, *Invektive*, 16–18; see also Jacqueline Long, *Claudian's In Eutropium*, 66–67 and Wilhelm Süß, *Ethos. Studien zur älteren griechischen Rhetorik* (Leipzig: B.G. Teubner, 1910), 247–54.

30. Theon, *Progymnasmata*, in *Rhetores Graeci*, vol. 2, ed. Leonard Spengel, Bibliotheca Scriptorum Graecorum et Romanorum Teubneriana (Leipzig: Teubner, 1854), 109–12. This outline of Theon's advice may be found in Marrou, *A History of Education*, 198–99.

31. "1. den Vorwurf, Sklave und Sklavensohn zu sein, 2. nicht-griechischer Herkunft zu sein, 3. gewerbetreibend und 4. Dieb oder ähnliches zu sein, 5. in sexuellen Dingen Vorwürfe zu verdienen, 6. ein μισόφιλος und μισόπολις zu sein, 7. ein finsteres Wesen zu haben, 8. in Aussehen, Kleidung und Auftreten ungebührlich aufzufallen, 9. ein 'Schildwegwerfer' zu sein und 10. schließlich ganz heruntergewirtschaftet zu haben," Süß, *Ethos*, 247–54.

32. Ilona Opelt, *Die lateinischen Schimpfwörter und verwandte sprachliche Erscheinungen. Eine Typologie* (Heidelberg: Carl Winter Universitätsverlag, 1965), 125–89. For a summary of the summaries, see Long, *Claudian's In Eutropium*, 66–67.

33. For further discussion of the models for praise and blame used during the so-called Second Sophistic, roughly identified as a period of highly polished rhetoric corresponding to the first three centuries C.E., see Graham Anderson, *The Second Sophistic: A Cultural Phenomenon in the Roman Empire* (New York: Routledge, 1993), 47.

34. See Theodore C. Burgess, "Epideictic Literature," *University of Chicago Studies in Classical Philology* 3 (1902): 89–102. Burgess traced the development of epideictic literature from Gorgias to Christian homiletic, arguing that it remained consistent throughout this very long period. The formulas of Menander Rhetor, Dionysius Halicarnassensis, Anaximenes, Theon, and Nicolaus Sophista varied slightly in detail but were all basically similar. See also Long, *Claudian's In Eutropium*, 78.

35. See, for example, Isoc. 3.10–14; 6.18–21, 39–42; 8. 36–37; Dem. 21.133–34, 158; 22.62–63; 36.45; 38.27.

36. On Isocrates as "the educator first of Greece and then of the whole ancient world," see Marrou, *A History of Education*, 194–96. See also Kennedy, *Classical Rhetoric*, 31–35. Between the third-century B.C.E. and the second-century C.E., a "canon of ten Attic orators"—held to be most representative of well-formed Greek oratory—may have been established. They included: Antiphon, Andocides, Lysias, Isocrates, Isaeus, Demosthenes, Aeschines, Hyperides, Lycurgus, and Dinarchus. See Ian Worthington, "The Canon of the Ten Attic Orators," in *Persuasion: Greek Rhetoric in Action*, ed. Ian Worthington (London: Routledge, 1994), 244–63.

37. Kennedy, *Classical Rhetoric*, 35.

38. The importance of this speech to later oratory, especially to epideictic, is made apparent by the use of the term "panegyric" to refer to encomia and invectives in general. See discussion in C. E. V. Nixon and Barbara Saylor Rodgers, *In Praise of Later Roman Emperors: The Panegyrici Latini* (Berkeley: University of California Press, 1994), 1.

39. Compare Plato *Rep.* 22a, where wealth is said to lead to luxury and idleness.

40. According to Kenneth J. Dover, "hubris" and related terms carried special, inflammatory weight: "Hubris is a term applied to any kind of behavior in which one treats other people just as one pleases, with an arrogant confidence that one will escape paying any penalty.... . Speakers in Athenian courts made lavish use of this group of words in castigating what they wished to portray as outrageous, arrogant or contemptuous behavior, for the words carry an emotive charge." *Greek Homosexuality* (Cambridge, Mass.: Harvard University Press, 1978), 34–35.

41. On extravagance as a vice, at least in the eyes of fourth-century Greeks, see Dover, *Greek Popular Morality*, 178–80. Dover suggests that the charge of extravagance usually concerned overindulgence in illicit sex. Wealth is squandered on flute-girls, courtesans, gambling, and expensive dinners. For examples, see Aeschin. *In. Tim.* 42, Dem. 36.39, Plut. *Lys.* 19.9.

42. Marrou, *A History of Education*, 164.

43. Aeschines questioned Demosthenes' claim that he had enjoyed an upright youth with a proper education, *In Tim.* 125–31.

44. Aeschin. *In Tim.*, thoroughly discussed by Dover, *Greek Homosexuality*, 19–109.

45. Translation by Dover, *Greek Homosexuality*, 20.

46. Brown, *Body and Society*, 24.

47. Translation my own.

48. On this term and its cognates, see Dover, *Popular Morality*, 205, and *Greek Homosexuality*, 63–65.

49. Compare Plato on the "tyrannical man," insatiable in his appetites, who has no self-control (*sōphrosynē*), and who therefore cannot be trusted (*Rep.* 578e–580c). See also Plut. *Mor.* 498D–E and Dio Chrys. *Or.* 14.1.18

50. On Lucian's tendency to "overwork the conventions" for the sake of amusement, such as the list of vices here described, see Graham Anderson, *Lucian: Theme and Variation in the Second Sophistic* (Netherlands: E. J. Brill, 1976), 1–22.

51. On "parasites" in Greek literature and in Roman comedy, see Cynthia Damon, *The Mask of the Parasite: A Pathology of Roman Patronage* (Ann Arbor: University of Michigan Press, 1997).

52. In other words, participating in orgiastic Dionysiac rites.

53. Translation my own.

54. Cora B. Lutz, ed. and trans., "Musonius Rufus, 'The Roman Socrates,'" *Yale Classical Studies* (1947): 35.

55. For a general discussion of status in the context of empire, see John H. Kautsky, *The Politics of Aristocratic Empires* (Chapel Hill: University of North Carolina Press, 1982), esp. 169–210. Kautsky outlines the principal values of aristocratic societies cross-culturally and notes the various ideologies that support the theory of a pure, deserving ruling class. These include: service, duty, honor, and glory; contempt for work and money-making; conspicuous consumption and display of wealth; nobility and superiority; pure blood, intermarriage, and sex relations. He associates concern for sexual behavior with the theory of "noble blood." In order to maintain "purity," aristocrats outlaw intermarriage with nonaristocrats, attempt to define themselves as racially distinct, hold daughters and wives to strict rules regarding the exercise of their sexuality and permit sex between aristocratic males and nonaristocratic females so long as the woman is not viewed as a legitimate wife (she is a mistress or a concubine, for example) (205–10).

56. Keith Bradley, *Slave and Society at Rome* (Cambridge: Cambridge University Press, 1994), 65–66.

57. For example, see Ach. Tat. 7.10, Plin. *HN* 35. On the (similar) views of Aristotle's Greek contemporaries, see Dover, *Greek Popular Morality*, 114–15. Some Stoic philosophers argued that slaves could achieve wisdom and cultivate virtue (see, for example, Sen. *Ep.* 47). Yet, the fact that the questions "are slaves fully human?" or "can slaves cultivate virtue and wisdom?" were raised emphasizes that slaves were commonly assumed to be deficient in virtue, wisdom, and humanity. On the supposed moral deficiencies of freedmen, see Petronius' satirical portrait of the vulgar freedman Trimalchio, who "would wish as a matter of course to ape the lifestyles of the rich and famous ... a former slave like Trimalchio would show no hesitation at all in submitting a host of underlings to the sorts of indignities of which he had first-hand experience himself" (Bradley, *Slave and Society*, 64, on Petron. *Satyr.* 26).

58. P. R. C. Weaver, "Social Mobility in the Early Roman Empire: The Evidence of the Imperial Freedmen and Slaves," *Past and Present* 37 (1967): 3–20.

59. Epictetus began his life as a slave. On the crossing of social categories by people in the Roman world, see Moses I. Finley, *The Ancient Economy* (Berkeley: University of California Press, 1973).

60. See Sarah B. Pomeroy, *Families in Classical and Hellenistic Greece* (Oxford: Clarendon Press, 1997), 21; P. R. C. Weaver, "Children of Freedmen (and Freedwomen)," in *Marriage, Divorce, and Children in Ancient Rome*, ed. B. Rawson (Oxford: Clarendon Press, 1991), 178; Susan Treggiari, *Roman Marriage* (Oxford: Clarendon Press, 1991), 301.

61. Keith Bradley, *Slave and Society*, 50; Treggiari, *Roman Marriage*, 52–54; and William L. Westermann, *The Slave Systems of Greek and Roman Antiquity* (Philadelphia: American Philosophical Society, 1955), 119. Treggiarri argues, on the basis of inscriptions, that slaves could think of themselves as married, though legally they were not recognized as such. On the basis of papyrological evidence from Roman Egypt, Westermann concludes that most "house-born slaves" were "children of slave parents upon both sides who had been permitted to live in quasi-marital relations," but see Keith Bradley, "On the Roman Slave Supply and Slavebreeding," *Slavery and Abolition* 8 (1987): 42–64; and William V. Harris, "Child Exposure in the Roman Empire," *JRS* 84 (1994): 18–19. See the excellent discussion of the sexual use of slaves in Jennifer A. Glancy, *Slavery in Early Christianity* (Oxford: Oxford University Press, 2002), 21–24.

62. Lovers of slave women who engaged in sexual activity without the approval of the women's masters could be prosecuted for insult and for violating the master's property. Furthermore, masters could sue men who violated their female slaves. *D* 48.5.6. Compare Plut. *Cat. Mai.* 21.2. Plutarch reports that Cato allowed each of his male slaves to choose one of his female slaves as his sexual partner for a fixed price. Each slave was allotted one woman only.

63. Apparently, adultery between a free woman and a slave could result in the legal murder of the slave by the husband, *D* 48.5.25; see discussion in Treggiari, *Roman Marriage*, 281.

64. Garlan, *Slavery in Ancient Greece*, 146; Westermann, *The Slave Systems*, 118–19. Diethart and Kislinger located three papyri that may be the transaction records between the family of a prostitute and her pimp, suggesting that some women or their families turned to prostitution out of poverty. P. Vindob. G 40796, P. Cairo Masp. 67097 2.41 (s.4), P. Lond 3.604 (a. 47), discussed in Johannes Diethart and Ewald Kislinger, "Papyrologisches zur Prostitution im Byzantinischen Ägypten," *Jahrbuch der Österreichischen Byzantinistik* 41 (1991): 21. See also BGU 4.1024 in which the mother of a prostitute requests that the murderer of her daughter be compelled to provide for her since, without the earnings from her daughter's prostitution, she has been left destitute. See discussion in Roger S. Bagnall, *Egypt in Late Antiquity* (Princeton, N.J.: Princeton University Press, 1993), 197; and Joëlle Beaucamp, *Le Statut de la femme à Byzance (4e–7e siècle)* (Paris: De Boccard, 1990), 1:81.

65. See discussion in Bradley, *Slave and Society*, 65.

66. On the importance of "status" in the Roman Empire and the ancient world more generally, see Finley, *The Ancient Economy*, 45; Géza Alföldy, *The Social History of Rome*, trans. David Braund and Frank Pollock (London: Croom Helm, 1985), 94–220; G. E. M. de Ste. Croix, *The Class Struggle in the Ancient Greek World* (London: Duckworth, 1981), 80–98; and William V. Harris, "On the Applicability of the Concept of Class in Roman History," in *Forms of Control and Subordination in Antiquity*, ed. Toru Yuge and Masaoki Doi (New York: E. J. Brill, 1988), 598–610. See also Wayne Meeks, *First Urban Christians: The Social World of the Apostle Paul* (New Haven, Conn.: Yale University Press, 1983), 20–21, 53–55.

67. In her discussion of "gossip" among the Athenian elite, for example, Virginia Hunter argues that stereotypes of the good or bad citizen "reflected and sustained the status quo" and were used to define, constitute, and police the Athenian elite. She identifies categories of gossip, drawn from Athenian law suits, that she calls "stereotypes." These are: level of public expenditure (generous or miserly?), military service (courageous or cowardly?), treatment of kin, and private life and conduct, especially sexual mores, categories that are very similar to those we observed in our survey of rhetorical theory, 110–111. See also Winkler, *Constraints*, 45–70. Similarly, Catherine Edwards argues that accusations of immorality in Rome defined "what it meant to be a member of the Roman elite, in excluding outsiders from this powerful and privileged group and in controlling insiders" (*The Politics of Immorality*, 12).

68. Halperin, *One Hundred Years*, 5.

69. Dover's view that intercrural intercourse was the primary act between the adult lover (whom Dover consistently calls the "*erastes*") and his junior partner ("*eromenos*") has recently been challenged by Cantarella who argues that, on the contrary, anal intercourse was the norm (*Bisexuality*, 46–47).

70. Halperin, *One Hundred Years*, 30.

71. Cantarella, *Bisexuality*, 50–51.

72. Amy Richlin, *The Garden of Priapus: Sexuality and Aggression in Roman Humor* (New Haven, Conn.: Yale University Press, 1983), 225. Yet, in contrast to Halperin, Richlin argues that "homosexuality" is a constant category and that Roman critiques of the pathic homosexual demonstrate that the homosexuality/heterosexuality paradigm can apply to ancient as well as modern evidence. See Richlin, "Not Before Homosexuality: The Materiality of the *Cinaedus* and the Roman Law Against Love Between Men," *Journal of the History of Sexuality* 3 (1992–93): 523–73. See also John Boswell, *Christianity, Social Tolerance, and Homosexuality: Gay People in Western Europe from the Beginning of the Christian Era to the Fourteenth Century* (Chicago: University of Chicago Press, 1980).

73. Williams, *Roman Homosexuality*, 125. See also Paul Veyne, "Homosexuality in Ancient Rome," in *Western Sexuality*, ed. Philippe Ariès and André Béjin, trans. Anthony Forster (Oxford: Basil Blackwell, 1985), 25–27; David Cohen and Richard Saller, "Foucault on Sexuality in Greco-Roman Antiquity," in *Foucault and the Writing of History*, ed. Jan Goldstein (Oxford: Blackwell, 1994), 55; Thomas Laqueur, *Making Sex: Body and Gender from the Greeks to Freud* (Cambridge, Mass.: Harvard University Press, 1990); Bernadette J. Brooten, *Love Between Women: Early Christian Responses to Female Homoeroticism* (Chicago: University of Chicago Press, 1996), 126–28, 140–41; Duncan F. Kennedy, *The Arts of Love: Five Studies in the Discourse of Roman Love Elegy* (Cambridge: Cambridge University Press, 1993), 31, 38–39.

74. Maud W. Gleason, *Making Men: Sophists and Self-Presentation in Ancient Rome* (Princeton, N.J.: Princeton University Press, 1995), 58–60; Laqueur, *Making Sex*, 19.

75. Polemon *Phys.* 2.1.194F. Translated and discussed by Gleason, *Making Men*, 60.

76. The following discussion is indebted to Brooten, *Love Between Women*, 45–48, 50, 171–73, 179, 183–86.

77. Describing her experience with Megilla to her male lover, Leaina remarks, "But I am ashamed, for it is unnatural" (5.1). See discussion in Brooten, *Love Between Women*, 52–53; and Ann Pellegrini's response, "Commentary on *Love Between Women*, by Bernadette J. Brooten," in "Lesbian Historiography Before the Name," ed. Elizabeth A. Castelli, *GLQ* 4 (1998): 578–89.

78. English translation by Richard M. Gummere, *Seneca: Moral Epistles*, vol. 2, LCL (Cambridge, Mass.: Harvard University Press, 1925). Cited by Brooten, *Love Between Women*, 45.

79. In light of this scenario, Ann Pellegrini notes, "the 'problem' of the masculine, sexually assertive *tribas* was first and foremost a problem of *gender* deviance, or status transgression, and only secondarily and symptomatically a matter of sexual deviance" (in Castelli, ed. "Lesbian Historiography," 582).

80. Brooten, *Love Between Women*, 55.

81. In both cases, the essential presence of a phallus or a phallic substitute is required, as is the correspondence of sexual and social position (Pellegrini, in Castelli, ed. "Lesbian Historiography," 580–83).

82. I use "sex" in a commonsense way to indicate biological identity of the actors, though I recognize that such a usage is problematic (see Judith Butler, *Gender Trouble*, 6–25). According to Laqueur, ancient medical texts confirm and extend this view of gender as hierarchical. These texts represent masculine and feminine as being a continuum, with male characteristics thought to be the more perfect and female considered deficient. Woman is understood as less than perfect, as a "colder" man, with the reproductive organs left within. "The vagina is an unborn penis, the womb a stunted scrotum, and so forth." Thus, "*man* is the measure of all things, woman does not exist as an ontologically distinct category. Not all males are masculine, potent, honorable, or hold power, and some women exceed some men in each of these categories. But the standard of the human body and its representations is the male body" (Laqueur, *Making Sex*, 28, 62). Pellegrini offers a similar analysis. Gender was configured on the basis of status: "What counted, then, was not the anatomical 'sex' of the sexual partners but their social genders—the degree, that is, to which their sexual roles did or did not

correspond to their respective positions in a rigid social hierarchy" (in Castelli, ed. "Lesbian Historiography," 580).

83. This brief summary of some of the recent work on what might be called the sex-gender systems of ancient Greece and Rome emphasizes difference—the difference between ancient Greco-Roman sexualities and genders and our own. This theory of difference, most famously articulated in Foucault's *History of Sexuality*, raises as many questions about categories assumed and discursive strategies employed by contemporary scholars as it does about the ancient world. Yet I find that the observation that Greece and Rome were different to be helpful when investigating the terms of the verbal sexual abuse I analyze below. (See Kennedy, *The Arts of Love*, 41: "In order to project sexuality or gender as culturally constructed and historically specific, it is necessary to project 'sexuality' and 'gender' as analytical terms of universal and transhistorical validity. Representing the past as fundamentally 'different' involves projecting it at some level … as also fundamentally the 'same.'")

84. See, for example, Cass. Dio 48.301; Muson. 4.20; Polyb. 31.25.5; Sall. *Cat.* 11.5; Suet. *Calig.* 37, 40, 41. On the prevalence of virtue and vice lists, see Anton Vögtle, *Die Tugend- und Lasterkataloge im Neuen Testament*, Neutestamentliche Abhandlungen 16 (Münster: Aschendorffschen, 1936). Vögtle is most interested in these lists as they appear in the New Testament. Nevertheless, he extensively compares the New Testament lists to those found in Greek and Roman sources.

85. On Plutarch's view of extravagance, see Alan Wardman, *Plutarch's Lives* (Berkeley: University of California Press, 1974), 79–86. We have already noted the view that luxurious living is the result of "foreign" influence. In the case of Isocrates, it is the "barbarians" who are condemned for the luxury that has made them "soft" and "slavish." See T. J. Haarhoff, *The Stranger at the Gate: Aspects of Isolationism and Cooperation in Ancient Greece and Rome*, 2nd ed. (Oxford: Oxford University Press, 1948). Representations of Antony suggest that succumbing to Cleopatra's "Eastern," lavish ways led to his downfall (see above).

86. Babbitt's translation.

87. In *Cat. Mai.* Plutarch praises Cato for the extremely strict manner in which he raised his son. "Cato's careful attention to the education of his son bore worthy fruit" (20.8).

88. Helen North, *Sophrosyne: Self-Knowledge and Self-Restraint in Greek Literature* (Ithaca, N.Y.: Cornell University Press, 1966), 134.

89. Translation my own.

90. For further discussion, see Kathy L. Gaca, *The Making of Fornication: Eros, Ethics, and Political Reform in Greek Philosophy and Early Christianity*, Hellenistic Culture and Society 40, (Berkeley and Los Angeles: University of California Press, 2003), esp. 87–92.

91. On terms referring to different types of prostitutes and the places where one could find them, see Diethart and Kislinger, "Papyrologisches zur Prostitution," 16–20.

92. See discussion in Kathleen Corley, *Private Women, Public Meals: Social Conflict in the Synoptic Tradition* (Peabody, Mass.: Hendrickson, 1993), 39–41.

93. The mid-second century P.Lond.inv. 1562 verso seems to be a receipt for a tax on a municipal brothel. See J. R. Rae, "P. Lond. inv. 1562 verso: Market Taxes in Oxyrhynchus," *ZPE* 46 (1982): 191–209. The relevant section reads, "From brothels, for each establishment, monthly." O. Berol. inv. 2574, O. Wilck 83, and O.Cair. GPW 6 are examples of tax receipts issued to individual prostitutes, dated from the first and second centuries. O. Wilck. 1157, SB 6.9545, no. 33, and SB 4.7399 represent permissions to individual prostitutes to ply their trade. A third-century papyrus suggests that a procurer could sublet his prostitute away from the brothel at the request of a customer, PSI 9.1055a. See discussion in Diethart and Kislinger, "Papyrologisches zur Prostitution," 19–20. See also Thomas A. J. McGinn, "The Taxation of Roman Prostitutes," *Helios* 16 (1989): 79–110; and McGinn, *Prostitution, Sexuality, and the Law in Ancient Rome* (Oxford: Oxford University Press, 1998). But see Roger Bagnall, "A Trick a Day to Keep the Tax Man at Bay? The Prostitute Tax in Roman Egypt," *Bulletin of the American Society of Papyrologists* 28 (1991): 5–12.

94. Plut. *Mor.* 140B. Garlan states: "The fact that a slave, whether female or male, could serve as a normal object of pleasure for his or her master within the *oikos* or for the general community of free men, after their banqueting in houses specializing in this field, really poses no problem, as is repeatedly borne out by the evidence" (*Slavery in Ancient Greece*, 152).

95. Compare Aeschin. *In Tim.* 1.42, 95–6. Timarchus enjoyed sumptuous meals, the company of flute-girls and prostitutes, and gambling (42). He spent his entire patrimony on his excessive love of luxury (95–96). Isoc. 3.40 claimed that it is an insult to one's wife to pursue sexual pleasure with prostitutes outside the home.

96. Aeschin. *In Tim.* 1.42, Dem. 18.296, 19.229, 36.39, 45; Isoc. 10.25. Dover comments: "Evidence of an unusual degree of enthusiasm for heterosexual or homosexual intercourse afforded manifold grounds for moral censure" (*Greek Homosexuality*, 23).

97. Alan Wardman, *Rome's Debt to Greece* (London: Paul Elek, 1976), 9; Earl, *Moral and Political Tradition of Rome*, 37–43.

98. For a discussion of Cicero's rhetorical use of stereotypical Roman attitudes toward Greeks and other non-Romans, see Ann Vasaly, *Representations: Images of the World in Ciceronian Oratory* (Berkeley: University of California Press, 1993), 191–243.

99. Translated and discussed by Edwards, *The Politics of Immorality*, 92. Note that Antony was also accused of succumbing to "foreign influence" by means of his lack of sexual self-control. His seduction by a foreign queen, his enjoyment of foreign luxuries, and his "un-Roman" association with Dionysius all supposedly led to his downfall.

100. Edwards, *The Politics of Immorality*, 93.

101. Donna Hurley comments: "The sequence of vices is similar to other biographies where lifestyle (extravagance, moderation, or stinginess) also follows lechery." *A Historical and Historiographical Commentary*, 139.

102. Thomas McGinn, following Suetonius and Dio, argues that Caligula instituted a new, more costly prostitution tax ("Taxation of Roman Prostitutes"). Yet citing lack of documentary evidence, Bagnall calls this argument into question. He notes: "Finally, it is important to remember (1) that Suetonius' description of Gaius' actions may not be wholly accurate; and (2) that even if it is, the tax may have been abolished or the rate changed after his fall. Suetonius clearly views these taxes as monstrosities, and Cass. Dio (60.4.1) tells us explicitly that Claudius undid Gaius' taxes bit by bit as opportunity arose" ("A Trick a Day," 11).

103. See discussion in Hurley, *A Historical and Historiographical Commentary*, 155.

104. See Hurley, *A Historical and Historiographical Commentary*, xv–xvi: "'Preference for the East' was in part at least a metaphor for an emperor's failure to deal graciously with the Rome-centered state."

105. Suetonius' interest in the virtues and vices of the emperors he discusses is further considered by Wallace-Hadrill, *Suetonius*, 142–72. On Greek and Roman historiography, M. J. Wheeldon comments, "both the *historicus* and his audience explained and evaluated historical reality not in terms of social and economic forces but almost entirely in terms of the moral attributes of the characters involved. It was a common justification of history-writing that it provided examples of ethical conduct which the reader should avoid or imitate as appropriate" ("'True Stories,'" 38). Compare Lucian's parody "How to Write History" (*Quomodo historia conscribenda sit*) in which he laments that most historians do not know the difference between history and panegyric (7).

106. Rolfe's translation. Further examples of Roman condemnation of luxury and extravagance include Polyb. 31.25a; Cic. *De or.* 2.283; Pliny *HN* 18.32; Cic. *Fam.* 97.

107. Cicero includes among his condemnations of Verres the accusation that Verres relied on disreputable women to do all of his tax collecting. He did his business in the bedroom and left these women, whom he bedded regularly, to squeeze as many taxes as they could out of the oppressed populace. Cic. *Verr.* 2.33–34. See also Scipio Aemilianus' invective against Claudius Asellus. Claudius Asellus is accused of squandering a third of his wealth on luxury and prostitutes, Gell. 6.11.9 = *ORF⁴*, fr. 19. Discussed in Alan E. Astin, "*Regimen Morum*," *JRS* 78 (1988):

24. Astin discusses the censorial concern with *mores* during the late republic. He concludes, "When the censors concerned themselves with *mores* they in effect drew attention—unsystematically but forcefully—to some of these values (the values of the aristocracy) and thereby tended to reinforce them" (33).

108. On the historians' use of anecdotes about the emperors, designed to serve as moral exempla for the edification of the audience, see Richard Saller, "Anecdotes as Historical Evidence for the Principate," *Greece and Rome* 27 (1980): 69–83. Cantarella makes the following helpful observation in her analysis of Suetonius: "Clearly, when it comes to the reliability of imperial biographies, doubts may plausibly be entertained. Evil doing is part of the essential material for writing such a biography, and the stereotype of the tyrant demands that he should be devoted to all types of vice, with sexual vice taking pride of place" (*Bisexuality*, 161).

109. The idea that the Persians were slavish due to (a) their extreme wealth, and (b) being ruled by a king/tyrant rather than a democracy is at least as old as the Persian wars. Aeschylus, *Persae*, in *Aeschyli Persae*, ed. Martin L. West, Bibliotheca scriptorum Graecorum et Latinorum Teubnerania (Stuttgart: Teubner, 1991), argues that the Greeks are free but the Persians are slaves (242–44); Herodotus records the Spartans as telling to Persians that they know how to be slaves but have never tasted freedom (7.135); and Euripides has Helen state that all barbarians (i.e., Persians) are slaves, with the exception of their king (1.276). For discussion, see Garlan, *Slavery in Ancient Greece*, 120.

110. Dover, *Greek Homosexuality*, 27.

111. Actors were considered to be licentious by definition.

112. Self-prostitution was indicated by *pornevō* in various passive forms; the (loaded and difficult term) *kinaidos* seems to refer to a man who enjoys penetration; the labels *malakos*, *habos*, *trypheros*, and *thēlytēs* indicated "womanly" or "effeminate" behavior.

113. See discussion in Gleason, *Making Men*, 65; Winkler, *Constraints*, 50. Dover was less willing to define *kinaidos*. Calling the term "vague" and "etymologically mysterious," he nevertheless comments (on Aeschin. 1.131 and 2.99) that "Aiskhines means ... to accuse Demosthenes of homosexual submission" (*Greek Homosexuality*, 17, 75). David Halperin sides with Gleason and Winkler, concluding that a "*cinaedus*, by contrast (to a respectable boy), was a male possessed of a supposedly feminine love of being sexually penetrated or dominated. This was the most disgraceful, most stigmatized identity a free male could acquire, and it carried with it a number of devastating social disqualifications": Halperin, "Commentary on *Love Between Women*, by Bernadette J. Brooten," in "Lesbian Historiography Before the Name," ed. Elizabeth A. Castelli, *GLQ* 4 (1998): 569.

114. See discussion in Dover, *Greek Homosexuality*, 75–6.

115. The second-century lexicographer Pollux mentioned the following terms related to loathsome, licentious, or reprehensible: βδελυρός, ἀσελγής, ἐπίψογος and μαλθακός, ἐκτεθηλυσμένος, γύννις. Some refer to softness and effeminacy, others to the passive role in homoerotic male sex. "Vendor of his youthful beauty" and "prostitute's colleague"(καταπύγων, τὴν ἡλικίαν πεπρακώς, ταῖς πόρναις ὁμότεχνος) were particularly sharp charges implying that a man had been penetrated "like a prostitute." Citied and discussed by Gleason, *Making Men*, 65. For a discussion of the Latin vocabulary, see Williams, *Roman Homosexuality*, 142–59.

116. "The *kinaidos* is a scare-image standing behind the more concrete charges of shaming one's integrity as a male citizen by hiring out one's body to another man's use" (Winkler, *Constraints*, 46).

117. Butler's translation, 121.

118. Discussed in Williams, *Roman Homosexuality*. Williams argues that denunciations of "Greek vice" in the writings of Tacitus and other Romans were not intended as condemnations of pederasty per se. Rather, these writers sought to signal their more general distaste for violations of the discipline and dignity appropriate to free Roman men by targeting Greeks who, presumably, had already relinquished a measure of their male "dignity" (70–72).

119. On the *gens togata* see E. Courtney, *A Commentary on the Satires of Juvenal* (London: Athlone Press, 1980), 23.

120. Even worse than a youth bought for his master's enjoyment, he chose to enslave himself to his "master" Curio. Cic. *Phil.* 2.44–5. Discussed by Edwards, *The Politics of Immorality*, 64–65.

121. Effeminate men (the *effeminati*) pluck out their hair, use depilatories, and fuss over their hair (Quint. *Inst.* 2.5.12). They touch their heads with a finger, walk in an unmanly fashion, and shift their eyes (Sen. *Ep.* 52.12). See Edwards, *The Politics of Immorality*, 63. Juvenal harangues against "soft" men. In *Satire 2*, he presents a Roman matron, Laronia, who inveighs against male effeminates, those who have a feminine gait (17, 20), use perfume (40–42), and enjoy performing oral sex (50). These men dress in gauze (65–76) and paint their eyes (97). See discussion in Richlin, *The Garden of Priapus*, 201–22; and S. H. Braund, "A Woman's Voice? Laronia's Role in Juvenal *Satire 2*," in *Women in Antiquity: New Assessments*, ed. Richard Hawley and Barbara Levick (London: Routledge, 1995), 207–19. Courtney suggests that Juvenal approves of Laronia's complaint (*A Commentary*, 32). Braund argues that Laronia is meant to be a woman of high social status who has committed adultery, not a prostitute, as some contemporary scholars have alleged ("A Woman's Voice?" 208).

122. He supposedly castrated a boy named Sporus, dressing him up like a woman, and "marrying" him. According to Williams, sexual involvement with youths was acceptable in the Roman context, as long as they were slaves or foreigners. As in Athens, boys were thought to be objects of adult male desire. As a result, men had to be kept away from Roman boys. In contrast to classical Athens, freeborn youths were off limits (*Roman Homosexuality*, 86–95, 123–24).

123. Men who adopt a feminine style have become "slaves of luxurious living and are completely enervated, men who can endure being seen as womanish creatures, hermaphrodites, something which real men would avoid at all costs" (Muson. 21.32–35; Lutz translation, 120). Dover suggests that the Greeks believed that the passive partner in anal sex did not receive, or should not receive, any pleasure from the act. If he does, he must be a *pornos* or he is perverted (*Greek Homosexuality*, 52–54, 103, 169). Edwards makes a similar observation regarding the Romans (*The Politics of Immorality*, 71–72).

124. Thus, in classical Athens, Athenian males could be threatened with the "scare-image" of the *kinaidos*, the "dreaded, anti-type of masculinity behind every man's back" (Winkler, *Constraints*, 46).

125. For the necessity of protecting freeborn youths from depraved adult males, see Quint. *Inst.* 1.15. For a lampoon of moralists who enjoy being penetrated, see Juv. 2.9–19. See discussion of these twin charges: "he enjoys penetration" and "he corrupts boys" in Richlin, *The Garden of Priapus*, 138–39, Gleason, *Making Men*, 405–8, and Edwards, *The Politics of Immorality*, 73.

126. Veyne, "Homosexuality in Ancient Rome," 29.

127. Jo Ann McNamara, "Gendering Virtue," in *Plutarch's Advice to the Bride and Groom and A Consolation to His Wife*, ed. Sarah B. Pomeroy (Oxford: Oxford University Press, 1999), 151–61. For a discussion of ἀνδρεία and *virtus* in Greek and Roman lists of virtues from classical Athens to early Christianity, see North, "Canons and Hierarchies," 165–83. On the link between cowardice and effeminacy in Roman texts, see Cic. *Mur.* 31; Suet. *Otho* 12; Plut. *Otho* 9; Tac. *Ann.* 13.30, discussed by Edwards, *The Politics of Immorality*, 77. On the hoplite warrior as the ideological opposite to the κίναιδος, see Winkler, *Constraints*, 46–54.

128. On this view in classical Greek sources, see Dover, *Popular Morality*, 96–102; in Hellenistic Greek sources, see Cantarella, *Pandora's Daughters: The Role and Status of Women in Greek and Roman Antiquity*, trans. Maureen B. Fant (Baltimore, Md.: Johns Hopkins University Press, 1987), 92–97; in Roman sources, see Treggiari, *Roman Marriage*, 205–28; in late antiquity, see Beaucamp, *Le Statut*, 1:26–27.

129. Translation my own, but I follow the suggestion of Lutz here by translating *sōphrona* as "chaste and self-controlled."

130. Helen F. North, *From Myth to Icon: Reflections of Greek Ethical Doctrine in Literature and Art* (Ithaca, N.Y.: Cornell University Press, 1979), 42.

131. Translation my own. Compare Plut. *Mor.* 141e, 142b–c, 145a–c. Plutarch assumes that women are especially vulnerable to an excessive love of adornment. It is therefore the husband's responsibility to refrain from luxury so that he does not corrupt his much more vulnerable wife.

132. A second-century epitaph to Ameyone listed the following virtues: *optima et pucherrima, lanifica, pia, pudicia, frugi, casta, domiseda.* According to Treggiari, this is a fairly stereotypical list (*Roman Marriage*, 248). For a similar list, see Karen Jo Torjesen, "In Praise of Noble Women," *Semeia* 57 (1992): 52. See also Plut. *Mor.* 139b–e. As the third-century jurist Ulpian put it, the true Roman matron, a *materfamilias*, deserves to be so because of her exemplary morals: "We ought to take *materfamilias* to mean a woman who does not live dishonorably: it is morals which distinguish and separate the *materfamilias* from all other women. So it will make no difference whether she is married or widowed or divorced, freeborn, or a freedwoman: for it is not marriage or birth which makes a *materfamilias* but good morals" (*D* 50.16.46.1; Watson's translation). About this passage, Treggiari remarks (280), "He protests too much.... But it is understandable when we consider how second- and third-century emperors and jurists had extended the scope of the statute" (i.e., the *lex Julia*, discussed in more detail below).

133. For discussion, see Susannah H. Braund, "Juvenal—Misogynist or Misogamist?" *JRS* 82 (1992): 75.

134. Following the translation of Lutz (43). After a discussion of Musonius' "revolutionary" view that women should study philosophy, James Francis cites this same line and comments "so much for the revolution" (*Subversive Virtue*, 14).

135. For further descriptions of this "good woman," see Xen. *Oec.* 7.3; 7:35–9.19. North states, "feminine *sophrosyne* (chastity, modesty, obedience, inconspicuous behavior) remains the same throughout Greek history" (*Sophrosyne*, 1). Treggiari finds a similar stereotype in the Roman sources (*Roman Marriage*, 209–34).

136. Dem. 21.158; Isoc. 21.19–20; Cass. Dio 55.12–16; Plut. *Luc.* 6.2–4; Plut. *Sol.* 23; Cic. *Cael.* 49; Hor. *Carm.* 3.6.17–32; Juv. 6.82–113; Livy 39.15.9; Sall. *Cat.* 25; Sen. *Ben.* 6.32.1; Suet. *Aug.* 65.1–2.

137. For another example of the association of women with suspect religion, see Plut. *Alex.* 2.4–5, 3.1–2. According to Plutarch, rumor had it that Philip of Macedon feared his wife Olympias because of her strange religious practices. This was not surprising, since all the women were addicted to the Orphic rites and Dionysiac orgies, engaging in extravagant and superstitious ceremonies. The result of Olympias' wild divine possessions, however, was the conception of Alexander by means of the god Ammon, or so some people say.

138. On *pornē* as a slur in the papyri, see Diethart and Kislinger, "Papyrologisches zur Prostitution," 16.

139. Prostitute (*pornē*), courtesan (*hetaira*), musician, actress—all of these can refer to a woman assumed to be sexually available, usually for a price. On the conflation of these categories in Roman law, see Beaucamp, *Le Statut*, 1:122–23. On the status of actresses during the late empire, see Dorthea R. French, "Maintaining Boundaries: The Status of Actresses in Early Christian Society," *Vigiliae Christianae* 52 (1998): 293–318, esp. 296–300.

140. See Braund, "Juvenal," 72–78. Braund places this satire in the context of a commonplace topic discussed in Greek and Latin rhetorical schools, "Should one marry?" (78–82).

141. The late-third- or early-fourth-century rhetorician "Menander" makes this point explicit by defining the signs of "the good emperor" in the following way: "Because of the emperor, marriages are chaste, fathers have legitimate offspring, spectacles, festivals and competitions are conducted with proper splendor and due moderation" (Men. Rhet. 376.10; Russell and Wilson's translation.

142. On the "rhetoric of conjugal unity," see Paul Veyne, "La Famille et l'amour sous le Haut-Empire romain," *Annales ESC* 33 (1978): 35–63.

143. The discussion that follows relies upon the preservation of these laws in the legal discussions of Ulpian, Paul, Macen, and other late-antique jurists. When citing the *Digest*, I will refer

to the text edition, with English translation, of Alan Watson, *Digest of Justinian*. A cautionary note: the *Digest* was compiled in 530 C.E. to bring into intelligibility an incredibly vast array of materials written by jurists from the Antonine and Severan periods about earlier legislation (such as the Augustan marriage laws). Thus, it is difficult to determine what portions of the *Digest* reflect the intentions of the original laws, the needs of the Antonine and Severan periods, and the interests of the compilers for Emperor Justinian. For further discussion, see P. Garnsey, *Social Status and Legal Privilege in the Roman Empire* (Oxford: Clarendon Press, 1970), 7–10.

144. Gardner, *Women in Roman Law and Society* (Bloomington: University of Indiana Press, 1991), 35; see also Syme, *Roman Revolution*, 444–45; Treggiari, *Roman Marriage*, 277–98.

145. For a discussion of *patria potestas* see Treggiari, *Roman Marriage*, 15–16.

146. See discussion in Treggiari, *Roman Marriage*, 282.

147. See Treggiari, *Roman Marriage*, 283–84.

148. Concubinage bore many resemblances to marriage. For example, a concubine could be charged with adultery, though, Ulpian states, the *lex Julia* will not apply. The main distinction between a wife and a concubine seems to be status: "He who keeps a free woman for the sake of a sexual relationship, and not for marriage, commits unlawful intercourse, unless to be sure, she is a concubine" (*D* 48.5.35, Modestinus).

149. Watson's translation. See McGinn, *Prostitution*, 123–38, (on prostitution as a disgrace, tied to juristic definitions of "prostitute") and 156–71 (on the explicit association of adulteresses with prostitutes).

150. Garnsey, *Social Status and Legal Privilege*, 23–24.

151. L. F. Raditsa, "Augustus' Legislation Concerning Marriage, Procreation, Love Affairs and Adultery," *ANRW* 2.13 (1980): 288.

152. Rousselle, *Porneia*, 78–79.

153. McGinn, *Prostitution*, 209.

154. Treggiari, *Roman Marriage*, 292–93. Treggiari, however, is less interested in the intent of the marriage legislation than in its potential effects. For example, did it prevent or diminish the frequency of adultery? The evidence is inconclusive (294–98). Compare D. C. Feeney, "*Silicit et fastest*: Ovid's *Fasti* and the Problem of Free Speech under the Principate," in *Roman Poetry and Propaganda in the Age of Augustus*, ed. Anton Powell (London: Bristol Classical Press, 1992), 3: "Augustus' very attempt to promote traditional Roman values clashed head on with traditional Roman values, by obtruding the government into the pater familias' area of responsibility."

155. Sall. *Cat.* 25; discussed by Edwards, *The Politics of Immorality*, 43.

156. Livy 39.15.9; discussed by Edwards, *The Politics of Immorality*, 44.

157. Edwards, *The Politics of Immorality*, 47.

158. Suggested by Courtney, *A Commentary*, 252. Again, the link between female license and horrific impiety is made, with Juvenal depicting the rites of Bona Dea as utterly corrupted by orgiastic women (*Sat.* 6. 315–45). Juvenal alluded to an earlier profanation of Bona Dea by Clodius.

159. Zanker, *Power of Images*, 157–58.

160. Pliny the Younger described the harmony of his marriage to his dutiful wife Calpurnia: She was domestic, loyal, supportive, and exceedingly modest; she expressed a profound interest in Pliny's intellectual endeavors; she hid behind a curtain whenever Pliny gave a reading so that she could listen to every word (*Ep.* 4.19). Cassius Dio placed a speech extolling the joys of marriage in the mouth of Augustus: "Is there anything better than a wife who is discreet, domestic, a good manager and child bearer; a woman to rejoice with you in times of health and look after you in illness, to join you in prosperity and console you in misfortune; to restrain the very impetuosity of youth, and to temper the untimely harshness of age?" (56.3.3–4). Lucretia, a heroine who preferred death to defilement, offers a further example of Roman stereotypes of the dutiful wife. The story of Lucretia's rape and suicide is told in Livy 10.23 and remembered fondly by Val. Max. 6 and Dion. Hal. *Ant. Rom.* 4.64.4. On Lucretia as a "hero of *sōphrosynē/pudicitia*," see North, *From Myth to Icon*, 49–52. See also Plutarch's *Consolation to His Wife* (*Mor.* 608A).

161. For an interesting parallel example, see Joan Wallach Scott, "'L'ouvrière! Mot impie, sordide ... ': Women Workers in the Discourse of French Political Economy, 1840–1869," in *Gender and the Politics of History* (New York: Columbia University Press, 1988), 139–63: "The implications of the discussion [of female workers] went well beyond references to the reality of women's lives. *Femmes isolées* represented the domain of poverty, a world of turbulent sexuality, subversive independence, and dangerous insubordination. They embodied the city itself" (147).

162. Hunter, *Policing Athens*, 115.

163. Discussed by Giula Sissa, "Maidenhood Without Maidenhead: The Female Body in Ancient Greece," in *Before Sexuality*, ed. David M. Halperin, John J. Winkler, Froma I. Zeitlin (Princeton, N.J.: Princeton University Press, 1990), 346–47.

164. Kate Cooper, "Insinuations of Womanly Influence: An Aspect of Christianization of the Roman Aristocracy," *JRS* 72 (1992): 151. The rising importance of *concordia* within marriage has been considered by Veyne and, following him, Foucault (Veyne, "La Famille et l'amour," 35–63. Michel Foucault, *History of Sexuality*, vol. 3, *The Care of the Self*, 74). During this period, Foucault states, the marriage bond, the "art of married living," was "*dual* in its form, *universal* in its value, and *specific* in its intensity and strength" (150; emphasis in the original). In this new discursive situation, promoted most forcefully by Musonius Rufus, "the woman as spouse is valorized within it as the other par excellence. But the husband must also recognize her as forming a unity with himself. Compared with the traditional forms of matrimonial relations, the change was considerable" (164). Yet neither Veyne nor Foucault give adequate consideration to the rhetorical use of "woman" and marriage in this context; nor do they take much note of the explicitly hierarchical thrust of all of the texts they site, texts that in every instance assume that women and wives are subordinate to men (also noted by Cohen and Saller, "Foucault on Sexuality," 35–59). Nevertheless, the observation that discussions of marriage and "the good wife" are particularly important in this period seems correct. See further Suzanne Dixon, "The Sentimental Ideal of the Roman Family," in *Marriage, Divorce, and Children in Ancient Rome*, ed. Beryl Rawson (Oxford: Clarendon Press, 1991), 105.

165. Syme, *Roman Revolution*, 150–54.

166. *Exempla* consisted of anecdotes telling of the exemplary deeds of famous Romans. These *exempla* are found throughout Roman historical sources, were utilized in forensic and political oratory, and were memorized by students in the course of their rhetorical training. See Saller, "Anecdotes as Historical Evidence," 69–83.

167. See Zanker, *Power of Images*, 156–210; Edwards, *The Politics of Immorality*, 34–62. On *mores maiorum*—a slogan referring to the supposed strict morality of the early Romans, exemplified by their simplicity, self-sufficiency, strict upbringing, order in the family, diligence, and bravery—see Zanker, *Power of Images*, 156; and Earl, *Moral and Political Tradition of Rome*, 28–30. See also Plut. *Cat. Mai.* 3.6, 4.2. Plutarch depicts the elder Cato as lamenting the sad state of the Roman republic which had "grown too large to keep its primitive integrity," especially following the introduction of foreign ways. On Cato as the embodiment of the *mos maiorum* (ways of the ancestors) see Williams, *Roman Homosexuality*, 17, 46–47.

168. According to Augustus' later marriage legislation, Cleopatra could not be a legitimate wife to Antony since she was a non-Roman. The most she could legally aspire to was concubinage. The legal capacity to marry, *conubium*, required that both partners be of marriageable age, of citizen status, and not be too closely related.

169. Wyke, "Augustan Cleopatras," 109.

170. Zanker, *Power of Images*, 3, 101–139, 143–215. See Suet. *Aug.* 29–31, 34, 40 on the temples Augustus built, the legislation he enacted to guard against extravagance and adultery, and his efforts to keep the people "pure and unsullied by any taint or foreign of servile blood" (Rolfe's translation, vol. 1).

171. See Maureen Flory, "*Sic exempla parantur:* Livia's Shrine to Concordia and the Porticus Liviae," *Historia* 33 (1984): 309–30. For further examples of public honorific statues in the Livia tradition, see Maureen Flory, "Livia and the History of Public Honorific Statues for Women in Rome," *Transactions of the American Philological Association* 123 (1993): 287–308.

172. Wyke, "Augustan Cleopatras," 98–140.

173. On Roman stereotypes for the ideal Roman aristocrat versus his debauched opposite, see Earl, *Moral and Political Tradition of Rome*, 11: "On the one side stand grave and revered senators, unbendingly devoted to the public service and administering a world empire with severe and impartial justice. On the other recline abandoned voluptuaries, given over to orgiastic corruption and the more recondite delights of the most exquisite depravity."

174. For a more detailed description of statuary of Livia and the connection of this statuary to various moments in the career of her husband Augustus, see Flory, "Honorific Statues," 294. Flory argues that the statues of Livia and Octavian's sister Octavia, erected during the period of major conflict between Antony and Octavian, could have "had some propagandistic functions related to the events of 35 BC and in particular to the emergence of Cleopatra as a major focus of Octavian's attempt to undercut Antony" (295).

175. On Livia as a political actor, see Flory, "Livia and the History," 305.

176. See discussion in Zanker, *Power of Images*, 65–73.

177. Flory, "Livia and the History," 295; and Zanker, *Power of Images*, 61.

178. Could the reports of Julia's infidelities also be linked to the invective tradition? Amy Richlin suggests as much in "Julia's Jokes, Galla Placidia, and the Roman Use of Women as Political Icons," in *Stereotypes of Women in Power*, ed. Barbara Glicken, Suzanne Dixon, and Pauline Allen (New York: Greenwood Press, 1992), 65–84. Richlin notes two extremes in the iconography of Roman imperial women: the perfect wife and mother, modest in comportment, dutiful, and the producer of legitimate heirs vs. promiscuous adulteresses with questionable dress and comportment. She concludes, "only occasionally can we tell how much of an image stems from real behavior, how differently the women involved perceived themselves, whether the image was deliberately sought by them or created by their families or enemies" (66).

179. Basore's translation. Compare Pliny *HN* 7.149; 21.9; Cass. Dio 55.12–16; Macrob. *Sat.* 2.5.

180. Ronald Syme suggests that the charge of adultery was a pretext designed to foil a treasonous plot. "The Crisis of 2 BC," *Bayerische Akademie der Wissenschaften* 7 (1974): 3–34.

181. On the significance of this statue, see Syme, *Roman Revolution*, 426.

182. Richlin, "Julia's Jokes," 66.

183. On representations of women in Plutarch, McNamara remarks, "Women's virility naturally found expression when men faltered" ("Gendering Virtue," 153). On the voracious sexual appetites of women, see Richlin, *The Garden of Priapus*, 109–16. Richlin discusses the theme in Roman invective of the sexually insatiable old woman.

184. "We virtually enrolled [Cloelia] as a man because of her outstanding courage," Sen. *Dial.* 6.16.2. Cloelia preserved her chastity *and* rescued hostages. See discussion in North, *From Myth to Icon*, 49.

185. This positive "masculinity" is in contrast to the phallic women discussed above who, rather than embracing their "natural" passivity, sought to penetrate their sexual partners. See discussion in Brooten, *Love Between Women*, 50–71; Verna E. F. Harrison, "The Allegorization of Gender: Plato and Philo on Spiritual Childbearing," in *Asceticism*, ed. Vincent L. Wimbush and Richard Valantasis (New York: Oxford University Press, 1995), 520–34.

186. On the meaning of *stuprum*, see J. N. Adams, *Latin Sexual Vocabulary* (Baltimore, Md.: Johns Hopkins University Press, 1982), 200–201.

187. Treggiari, *Roman Marriage*, 264–90, Rousselle, *Porneia*, 78–79; Judith Evans Grubbs, *Law and Family in Late Antiquity* (Oxford: Clarendon Press, 1995), 62.

188. See the discussion of *moicheia* in Athenian forensic speeches in Rosanna Omitowoju,

"Regulating Rape: Soap Operas and Self-Interest in the Athenian Courts," in *Rape in Antiquity,* ed. Susan Deacy and Karen F. Pierce (London: Duckworth, 1997), 14–18.

189. See, for example, Dover, *Greek Homosexuality,* 88–89. Dover points out that in the Greek case, freeborn youths were also acceptable lovers. Indeed, he views the Greek double-standard regarding women to be a contributing factor to the importance of homosexual liaisons during the classical Greek period. He states, "on the one hand, the Athenian father of a handsome boy did not have to worry about the financial and organizational problems which are created by the birth of an illegitimate baby, and to the extent we might have expected him to take a less repressive attitude towards the boy's homosexual affairs. On the other hand, whereas a woman insulated from contact with men throughout her youth and encouraged to treat all men alike with mistrust may find it hard to make the transition from the approved role of virgin daughter to the approved roles of bride, housewife, and mother, a boy who rejects the advances of erastai will nevertheless turn into an adult male citizen, and his performance of that role will not be impaired by his past chastity." On the double standard for Roman men and women, see Treggiari, *Roman Marriage,* 221–22 and Richlin, *The Garden of Priapus,* 216. In contrast to the Greeks, however, freeborn male youths were also off-limits, yet a double standard for men and women prevails (Williams, *Roman Homosexuality,* 50).

190. See discussion in Lisette Goessler, "Advice to the Bride and Groom," in *Plutarch's Advice to the Bride and Groom and A Consolation to his Wife,* ed. Sarah B. Pomeroy (Oxford: Oxford University Press, 1999), 102–3.

191. Discussed in Williams, *Roman Homosexuality,* 50.

192. See, for example, Quint. *Inst.* 1.2.4, 1.3.17. In Athens, sex between a free citizen male and a freeborn boy was also acceptable, though Romans seem to have regarded sexual activity with freeborn boys as a disgrace.

193. Francis, *Subversive Virtue,* 11. See also Foucault, *History of Sexuality,* vol. 3, *Care of the Self,* 167; and Gaca, *The Making of Fornication,* 90–92. Though Musonius Rufus went further than other authors from this period in his outright rejection of extramarital sex, his recommendations can be seen within a larger trend in which the restriction of sexual activity for men as well as women became newly important. Love of boys was called into question, as was sexual indulgence with prostitutes.

194. According to Ulpian, "The crime of pimping [i.e., procuring] is included in the law of adultery, as a penalty has been preserved against a husband who profits pecuniarily by the adultery of his wife, as well as against one who retains his wife after she has been taken in adultery" (*D* 48.5.2).

195. According to Seneca, Clodius got off from the charge of polluting the rites of the Bona Dea because he was able to offer the many matrons and youths he had corrupted as a bribe to the jury. Sen. *Ep.* 92. See discussion in Edwards, *The Politics of Immorality,* 47.

196. On the meaning of "virgin" (*parthenos*) in the context of Greek medical writings, see Sissa, "Maidenhood Without Maidenhead," 346–54.

197. Discussed by Ian Worthington, *A Historical Commentary on Dinarchus: Rhetoric and Conspiracy in Later Fourth-Century Athens* (Ann Arbor: University of Michigan Press, 1992), 327–29.

198. Dover remarks that Aeschines is guilty here of "a double falsehood. The laws which have been read out say no such thing.… . The fresh statement that 'anyone who hires an Athenian to use as he pleases' is liable to punishment again omits the essential specification of 'an Athenian' as a boy hired out by father or guardian" (*Greek Homosexuality,* 27).

199. That these categories are related (free woman, girl, and boy) and constitute the groups that must be protected and are in danger of violation is evident in the argument of Lysias 1.32–33. Lysias here makes a distinction between men who forcibly disgrace a free person, male or female, and those who persuade wives to go along. Such a distinction seems to be exceptional, however, since Athenian law treated rape and adultery as similar offenses. See discussion in Daniel Ogden, "Rape, Adultery, and the Protection of Bloodlines in Classical Athens," in *Rape in Antiquity,* ed. Susan Deacy and Karen F. Pierce (London: Duckworth, 1997), 32–36.

200. Dover, *Greek Homosexuality,* 36, and *Popular Morality,* 119–23.

201. Cic. *Phil.* 2, Plut. *Pomp.* 2, Suet. *Iul.* 49.4–52.3, Suet. *Claud.* 26.2, Suet. *Tit.* 10.2, Suet. *Dom.* 1.3, 22, Juv. 2.29. See Richlin, *The Garden of Priapus*, 217.

202. See, James A. Arieti, "Rape and Livy's View of Roman history," in *Rape in Antiquity*, ed. Susan Deacy and Karen F. Pierce (London: Duckworth, 1997), 212–14. Compare Seneca's critique of Rome as it appeared during his lifetime (c. 5 B.C.E.—65 C.E.): "They make a laughing-stock of other men's wives, not even secretly, but openly, and then surrender their own wives to others.... The result is that adultery has become the most seemly sort of betrothal" (*Ben.* 1.9.4–5; Basore's translation).

203. Rolfe's translation.

204. As Edwards puts it, "better to have committed adultery from calculation, *ratione*, than from lust, *libidine*." Using sex for political ends was a much more acceptable practice (*Politics of Immorality*, 48).

205. Dover, *Popular Morality*, 88; Edwards, *Politics of Immorality*, 48–49; Williams, *Roman Homosexuality*, 132.

206. Ogden, "Rape," 25; and, more generally, Kautsky, *Aristocratic Empires*, 83–90.

207. Once again, Caligula and Nero offer excellent examples.

208. Gleason, *Making Men*, 42.

209. A speech of Thersander, the villain of the second-century romance *Leucippe and Clitophon*, makes this point to humorous effect: "Whenever adulterers murder other people's female slaves, whenever murderers debauch other people's wives, whenever pimps break up sacred assemblies, whenever whores pollute the holiest of temples, whenever a man is in the act of fixing the trial date between slave girls and their master, what more could anyone do in excess of this farrago of lawlessness, adultery, impiety and bloodguilt?" Ach. Tat. 8.8.3. See discussion in Anderson, *The Second Sophistic*, 66–67.

210. One potential objection to my analysis is that I have treated "Greece" and "Rome" as reified categories in need of no further explanation. Beryl Rawson, "From 'Daily Life' to 'Demography,'" in *Women in Antiquity: New Assessments*, ed. Richard Hawley and Barbara Levick (London: Routledge, 1995), 4, notes that these two labels, "Greek" and "Roman," are "too general to be useful. It is important to differentiate regionally and chronologically, e.g. fifth-century BC Athens, Bronze Age Mycenae, Greek-speaking provinces of the Roman empire in the second century AD; the huge city of Rome, or country towns in Italy, or other parts of the empire which had different cultural traditions. These differentiations are too often ignored."

211. For a discussion of what may have been at stake for Aeschines, see John J. Winkler, "Laying Down the Law: The Oversight of Men's Sexual Behavior in Classical Athens," in *Before Sexuality*, ed. David M. Halperin, John J. Winkler, Froma I. Zeitlin (Princeton, N.J.: Princeton University Press, 1990), 192–94. On Cicero and Catiline, see Lily Ross Taylor, *Party Politics in the Age of Caesar*, Sather Classical Lectures 22 (Berkeley: University of California Press, 1949), 124; and Vasaly, *Representations*, 49–59.

212. A comment by Winkler seems apt here: "The word 'unnatural' in contexts of human behavior quite regularly means 'seriously unconventional,' and is used like a Thin Ice sign to mark off the territory where it is dangerous to go" ("Laying Down the Law," 172).

213. In classical Greece, love of freeborn boys was permissible. See above.

214. Carey and Reid, eds., *Demosthenes*, 9.

215. See especially Fergus Millar, *The Emperor in the Roman World* (Ithaca, N.Y.: Cornell University Press, 1977).

216. *Auctoritas* was highest form of prestige available to a Roman politician. See Earl, *Moral and Political Tradition of Rome*, 33, 73. With Augustus, "all real power and position, *auctoritas*, *dignitas* and *gloria* had passed into the possession of one man."

217. Many scholars of early Christianity have made a similar claim. See, for example, Klaus Wengst, *Pax Romana*, trans. John Bowden (Philadelphia: Fortress Press, 1987). For a discussion of Christian discourse in the context of imperial rhetorics, see Cameron, *Christianity and the Rhetoric of Empire*.

2. PAUL, THE SLAVES OF DESIRE,
AND THE SAINTS OF GOD

1. Justin went on to argue that these worthless demons defile women and corrupt boys. For him, "demons" were the gods of the Greeks.

2. Athenagoras further observed that the Greeks and Romans promote male prostitutes and attribute such vile deeds to their own gods. According to yet another apologist, the depravity of the Greeks was proven by their admiration of actors who posture obscenely and demonstrate adultery on stage (Tatian *Or.* 22). For further discussion, see chapter 3.

3. "He must manage his own household well, keeping his children submissive and respectful in every way, for if a man does not know how to manage his own household, how can he care for God's church?" (1 Tim 3:4–5). For discussion, see esp. Mary Rose D'Angelo, "Εὐσέβεια: Roman Imperial Family Values and the Sexual Politics of 4 Maccabees and the Pastorals," *Biblical Interpretation* 11, no. 2 (2003): 139–65.

4. Also see 1 Thess 4:4. "Idolatry" stands in a metonymic relationship with "fornication" throughout ancient Jewish and Christian literature, as noted below. Clement of Alexandria explained: "For as covetousness [πλεονεξία] is called fornication because it is opposed to contentment with what one possesses, and as idolatry is an abandonment of the one God to embrace many gods, so fornication is apostasy from single marriage to several" (*Strom.* 3.12.89; Oulton and Chadwick's translation).

5. See Ign *Poly,* 5.1–2; Justin *1 Apol,* 15. Such a practice was not universally accepted (see, for example, 1 Tim 5:3–16). Note also Paul's complicated stance on the issue in 1 Cor 7:1–40. For a discussion of Paul's views on marriage and continence, see, for example, Dale B. Martin, *The Corinthian Body* (New Haven, Conn.: Yale University Press, 1995), esp. 200–249; Daniel Boyarin, *A Radical Jew: Paul and the Politics of Identity* (Berkeley: University of California Press, 1994), esp. 59–69, 162–64, 170–79, 191–96; Vincent L. Wimbush, *Paul: The Worldly Ascetic* (Macon, Ga.: Mercer University Press, 1987); Mary Rose D'Angelo, "Veils, Virgins and the Tongues of Men and Angels: Women's Heads in Early Christianity," in *Off with Her Head! The Denial of Women's Identity in Myth, Religion, and Culture,* ed. Howard Eilberg-Schwartz and Wendy Doniger (Berkeley: University of California Press, 1998), 131–34; Yarbrough, *Not Like the Gentiles*; and Antoinette Clark Wire, *Corinthian Women Prophets: A Historical Reconstruction through Paul's Rhetoric* (Minneapolis: Fortress Press, 1990).

6. See 1 Thess 4:1–7; 1 Cor 5:1–13, 6:9–20, 7:1–40, 10:7–22, 11:2–15; 2 Cor 6:14–18; Gal 5:16–26; and Rom 6:12–23.

7. Paul and Polycarp, for example, argued that if a believer is unable to control his lusts "like the gentiles," then he will be judged as if he were among them. See 1 Cor 5:13, and Poly. *Phil.* 11.1–2. Compare *Did.* 3.3, 5.1.

8. Jaeger, *Early Christianity,* 7; Gamble, *Books and Readers,* 35: "early Christian literature is deeply indebted to the techniques, forms, and modes of ancient rhetoric." On Paul in particular, see also W. Wuellner, "Greek Rhetoric and Pauline Argumentation," in *Early Christian Literature and the Classical Tradition,* ed. W. R. Schoedel and R. L. Wilken (Paris: Beauchesne, 1979), 177–88; F. W. Hughes, *Early Christian Rhetoric and 2 Thessalonians* (Sheffield: JSOT Press, 1989), 19–30.

9. See Robert M. Grant, *Greek Apologists of the Second Century* (Philadelphia: Westminster Press, 1988), 54–55; Frances Young, "Greek Apologists of the Second Century," in *Apologetics in the Roman Empire: Pagans, Jews, and Christians,* ed. Mark Edwards, Martin Goodman, and Simon Price (Oxford: Oxford University Press, 1999), 82–85.

10. George Kennedy, *Greek Rhetoric Under Christian Emperors* (Princeton. N.J.: Princeton University Press, 1983), 258–60; Robert Dick Sider, *Ancient Rhetoric and the Art of Tertullian* (London: Oxford University Press, 1971).

11. See esp. Stanley K. Stowers, *Letter Writing in Greco-Roman Antiquity,* Library of Early Christianity (Philadelphia: Westminster Press, 1986).

12. Christian vice lists include those found in Rom 1:29–32; 2:20; Gal 5:19–23; Phil 4:8–9; 1 Cor 5:11; 2 Tim 3:1–8; Col 3:5–10; Eph 4:31; 1 Pet 4:3; Rev 9:21, 21:8, 22:15; Poly. *Phil* 5.2; and 1 Clem 21.6–8. For virtue and vice lists in non-Christian Greek sources, see, for example: Diog. Laert. 7.110–114; Dio Chrys. *Or.* 1.15–35, 2.75; Arr. *Epct. diss.* 2.16.11–17; and Muson. 33.7–39.1. Comparative lists are also found in Philo *Mos.*1.152–54, 2.19; Philo *Ios.* 70; and Philo *Spec.* 4.84. See also Cic. *Tusc.* 4.3.5, 4.6.11–14. See discussion in Hans Lietzmann, *An die Römer*, HNT 9 (Tübingen: J. C. B. Mohr, 1906); Martin Dibelius, *An die Kolosser, an die Epheser, an Philemon*, 3rd. ed., HNT 12 (Tübingen: J. C. B. Mohr, 1913); Harold W. Attridge, *The Epistle to the Hebrews*, Hermeneia (Philadelphia: Fortress Press, 1989); Wayne A. Meeks, *The Moral World of the First Christians*, Library of Early Christianity (Philadelphia: Westminster Press, 1986), 131. The most comprehensive discussion may be found in Vögtle, *Die Tugend- und Lasterkataloge*.

13. For example, Ignatius warned against false teachers who are "mingle Jesus Christ with themselves, as if giving a deadly drug mixed with honeyed wine" (*Trall.* 6.2. English translation Schoedel, in *Athenagoras: Legatio and De Resurrectione*), an image that William Schoedel relates to ancient medical imagery and metaphorical references to "evils dressed up to please" found in such authors as Diogenes Laertius (6.61). William R. Schoedel, *A Commentary on the Letters of Ignatius of Antioch* (Philadelphia: Fortress Press, 1985), 147. For a Pauline example, see A. J. Malherbe, "Gentle as a Nurse: The Cynic Background of 1 Thess 2," *NovT* 12 (1970): 203–17. Malherbe places Paul's claims about his gentleness within Cynic and Stoic arguments about their own gentleness. See also 1 Clem. 25, in which the author offers the phoenix as a sign of the resurrection. A thorough discussion of this issue, especially the influence of Stoic philosophy on the "fathers," may be found in Michael Spanneut, *Le Stoïcisme des pères de l'église: De Clément de Rome à Clément d'Alexandrie*, Patristica Sorbonensia 1 (Paris: Éditions du Seuil, 1957).

14. See, for example, Lev 18:24–30, 20:1–9; Exod 23:32–33, 34:15–16; Deut 31:16, Judg 2:17, 8:27; 1 Chr 5:25; 2 Kgs 9:22. Cf. Wis. Sol. 14:12; Ep. Jer. 9–10, 42–43; *Sib. Or.* 3.590–600; Philo *Virt.* 34.182; Joseph *Ap.* 2.273–275; *L. A.B.* 18.13, 30.1.

15. By designating postbiblical writing by authors who identified themselves as belonging to the category *Ioudaios*, "Jews," I do not mean to imply that "Jew" or "Jewishness" is a monolithic, obvious category.

16. Johnson, "The New Testament's Anti-Jewish Slander," 419–41.

17. See also Lev 17:7, 20:1–9; Deut 31:16; Judges 2:17, 8:27; 1 Chron 5:25; Ez 6:9, 20:30; 2 Kgs 9:22. For discussion, see. Bird, "'To Play the Harlot,'" 75–94. Bird challenges the notion that sacred or cult prostitution lies behind these accusations, arguing that the identification of the Canaanites with prostitution is polemical. See also Bird, "The Harlot as Heroine," 197–218; Dijk-Hemmes, "Metaphorization of Women in Prophetic Speech," 167–76; Eilberg-Schwartz, *God's Phallus*, 97–105; Sherwood, *The Prostitute and the Prophet*, 19–20; Freymer-Kensky, "Law and Philosophy," 293–304.

18. Compare Deut 31:16: In a dream, the coming idolatry of the people is predicted. The Hebrew people, following Moses' death "play the harlot after the strange gods of the land." On the Ezekiel passage, see Weston W. Fields, *Sodom and Gomorrah: History and Motif in Biblical Narrative*, JSOT Supplement Series 231 (Sheffield: Sheffield Academic Press, 1997), 124, 158, 171–78.

19. "Sometimes the [gentile] priests secretly take gold and silver from their gods and spend it on themselves, or even give some of it to the prostitutes on the terrace" (English translation NRSV).

20. *Jubilees*, in *The Book of Jubilees*, ed. James C. Vanderkam, 2 vols., Corpus Scriptorum Christianorum Orientalium 510–11, Scriptures Aethiopici 88–89 (Louvain: Peeters, 1989); English translation O. S. Wintermute, "Jubilees," *Old Testament Pseudepigrapha*, vol. 2, ed. James H. Charlesworth (New York: Doubleday, 1985). Jubilees is a pseudepigraphical work usually dated to the mid-second century B.C.E. Though the full text survives only in Ethiopic (Ge'ez), portions survive in Hebrew, Greek, and Latin. Apparently, the text was quite popular among the sectarian Jews at Qumran, as fragments of fifteen separate copies were found there. It was also

cited by various church fathers. A basic introduction to the work may be found in Emil Schürer, *The History of The Jewish People in the Age of Jesus Christ (175 B.C.–A.D. 135)*, ed. Geza Vermes and Fergus Millar (Edinburgh: T. & T. Clark, 1973), vol. 3, part 1, 308–18.

21. Compare *Sib. Or.* 3.762–765: the Jews were exhorted to shun unlawful worship, avoid adultery and intercourse with males, and to rear their own children. See discussion in Erich S. Gruen, "Jews, Greeks, and Romans," 15–36.

22. On Josephus' polemic against idolatry, see Kasher, "Polemic and Apologetic Methods," 147–50.

23. 4Q166–7, in J. M. Allegro and A. A. Anderson, eds., *Discoveries in the Judaean Desert of Jordan, V:I (4Q158–4Q186)* (Oxford: Oxford University Press, 1968); English translation with commentary Geza Vermes, *The Complete Dead Sea Scrolls in English* (New York: Penguin Books, 1997); see also corrections to the edition published in *DJD V* in John Strugnell, "Notes en marge du volume V des *Discoveries in the Judaean Desert of Jordan*," *RQ 7* (1970):163–276. Also see CD 1.13–15, 4.13–18.

24. See discussion in Louis H. Feldman, *Jew and Gentile*, 79–83. On the problem of identifying Philo as representative of "Hellenistic Judaism," see Judith Romney Wegner, "Philo's Portrayal of Women—Hebraic or Hellenic," in *Women Like This: New Perspectives on Jewish Women in the Greco-Roman World*, ed. Amy-Jill Levine (Atlanta: Scholars Press, 1991), 41–66.

25. Who were these women? Eskenazi and Judd argue that their identity is not actually specified since the women are said to be *like* the people of the land, not necessarily identical to them. Still, this nuance was not preserved in the Septuagint. See Tamara C. Eskenazi and Eleanore P. Judd, "Marriage to a Stranger in Ezra 9–10," in *Second Temple Studies*, vol. 2, *Temple Community in the Persian Period*, ed. Tamara C. Eskenazi and Kent H. Richards, JSOT Supplement Series 175 (Sheffield: JSOT Press, 1994), 266–72. Shaye J. D. Cohen, *The Beginnings of Jewishness: Boundaries, Varieties, Uncertainties* (Berkeley and Los Angeles: University of California Press, 1999), notes that these women cannot have been Canaanites, Hittites, Perizites, or Jubusites for these peoples no longer existed in Israel (244). Whether these women were truly "foreign" (members of other nations) or Judean/Israelite women, they were identified as unacceptable by a discursive link to the (allegedly abominable) practices of gentiles. In other words, "foreign" or not, they had become *like* foreigners and hence could not be tolerated. Or so Ezra's biographer suggested.

26. The author of Ezra seems to have invented a suitable commandment by paraphrasing Leviticus 18:24–30 and Deuteronomy 7:3–4. Leviticus 18 condemns the (alleged) abominations of the Canaanites and the Egyptians; Deuteronomy 7 forbids Israelites to marry members of the seven Canaanite nations they were instructed to destroy. For discussion, see Cohen, *Jewishness*, 243–44; Christine Hayes, "Intermarriage and Impurity in Ancient Jewish Sources," *Harvard Theological Review* 92, no. 1 (1999): 10–13; Jonathan Klawans, *Impurity and Sin in Ancient Judaism* (Oxford: Oxford University Press, 2000), 43–45.

27. For an interesting reading of the use of these terms ("holy seed," "menstruous"), see Harold C. Washington, "Israel's Holy Seed and the Foreign Women of Ezra-Nehemiah: A Kristevan Reading," *Biblical Interpretation* 11 (2003): 427–37.

28. Hayes, "Intermarriage," 13.

29. Klawans, *Impurity*, 45.

30. Klawans, *Impurity*, 43–66.

31. Michael Satlow also views Ezra's wholesale denunciation of "foreign wives" as novel: "Ezra rocked the boat. He came to Judah waving a flag of ideological purity, bearing the latest platform of the 'YHWH alone' party." From Satlow's perspective, this insistence on endogamy helped Ezra to realize his revolutionary agenda; he united his sympathizers and ostracized his critics by claiming to revive the "old" traditions of the "good" men of Israel who obeyed God's endogamous commands; see Satlow, *Jewish Marriage in Antiquity* (Princeton, N.J.: Princeton University Press, 2001), 138–39. Ezra seems to have shared a strategy that would later be adopted by the Emperor Augustus, if Catherine Edwards and Thomas McGinn are correct. See discussion of the Augustan marriage legislation in chapter 2.

32. Claudia V. Camp, *Wise, Strange, and Holy: The Strange Woman and the Making of the Bible*, JSOT Supplement Series 320 (Sheffield: Sheffield Academic Press, 2000), 32. Shaye J. D. Cohen suggests that the context of post-exilic Judaism led to this new condemnation of intermarriage, "In the wake of the destruction of the temple in 587 B.C.E., Judaea lost any semblance of political independence, the tribal structure of the society was shattered, and the Israelites were scattered among the nations. In these new circumstances marriage with outsiders came to be seen as a threat to Judaean (Jewish) identity and was widely condemned. The Judaeans sensed that their survival depended upon their ideological (or religious) and social separation from the outside world" (*Jewishness*, 261). A similar interpretation is offered by Philip F. Esler, "Ezra-Nehemiah as a Narrative of (Re-invented) Israelite Identity," *Biblical Interpretation* 11 (2003): 413–26. See also Daniel L. Smith-Christopher, "The Mixed Marriage Crisis in Ezra 9–10 and Nehemiah 13: A Study of the Sociology of the Post-Exilic Judaean Community," in *Second Temple Studies*, vol. 2, *Temple Community in the Persian Period*, ed. Tamara C. Eskenazi and Kent H. Richards, JSOT Supplement Series 175 (Sheffield: JSOT Press, 1994), 243–65. With the assistance of sociological theory, Smith-Christopher argues that the "mixed marriage crisis," as represented in Ezra, may reflect an inter-Judaean debate regarding the identity of the community itself.

33. See Amy-Jill Levine, "Diaspora as Metaphor: Bodies and Boundaries in the Book of Tobit," in *Diaspora Jews and Judaism: Essays in Honor of and in Dialogue with Thomas A. Kraabel*, ed. J. Andrew Overman and Robert S. MacLenham (Atlanta: Scholars Press, 1992), 105–17.

34. Pseudo-Aristeas, in *Aristeae Ad Philocratum epistula cum ceteris de orignie versions LXX interpretum testimonis*, ed. Paul Wendland, Bibliotheca scriptorum Graecorum et Romanorum Teubneriana (Leipzig: Teubner, 1900), 129. For background, see Schürer, *The History*, 677–87.

35. See discussion in Betsy Halpern Amaru, *The Empowerment of Women in the Book of Jubilees*, Supplements to the Journal for the Study of Judaism 60 (Leiden: E. J. Brill, 1999), 5–7, 27–28, 37, 114, 147.

36. See esp. Alice Bach, *Women, Seduction, and Betrayal in Biblical Narrative* (Cambridge: Cambridge University Press, 1997), 28–32. On the Jews of Qumran, see Klawans, *Impurity*, 67–88. He concludes that, to the Qumran sectarians, "What is evil is impure, what is impure is demonic, and foreigners are impure." See also Hayes, "Intermarriage," 24–34.

37. See Sacha Stern, *Jewish Identity in Early Rabbinic Writings*, Arbeiten zur Geschichte des antiken Judentums und des Urchristentums 23 (Leiden: E. J. Brill, 1994), 159–70. But, according to Shaye J. D. Cohen, the Talmudim were aware that a blanket prohibition of marriage to gentiles was a departure from the Torah and debated its relevance. In the end, marriage to a non-Israelite woman was "rendered unproblematic by rabbinic exegesis: the woman, of course, had to convert to Judaism first," see *Jewishness*, 242–62, quotation from 262.

38. I borrow the term "moral impurity" from Klawans. He distinguishes between those acts deemed morally impure and those deemed ritually impure. Moral impurity "results from committing certain acts so heinous that they are explicitly referred to in biblical sources as defiling." Such acts lead to the expulsion of the people from the land. This type of impurity is to be contrasted with ritual impurity that is impermanent and can be ameliorated. Klawans, *Impurity and Sin*, 26–31.

39. Compare *T. Naph.* 3.5: "Do not become like Sodom, which departed from the order of nature." *T. Levi.* 14.8, becoming "like Sodom and Gomorrah" results in God's wrath; Jude 7; 2 Pet 2:6; Rev 11:8. See discussion in Fields, *Sodom and Gomorrah*, esp. 181–82. The origin and date of the *Testament of the Twelve Patriarchs* is disputed. See H. D. Slingerland, *The Testaments of the Twelve Patriarchs: A Critical History of Research* (Missoula, Mont.: Scholars Press, 1977). The assertion by Philo that the sins of Sodom were, by and large, sexual in nature may have been a departure from earlier interpretations that stressed the power of God's wrath rather than Sodom's sin; see, for example, Amos 4:11; Isa 1:9–10, 13:19; Jer 49:18; Lam 4:6; Zeph 2:9; Deut 29:22, 32:32.

40. Philo *Contempl.* 59–63. For a discussion of the meaning of the condemnation of Sodom in Genesis, see Robin Scroggs, *The New Testament and Homosexuality* (Philadelphia: Fortress

Press, 1983), 73–75 and Boswell, *Christianity, Social Tolerance, and Homosexuality*, 92–97. Boswell argues that the original story did not imply a judgment on the basis of sexual or homosexual sin.

41. In a study of the construction of gender in Philo, Judith Romney Wegner notes that Philo adopted a whole host of Greek cultural assumptions when discussing men and women. Men have "masculine thoughts" that are "wise, sound, just, prudent, pious, filled with freedom and boldness and kin to wisdom." Women, on the other hand, have "irrational" and "bestial passions." "Philo's Portrayal of Women," 53–55 (discussing Philo *Quaest. Gen.* 4.15).

42. "The [Jewish] law recognizes no sexual intercourse except the natural union of man and wife, and that only for the procreation of children. And it abhors that of men towards men" (Joseph *Ap.* 199).

43. David Baile, *Eros and the Jews: From Biblical Israel to Contemporary America* (New York: Basic Books, 1992), 37–40. The degree to which Jews of the Hellenistic and Roman periods shared the sex-gender assumptions of their Hellenized and Romanized neighbors cannot easily be determined. As Wegner has noted, both Greco-Roman culture and rabbinic Judaism tended to polarize male and female attributes, identifying "male" with "wise" or "wisdom" and "female" with "perception" or "intuition," but the cultural-historical workings of these polarizations should not be assumed to be identical. Nevertheless, she attempts to discern which of Philo's attitudes about gender reflect Greek concerns and which were distinctively Jewish. Some of Philo's language and assumptions appear to be derived from his Greek education. For example, Philo adopted the Aristotelian view that females are weaker, colder, and less capable of virtue (which is, after all, a male attribute). Still, his views on sexual morality and the arrangement of the family were, she argues, "clearly not Hellenic but uncompromisingly Judaic" (Wegner, "Philo's Portrayal," 53–66).

Which is it, then, "Jewish" or "Hellenic"? Still, Wegner is responding here to an argument of some Christian feminists that Pauline strictures on women reflect Paul's "Jewishness." By arguing that Greco-Roman cultural norms were as restrictive, if not more restrictive, than those of rabbinical Jews, placing Philo's arguments about the inherent weaknesses of women in the context of Greco-Roman rather than Jewish norms, Wegner does serious damage to these Christian interpretations, which is, I suspect, her larger goal; see Judith Plaskow, "Anti-Judaism in Feminist Christian Interpretation," in *Searching the Scriptures*, vol. 1, *A Feminist Introduction*, ed. Elizabeth Schüssler Fiorenza (New York: Crossroad Publishing Company, 1997), 117–29. Similarly, an analysis of the portrayal of women in Josephus's *Biblical Antiquities* found that Josephus refashioned female Biblical characters in light of Greco-Roman ideals of womanhood; Betsy Halpern Amaru, "Portraits of Biblical Women in Josephus' *Biblical Antiquities*," *Journal of Jewish Studies* 39 (1988): 143–70. Still, there can be no doubt that Josephus wrote his *Biblical Antiquities* as a Jew. After all, *Biblical Antiquities* is a retelling of the stories of the Hebrew Bible! Perhaps attempts to discern what is "Jewish" or "Greek" or "Greco-Roman" within the writings of a particular Jewish author, in the end, obfuscates rather than clarifies matters.

44. Michael L. Satlow, "Rhetoric and Assumptions: Romans and Rabbis on Sex," in *Jews in a Graeco-Roman World*, ed. Martin Goodman (Oxford: Clarendon Press, 1998), 138.

45. Satlow, "Rhetoric," 137–44.

46. Satlow, "Rhetoric," 143; Michael L. Satlow, *Tasting the Dish: Rabbinic Rhetorics of Sexuality*, Brown Judaic Studies 33 (Atlanta: Scholars Press, 1995), 315–19. And yet the rabbis also imagined themselves as the wives of God, the feminine partner in an erotic relationship with an active male deity, an anxiety-producing fantasy that requires the hiding of God's genitals, the displacement of this "love" onto a feminized attribute of God (wisdom, for example), through feminizing the man by means of circumcision, and other strategies. See Eilberg-Schwartz, *God's Phallus*, esp. 163–96.

47. Additions to the Book of Esther 14:15–16 (NRSV). The rabbis also found it necessary to emphasize the "Jewishness" of Esther; see Leila Leah Bronner, "Esther Revisited: An Aggadic Approach," in *A Feminist Companion to Esther, Judith, and Susanna*, ed. Athalya Brenner, Feminist Companion to the Bible 7 (Sheffield: Sheffield Academic Press, 1995), 176–97.

48. I have been influenced here by the comparison of Esther and Judith in Bach, *Women, Seduction, and Betrayal,* 189–204.

49. Amy-Jill Levine offers a similar analysis of these Hellenistic Jewish texts, with particular attention to Susanna, a Hellenistic addition to Daniel. See her "'Hemmed in on Every Side': Jews and Women in the Book of Susanna," in *A Feminist Companion to Esther, Judith, and Susanna,* ed. Athalya Brenner, Feminist Companion to the Bible 7 (Sheffield: Sheffield Academic Press, 1995), 303–23.

50. This argument is also employed by 3 Maccabees. When the Greek-Egyptian General Ptolemy threatened to enter the temple, "Young women who had been secluded in their chambers rushed out with their mothers, sprinkled their hair with dust, and filled the streets with groans and lamentations" (3 Macc 1:18; NRSV). In other words, the chaste virgins of Jerusalem were forced by Ptolemy's shocking threat to abandon their modesty. This act was interpreted as shaming Ptolemy, not the virgins.

51. On Potipher's wife, see Bach, *Women, Seduction, and Betrayal,* 34–81; on Jezebel, see esp. Phyllis Trible, *God and the Rhetoric of Sexuality* (Philadelphia: Fortress Press, 1978).

52. Levine, "'Hemmed in on Every Side,'" 310.

53. Later rabbinic literature continued the same theme. Desire was viewed as an "evil impulse" that must be controlled through a disciplined study of Torah, similar to the position held by Greek moralists who argued that the passions should be disciplined through the study of philosophy. The condemnation of male homoerotic sex for reasons of purity in Leviticus gave way in rabbinic discourse to a more pointed critique of the passive partner in the sexual act, analogous to the Greek and Roman concern with the *kinaidos* (Satlow, "Rhetoric," 142; Satlow, *Tasting,* 194–97; Plaskow, *Standing Again,* 179. Compare Muson. 3, 4, 6, 8, 12; [Plutarch] *Mor.* 1a–14c). John Boswell has called into question the notion that Leviticus intended to condemn male homosexual sex per se. Rather, Leviticus was more interested in ritual uncleanliness and producing Jewish distinctiveness (*Christianity, Social Tolerance, and Homosexuality,* 99–101). Unlike Greek and Roman moralistic and medical texts, however, biblical texts do not mention female homoerotic acts at all, and rabbinic texts only rarely. Noted by Rebecca Alpert, *Like Bread on the Seder Plate: Jewish Lesbians and the Transformation of Tradition* (New York: Columbia University Press, 1997), 36; and Plaskow, *Standing,* 182. Also see Rachel Biale, *Women and Jewish Law: The Essential Texts, their History, and their Relevance for Today* (New York: Schocken Books, 1995), 192–97. When female homoerotic sex is mentioned, it is to compare Jewish and gentile practices: "You shall not copy the practices of the land of Egypt ... or the land of Canaan ... Scripture says, 'nor shall you follow their laws.' I am only talking about those laws that are legislated for them and for their fathers and for their fathers' fathers. And what would they do? A man would marry a man; a woman [would marry a] woman; and a man would marry a woman and her daughter; and a woman would marry two [men]" (*Sifra Ahare* 9:8, cited and translated by Satlow, *Tasting,* 188). Also see Mark D. Smith, "Ancient Bisexuality and the Interpretation of Romans 1:26–27," *JAAR* 64 (1996), 242.

54. Stern, *Jewish Identity,* 23–26. By contrast, Jews are nonpromiscuous, the paternity of Jewish children is never in doubt, Jewish men never commit adultery in the presence of their wives, and incest never occurs.

55. Compare Paul's use of παραδίδωμι in Rom 1:18–32 to indicate the punishment that idolaters receive—abandonment to their lusts (discussed in more detail below).

56. For an indication of the influence of Paul among later "church fathers," see the numerous citations of Paul listed in the *Biblia Patristica: Index des citations et allusions bibliques dans la litterature patristique,* 3 vols. (Paris: Université des science humaines de Strasbourg, 1975). See also William S. Babcock, ed., *Paul and the Legacies of Paul* (Dallas, Tex.: Southern Methodist University Press, 1990).

57. The purpose and intended audience of Romans is a topic of considerable debate. Paul himself states that his purpose is to "share some spiritual gift to you," "to reap some harvest among you," and "to proclaim the gospel to you in Rome" (1:11, 13, 15). I am persuaded by the

work of those scholars who argue that all of Paul's letters, including Romans, were intended primarily for a gentile audience; see Stanley Stowers *Rereading Romans: Justice, Jews, and Gentiles* (New Haven, Conn.: Yale University Press, 1994), 227–50; Lloyd Gaston, *Paul and the Torah* (Vancouver: University of British Columbia Press, 1987;) John Gager, *Reinventing Paul* (Oxford: Oxford University Press, 2000). Indeed, this perspective helps to explain why Paul never singles out Judean sexual practice for condemnation. Paul seems to have accepted the view that Judeans were by definition more capable of sexual morality than other people. This may be taken as further evidence that Paul was seeking to distinguish between Judean practice and gentile practice while simultaneously inviting gentiles to become a special sort of Judean-in-Christ, a new category that enabled gentiles to adopt "good" morals one they became the adopted sons of God. See further Hodge, " 'If Sons, Then Heirs,' " esp. 56–89. For a summary of earlier scholarship regarding the purpose of Romans, see the helpful summary by James D. G. Dunn, *Romans 1–8*, Word Biblical Commentary 38 (Dallas, Tex.: Word Books, 1988).

58. See John Ziesler, *Paul's Letter to the Romans* (London: SCM Press; Philadelphia: Trinity Press International, 1989), 33–35; Dunn, *Romans 1–8*, lix; R. Dean Anderson Jr., *Ancient Rhetorical Theory and Paul*, rev. ed. (Leuven: Peeters, 1998), 207–8. All of Paul's letters contain common epistolary formulae (introduction, thanksgiving, reproof, disclosure, request, transition, greeting, and farewell, for example); see John Coolidge Hurd Jr., *The Origin of 1 Corinthians* (London: S.P.C.K., 1965; reprint, Atlanta: Mercer University Press, 1983), xix (page citations are to the reprint edition); Stowers, *Letter Writing*.

59. Robert Jewett, "Romans as an Ambassadorial Letter," *Interpretation* 36 (1982): 5–20. Jewett argues that Paul's letter combines several genres, but, overall, it should be identified as an "ambassadorial letter." See also Robert Jewett, "Following the Argument of Romans," in *The Romans Debate*, ed. Karl Donfried, rev. ed. (Peabody, Mass.: Hendrickson, 1991), 265–77. Stowers has also connected Paul's letters to Greek letter-writing techniques (*Letter Writing*).

60. The Cynic-Stoic scheme was argued most famously by Rudolf Bultmann, *Der Stil der Paulischen Predigt und die kyniche-stoische Diatribe* (Göttingen: Vandenhoeck & Ruprecht, 1910). Bultmann's original thesis received a thorough critique and reformulation by Stanley Stowers, *The Diatribe and Paul's Letter to the Romans*, SBL Dissertation Series 57 (Atlanta: Scholars Press, 1981). But, see the critique of Bultmann in Karl Paul Donfried, "False Presuppositions in the Study of Romans," *Catholic Biblical Quarterly* 36 (1974): 232–355, and the critique of both Bultmann and Stowers found in R. Dean Anderson, *Ancient Rhetorical Theory and Paul*, 201–5, 242–44.

61. Mark D. Jordan, "Ancient Philosophic Protreptic and the Problem of Persuasive Genres," *Rhetorica* 4 (1986): 309–33; David Aune, "Romans as a Logos Protreptikos in the Context of Ancient Religious and Philosophical Propaganda," in *Paulus und das antike Judentum*, ed. Martin Hengel and Ulrich Heckel (Tübingen: Mohr/Siebeck, 1992), 91–121; Anthony J. Guerra, *Romans and the Apologetic Tradition: The Purpose, Genre, and Audience of Paul's Letter*, Society for New Testament Studies Monograph Series 81 (Cambridge: Cambridge University Press, 1995).

62. For example, suggesting that Romans contains three Pauline protreptic speeches, revised and then combined into a letter, David Aune proposed the following textual units: 1:16–4:25, 5:1–8:39, 12:1–15:13, with 9–11 containing an extended digression; see Aune, "Romans," 120. Ernst Käsemann avoided identifying Romans with a particular type of speech-letter genre, yet he offered similar divisions in his analysis of the letter (1:1–17, 1:18–3:20, 3:21–4:25, 5:1–8:39, 9:1–11:36, 12:1–15:13, 15:14–33, 16:1–27); Käsemann, *Commentary on Romans*, trans. Geoffrey W. Bromily (Grand Rapids, Mich.: William B. Eerdmans, 1980), 4–21, 33, 91, 131, 253, 323, 389, 409. See also Joseph A. Fitzmyer, *Romans*, Anchor Bible (New York: Doubleday, 1993), 98–101. Paul's letters are sometimes interpreted in light of the conventions of school rhetoric; see, for example, F. W. Hughes, "The Rhetoric of 1 Thessalonians," in *The Thessalonian Correspondence*, ed. Raymond F. Collins (Belgium: Leuven University Press, 1990), 94–116; W. Wuellner, "The Argumentative Structure of 1 Thessalonians as Paradoxical Encomium," in *The Thessalonian Correspondence*, ed. Raymond F. Collins (Belgium: Leuven University Press, 1990), 117–36; W. Wuellner, "Paul's

Rhetoric of Argumentation in Romans: An Alternative to the Donfried-Karris Debate Over Romans," *Catholic Biblical Quarterly* 38 (1976): 330–51; Jewett, *The Thessalonian Correspondence: Pauline Rhetoric and Millenarian Piety* (Philadelphia: Fortress Press, 1986); and Jewett, "Following the Argument." Others are skeptical of this sort of approach; see, for example, R. Dean Anderson, *Ancient Rhetorical Theory,* and Ziesler, *Paul's Letter.*

63. For example, Paul was fond of rhetorical questions that are similar to those found in Epictetus (Arr. *Epct. diss.* 1.29.64; 2.22.3–4). See Rom 2:3, 4, 21, 22; 3:1, 9; 4:1, 9, 10; 6:1; 15; 7:1, 7, 13; 8:31, 33, 34, 35; 9:14, 19, 20, 30; 10:14, 15; 11:7, 11; 14:4, 10. For further discussion, see Stowers, *Diatribe,* 125–54.

64. Various proposals regarding *the* central point of Romans (and of Paul's gospel more generally) have been offered. Perhaps the most influential have been Protestant readings of Paul that, following Martin Luther, find the doctrine of justification by grace through faith to be Paul's central message. For an overview, see Karl Donfried, ed., *The Romans Debate,* rev. ed. (Peabody, Mass.: Hendrickson, 1991). On the problems with these readings, see Gager, *Reinventing Paul;* Stowers, *Rereading;* Krister Stendahl, *Paul Among Jews and Gentiles* (Philadelphia: Fortress Press, 1976).

65. See Elizabeth A. Castelli, "Romans," in *Searching the Scriptures,* vol. 2, *A Feminist Commentary,* ed. Elizabeth Schüssler Fiorenza (New York: Crossroad, 1994), 280–84, 293–95.

66. Daniel Boyarin has presented a persuasive argument, parallel to my own, regarding the centrality of sex to Paul's argument in Romans, particularly in the context of Romans 5–7. In reference to Romans 7, Boyarin observes, "In my opinion, only the interpretation that Paul is speaking of sexual lust, inflamed by the positive commandment to procreate, which 'Sin' does indeed know how to exploit, accounts for such expressions as 'Law of Sin in our members' and all the talk here about inflamed passions." See his *Radical Jew,* 164.

67. The "unnatural lusts" discussed by Paul have received a great deal of attention in recent years, most prominently in the important study by Bernadette Brooten, *Love Between Women.* During the course of her study, Brooten argues that Paul adopted a widespread definition of "natural" gender, an argument that is fundamental to my own interpretation of this passage (see esp. 241–58, 264–80). I rely heavily on Brooten's treatment of this material throughout the discussion that follows. Nevertheless, my focus is slightly different. Rather than concerning myself with a description of what Paul meant when he denounced homoeroticism, I am interested in how Paul's polemic helped to construct difference between Christ followers and others in sexual terms. For an excellent collection of responses to Brooten, discussing the importance of her work and outlining various objections to it, see Elizabeth A. Castelli, ed., "Lesbian Historiography Before the Name?" *GLQ* 4 (1998): 557–630.

68. See Stowers, *Rereading,* 83–125; Brooten, *Love Between Women,* 215–66; Deirdre Good, "Commentary on *Love Between Women,* by Bernadette Brooten," in "Lesbian Historiography Before the Name?" ed. Elizabeth A. Castelli, *GLQ* 4 (1998): 604: "Romans 1.18–32 speaks not of original sin but of the consequences of earthly existence." This disagrees with Dunn; see C. K. Barrett, *A Commentary on the Epistle to the Romans,* 2nd ed. (London: Black, 1991); Douglas J. Moo, *The Epistle to the Romans* (Grand Rapids, Mich.: Eerdmans, 1996); Richard B. Hays, *The Moral Vision of the New Testament: A Contemporary Introduction to New Testament Ethics* (San Francisco: HarperCollins, 1996). I am in agreement with Good and Stowers that Romans 1:18–32 does not refer to Adam or the results of an original sin.

69. I am hardly the first scholar to notice these connections. See, for example, E. P. Sanders, *Paul, the Law, and the Jewish People* (Philadelphia: Fortress Press, 1983), 123–35. Sanders concludes: "I think that the best way to read 1:18–2:29 is as a synagogue sermon.... . I find, in short, no distinctively Pauline imprint in 1:18–2:29" (129). For a similar argument, see Scroggs, *The New Testament and Homosexuality,* 109–18. Yet, on the identification of Rom 1:18–32 with "Jewishness," see Stowers, *Rereading,* 124–25: Describing Romans 1–2 as a "synagogue sermon," Sanders is able to eliminate it as having any bearing on Paul's *real* thought, which, to Sanders, cannot include the view that salvation depends upon obedience to the law. I find it interest-

ing that Sanders chooses to eliminate Romans 1–2 from his discussion of Paul and the law by claiming that Paul is utilizing entirely Jewish, pre-Christian traditions. Sanders's interpretation implies that Christianity supersedes Judaism and, therefore, Jewish arguments can be put aside, even Paul's Jewish arguments.

70. Questions of Paul's "Jewish identity" have been framed in a variety of ways, especially around the issue of the pre-Christian Jewish Paul and the postconversion Christian Paul. How Jewish was Paul once he came to view Jesus as the Messiah? How great a "conversion" was there? Responses to these questions include: (1) Paul remained a Jew but underwent a "cognitive shift" when he became a Messianic Jew who believed that Jesus was the Messiah. This shift "transformed" Paul's understanding of God and God's actions in the world: Beverly Gaventa, *From Darkness to Light* (Philadelphia: Fortress Press, 1986), esp. 33–46. (2) Paul remained a Jew, but a Jew who was called to be "apostle to the gentiles." He did not experience some dramatic conversion away from Judaism, rather, he experienced a special call: Stendahl, *Paul Among Jews and Gentiles*. (3) Paul did not reject Judaism entirely. He preserved the emphasis on obedience but made the basis of obedience of faith in God: Rudolf Bultmann, "Christ the End of the Law," *Beiträge zur Evangelischen Theologie* I (1940): 3–27. (4) Paul's ecstatic experiences, those that led him to "covert" to Messianic belief in Jesus, were thoroughly Jewish, as was his apocalypticism, though he gave up the law when he left Pharisaic Judaism for the sake of Christianity: Alan F. Segal, *Paul the Convert: The Apostolate and Apostasy of Saul the Pharisee* (New Haven, Conn.: Yale University Press, 1990). (5) Paul should be read as both Greek and Jew within the context of the "inner discourse of Jewish culture" (Boyarin, *A Radical Jew*, 12). Boyarin's positioning of Paul as always both Jewish and Greek, both Greek and Jewish, is helpful. Nevertheless, as Gager points out, Paul understood himself to be bringing gentiles in rather than rejecting Judaism in any way. Indeed, Paul presumes Judean privilege vis-à-vis God (Gager, *Reinventing*).

71. Joseph Fitzmyer thinks that, given the explicit reference to the Jews in Rom 2:1, Paul must have had non-Jewish humanity in mind (*Romans*, 270). Fitzmyer calls this section "God's Wrath Against Pagans." If it is true, as Malherbe, Stowers, and others have argued, that Paul was well acquainted with Greek rhetorical and philosophical traditions, then the fact that Paul never actually mentions "the Greeks" or "the gentiles" in this passage may mean that he particularly wanted his audience to think of them. Frederick Ahl has noticed that ancient authors, when they wanted to get a point across, often did the exact opposite of what contemporary authors are trained to do—they did not mention the point explicitly at all: Frederick Ahl, "The Art of Safe Criticism in Greece and Rome," *American Journal of Philology* 105, no. 2 (1984): 174–208. Rather, by means of "figured speech," (Demetr. *Eloc.* 289; Quint. *Inst.* 9.2.65–72) these authors sought to reproach without ever committing to an outright statement.

72. See, for example, Wis. Sol. 15:18, Philo *Decal.* 76–80 and *Contempl.* 8. See discussion in Brooten, *Love Between Women*, 231–32.

73. In addition to the sources discussed above, see *2 Apoc. Bar.* 54.17–18 and the Ep. Jer.

74. See, for example, Rom 3:24–26; 4:23–25; 5:1–6, 18–21; 6:12–14.

75. Käsemann, *Romans*, rejects the view that *ta melē* refers to bodily parts here, preferring the interpretation "our capabilities" on the basis of 1 Cor 12:12–25. But see Martin, *Corinthian Body*, 92–96.

76. Stowers, *Rereading*, 255–58, sees the language and argumentation of Rom 6 as intentionally linked to the language and imagery of Rom 1:18–32.

77. Boyarin, *A Radical Jew*, 158–70, suggests that, in Rom 5–8, "sin" is "sex."

78. Bradley, *Slave and Society at Rome*, 66. Also see Peter Garnsey, "Legal Privilege in the Roman Empire," in *Studies in Ancient Society*, ed. Moses I. Finley (London: Routledge and Kegan Paul, 1974), 141–65.

79. Arist. *Pol.* 1260a4–1260b8; Ach. Tat. 7.10; Plin. *HN* 35

80. According to Paul, the Roman gentiles in Christ seem to have emulated the miseducated sons described by an anonymous non-Christian moralist in their previous life (cited in chapter 1 above). That author's solution to the problem—careful education and upbringing, training

in philosophy—contrasts with Paul's "enslavement to God." According to this contemporary of Paul, good training (*agōgē spoudaia*) and a proper education (*paideia nomimos*) will establish virtue (*arethē*) and lead towards happiness, preventing sons from falling into the licentious, "slavish" excess ([Plutarch] *Mor.* 5D).

81. See Glancy, *Slavery*, 9–38.

82. Epictetus (Arr. *Epct. diss.* 2.1.28) makes a similar point: "Have you no master? Have you not as your master money, or a girl, or a boy, or the tyrant or some friend of the tyrant?" To Epictetus, "slave" and "master" hold, ultimately, an improper and unimportant distinction, since all are sons of Zeus yet can become enslaved by desire: "How can you be my master? Zeus has set me free. Or do you really think that he was likely to let his own son be made a slave? You are, however, master of my dead body, take it" (1.9.9; Oldfather's translation). Compare Rom 8:9–17 and Gal 3:21–4:7.

83. Rom 7:5, 6:6, 6:19, 6:21: "But then what fruit did you get for the things about which you are now ashamed?"

84. Dale B. Martin, "Paul Without Passion: On Paul's Rejection of Desire in Sex and Marriage," in *Constructing Early Christian Families*, ed. Halvor Moxnes (London: Routledge, 1997), 207–10.

85. Rom 7:5. Compare Sen. *Ep.* 16, 17; Plut. *Mor.* 76b–d, 78e–79, 83a–e; Muson. 4, 6.

86. Compare 1 Cor 7:22: "For whoever was called in the Lord as a slave is a freed person belonging to Lord. Likewise, just as whoever was free when called is a slave of Christ." Gal 3:28: "There is neither Jew nor Greek, there is neither slave nor free, there is not male or female; for you are all one in Christ Jesus" (NRSV). Gal 4:7: "So through God you are no longer a slave but a son, and if a son then an heir."

87. Dale B. Martin, *Slavery as Salvation: The Metaphor of Slavery in Pauline Christianity* (New Haven, Conn.: Yale University Press, 1990), 30–49.

88. Castelli, "Romans," 293–95, and Martin, *Slavery*, 50–51.

89. Martin, *Slavery*, 63.

90. Martin, *Slavery*, 148. I agree with Martin that Paul's references to slavery can be read as a challenge to status assumptions. Still, in my opinion, Martin's analysis does not adequately account for the problems raised by Paul's attempt to level or even reverse the status of the brothers and sisters "in Christ" while, at the same time, making strict sexual, gender-normative behavior an important mark of Christian identity (see my discussion of 1 Corinthians, below). My reading of Paul, especially of his letters to the Romans and the Corinthians, suggests that Paul worked within his larger cultural framework—a framework in which sex, gender, and status are inextricably linked—in such a way that hierarchical distinctions were often maintained, not challenged. Paul may have metaphorically referred to slavery as a positive state, yet he did so not only (or even principally) to undermine the status presuppositions that supported slave ownership within Greco-Roman households.

91. Hans Dieter Betz warns against reading Galatians through Romans, arguing that the passage in Romans is much more subtle and complex than what Paul presents in Galatians 5. See his *Galatians: A Commentary on Paul's Letter to the Churches of Galatia*, Hermeneia (Philadelphia: Fortress Press, 1979), 272 n. 16. Still, I would counter that the similarity in language, if not complexity, can aid in understanding Paul's use of the flesh/spirit dualism, even if Paul offers a much less complete argument in Galatians. Betz himself recognizes this, stating that the flesh/spirit dichotomy as it appears in Galatians represents "in a very concise form one of the fundamental anthropological doctrines of Paul" (278).

92. Are Christian women included here? Can they too become "sons"? Castelli, "Romans," 291–92, relying upon an unpublished paper of Kathleen Corley, suggests not.

93. See Hodge, "If Sons, Then Heirs," esp. 58–75. She suggests that Paul employed a language of kinship and ethnicity to assert that the gentiles-in-Christ have become the "sons of Abraham" and the "sons of God." To Paul, then, becoming a Christ follower meant becoming a descendant of Abraham since "the concept of replacing Israel with a new people would never have occurred to Paul" (223).

94. See also Rom 5:1–5, 18–19; 6:6–7, 11, 12–14, 18, 22; 8:2–4, 9, 11, 14, 30; 10:11–12; 12:1, 6–8, 9–13, 16–18; 13:9–10.

95. Women within the Christian community ought to submit to men while maintaining control (*exousia*) over themselves and their desires (1 Cor 11:2–16). Likewise, men ought to have authority over their desires, and all Christians should submit their "members" to God, choosing God as their master rather than food or sexual desire (1 Cor 6:1–20). Moreover, slaves ought to remain enslaved even though they have gained new status as "slaves," "freedmen," and even "sons" of Christ (1 Cor 7:17–24).

96. Rom 1:18, 2:5, 5:9, 9:22, 12:19; 1 Thess 1:10, 2:16. Compare 1 Cor 5:5, 6:9–11. On Paul's eschatological viewpoint, see J. Christiaan Beker, *Paul the Apostle: The Triumph of God in Life and Thought* (Philadelphia: Fortress Press, 1980); and also Beker, *Paul's Apocalyptic Gospel* (Philadelphia: Fortress Press, 1982).

97. On Hellenistic theories of kingship that justify rule, in part, on the basis of virtue, see the essays collected in Per Bilde et al., eds. *Aspects of Hellenistic Kingship*, Studies in Hellenistic Civilization 7 (Aarhus: Aarhus University Press, 1996); Richard A. Billows, *Kings and Colonists: Aspects of Macedonian Imperialism*, Columbia Studies in the Classical Tradition 22 (Leiden: E. J. Brill, 1995), 56–70; and Helen S. Lund, *Lysimachus: A Study in Early Hellenistic Kingship* (London: Routledge, 1992), 153–83.

98. Hor. *Carm.* 4.5.

99. See Simon Price, *Rituals and Power: The Roman Imperial Cult in Asia Minor* (Cambridge: Cambridge University Press, 1984), esp. 2–5, 49–51, 53–62, 243–46; Fears, "The Cult of the Virtues"; Beard, North, and Price, *Religions of Rome*, 313–63.

100. English translation, Smallwood.

101. In this way, he adopted a strategy such as was recommended by the treatise "On Style" (Περὶ ἑρμηνείας). The author of "On Style" suggests that, when seeking to persuade a tyrant, one ought to either inveigh against the faults of some other tyrant or praise persons who have acted in an opposite way, thereby avoiding direct reference to the faults of the addressee while commending the behavior one seeks to encourage (Demetr. *Eloc.* 477). See Ahl, "The Art of Safe Criticism"; and D. M. Schenkeveld, *Studies in Demetrius* (Amsterdam: Adolf M. Hakkert, 1964), 116–34. For a description of the circumstances surrounding Philo's *Legatio*, see Mary E. Smallwood, introduction to *Philonis Alexandrini: Legatio ad Gaium* (Leiden: E. J. Brill, 1961), 3–31. See also Emil Schürer, *The History of The Jewish People*.

102. See also Men. Rhet. 367.5–8; Dio Chrys. *Or.* 1.14. For discussion, see Nixon and Rodgers, *In Praise of Later Roman Emperors*, 22–23; North, "Canons and Hierarchies," 177–80.

103. See, for example, Martin Luther, "Admonition to Peace, A Reply to the Twelve Articles of the Peasants of Swabia, 1525" in *Luther's Works*, trans. Charles M. Jacobs, rev. and ed. Robert C. Schultz, American Edition (Philadelphia: Fortress Press, 1967), 46:25: "The fact that the rulers are wicked and unjust does not excuse disorder and rebellion, for the punishing of wickedness is not the responsibility of everyone, but of worldly rulers who bear the sword. Thus Paul says in Romans 13 and Peter in 1 Peter, that the rulers are instituted by God for the punishment of the wicked." Also see Martin Luther, "Temporal Authority," in *Luther's Works*, trans. Charles M. Jacobs, rev. and ed. Robert C. Schultz, American Edition (Philadelphia: Fortress Press, 1967), 1.1, 5. More recently, Anthony Guerra argues that Rom 13:1–7 should be read as a piece of traditional political apologetic in which Paul, responding to the concrete sociopolitical conditions in Rome, urges the Roman Christians to remain loyal and dutiful in their fulfillment of their civic obligations (*Romans*, 160–64).

104. For further discussion of Rom 13:1–7, see Walter E. Pilgrim, *Uneasy Neighbors: Church and State in the New Testament* (Minneapolis: Fortress Press, 1999), 8–12, 27–35. Pilgrim assesses the most common approaches to this passage and places Paul's argument within Jewish and early Christian "loyalty traditions." See also Wengst, *Pax Romana*, 76–82; Richard A. Horsley, ed. *Paul and Empire: Religion and Power in Roman Imperial Society* (Harrisburg, Penn.: Trinity Press International, 1997); and Dieter Georgi, "Who is the True Prophet?" *Harvard Theological*

Review 79 (1986): 100–126. For a discussion of Paul's relativizing attitude toward living in the world, see Wimbush, *Paul*, 66–96. See also Richard Valantasis, "Competing Ascetic Subjectivities in the Letter to the Galatians," in *The New Testament and Asceticism*, ed. Leif E. Vaage and Vincent L. Wimbush (New York: Routledge, 1999), 211–25.

105. For example, "It is well for a man not to touch a woman," 1 Cor 7:1 and "All things are lawful," 1 Cor 10:23. But see Bruce N. Fisk, "Πορνευειν as Bodily Violation: The Unique Nature of Sexual Sin in 1 Corinthians 6.18," *New Testament Studies* 42 (1996): 540–41. For a summary of various proposals regarding instances when Paul may be quoting the Corinthian Christians, see Hurd, *The Origin of 1 Corinthians*, 68; Barrett, *A Commentary*, 144–46; Hans Conzelmann, *1 Corinthians*, trans. James W. Leitch, Hermeneia (Philadelphia: Fortress Press, 1975), 108.

106. 1 Cor 7:1: "concerning the matter about which you wrote"; 1 Cor. 1:11: "it has been reported to me"; 1 Cor 5:1: "it is actually reported that." Paul's responses to reports and letters may include: reports about divisions (1:10–4:21), sexual immorality among the Christians (5:1–12), and visits to law courts (6:1–11); a letter with questions about sexual asceticism (7:1–40), food and eating (8:4–12, 11:17–34), idolatry (8:1–12, 10:1–11:1), veiling (11:2–16), spiritual gifts (12:1–31), and proper behavior during worship (14:1–33). For an analysis of the Paul-Corinthian correspondence, positing four letters from Paul (now incorporated into 1 and 2 Cor, with portions missing) and an imaginative reconstruction of the Corinthian side of this dialogue, see Calvin J. Roetzel, *The Letters of Paul: Conversations in Context* (Atlanta: John Knox Press, 1975), 42–51.

107. 1 Cor 7:1, 7:25, 8:1, 12:1, 16:1, 16:12. See Hurd, *The Origin of 1 Corinthians*, 63. See also Conzelmann, *1 Corinthians*, 6–15.

108. For example, Margaret Y. MacDonald, "The Social Setting of 1 Corinthians 7," *New Testament Studies* 36 (1990): 169–173; and Wire, *Corinthian Women Prophets*.

109. For example, Dieter Georgi, *The Opponents of Paul in Second Corinthians: A Study of Religious Propaganda in Antiquity* (Philadelphia: Fortress Press, 1986).

110. See, for example, Hurd, *The Origin of 1 Corinthians*; Conzelmann, *1 Corinthians*; Ben Witherington III, *Conflict and Community in Corinth: A Socio-Rhetorical Commentary on 1 and 2 Corinthians* (Grand Rapids, Mich.: Eerdmans, 1995); Ralph Bruce Terry, *A Discourse Analysis of First Corinthians* (Arlington, Tex.: Summer Institute of Linguistics, 1995).

111. 2 Cor 6:14–7:1 may be a non-Pauline tradition that was inserted into the letter, perhaps even by Paul. See discussion in Schüssler Fiorenza, *In Memory of Her*, 194–96. I am following Schüssler Fiorenza in interpreting this passage to be a prohibition against marriage with gentile outsiders. 2 Cor 6:14 finds an echo in 1 Cor 7:39, which suggests that a believing widow, if she marries again, should marry "in the Lord."

112. The integrity of the Paul's Corinthian letters, especially of 2 Cor, is sometimes questioned. Some scholars have argued that 1 and 2 Cor contain not two relatively complete Pauline letters, but four or more letters that were later combined in a haphazard manner. For a summary of these arguments, see Roetzel, *The Letters of Paul*; Conzelmann, *1 Corinthians*, 3–6; and Hurd, *The Origin of 1 Corinthians*, 68. The coherence of 1 Cor is more commonly accepted (see Witherington, *Conflict and Community*, 73–77).

113. See Elizabeth A. Castelli, *Imitating Paul* on the impact and intent of this sort of language.

114. The NRSV renders "a man has his father's woman" as "a man is living with his father's wife" but this translation is misleading. Though "gunē" may mean "wife," it also means simply "woman"; no contextual clues to indicate that she was a "wife." See further Wire, "1 Corinthians," in *A Feminist Commentary*, vol. 2, *Searching the Scriptures*, ed. Elisabeth Schüssler Fiorenza (New York: Crossroad, 1996), 166–7, Glancy, *Slavery*, 63–64.

115. See Lev 18:7–8; Deut 22:30, 27:20; *D* 23.8.12, Ulpian; *D* 23.14, Paul.

116. See, for example, Walter Schmithals, *Paul and the Gnostics*, trans. John E. Steely (Nashville: Abingdon Press, 1972), 96–100, 111; Jerome Murphy-O'Conner, *1 Corinthians*, New Testament Message 10 (Wilmington, N.C.: Michael Glazier, 1979), 40–42, 60; John J. Kilgallen, *First Corinthians: An Introduction and Study Guide* (New York: Paulist Press, 1987), 40–43, 67; Barrett, *A Commentary*, 120–21, 153.

117. A number of scholars have suggested that a significant age gap between husbands and wives was common during this period; moreover, eligible girls were frequently married quite young (perhaps as young as twelve in some cases, though this is debated). See, for example, Gardner, *Women In Roman Law*, 38; Raditsa, "Augustus' Legislation," 317; Tim G. Parkin, *Demography and Roman Society* (Baltimore, Md.: Johns Hopkins University Press, 1992), 125; M. Keith Hopkins, "The Age of Roman Girls at Marriage," *Population Studies* 18 (1965): 309–27. On marriage to a former slave, see P. R. C. Weaver, "Children of Freedman (and Freedwomen)," in *Marriage, Divorce, and Children in Ancient Rome*, ed. Beryl Rawson (Oxford: Clarendon Press, 1991), 178–79; Treggiari, *Roman Marriage*, 52–54; Beryl Rawson, "Family Life Among the Lower Classes at Rome in the First Two Centuries of the Empire," *Classical Philology* 61 (1966): 71–83. On the inheritance of slaves (for example, a son inheriting the slaves of his father), see Glancy, *Slavery*, 10–11, 73–74.

118. See Conzelmann, *1 Corinthians*, 95. Still, the man will be the victim, should the Corinthians take his advice to "drive the wicked from among you" (1 Cor 5:13).

119. McGinn, *Prostitution, Sexuality, and the Law*, 78–82, 90.

120. For example, the Roman senate instructed the praetor of the province of Asia to "send letters to the people and states and to the kings written down above.... And he is to see, insofar as it be possible, that whatever letters he sends according to this statute, to whomever he sends them, be delivered according to this statute": M. Crawford, ed., *Roman Statutes* 12, Delphi copy, column B, II.20–26; cited, translated, and discussed by Clifford Ando, *Imperial Ideology and Provincial Loyalty*, Classics and Contemporary Thought 6 (Berkeley: University of California Press, 2000), 81–83 and 81 n. 26; Ando offers further examples, 82–90.

121. For example, Deut 22:24 (a man who lies with the betrothed of another shall be stoned, he and the woman both, "so shall you drive the wicked from among you"); compare *Jubilees* 33.13 (discussed by Gaca, *The Making of Fornication*, 141 n. 59). Gaca speculates that Paul may have intended for the community to kill this man, along the lines recommended in Deuteronomy: "It cannot be ruled out, however, that Paul aims to stir up zealots in the community to kill the man outright, problematic though such a procedure might be if the Roman authorities were to find out. Deuteronomic precedent requires the death penalty, which Paul cites in delivering his condemnation" (140). Conzelmann suggests that this man is to be "thrust out into the realm of wrath," meaning that Paul will let supernatural forces take care of the problem (*1 Corinthians*, 96).

122. These may be sayings popular among some in the Corinthian community; see Martin, *The Corinthian Body*, 175; Barrettt, *A Commentary*, 144; Conzelmann, *1 Corinthians*, 108; Hurd, *The Origin of 1 Corinthians*, 86; Raymond F. Collins, *First Corinthians*, Sacra Pagina Series 7 (Collegeville, Minn.: Liturgical Press, 1999), 241.

123. Muson. 18. See also Philo *Abr.* 133 on the gluttony and lasciviousness of the Sodomites. For an additional Pauline example, see Phil 2:17–21 ("their god is the belly and they glory in their shame").

124. Lucian *Nigr.* 15–16; [Plutarch] *Mor.* 5b–c; Plut. *Mor.* 145b; Plut. *Luc.* 39–41; Muson. 4; Poly. *Phil.* 31.25.5.

125. Dio Chrys. *Or.* 1.12–14.

126. For a careful discussion of Paul's language here—sinning against one's own body—see Fisk, "Πορνευειν as Bodily Violation," 545–50, 553–558. Fisk notes the parallel between this passage in Paul and the "sin against oneself" mentioned in Sir 19.2.

127. As Castelli puts it, "From the discussion of *porneia* beginning in chapter 5 and concluding in chapter 7, individual human bodies appear as sites of danger and contest, open to the powerful resignifying force of other bodies" : "Interpretations of Power in 1 Corinthians," *Semeia* 54 (1992): 210.

128. For an excellent discussion of the significance of this argument for slaves, see Jennifer A. Glancy, "Obstacles to Slaves' Participation in the Corinthian Church," *JBL* 117 (1998): 481–501.

129. The μαλακοί will not inherit the kingdom of God (1 Cor 6:9). Compare Rom 1:26–27. Brooten suggests that, to Paul, homoerotic sex violates "nature" because it violates hierarchical gender constructions that assume that the male must be the active, penetrating partner in sexual intercourse. See her *Love Between Women*, 275–80, 293–94, 300–302. See also 1 Cor 11:2–16 (Women ought to wear veils for, by nature and by creation, they are subordinate to men).

130. Paul's extended discussion of marriage, desire, virgins, and self-control in 1 Cor 7 received a great deal of attention among ancient Christians and it continues to fascinate scholars interested in Christian or Pauline approaches to marriage, celibacy, asceticism, women, and desire. For example, Vincent Wimbush views this passage as important evidence for Paul's principle of *hōs mē* (living in the world "as not"), a relativizing of the structures and demands of the world in favor of "the things of the Lord" (*Paul*, 73–98). Margaret MacDonald finds in 1 Cor 7 early evidence for pneumatic women who sought autonomy and spiritual authority by means of celibacy ("The Social Setting," 169–73). For a similar interpretation, see Joette Bassler, "1 Corinthians," in *The Women's Bible Commentary*, ed. Carol A. Newsom and Sharon H. Ringe (London: SPCK, 1992), 322. See also Boyarin, *A Radical Jew*, 191–93; and Wire, *Corinthian Women Prophets*.

131. Some scholars view this as a statement of the Corinthian community that Paul is quoting. See, for example, Conzelmann, *1 Corinthians*, 115 and Yarbrough, *Not Like the Gentiles*, 95–96. Hurd, *The Origin of 1 Corinthians*, 275, on the other hand, thinks this is a statement of Paul's that has been misused by the Corinthians.

132. On "burning," see Martin, "Paul Without Passion," 202, and *The Corinthian Body*, 212–16. "Burning" may refer to both the coming wrath of God as well as out-of-control desire.

133. "None of these instructions say anything about human sexuality being good or about realizing one's divinely ordained sexuality or living up to some human psychological potential as a 'sexual being.' Rather, in 7:2 marriage is merely a prophylaxis against *porneia*; in 7:3 it is a duty or debt owned by spouses to one another; and in 7:5 it is a prophylaxis against Satanic testing" (Martin, *The Corinthian Body*, 209).

134. 1 Cor 7:7: "I wish that all were as I myself am." 1 Cor 7:38: The one who marries his virgin does well and the one who does not marry will do better."

135. One should stay married to an unbeliever "for God has called us to peace," and, besides, the believing spouse may save the unbeliever (1 Cor 7:15–16). Paul recommends that virgins remain as they are "in view of the present distress" (1 Cor 7:26).

136. The words "θέλημα" and "θέλω" replace the Attic "ἐθέλω," which never occurs in the NT and LXX. In this verse, it refers to the act of willing or desiring and, by extension, to sexual desire. Compare 1 John 1:13. For discussion, see BDF § 101 and BAGD, s.v. "θέλημα" and "θέλω."

137. Castelli, "Interpretations of Power," 211.

138. Some have argued that outright rejection of marriage was a policy of some of the Corinthian Christians, a policy that Paul cautiously endorsed. See Yarbrough, *Not Like the Gentiles*, 93–96; MacDonald, "The Social Setting," 171; Martin, *The Corinthian Body*, 205–8. Some women, "the virgins," may have claimed special pneumatic authority on the basis of their sexual renunciation. See Wire, *Corinthian Women Prophets*, 240–45, 260–67; and MacDonald, "The Social Setting," 171–73. Some married couples may have renounced sexual intercourse even while remaining married, a practice that Paul rejected "because of *porneia*." Bassler, "1 Corinthians," 323; Richard Horsley, *1 Corinthians* (Nashville: Abingdon Press, 1998), 97–99.

139. On the importance of Pauline injunctions to "imitate me," see Castelli, *Imitating Paul: A Discourse of Power* (Louisville: Westminster/John Knox Press, 1991), esp. 97–117.

140. Thess 4:1–7; Rom 6–8; Gal 5:16–26.

141. On the "shameful parts," see 1 Cor 12:23.

142. These verses have been called chaotic, irrational, conflicted, and confusing. For example, Bassler, "1 Corinthians," 327: "One senses conflicting views within Paul shutting down the rational process, and where reason fails, emotion and tradition take over." Neil Elliott, *Liberating*

Paul: The Justice of God and the Politics of the Apostle (Maryknoll: Orbis Books, 1994), 209: "his supposed argument appears particularly inept." What, precisely, Paul was so exercised about when he composed this passage continues to be debated. For example, could Paul be arguing against the practice, familiar within Greco-Roman mystery cults, of women wearing their hair unbound during ecstatic worship? (Schüssler Fiorenza, *In Memory of Her*, 226–27). Or perhaps Paul's real concern was with men who prayed with their heads covered, an activity reserved for elite men alone (Elliott, *Liberating Paul*, 210–11). Or, perhaps, Paul sought to quiet and subordinate the pneumatic women, the same group that upset him in 1 Cor 7, by reasserting gender hierarchies via hairstyles and veiling (Wire, *Corinthian Women Prophets*, 116–34, 181–88). As interesting as the first two propositions are, I find that the latter—Paul seeks here to reassert gender hierarchies—is the most persuasive, especially given Paul's repeated reference to the problem of desire, the danger of sex, and the need for self-control among the Christians.

143. See Barrettt, *A Commentary*, 249: "Thus a chain or originating and subordinating relationships is set up: God, Christ, man, woman. From this proposition practical consequences are deduced." According to Conzelmann, *1 Corinthians*, 182, this verse seeks to provide "a *fundamental* ground on which to argue the special problem" (emphasis in the original). According to Collins, *First Corinthians*, 399, Paul's "forceful" use of the phrase "I want you to understand," "introduces a statement of principle on the basis of which Paul formulates a limited dress code."

144. See Joseph Fitzmyer, "Another Look at KEPHALE in 1 Corinthians 11:3," *New Testament Studies* 35 (1989): 503–11. But see Witherington, *Conflict and Community*, 237–38.

145. On the meaning of "glory" and the attribution of glory to men, see Wire, "1 Corinthians," 177.

146. D'Angelo, "Veils, Virgins and the Tongues of Men," 133.

147. Compare 1 Tim 2:13–15: "For Adam was formed first, then Eve; and Adam was not deceived, but the woman, being deceived, became a transgressor. And she will be saved through (bearing) a child, if she remains in faith and love and holiness with chastity [*sōphrosynē*]."

148. Sen. *Contr.* 1.8–9. See discussion of the Roman representations of the womanish and long hair of the barbarians and *cinaedi* in Amy Richlin, "Making Up a Woman: The Face of Roman Gender," in *Off with Her Head! The Denial of Women's Identity in Myth, Religion, and Culture*, ed. Howard Eilberg-Schwartz and Wendy Doniger (Berkeley: University of California Press, 1998), 201–4.

149. Among other signs. Dio Chrys. *Or.* 33.52.

150. Pseudo-Phocylides, *Admonitions*, in *The Sentences of Pseudo-Phokylides*, ed. and trans. Pieter W. van der Horst, Studia in Veteris Testamenti Pseudepigrapha 4 (Leiden: E. J. Brill, 1978), 210–12. Cited and discussed by Brooten, *Love Between Women*, 63.

151. Arr. *Epct. diss.* 1.16.9–14, in which Epictetus notes that "nature" has given us a wonderful way to distinguish between men and women, the beard. Women are granted a softer voice and hairless chins. Men, in their beards, have the fair and dignified sign of their gender. Therefore, men ought not to pluck their beards for such an action may confuse the sexes. For a discussion of the importance of hair and beards in determining masculine and feminine styles, see Maud Gleason, "The Semiotics of Gender: Physiognomy and Self-Fashioning in the Second Century C.E.," in *Before Sexuality: The Construction Erotic Experience in the Ancient Greek World*, ed. David Halperin, John J. Winkler, and Froma L. Zeitlin (Princeton, N.J.: Princeton University Press, 1990), 399–400. On the possible association between long hair and effeminacy in ancient Greece, see Dover, *Greek Homosexuality*, 74–7.

152. MacLeod's translation.

153. This passage linked to 1 Cor 11:2–16 by Brooten, *Love Between Women*, 238, 240, 266, 275.

154. Castelli, "Romans," 282; Brooten, *Love Between Women*, 271–80.

155. Brooten, *Love Between Women*, 257–8. Compare Arr. *Epct. diss.* 2.10.17–18: "What is ruined by the one who suffers the things of the *kinaidos*? His manhood. But what of the one

who handled him? Many other things, but he also loses his manhood just as much" (translation my own).

156. Stowers, *Rereading*, 94.

157. Wire, "1 Corinthians," 179, and *Prophets*, 117. See also Jason BeDuhn, "'Because of the Angels': Unveiling Paul's Anthropology in 1 Corinthians 11," *JBL* 118 (1999): 295–320.

158. See discussion in Boyarin, *A Radical Jew*, 181–91; Schüssler Fiorenza, *In Memory*, 205–36; Betz, *Galatians*, 181–201; Wayne Meeks, "The Image of the Androgyne: Some Uses of a Symbol in Earliest Christianity," *History of Religions* 13 (1974): 165–208; Robin Scroggs, "Paul and the Eschatological Woman," in *The Text and the Times: New Testament Essays for Today* (Minneapolis: Fortress Press, 1993), 79–83. For a helpful discussion on whether or not the "not male or female" distinction in Pauline Christianity should be understood as an indicator of gender equality, see Martin, *The Corinthian Body*, 229–33. Note that Paul eliminates the third pair in 1 Cor 12:13: "For by one spirit we were all baptized into one body, whether Jews or Greeks, whether slaves or free, and we were all made to drink of one spirit."

159. D'Angelo, "Veils, Virgins and the Tongues of Men," 139–40. D'Angelo suggests that a woman's head stands for her genitals "by a kind of erotic metonymy."

160. Gen 6:2–3; compare 1 Enoch 6.

161. See discussion in D'Angelo, "Veils, Virgins and the Tongues of Men," 134–36, 146–47.

162. I borrow the term "prophylactic" from Dale Martin. Still, as Roger Bagnall has pointed out to me, our knowledge of the geographical range and cultural significance of the veiling of women is limited.

163. Witherington notes that head covering was "means to warn men (and angels?) that the wearer was a respectable woman and thus untouchable. If so, then the head covering would serve as a sign of respectability, not subordination" (*Conflict and Community*, 234 n. 15). In my opinion, the problem with this analysis is that it does not recognize that respectability for women in this cultural context requires their subordination.

164. As Paul warned in 1 Cor 5:3–4: "For though absent in body, I am present in spirit; and as if present I have already pronounced judgment in the name of Lord Jesus on the man who has done such a thing" (NRSV).

3. SEXUAL VICE AND CHRISTIAN *APOLOGIA*

1. Robert Grant, *Greek Apologists*, esp. 1–33. Also see Emily J. Hunt, *Christianity in the Second Century: The Case of Tatian* (London: Routledge, 2003), 9–10, 56–59.

2. See, for example, Anthony J. Guerra, "The Conversion of Marcus Aurelius and Justin Martyr: The Purpose, Genre, and Content of the First Apology," *Second Century* 9 (1992): 171–87. Guerra speculates that Justin had some reason to hope that at least Marcus Aurelius would convert, given his well-known conversion to Stoic philosophy. See also L. W. Barnard, *Athenagoras: A Study in Second Century Christian Apologetic*, Théologie Historique 18 (Paris: Beauchesne, 1972), 11–13, 22–24. Barnard argues that Athenagoras may have prepared his *Legatio* as an address to be delivered in the emperor's presence: "Is it fanciful to suggest that Athenagoras was favourably impressed with the Emperor's philosophic bearing in Alexandria and felt that, at least, he would give him a hearing as a Christian philosopher?" (24). On the difficulties faced by Stoic philosophers who were perceived to go too far in their critique of the emperor, see Francis, *Subversive Virtue*, esp. the discussion of Musonius Rufus, 13–14. See also Ramsay MacMullen, *Enemies of the Roman Order: Treason, Unrest, and Alienation in the Empire* (London: Routledge, 1966), 63–65.

3. L.W. Barnard, *Justin Martyr: His Life and Thought* (Cambridge: Cambridge University Press, 1967), 1–4, 12–13.

4. Noted by Grant, *Greek Apologists*, 54.

5. The *Legatio* is usually dated between 176–78 C.E. See William R. Schoedel's introduction to Athenagoras *Leg.* ix–xii.

6. Interestingly, Marcus Aurelius had argued the opposite in his *Meditations*: Zeus, the principal god of the pantheon, made it possible for him to lead the ideal Stoic "life according to Nature" (*Med.* 1.17, 5.8). Clearly, Marcus Aurelius was not ready to abandon the worship of Zeus, though not for the reasons Athenagoras suggested. See discussion in R. B. Rutherford, *The Meditations of Marcus Aurelius: A Study* (Oxford: Clarendon Press, 1989), 188–93.

7. Schoedel's translation.

8. McGehee argues that Tatian's *Oratio ad Graecos* was intended to be read as a *protreptikos*, a speech designed to attract students. See his "Why Tatian Never 'Apologized' to the Greeks," *JECS* 1 (1993): 143–58.

9. Whittaker's translation.

10. In other words, the actor teaches men to adopt the passive position in sexual acts.

11. Whittaker's translation.

12. Beard, North, and Price, *Religions of Rome*, 1:310. See further Millar, *Emperor and the Roman World*, 562–63; Mark J. Edwards, "Justin's Logos and the Word of God," *JECS* 3 (1995): 279–80. It is possible that some of these treatises were intended as protreptic, speeches seeking to recruit students. See Anthony J. Guerra, *Romans and the Apologetic Tradition*, 3–21; and Michael McGehee, "Why Tatian Never 'Apologized,'" 143–58. Even so, I would argue that an in-group audience is probably to be imagined.

13. Young, "Greek Apologists," 81. Furthermore, the diversity of the titles given to these works by their authors (petitions, orations, appeals) signifies that the circumstances in which they were produced were different and that they were governed by different literary genres (90–91).

14. Young, "Greek Apologists," 84.

15. Justin's familiarity with and sympathy towards Greek philosophy has been a particular interest of scholars. See the classic work of Robert Joly, *Christianisme et philosophie: Etudes sur Justin et les Apologistes grecs du deuxième siècle* (Paris: Editions de L'Universite de Bruxelles, 1973), esp. 9–78. Joly also considers the Epistle to Diognetus, Tatian, Aristides, Athenagoras, Melito, Theophilus of Antioch, and Tertullian. See further Mark J. Edwards, "On the Platonic Schooling of Justin Martyr," *Journal of Theological Studies* 42 (1991): 17–34; Arthur J. Droge, *Homer or Moses? Early Christian Interpretations of the History of Culture* (Tübingen: Mohr/Siebeck, 1989), 49–71.

16. Taking a different approach, Tatian argued that Christianity, the "barbarian philosophy," was far superior to Greek philosophy, which is entirely corrupt. For discussion, see McGehee, "Why Tatian never 'Apologized,'" 143–58.

17. Theophilus singles out Epicurus, Chrysippus, and Plato for critique.

18. Athenagoras cited Plato in *Leg.* 6.2, 16.4, 19.2, 23.5–9. In paragraph 6, Athenagoras notes with approval Plato's opinion that it is difficult to discover the creator of the universe (Plato, *Timaeus*, 28c, 41a); in section 16 Athenagoras employs the authority of Plato to buttress his argument that one ought to examine the beauty of the universe to understand the powers of God (Plato, *Timaeus*, 33c); in 19 he further observes that Plato believed in an eternal, uncreated God (Plato, *Timaeus*, 27d); in 23 Athenagoras reminds his audience of Plato's previous critique of the idea that the gods could beget offspring (Plato, *Timaeus*, 40d–e).

19. Justin adopted this argument from others. There was already a traditional argument claiming that the Greeks had stolen their ideas from Jewish scriptures. See Monique Alexandre, "Apologétique judéo-hellénistique et premières apologies chrétiennes," in *Les apologistes chrétiens et la culture grecque*, ed. Bernard Pouderon and Joseph Doré (Paris: Beauchesne, 1998), 1–40.

20. Justin mentions these "good" philosophers, at least in part, so that he can claim that those who proclaimed the truth were often persecuted in a manner similar to the Christians, concluding that the same gods or demons that now inspire the current crop of rulers to abuse the Christians once inspired former, corrupt rulers to persecute the few good philosophers (*1 Apol.* 5). This argument is hardly a ringing endorsement of non-Christian philosophy.

21. Rebecca Lyman, "2002 NAPS Presidential Address: Hellenism and Heresy," *JECS* 11, no. 2 (2003): 209–22.

3. SEXUAL VICE AND CHRISTIAN APOLOGIA 207

22. Lyman, "2002 NAPS Presidential Address," 218. See also Tessa Rajak, "Talking at Trypho: Christian Apologetic as Anti-Judaism in Justin's *Dialogue with Trypho the Jew*," in *Apologetics in the Roman Empire*, ed. Mark J. Edwards, Martin Goodman, and Simon Price (Oxford: Clarendon Press, 1999), 58–80. Rajak notes that Justin discusses Platonism at length in his *Dialogue*, only to dismiss it: "So Platonic philosophy is momentarily elevated; but only to lend force to the exposure of its pretensions" (67).

23. See Alain le Boulluec, *La notion d'hérésie dans la littérature greque, IIe–IIIe siècles*, vol. 1, *De Justin à Irénée* (Paris: Études Augustiniennes, 1985), 52–54, 58–64: "les anciens philophes ont connu une vérité partielle, la vérité entière étant celle du Logos, révélée aux prophètes plus anciens que les philosophes" (59).

24. Discussed by Lyman, "2002 NAPS Presidential Address," 218–19.

25. A point made previously by R. M. Price. Price observes that though Justin was willing to acknowledge that some philosophers were inspired by the Logos (the persecuted philosophers Socrates, Heraclitus, and Musonius Rufus in particular), his primary object was to demonstrate that "good" philosophers always suffer persecution at the hand of men who allow themselves to be swayed by demons. He was not interested in arguing that these philosophers could actually achieve virtue without Christ. See R. M. Price, "Are there 'Holy Pagans' in Justin Martyr?" *Studia Patristica* 31 (1997): 153–69.

26. Whether or not he had access to Paul's letters, Justin never cited Paul explicitly. His knowledge of Paul's letters, therefore, cannot be assumed.

27. With most scholars, I read Ephesians, Colossians, 1 and 2 Timothy, and Titus as pseudonymous.

28. On the pseudonymity of Titus and the other "Pastoral Epistles" (1, 2 Timothy and Titus), see Lewis R. Donelson, *Pseudepigraphy and Ethical Argument in the Pastoral Epistles* (Tübingen: Mohr/Siebeck, 1986), 7–66.

29. Further evidence that this is a pseudonymous letter since Paul, a "Hebrew born of the Hebrews and as to the law a Pharisee"(Phil 3:5), would hardly include himself among the gentiles, before they found Christ, who had been "slaves to various desires and pleasures."

30. A move that was famously described as "love patriarchy" (*Liebespatriarchalismus*) by Gerd Theissen. See the critique of Theissen's perspective in Schüssler Fiorenza, *In Memory of Her*, 76–80

31. "By constructing submission as the natural relationship of wife to husband and justifying it by analogy to Christ and the church, the author [of Ephesians] has made obedience to husbands a requirement for wives": Cynthia Briggs Kittredge, *Community and Authority: The Rhetoric of Obedience in the Pauline Tradition*, Harvard Theological Studies 45 (Harrisburg, Penn.: Trinity Press International, 1998), 139. See also Schüssler Fiorenza, *In Memory of Her*, 251–79

32. Bishops and deacons were required to be "the husband of one wife," a reference to one marriage, not to polygamy: 1 Tim 3:2, 12. For further discussion of the "widows" in the Pastorals (who may not be "widows" at all but young women who have adopted celibacy and demanded the authority that came with their vow), see Dennis R. MacDonald, *The Legend and the Apostle: The Battle for Paul in Story and Canon* (Philadelphia: Westimster Press, 1983); Margaret MacDonald, "Rereading Paul: Early Interpreters of Paul on Women and Gender," in *Women and Christian Origins*, ed. Ross Shepard Kraemer and Mary Rose D'Angelo (Oxford: Oxford University Press, 1999), 236–53; Gail Corrington Streete, "Askesis and Resistance in the Pastoral Episles," in *The New Testament and Asceticism*, ed. Leif Vaage and Vincent Wimbush (New York: Routledge, 1999), 299–316. Antoinette Clark Wire envisions a community of celibate women—the "widows" of the Pastorals—already in place when Paul wrote 1 Corinthians, (see her *Corinthian Women Prophets*).

33. As Corrington Streete has noted, this "Paul" instructs gentiles-in-Christ to display a sort of "householder asceticism," whereby *sōphrosynē* was practiced within a harmonious, hierarchical household (309). See further Schüssler Fiorenza, *In Memory of Her*, 284–91: "The patriarchal order of the house, when applied to the order of the church, restricts the leadership of wealthy

women and maintains the social exploitation of slave-women and men, even within the Christian household community" (291). See also David Horrell, "From *adelphoi* to *oikos theou*: Social Transformation in Pauline Christianity," *JBL* 120, no. 2 (2001): 293–311.

34. For a detailed discussion of the commonplace "Concerning Household Management" as found in Stoic, Hellenistic Jewish, and Neopythagorean authors during the period in which these texts were written, see David Balch, *Let Wives be Submissive: The Domestic Code in 1 Peter*, SBL Monograph Series 26 (Chico, Calif.: Scholars Press, 1981), 51–62. Some would argue that the household code found in Colossians and taken up and expanded in Ephesians challenges traditional Greco-Roman hierarchical notions about the household by demanding mutual subjection. I am not convinced by these readings. As seen in the Greco-Roman literature already surveyed, the "rhetoric of conjugal unity" was (a) not limited to Christians and (b) did not erase hierarchical distinctions. Rather, these rhetorics, while recommending love and reciprocity between the spouses, assumed the secondary, derivative status of wives. See further Cohen and Saller, "Foucault on Sexuality," 35–59.

35. Plut. *Mor.*144C. Indeed, Plutarch concluded, it is more important for a man to enforce harmony in his household than to protect "his" women from outside harm since it is easier to conceal a rape than the misdeeds of an openly promiscuous daughter: "For it is much more likely that the sins of women rather than sins against women will go unnoticed by most people." For discussion, see Sarah B. Pomeroy, ed., *Plutarch's Advice to the Bride and Groom and a Consolation to his Wife* (Oxford: Oxford University Pres, 1999). On the wife and mother as "a moral barometer for the household," see Richard Hawley, "Practicing What You Preach: Plutarch's Sources and Treatment," in *Plutarch's Advice to the Bride and Groom and a Consolation to his Wife*, ed. Sarah B. Pomeroy (Oxford: Oxford University Press, 1999), 116–17.

36. Philo *Spec.* 3.169–171; Philo *Post.* 181; Joseph *Ap.* 2.199–126; M. Aur. *Med.* 1.9. For further relevant examples, see those listed and explained by Balch, *Let Wives be Submissive*, 52–56.

37. The *Acts of Paul and Thecla* has been the subject of much scholarly debate. Some have found in the story evidence for a community of women who embraced virginity, sought autonomy from the strictures of patriarchal households, and embraced Thecla as their hero. See, for example, Burrus, *Chastity as Autonomy*; Stevan L. Davies, *The Revolt of the Widows: The Social World of the Apocryphal Acts* (Carbondale: Southern Illinois University Press, 1980); Ross Shepard Kraemer, "The Conversion of Women to Ascetic Forms of Christianity," *Signs* 6 (1980): 298–307. Dennis MacDonald has famously argued that the Pastoral Epistles were written, in part, to oppose the emphasis on female virginity and independence promoted by the *Acts of Paul*; see MacDonald, *The Legend and The Apostle*. Some have questioned the possibility that much, if any, historical evidence about the lives of women can be gleaned from the tale. Kate Cooper has offered the most extensive case for this position; see Cooper, *The Virgin and the Bride*, esp. 45–67. See also Lynne C. Boughton, "From Pious Legend to Feminist Fantasy: Distinguishing Hagiographical License from Apostolic Practice in the *Acts of Paul/Acts of Thecla*," *JAAR* 71 (1991): 362–83.

38. *Acta Pauli et Theclae*, Ed. R. Lipsius, in *Acta apostolorum apocrypha*, ed. R. Lipsius, Vol. 1 (Leipzig: Mendelssohn, 1891; repr., Hildesheim: Olms, 1972), 235–71. English translation by J. K. Elliott, *The Apocryphal New Testament: A Collection of Apocryphal Christian Literature in an English Translation* (Oxford: Clarendon Press, 1993).

39. This model—a proper Greek virgin daughter or chaste wife rejects the demands of her family and city in favor of the call of virginity in Christ—was standard fare in the *Apocryphal Acts*. Mygdonia and Tertia refused further intercourse with their husbands after hearing Christ preached by Thomas; Maximilla rejected the advances of her husband with the assistance of the apostle Andrew; Drusiana died just in time to escape the amorous desires of her husband's slave Callimachus, only to be resurrected by the apostle John (*Acts of Thomas*, 82–138; *Acts of Andrew*, 13–64; *Acts of John*, 63–86). Thecla's enormous and lasting popularity is attested in several early Christian sources. She served as a model in Christian celebrations of female askesis: later Christian saints were compared to her, early Christian art depicted her triumphs in the amphitheater,

and her story received a series of elaborations, culminating in a fifth-century *Life of Thecla*. For discussion of the development of the "cult of Saint Thecla," see Stephen J. Davis, *The Cult of Saint Thecla: A Tradition of Women's Piety in Late Antiquity* (New York: Oxford University Press, 2001). The text of the *Life of Thecla* has been edited, with French translation, by Gilbert Dagron, *Vie et miracles de Sainte Thècla: Texte grec, traduction et commentaire*, Subsidia Hagiographica 62 (Brussels: Société des bollandistes, 1978). See also the excellent discussion of the rewriting of Thecla's memory in Elizabeth A. Castelli, *Martyrdom and Memory: Early Christian Culture Making* (New York: Columbia University Press, 2004).

40. On the romance, see esp. Simon Goldhill, *Foucault's Virginity: Ancient Erotic Fiction and the History of Sexuality* (Cambridge: Cambridge University Press, 1995); Niklas Holzberg, *The Ancient Novel: An Introduction*, trans. Christine Jackson-Holzberg (New York: Routledge, 1995); David Konstan, *Sexual Symmetry: Love in the Ancient Novel and Related Genres* (Princeton, N.J.: Princeton University Press, 1994); B. P. Reardon, *The Form of Greek Romance* (Princeton, N.J.: Princeton University Press, 1991). A handy collection of the romances in English translation has been compiled by B. P. Reardon, *Collected Ancient Greek Novels* (Berkeley: University of California Press, 1989). Cooper discusses the novels as well, *The Virgin and the Bride*, 20–43. Reardon sums up the novel as follows: "The pattern of Greek love-romance, then, is as simple as it could be. Loving couple, their travels and trials; the vicissitudes of Fortune, which may take on a providential aspect; the happy ending. A perennial pattern" (Reardon, *The Form of Greek Romance*, 34). The expected "happy ending" is, of course, marriage.

41. Cooper, *The Virgin and the Bride*, 55.

42. Cooper's claim that the Apocryphal Acts were not "about women" has been challenged by Shelly Matthews. She remarks, "How is it conceivable that in the early church, which was never an exclusively male sect, questions about authority and social order could have *nothing to do with women*?" See her "Thinking of Thecla: Issues in Feminist Historiography," *JFSR* 17, no. 2 (2001): 50 (emphasis in the original). Matthews offers an important critique of Cooper's perspective. Still, I agree with Cooper that, rhetorically speaking, these stories could have been intended as weapons in a battle for prestige, whatever the gender of the participants.

43. Cooper, *The Virgin and the Bride*, 58–59.

44. Donelson, *Pseudepigraphy*, 174.

45. Compromise positions were possible. For example, Ignatius of Antioch encouraged the "sisters" to love the Lord and be satisfied with their husbands in the flesh. The "brothers" were exhorted to love their wives as the Lord loves the church, an echo of the earlier Pauline letters Colossians and Ephesians. Still, Ignatius was quite pleased with those who chose celibacy over marriage, so long as they did not boast of their exceptional self-control—"if anyone is able to honor the flesh of the Lord by maintaining a state of purity, let him do so without boasting"— and he celebrated his own triumph over desire (Ign. *Pol.* 5.2; Ign. *Rom.* 7.2–3). See Schoedel, *A Commentary*; Ehrman's translation. The extent to which Ignatius was actually acquainted with the Pauline epistles, including the deutero-Pauline epistles Colossians and Ephesians, continues to be debated. Nevertheless, Ignatius clearly recognized the authority of Paul and, on several occasions, claimed Paul's authority to legitimate his position. See Andreas Lindemann, "Paul in the Writings of the Apostolic Fathers," in *Paul and the Legacies of Paul*, ed. William Babcock (Dallas: Southern Methodist University Press, 1990), 25–45; and *Paulus im ältesten Christentum: Das Bild des Apostels und die Rezeption der paulinischen Theologie in der frühchristlicen Literatur bis Marcion*, Beiträge zur historischen Theologie 58 (Tübingen: J. P. Mohr, 1979).

46. *1 Apol.* 27. William Harris offered the following comment on this passage: "[Justin] wanted to turn the charge back on the accusers, and as far as reproduction and sexuality were concerned, child-exposure was their most vulnerable point…. This was a rhetorical dispute, but one of some importance in the struggle of Christians to dominate the sphere of sexuality" ("Child-Exposure," 11).

47. Unless otherwise noted, English translation from L. W. Barnard, *St. Justin Martyr: The First and Second Apologies*, Ancient Christian Writers 56 (New York: Paulist Press, 1997).

48. The husband of such a woman was free to kill any slave paramour of his wife and he was required to divorce her, *D* 48.5.21.1, Papinian; *D* 48.5.24.1, Ulpian; *D* 48.5.25.1, Macer. For discussion, see Treggiari, *Roman Marriage*, 283–84.

49. Barnard's translation, with slight emendations.

50. See the discussion of the *lex Julia de adulteriis coercendis*, the *lex Julia de maritandis ordinibus*, and the *lex Papia Poppaea* in Gardner, *Women in Roman Law*, 35; Treggiari, *Roman Marriage*, 277–98.

51. She believed it would be wicked to continue to lie with such a man. Perhaps Justin had Paul's injunction to avoid joining the "members" of a Christ follower with the "members" of a prostitute (1 Cor 6:15–17), though Justin never quoted Paul explicitly.

52. See Williams, *Roman Homosexuality*, 86–95, 123–25, Veyne, "Homosexuality," 25–27; Richlin, *The Garden of Priapus*, 138–39; Gleason, *Making Men*, 405–8.

53. Elaine Pagels, "Christian Apologists and 'The Fall of the Angels': An Attack on Roman Imperial Power," *Harvard Theological Review* 78 (1985): 304. Everett Ferguson offers a helpful summary of Justin's beliefs regarding the demons: the demons are identified with the Watchers, angels who lusted after women (Gen 6:2–3; 1 Enoch 6—see discussion in chapter 2); they are the "gods" worshiped by non-Christians; they are responsible for the evils suffered by humanity, including the persecution of the Christians; Christ is/will be victorious over them. See Ferguson, *Demonology of the Early Christian World*, Symposium Series 12 (New York: Edwin Mellen Press, 1980), 105–34.

54. For example, Octavian Augustus hoped that he would be remembered for his *virtus, clementia, iustitia,* and *pietas,* composing a list of his moral, social, and military "achievements" to be erected following his death (*RG* 8.5, 10.1–2, 27.3, 35.1). On the erection of this record of his achievements, written on golden tablets and displayed before his mausoleum, see Suet. *Aug.* 101.4. On the relationship between the *Res Gestae* and Hellenistic theories of kingship, see Brian Bosworth, "Augustus," 1–18. Bosworth argues that a sophisticated, educated audience would immediately understand the *Res Gestae* for what it was: an elaborate justification of the deification of Augustus. Augustus, Tiberius, Trajan—each emperor was, at one time or another, said to personify virtue, at least in theory. As we observed in chapter 1, by the second century the good emperor had come to represent the justice, peace, concord, abundance, and prosperity of the empire, at least in theory; his virtues were said to secure the well-being of the empire and to guarantee the favor of the gods.

55. Justin wrote his "apologies" in Rome. The latter addition to the first petition was addressed to the Roman Senate in light of what Justin viewed as the outrageously unjust behavior of Urbicus, prefect of Rome.

56. Barnard's translation.

57. Justin understood Christianity to be the fulfillment of Judaism. He argues that the Hebrew prophets pre-dated the Greek philosophers, that the prophets directly foretold the coming of Christ, and that Jews who did not accept Christ had been rejected by God. From Justin's perspective, the old law of Israel has been abrogated by Christ. See *1 Apol.* 30–45 (the prophets foretold Christ), 59–64 (Plato copied his insights from Moses); *Dial.*, esp. 11–15, 71–74, 112–14. For discussion, see esp. Rajak, "Talking at Trypho," 9–80. On Justin's use of Hebrew Bible sources, see the extensive study by Oskar Skarsuane, *The Proof from Prophecy: A Study of Justin Martyr's Proof-Text Tradition: Text-Type, Provenance, Theological Profile*, Supplements to Novum Testamentum 56 (Leiden: E. J. Brill, 1987).

58. See, for example, Plato, *Timaeus,* 40d–e.

59. On Hadrian's munificence, see Cass. Dio 69.5.2–3. Hadrian's impressive building and restoration projects are discussed by Mary T. Boatwright, *Hadrian and the Cities of the Roman Empire* (Princeton, N.J.: Princeton University Press, 2000). The temple of Venus and Rome was "the largest temple ever built in the city." See discussion in Beard, North, and Price, *Religions of Rome*, 1:256–59.

60. Justin mentions Antinous in the context of his attack on the Romans for their participation in homoerotic sex. He ends this section with a rather barbed reference to Antinous and

Hadrian: "And it is not out of place, we think, to mention here Antinous, who was recently alive, and whom everybody, with reverence, hastened to worship as a god, though they knew who he was and what was his origin" (*1 Apol.* 29; Barnard's translation). Craig Williams views Hadrian's devotion to Antinous as evidence of the relative acceptance of male homoerotic sex between a superordinate man (in this case, Hadrian) and his subordinate (in this case, Antinous, a young male slave; Williams, *Roman Homosexuality*, 60–61). Perhaps Hadrian's public declaration of his love for Antinous—celebrated in the city and religious cult Hadrian founded in his honor following Antinous' untimely death—is best understood in light of Hadrian's effort to associate himself with Greek philosophy, in this case by associating himself with "Greek love." See Jaś Elsner, *Imperial Rome and Christian Triumph: The Art of the Roman Empire, 100–450* (Oxford: Oxford University Press, 1998), esp. 177–83. Though Christians often made snide remarks regarding Antinous, Hadrian clearly believed that celebrating his youthful male lover could recommend him to his subjects. For further Christian critique, see also Athenagoras *Leg.* 30.2; Tatian *Or.* 10.1–2. Interestingly, Celsus compared the alleged impropriety of the Christians with the iniquity of the "revelers of Antinous in Egypt"; see Origen, *Contra Celsum*, in *Origen: Contra Celsum*, 5 vols., ed. with French translation by Marcel Borret, Sources Chrétiennes (Paris: Éditions du Cerf, 1967–76), English translation by H. E. Chadwick, *Origen: Contra Celsum* (Cambridge: Cambridge University Press, 1965), 5.63.

61. On the apotheosis of *divus* Antoninus and other divine emperors, see Simon Price, "From Noble Funerals to Divine Cult: The Consecration of Roman Emperors," in *Rituals of Royalty: Power and Ceremonial in Traditional Societies*, ed. D. Cannadine and S. Price (Cambridge: Cambridge University Press, 1987), 56–105. For a discussion of a famous column depicting the apotheosis of Antoninus Pius and the empress Faustina, see Lise Vogel, *The Column of Antoninus Pius* (Cambridge, Mass.: Harvard University Press, 1973).

62. Cass. Dio 71.36.4. Famously, Marcus Aurelius seems to have penned his own set of moral reflections grounded in Stoic philosophy. Usually identified as the *Meditations*, this work was not well known in antiquity (copies today are made from a MS of sixteenth-century origin though most scholars accept it as authentic). See discussion by P. A. Brunt, "Marcus Aurelius in his *Meditations*," *JRS* 64 (1974): 1–20.

63. According to at least one interpreter, the inclusion of Marcus Aurelius in this list of addressees was no accident. Marcus Aurelius' well-known adherence to Stoic thought could have given peculiar weight to Justin's appeal to philosophy. Indeed, six Christian apologists referred directly to Aurelius in their pleas; see Guerra, "The Conversion of Marcus Aurelius," 171–87; Robert Grant, "Five Apologists and Marcus Aurelius," *Vigiliae Christianae* 42 (1988): 1–17. This interpretation seems to me to be highly improbable.

64. For Origen, *Contra Celsum*, see note 60.

65. Celsus' work "constitutes a fairly extensive compendium of arguments against Christianity," some that had been put forward earlier and some that Celsus himself developed: Micahel Frede, "Origen's Treatise *Against Celsus*," in *Apologetics in the Roman Empire: Pagans, Jews, and Christians*, ed. Mark Edwards, Martin Goodman, and Simon Price (Oxford: Oxford University Press, 1999), 133. See also Arthur Droge, *Homer or Moses?*, 72–81; Pierre de Labriolle, *La Réaction païenne: Etude sur la polémique antichrétienne du Ier au IVe siècle* (Paris: L'Artisan du Livre, 1934), 117–27; Grant, *Greek Apologists*, 133–39.

66. Schoedel's translation.

67. For further discussion of the "Thyestian banquets and Oedipean union" charge, see Henrichs, "Pagan Ritual," 18–20. See also Rives, "Human Sacrifice"; McGowan, "Eating People"; Jeffrey W. Hargis, *Against the Christians: The Rise of Early Christian Polemic*, Patristic Studies 1 (New York: Peter Lang, 1999), esp. 1–16.

68. Rives, "Human Sacrifice"; McGowan, "Eating People."

69. Plin. *Ep.* 10.96. See further Robert L. Wilken, *Christians as the Romans Saw Them* (New Haven, Conn.: Yale University Press, 1984); Stephen Benko, *Pagan Rome and the Early Christians* (Bloomington: Indiana University Press, 1986); Labriolle, *La Réaction païenne*.

70. Tac. *Ann.* 15.44. See discussion in Wilken, *Christians as the Romans Saw Them*, 49–50.

71. Suet. *Ner.* 16.

72. Lucian *De mort. peregr.* 11–13. On Lucian's relatively benign critique, see Labriolle, *La Réaction païnne*, 108: "Lucian est le *seul* écrivain païen que paraisse trouver cette folie à peu près inoffensive" (emphasis in the original).

73. Keith Hopkins, "Christian Number and Its Implications," *JECS* 6 (1998): 196.

74. Pliny, *Ep.* 96. For discussion, see also Wilken, *Christians as the Romans Saw Them*, 21–30.

75. Castelli, *Martyrdom and Memory*, 38.

76. On the need for a steady supply of prisoners for the amphitheater, see Kathleen M. Coleman, "Fatal Charades: Roman Executions Staged as Mythological Enactments," *JRS* 80 (1990), 47–55.

77. Holt N. Parker, "The Observed of All Observers: Spectacle, Applause, and Cultural Poetics in the Roman Theater Audience," in *The Art of Ancient Spectacle*, ed. Bettina Berhmann and Christine Kondoleon, National Gallery of Art Studies in the History of Art 56, Center for Advanced Study in the Visual Arts Symposium Papers 34 (New Haven: Yale University Press, 1999), 163–79; and Kathleen M. Coleman, "Informers on Parade," in *The Art of Ancient Spectacle*, ed. Bettina Berhmann and Christine Kondoleon, National Gallery of Art Studies in the History of Art 56, Center for Advanced Study in the Visual Arts Symposium Papers 34 (New Haven: Yale University Press, 1999), 231–45; David Potter, "Martyrdom as Spectacle," in *Theater and Society in the Classical World*, ed. Ruth Scodel (Ann Arbor: University of Michigan Press, 1993), 53–88, esp. 65–66; Garnsey, "Legal Privilege," 141–65; Garnsey, *Social Status and Legal Privilege*, 164–65. William Ian Miller has observed that victims tend to be coded as "female" and victimizers as "male": "Victimizers, according to our common notions, will tend to be male, and victims, if not female to the extent as victimizers are male, will, in many settings, be gendered female nonetheless. A male victim is a feminized male": William Ian Miller, *Humiliation: And Other Essays on Honor, Social Discomfort, and Violence* (Ithaca, N.Y.: Cornell University Press, 1993), 55. Though this is clearly an overstatement, the presupposition that dominance is "male" and submission "female" does inform ancient discourses about punishment, especially punishment of the body.

78. *D* 48.19.10.2, Macer: "*quia et solus fustium ictus grauior est quam pecniaris damnatio*"; Watson's translation. See also *D* 48.19.16.6, Claudius Saturninus. Saterninus cited a saying of Demosthenes, "the greatest of Greek orators," noting that the insult of being beaten is worse than the blow itself.

79. Callistratus clarified the policy: "It is not the custom for all persons to be beaten with rods, but only freemen of the poorer classes; men of higher status are not subject to beating with rods, as is specifically laid down in imperial rescripts" (*D* 48.19.28.2, Callistratus; Watson's translation). James Rives discusses the (unusual) decision of Hilarianus, the Roman procurator who ordered the execution of Perpetua, Felicitas, and their companions. Hilarianus arranged for Perpetua to be executed in the arena by beasts, a punishment normally reserved for *humiliores* (people of low status). Rives speculates that Perpetua was from Roman citizen family of the decurial class and hence a *honestior*. Hilarianus' decision to utterly humiliate her by sentencing her to the beasts, then, indicates how deeply offended he was at Perpetua's revocation of her status and duty when she declared herself to be a Christian. See Rives, "The Piety of a Persecutor," *JECS* 4, no. 1 (1996): 1–25.

80. Defined in the *Digest* as treason, murder, conspiracy against one's master, arson, sacrilege, and brigandage. See *D* 48.13.7, Ulpian ("I know indeed that many have been condemned to the wild beasts for sacrilege, some even burned alive, and others hanged on the gallows. But the penalty should be tempered to restrict condemnation to the beasts to those who have formed a band, broken into a temple, and carried off from there the god's offerings by night."); *D* 48.19.6.2, Ulpian (there are classes of punishments, the appropriate punishment is determined, in part, by the status of the person charged); *D* 48.19.8.2, Ulpian ("enemies of the state" and deserters are to be burned alive); 8.11 (younger men condemned to the hunting games are first

degraded to the status of *servi poenae*; compare *D* 48.19.12, Macer); *D* 48.19.11–12, Callistratus (slaves and free men of low rank are condemned to death by fire when they conspire against their masters, as are arsonists); *D* 48.19.28.15–16, Callistratus (brigands ought to be hung so that the spectacle of their death will deter others; notorious people and slaves ought to receive more severe punishments); *D* 48.19.38.2, Paul (those who insight a mob are either hanged, thrown to the beasts, or deported to an island, depending upon their status). I do not assume that these jurists describe the actuality of Roman punishment. Rather, their discussion of ideal practice reveals the status-based attitudes embedded in idealized Roman legal procedure. See also Coleman, "Fatal Charades," 55–58. Coleman notes that the practice of punishing low-status offenders more severely than those of higher status was in place at least by the time of Hadrian.

81. Kathleen Coleman, "Informers," 241–42; Potter, "Martyrdom," 65: "The body of the condemned became a vehicle for the reaffirmation of the public order, and, indeed, for a reaffirmation of the power of the central government, as only an imperial governor possessed the *ius gladii* which gave him the power to inflict capital sentences."

82. Elizabeth Castelli discusses the implications of the "male" gaze to Perpetua's representation of her martyrdom. By being looked at and victimized, Perpetua was gendered female, yet Perpetua imagined herself as "male." See her *Visions and Voyeurism: The Politics of Sight in Early Christianity*, Protocol of the Colloquy of the Center for Hermeneutical Studies (Berkeley: Center for Hermeneutical Studies, 1995). On the "male" gaze in the context of Roman spectacles, see Parker, "Observed of All Observers," 165, 168.

83. Parker comments: "The symbolism of sexual penetration underlies all these attacks on the body of the elite Roman, attacks which are directed especially at the face. And of all the penetrations of the body, the most degrading is *irrumatio*, oral rape. Anyone who is the victim, who submits to it, is *impurus*, a word which has marked overtones of oral sexual debasement" ("The Observed," 175). For the gendered implications of viewing deaths in the arena as "sacrifice," see Castelli, *Martyrdom and Memory*. Castelli notes that sacrifice is often coded for gender in such a way that those who perform the sacrifice are male and those who are sacrificed are female. Christian theorizing regarding martyrdom inverts these gendered categories, elevating passivity and submission to the level of "manliness."

84. *Martyrdom of Polycarp*, ed. and trans. Bart D. Ehrman, *The Apostolic Fathers*, vol. 1, LCL (Cambridge, Mass.: Harvard University Press, 2003), 9. "Thus begins a tradition whereby the martyr's endurance comes to be linked explicitly with masculinity and tied also to images of athleticism and militarism" (Castelli, *Martyrdom and Memory*).

85. *Martyrs of Lyons* (*Epistle of the Churches of Lyons and Vienne*), ed. and trans. Herbert Musurillo, *The Acts of the Christian Martyrs* (Oxford: Clarendon Press, 1972), 19.

86. *Martyrdom of Perpetua and Felicitas*, in *Passion de Perpétue et de Félicité suivi des Actes*, ed. with French translation by Jacqueline Amat, Sources Chrétiennes 417 (Paris: Éditions du Cerf, 1996), 10.7–15. For further discussion, see Castelli, *Martyrdom and Memory*, and *Visions and Voyeurism*, 14–16; Judith Perkins, *The Suffering Self: Pain and Narrative Representation in the Early Christian Era* (New York: Routledge, 1995), 109–21: "The martyrs are never portrayed as victims, but their ordeals are incorporated into the universal and traditional ideology of athletic games" (111). On the significance of naming Perpetua's rival as an Egyptian, see Gay L. Byron, *Symbolic Blackness and Ethnic Difference in Early Christian Literature* (London: Routledge, 2002), 45.

87. Justin's insistence that passive endurance was equivalent to manliness (ἀνδρεία) and that nobility (γενναία) remained possible throughout the humiliating process of public execution was hardly a traditional reading of these virtues. For further discussion, see Castelli, *Martyrdom and Memory*, and Brent Shaw, "Body/Power/Identity: Passions of the Martyrs," *JECS* 4 (1990): 269–312. See also Daniel Boyarin, *Dying for God: Martyrdom and the Making of Christianity and Judaism* (Stanford, Calif.: Stanford University Press, 1999), 74–81; and Virginia Burrus, "Reading Agnes," 25–46. Boyarin concludes that like the late-antique Christians described by Burrus, both the rabbis and the fathers identified with female virgins and martyrs as a way to disidentify with a Rome "whose power was stereotyped as a highly sexualized male" (79).

88. Babbitt's translation.

89. For discussion, see William V. Harris, *Restraining Rage: The Ideology of Anger Control in Classical Antiquity* (Cambridge, Mass.: Harvard University Press, 2001), 245.

90. Chapter 18 lists ten prescriptions against anger; see discussion in Rutherford, *The Meditations*, 34.

91. Plut. *Mor.* 6. English translation W. C. Helmbold,

92. See also Sen. *Clem.* 1.7.4: "Those placed in lowly station are more free to use force, to quarrel, to rush into a brawl, and to indulge their wrath; when the odds are matched, blows fall light; but in a king, even loud speech and unbridled words ill accord with his majesty" (Basore's translation).

93. Athenagoras added, "It is these demons who drag men to the images. They engorge themselves in the blood from the sacrifices and lick all around them" (*Leg.* 26.1). Tatian linked the murderous violence demanded by the gods with the spectacles demanded by crowds in the amphitheatre: "You [who sponsor spectacles] sacrifice animals in order to eat meat and you buy men to provide human slaughter for the soul, feeding it with bloodshed of the most impious kind. The bandit murders for the sake of what he can get, but the rich man buys gladiators for the sake of murder" (Tatian *Or.* 23.2).

94. Compare Theophilus *Ad Auto.* 3.14; Athenagoras *Leg.* 11.3.

95. According to Katherine Welch, a penchant for bloodthirsty violence and illicit sexual desire were also linked in Greek critiques of Roman rule. For example, Philostratus, Lucian, and Dio Chrysostom all decried the violent spectacles performed in Athens, comparing Athens to the Roman colony Corinth and calling the Athenians to reject the impious, perverse, and violent gladiatorial shows performed there. See her "Negotiating Roman Spectacle: Architecture in the Greek World: Athens and Corinth," in *The Art of Ancient Spectacle*, ed. Bettina Berhmann and Christine Kondoleon, National Gallery of Art Studies in the History of Art 56, Center for Advanced Study in the Visual Arts Symposium Papers 34 (New Haven, Conn.: Yale University Press, 1999), 125–45.

96. Grant proposes that Justin wrote his *Apology* in response to Polycarp's arrest and execution (*Greek Apologists*, 53). Musurillo surveys the evidence and concludes that the date of Polycarp's death cannot be fixed with any certainty: Herbert Musurillo, *The Acts of the Christian Martyrs* (Oxford: Clarendon Press, 1972), xiii.

97. Musurillo's translation.

98. *Acta Carpus*, in *The Acts of the Christian Martyrs*, ed. and trans. Herbert Musurillo (Oxford: Clarendon Press, 1972), 5, Greek recension. On the date of this martyrdom, see discussion in Musurillo, *The Acts of the Christian Martyrs*, xv–xvi. Eusebius placed the martyrdom during the reign of Marcus Aurelius (Eusebius *Hist. Eccl.* 4.15.48). Others argue that these Christians were executed during the Decian persecution. On the Decian persecution, see esp. James B. Rives, "The Decree of Decius and the Religion of Empire," *JRS* 89 (1999): 135–54.

99. Miller observes, "the violence of dandified decadence not only thwarts the usual gender typing of violence, it also bears the markings of the cruel. This kind of violence seldom pretends to moral justification; it is unaccompanied by excusing anger or justifying indignation. It is simply for the beauty of it, for the fun of it, the pleasure of it" (Miller, *Humiliation*, 88). Also see Lincoln, *Authority*, 75–76 on violence as a form of speech.

100. Perkins, *The Suffering Self*, 32.

101. Young, "Greek Apologists," 80–81.

4. THE FALSE TEACHERS OF THE END TIME

1. That the author intends the whore to stand for Rome is clear from his identification of "her" as "seated upon many waters" (17:1), "seated upon seven mountains" (17:9), and as "the great city which has dominion over the kings of the earth" (17:18). See Barbara R. Rossing, *The*

Choice Between Two Cities: Whore, Bride, and Empire in the Apocalypse, Harvard Theological Studies 48 (Harrisburg, Penn.: Trinity Press International, 1999), 6–9; Frederick J. Murphy, *Fallen Is Babylon: The Revelation to John* (Harrisburg, Penn.: Trinity Press International, 1998), 1–3, 5–7, 348–85; Catherine Keller, *Apocalypse Now and Then: A Feminist Guide to the End of the World* (Boston: Beacon Press, 1996), 74–77; Leonard L. Thompson, *The Book of Revelation: Apocalypse and Empire* (Oxford: Oxford University Press, 1990), 174–75; Elizabeth Schüssler Fiorenza, *Revelation: Vision of a Just World,* Proclamation Commentaries (Minneapolis: Fortress Press, 1991), 95–101. Schüssler Fiorenza suggests that the image of the great harlot derives from Isa 23:17, "which, especially in its Greek form, understands the international commerce and wealth of Tyre as the 'hire' paid to a harlot" (96).

2. Christopher Rowland's comments are helpful here. He suggests that in apocalyptic writing "the present has been suffused with a critical character." The language adopted offers those who use it a "sense of privilege and destiny" and gives "ultimate significance" to their historical actions. Rowland, "Apocalyptic and the New Testament," in *Apocalypse Theory and the Ends of the World,* ed. Malcolm Bull (Oxford: Blackwell, 1995), 38–57 (quotations drawn from pages 42, 49, and 55 respectively).

3. For discussion, see Murphy, *Fallen Is Babylon,* 215–22, 313–21; and Keller, *Apocalypse Now and Then,* 74–75.

4. Stephen O'Leary offers helpful definitions of "apocalypse," "eschatology," and "apocalyptic eschatology": Eschatology is "discourse about the last things ... the furthest imaginable extensions of human and cosmic destiny." Apocalypse is "that discourse that reveals or makes manifest a vision of ultimate destiny." Apocalyptic eschatology "argues for the imminence of this Judgment in which good and evil will finally receive their ultimate reward and punishment": O'Leary, *Arguing the Apocalypse: A Theory of Millennial Rhetoric* (Oxford: Oxford University Press, 1994), 5–6. As already observed, numerous Christian authors appealed to the last things and the end of time to buttress their argument that the (true) Christians are crucial actors in a cosmic drama in which the righteous (i.e., the Christians) will ultimately triumph. So, for example, Paul exhorts the Roman Christians to "give place to the wrath [of God]"(Rom 12:19) and praises the Thessalonian Christians for turning from idols to serve God while they wait for the return of the Son "who delivers us from the wrath to come" (1 Thess 1:10). The author of Colossians reminds his readers that when Christ appears, "then you, together with him, will appear in glory" (Col 3:3). The authors of the synoptic gospels include extended descriptions of the tribulations of the end times, warning the faithful to "watch" (Mark 13:1–37; Matt 24:3–44; Lk 21:7–36). This warning is repeated in the *Didache,* together with the promise that the "saints" will receive salvation (*Did.* 16.1–8). Other examples include 1 Cor 15:20–57; Eph 1:9–14; 1 Thess 4:13–5:11; 2 Thess 2:1–12; 2 Tim 3:1–9; 1 Pet 4:3–7; 2 Pet 3:2–13; 1 John 2:18–20; *Barn.* 4–6, 9–14; Justin *1 Apol.* 28; Justin *2 Apol.* 7. The apocalyptic "genre" has been variously identified; the working definition used by the Society of Biblical Literature Genres Project has been influential. According to this definition, apocalypse is "a genre of revelatory literature with a narrative framework, in which revelation is mediated by an otherworldly being to a human recipient, disclosing a transcendent reality which is both temporal, insofar as it envisages eschatological salvation, and spatial insofar as it involves another, supernatural world." See John J. Collins, ed., "Apocalypse: The Morphology of a Genre," *Semeia* 14 (1979); and Collins, *The Apocalyptic Imagination: An Introduction to Jewish Apocalyptic Literature,* 2nd ed. (Grand Rapids, Mich.: Eerdmans, 1998), 2–9. Though Revelation is the first example of a document calling itself an "apocalypse" (ἀποκάλυψις), elements of the genre appear in a number of earlier texts, for example: 4 Ezra; 1 Enoch; *Apoc. Ab.*; *Apoc. Bar.*; CD 5.8; 4Q181; 4Q521, fr. 2. The "Prophecies of the Potter" offers an interesting Egyptian example: text in Ludwig Koenen and Reinhold Merkelbach, "Die Prophezeiungen des 'Töpfers,'" *ZPE* 2, no. 3 (1968): 178–209, discussion in L. Koenen, "The Prophecies of a Potter: A Prophecy of World Renewal Becomes an Apocalypse," in *Proceedings of the Twelfth International Congress of Papyrology,* ed. Deborah H. Samuel (Toronto: Hakkert, 1970), 249–54. On "apocalypse" as an ancient literary designation, see Morton Smith, "On the History of ΑΠΟΚΑΛΥΠΤΩ and

ΑΠΟΚΑΛΥΨΙΣ," in *Apocalypticism in the Mediterranean World and the Near East*, Proceedings of the International Colloquium on Apocalypticism, ed. David Hellholm, 2nd ed. (Tübingen: Mohr./Siebeck, 1989), 9–20.

5. Most scholars suggest that this "John" cannot be John the apostle, John the author of the Gospel of John, or John the Baptist, but was another John altogether. See discussion in Murphy, *Fallen Is Babylon*, 33–41.

6. On the development of the figure of Satan and the association of Satan with "false" Jews or Christians by their opponents, see Elaine Pagels, *The Origin of Satan* (New York: Random House, 1995), esp. 47–49, 59–60, 147–49.

7. Translation my own. Compare 1 John 4:1–6. For discussion, see Gregory C. Jenks, *The Origins and Early Development of the Antichrist Myth*, Beihefte zur Zeitschrift für die neutestamentliche Wissenschaft 59 (Berlin: Walter de Gruyter, 1991), 351–53; L. J. Lietaert Peerbolte, *The Antecedents of Antichrist: A Traditio-Historical Study of the Earliest Christian Views on Eschatological Opponents*, Supplements to the Journal for the Study of Judaism 49 (Leiden: E. J. Brill, 1996), 96–113.

8. Grant's translation. Eusebius quotes the Greek original (Eusebius *Hist. Eccl.* 4.14.7–8). Irenaeus recounts this meeting between Polycarp and Marcion in order to exhort the Christians of his own day to follow the example of the apostles and early disciples. Polycarp and Paul, Irenaeus argues, avoided false teachers. If they encountered such deviants, they always offered a swift and pointed rebuke. Irenaeus quotes the "Paul" of Titus to confirm his position, "as Paul too says: 'After a first and second warning, avoid the heretic, knowing that such a man is perverted and when he sins is self-condemned' " (*Adv. Haer.* 3.3.4; compare Eusebius *Hist. Eccl.* 4.14.8 and Titus 3:10–11). Polycarp, in turn, was probably alluding to 1 John. In that epistle, the "little children" (*teknia*, i.e., Christians) are warned to watch out for antichrists and false prophets who are "of the world" and say what is "of the world." These antichrists commit sin and are "of the devil." Indeed, they are "the children of the devil" (*ta tekna tou diabolou*, 1 John 2:18–19, 3:7–10, 4:1–6). On the relationship between Poly. *Phil.* 7.1 and 1 John, see Peerbolte, *Antecedents of Antichrist*, 112–13.

9. Along similar lines, the author of Ephesians warns Christians to be on guard against the "sons of disobedience" who deceive "with empty words" and hide their deeds in darkness. These deeds are too shameful to mention—"it is a shame even to speak about the things they do in secret" (Eph 5:6, 11–12, quotation from 12). Because of them and their fornications, impurity, and idolatry, the wrath of God comes (Eph 5:6). The "sons of disobedience" and the "children of light" (i.e., the true Christians) are, "Paul" asserts, engaged in a contest with earthly and heavenly consequences (Eph 6:12: "For our struggle is not against flesh and blood but against the powers, against the authorities, against the rulers of this darkness, against the spirits of wickedness in the heavenly places.")

10. On the traditional character of these vices, see Martin Dibelius and Hans Conzelmann, *A Commentary on the Pastoral Epistles*, trans. P. Buttolph, A. Yarbro, and H. Koester, Hermeneaia (Philadelphia: Fortress Press, 1972), 115–16. Dibelius and Conzelmann question whether the author of this letter sought to accuse his opponents of being unchaste, arguing that he would have been much more specific had he intended to make such a charge. Still, his vice list implies licentiousness ("profligates," "lovers of pleasure") and the mention of "weak" or "little" women suggests to me that the accusation of sexual depravity is a subtext here. See also MacDonald, *The Pauline Churches*, 179–80.

11. MacDonald, *Early Christian Women*, 62–63. On the similarities between the polemic of the Pastoral Epistles and similar, equally stereotypical accusations lodged by Greek moralists against their opponents, see Abraham J. Malherbe, "Medical Imagery in the Pastoral Epistles," in *Paul and the Popular Philosophers* (Minneapolis: Fortress Press, 1989), 121–36.

12. Walter Bauer, *Orthodoxy and Heresy in Earliest Christianity*, 2nd German ed., ed. George Strecker, trans. Philadelphia Seminar on Christian Origins (Philadelphia: Fortress Press, 1971), originally published as *Rechgläubigkeit und Ketzerei im ältesten Christentum*, Beiträge zur historischen Theologie 10 (Tübingen: Mohr/Siebeck, 1934).

13. Bauer, *Orthodoxy and Heresy*, xxii. (this section trans. Robert A. Kraft); also see 35.

14. Baur, *Orthodoxy and Heresy*, xxiii–xxiv. On the situation in Edessa, Bauer concluded that there was "a foundation that rests on an unmistakably heretical basis. In relation to it, orthodoxy comes to prevail only very gradually and with great difficulty" (43). In terms of Egypt, Bauer finds no representative of "ecclesiastical" Christianity at all until 189 c.e. (53). Rome was the only place that was not dominated by a form of Christianity that was eventually deemed "heretical" (95–110).

15. Bauer, *Orthodoxy and Heresy*, 100.

16. In the second chapter, I discussed the very material from 1 Corinthians cited by Bauer to establish his claim that Gnostic ideas were present in Asia Minor as early as Paul.

17. Bauer never explicitly defines "heresy" but does state that "orthodoxy" implies adherence to apostolic teaching. "Heresy" and "heretic" then refer to the opponents of "the apostles" and those who claimed to preserve apostolic teaching. For a definition of "orthodoxy," see Bauer, *Orthodoxy and Heresy*, 38. Still, unlike the "church fathers," Bauer does grant the "heretics" the status of "Christian."

18. Examples of the suggestion that rival Christian teachers are innovators who do not conform to what was handed down by the apostles or, alternatively, that true Christians hold onto apostolic teaching, include Col 2:8; 2 Thess 2:2–3; 1 Clem 42.1–4, 47.1–7; Ign. *Eph.* 11.2; Ign. *Mag.* 13.1; Ign. *Smyrn.* 6.2; Iren. *Adv. Haer.* 3.1–4.3.

19. Marcel Simon, "From Greek Hairesis to Christian Heresy," in *Early Christian Literature and the Classical Intellectual Tradition: In Honorem Robert M. Grant*, ed. William R. Schoedel and Robert L. Wilken, Théologie Historique 54 (Paris: Éditions Beauchesne, 1979), 101–16.

20. As Pagels demonstrates, many so-called Gnostics claimed that their views were derived from the authentic writings of the apostle Paul. Elaine H. Pagels, *The Gnostic Paul: Gnostic Exegesis of the Pauline Letters* (Philadelphia: Fortress Press, 1975). Also see Pheme Perkins, *The Gnostic Dialogue: The Early Church and the Crisis of Gnosticism*, Theological Inquiries (New York: Paulist Press, 1980), 12.

21. See McGuire, "Women, Gender, and Gnosis," 262–66.

22. Bauer, *Orthodoxy and Heresy*, 135–41, on Eusebius *Hist. Eccl.* 5.17.2–18.11. However, this observation did not lead Bauer to question the reliability of the abuse heaped upon Paul's opponents in Corinth, the targets of the ire of the author of Revelation, or Justin's and Irenaeus' Gnostics. Instead, he accepts the suggestion that these particular "deviants" were libertine, free-thinking gluttons who could not resist their sexual impulses.

23. See, for example, King, *What is Gnosticism?*; Williams, *Rethinking "Gnosticism"*; Ehrman, *The Orthodox Corruption*, 15–17; Wisse, "The Epistle of Jude," 133–43; J.J. Buckley, "Libertines or Not: Fruit, Bread, Semen, and Other Bodily Fluids in Gnosticism," *JECS* 2 (1994): 15–31; Pagels, *The Gnostic Paul*; G.A.G. Stroumsa, *Another Seed: Studies in Gnostic Mythology*, Nag Hammadi Studies 24 (Leiden: E.J. Brill, 1984), 173; James E. Goehring, "Libertine or Liberated: Women in the So-called Libertine Gnostic Communities," in *Images of the Feminine in Gnosticism*, ed. Karen L. King (Philadelphia: Fortress Press, 1988), 329–44. Goehring notes that "there are no recognizable sources from these communities themselves by which to test the accounts of the heresiologists." He also observes that supposedly deviant religious sects are routinely accused of "sexual deviation." Nevertheless, he continues to assume that there were libertine Gnostic groups, though he refuses to suggest that "libertine" is a negative designation. See the helpful survey of approaches to Gnosticism by McGuire, "Women, Gender, and Gnosis," 257–60. For a discussion of the ideological function of the term "heretic," see Elizabeth A. Clark, "Ideology, History, and the Construction of Woman," *JECS* 2 (1994): 155–184; and Virginia Burrus, "The Heretical Woman as a Symbol in Alexander, Athanasius, Epiphanius, and Jerome," *Harvard Theological Review* 84 (1991): 229–48. Important proponents of the earlier view include Benko, *Pagan Rome*, 63–73; Hans Jonas, *Gnosis und spätaniker Geist*, vol. 1 (Göttingen: Vandenhoeck und Ruprecht, 1934), 170; and Stephen Gero, "With Walter Bauer on the Tigris: Encratite Orthodoxy and Libertine Heresy in Syro-Mesopotamian Christianity," in *Nag Hammadi, Gnosti-*

cism, and Early Christianity, ed. Charles W. Hedrick and Rogert Hodgson Jr. (Peabody, Mass.: Hendrickson, 1986), 287–307.

24. For the argument that the opponents of Paul in Corinth may have possessed an antinomian attitude, see Walther Schmithals, *Gnosticism in Corinth,* trans. J. Steely (Nashville: Abington Press, 1971); Hurd, *The Origin of 1 Corinthian;* Conzelmann, *1 Corinthians;* Witherington, *Conflict and Community;* Terry, *Discourse Analysis of First Corinthians.* On Jude, see J. Daryl Charles, *Literary Strategy in the Epistle of Jude* (Scranton: University of Scranton Press, 1993), 52; Richard J. Bauckham, *Jude, 2 Peter,* Word Biblical Commentary 50 (Waco, Tex.: Word Books, 1983), 11–12; Duane F. Watson, "The Letter of Jude," in *The New Interpreter's Bible,* vol. 12 (Nashville: Abingdon Press, 1998), 475; Charles Bigg, *A Critical and Exegetical Commentary on the Epistles of St. Peter and St. Jude,* International Critical Commentaries (New York: Scribner, 1922), 313–15; J. N. D. Kelly, *A Commentary on the Epistles of Peter and Jude,* Black's New Testament Commentaries (London: Adam & Charles Black, 1969), 265. On 2 Peter, see Bauckham, *Jude, 2 Peter,* 154–57; Donald Senior, *1 and 2 Peter* (Wilmington, N.C.: Glazier, 1980), 100; Kelly, *A Commentary,* 328. On the opponents of the Pastorals, see Dibelius and Conzelmann, *Pastoral Epistles,* 116. Dibelius and Conzelmann grant that the opponents may by libertine, though they call this hypothesis into question on the evidence of Gnostic tendency toward asceticism, not libertinism.

25. McGuire, "Women, Gender, and Gnosis," 264.

26. Justin *1 Apol.* 16, 26; Iren. *Adv. Haer.* 1.6.3; 1.28.2. See also Arist. *Apol.* 17.2; Tatian *Or.* 25.3; Athenagoras *Leg.* 3.1; Tertullian *Apol.* 7.1–8.9; Minicius Felix *Oct.* 9.5–7.

27. Given the centrality of sexualized language to the Christian (and non-Christian) discourses of legitimization examined in this book, it seems to me that these charges cannot be read as secure historical evidence of much of anything.

28. On the literary relationship between Jude and 2 Peter, see Neyrey, *2 Peter, Jude: A New Translation with Introduction and Commentary,* Anchor Bible 37c (New York: Doubleday, 1993), 135; Bauckham, *Jude, 2 Peter,* 141–43; Eric Fuchs and Pierre Reymond, *La Deuxième Épitre de Saint Pierre, l'Épitre de Saint Jude,* Commentaire de Noveau Testament 13b (Paris: Delachaux & Niestlé, 1980), 20–24; Hubert Frankemölle, *1. und 2. Petrusbrief, Judasbrief,* Die Neue Echter Bibel (Würtzburg: Echter Verlag, 1987), 82–84; A. R. C. Leaney, *The Letters of Peter and Jude: A Commentary on the First Letter of Peter, a Letter of Jude, and the Second Letter of Peter,* Cambridge Bible Commentary (Cambridge: Cambridge University Press, 1967), 100–104; Kelly, *A Commentary,* 225–37.

29. On the popularity of *The Shepherd* in the early church, see Carolyn Osiek, *The Shepherd of Hermas,* Hermeneaia (Minneapolis: Fortress Press, 1999), 4–7; Martin Dibelius, *Der Hirt des Hermas,* vol. 4 of *Die apostolishen Väter,* Handbuch zum Neuen Testament (Tübingen: Mohr/Siebeck, 1923), 421–23.

30. Bauckham, *Jude, 2 Peter,* 6; Neyrey, *2 Peter, Jude,* 27. Even if we accept the argument of Bauckham that the point of the letter is to be found in the concluding exhortation (Bauckham, "appeal"), the polemic against false teachers occupies sixteen of verses of the twenty-five verse letter (Bauckham, *Jude, 2 Peter,* 4). References to biblical and apocryphal traditions in Jude include Exodus (5), Watchers (6), Sodom and Gomorrah (7), Moses and the archangel Michael (9), Cain, Balaam, and Korah (11), and a quotation of 1 Enoch (14).

31. See Neyrey, *2 Peter, Jude,* 29, 35. See also the rhetorical analysis of Jude offered by Charles, *Literary Strategy,* 25–48; and Duane F. Watson, *Invention, Arrangement, and Style: Rhetorical Criticism of Jude and 2 Peter,* SBL Dissertation Series 104 (Atlanta: Scholars Press, 1988), 29–79.

32. There are fourteen words in Jude that appear no where else in the New Testament. The author demonstrates a familiarity with Greek idiom, and the diction of Jude has been favorably compared with Luke-Acts, Hebrews, and 2 Peter (which borrowed from Jude). See N. Turner, "The Literary Character of New Testament Greek," *NTS* 20 (1974): 107. On the use of Greek idiom in Jude, see Bauckham, *Jude, 2 Peter,* 6.

33. One recent study states, "Nothing definite can be said about the author, origin, or date of the Epistle of Jude" (Watson, *Invention,* 473).

34. Bigg, *A Critical and Exegetical Commentary*, 313–15; W. G. Kümmel, *Introduction to the New Testament*, 14th ed. (New York: Abingdon, 1966), 299; Kelly, *A Commentary*, 265; E. M. Sidebottom, ed., *James, Jude, and 2 Peter*, The Century Bible (London: Nelson, 1967), 75–76.

35. Bauckham, *Jude, 2 Peter*, 11–12; Neyrey, *2 Peter, Jude*, 32; Leaney, *Letters of Peter and Jude*, 83, 85.

36. Charles, *Literary Strategy*, 52. Bauckham, *Jude, 2 Peter*, 11–12. Bauckham further identifies this group as itinerant charismatics. Watson agrees, arguing that they are antinomian itinerant prophets (*Invention*, 475). Still, little can be said about the author's opponents or the purpose of his letter beyond the polemical evidence he himself offers. Thus all attempts to identify the specific place of writing, the identity of the author, and the occasion for its composition can only be speculative (Neyrey, *2 Peter, Jude*, 32).

37. Several commentators note Jude's polemical use of οὗτοι. See esp. Bauckham, *Jude, 2 Peter*, 45 and Charles, *Literary Strategy*, 33, 39–40, 168–69

38. The citation of "the predictions of the apostles" here in Jude suggests to some exegetes that this letter must be postapostolic (i.e., late first or early second century), but see Bauckham, *Jude, 2 Peter*, 103; and Watson, *Invention*, 474.

39. The source of this story is disputed, though it is loosely based on the tradition of the death of Moses (Deut 34). Bauckham argues that Jude 9 may reflect a lost section of the *Testament of Moses*. Bauckham, *Jude, 2 Peter*, 178–206. See also Charles, *Literary Strategy*, 149–53; D. H. Wallace, "The Semitic Origin of the Assumption of Moses," *Theologische Zeitschrift* 11 (1955): 321–28. I am following Bauckham's exegesis of this verse, preferring the Bauckham's translation and interpretation to that of, for example, the RSV. (Bauckham: "But when Michael the archangel, in debate with the devil, disputed about the body of Moses, he did not presume to condemn him for slander, but said, 'May the Lord rebuke you.'" RSV: "But when the archangel Michael, contending with the devil, disputed about the body of Moses, he did not presume to pronounce a reviling judgment upon him, but said, 'The Lord rebuke you.'") For an alternative view, see Kelly, *A Commentary*, 264–65. Whichever translation is preferred, the point seems to be that judgment is best left to God.

40. See discussion in Geza Vermes, "The Story of Balaam," in *Scripture and Tradition in Judaism* (Leiden: Brill, 1973), 127–77.

41. On the relationship between Jude and 1 Enoch, see James C. VanderKam, "1 Enoch, Enochic Motifs, and Enoch in Early Christian Literature," in *The Jewish Apocalyptic Heritage in Early Christianity*, ed. James C. VanderKam and William Adler, Compendia Rerum Iudaicarum ad Novum Testamentum 4 (Minneapolis: Fortress Press, 1996), 35–40.

42. The textual tradition is inconsistent here. Most manuscripts read "the Lord."

43. Kelly suggests that the use of "*to deuteron*" here is an implied reference to the rescue from Egypt (*A Commentary*, 256).

44. On this story in 1 Enoch 6–11, to which Jude most likely refers here, see Albert-Marie Denis, *Introduction aux pseudépigraphes Grecs d'Ancien Testament*, Studia in Veteris Testamenti Pseudepigrapha (Leiden: E. J. Brill, 1970), 15–30; George W. E. Nickelsburg, *Jewish Literature Between the Bible and the Mishnah: A Historical and Literary Introduction* (Philadelphia: Fortress Press, 1981), 48–55; Maxwell J. Davidson, *Angels at Qumran: A Comparative Study of 1 Enoch 1–36 and Sectarian Writings from Qumran*, Journal for the Study of the Pseudepigrapha Supplement Series 11 (Sheffield: JSOT Press, 1992), 31–78; D. S. Russell, *Divine Disclosure: An Introduction to Jewish Apocalyptic* (Minneapolis: Fortress Press, 1992), 37–42. According to VanderKam's careful analysis, Jude knew at least 1 Enoch 1 and 6–11 ("1 Enoch," 35). References to the "Watchers" who fornicated with women may also be found in *CD* 2.14–23, 2 Enoch 18, 2 *Apoc. Bar.* 56:12–15, *T. Reub.* 5.6–7, and Joseph *Ant.* 1.3.1.

45. On the composite character of "1 Enoch," see E. Isaac, introduction to the Ethiopic Apocalypse of Enoch, in *The Old Testament Pseudepigrapha*, vol. 1, ed. James H. Charlesworth (New York: Doubleday, 1983), 5–12. VanderKam argues that Jude may have known 1 Enoch 1.9 ("1 Enoch," 35).

46. The passage in Jude does not directly correspond to any of the Greek versions of 1 Enoch, however, and therefore may be an allusion rather than a direct citation. See H.J. Lawlor, "Early Citations from the Book of Enoch," *Journal of Philology* 25 (1897), 164–225. Bauckham reconsiders the issue carefully, concluding that Jude knew the Greek version but made his own translation from the Aramaic. This supports Bauckham's larger thesis that the author was fluent in Hebrew and Aramaic (*Jude, 2 Peter*, 94–96). Enoch was also cited by the author of the Epistle of Barnabas (*Barn.* 4.3), but that citation does not appear in any edition of Enoch currently available.

47. On this passage as a critique of the earthly priesthood, see Martha Himmelfarb, *Ascent to Heaven in Jewish and Christian Apocalypses* (New York: Oxford University Press, 1993), 20–23.

48. As we have seen, traditions about unfaithful Israel frequently described unfaithfulness in terms of illicit desire and sexual infidelity. The people lusted (*epithumeō*) after rich food. Their lack of faith was referred to as fornication/whoring (*porneuō* and cognates). Men of Israel were seduced into worshipping Baal when they fornicated with Moabite women. Paul's reference to these events is telling. Arguing that Christians should avoid idolatry, he warns the Corinthians not to "fornicate" (*porneuō*) like unfaithful Israel, for "twenty-three thousand fell in a single day" (1 Cor 10:8; Num 25:1–18. See also Heb 3:7–4:3; *CD* 3:6–10).

49. So Wisse, "The Epistle of Jude," 138; Kelly, *A Commentary*, 254–5. Bauckham and Charles would disagree.

50. I am in agreement with Bauckham here that the "strange flesh" that the men of Sodom and Gomorrah are accused of desiring does not necessarily refer to their desire for homoerotic intercourse but rather for the "strange flesh" of the angels. See Bauckham, *Jude, 2 Peter*, 54 (Watson disagrees: *Invention*, 489). Still, the sexual content of their sin is clear. They "fornicated" (*ekporneuō*) and "went after strange flesh." Sodom was said to be guilty of various other sins including hatred of strangers (Wis 19.14–15), selfishness (Ezek 16:46–50), and sexual immorality in general (*Jubilees*, 16.5–6; *T. Levi* 14.6). Interestingly, *T. Levi* also mentions Enoch, the marrying of foreign women by unfaithful Israelite men, and the dangers of becoming "like Sodom and Gomorrah" (14.1–8). See H.W. Hollander and M. de Jonge, *The Testaments of the Twelve Patriarchs*, Studia in Veteris Testamenti Pseudepigrapha (Leiden: E. J. Brill, 1985), 169–71.

51. My reading of the examples offered in Jude 5–7 privileges the (presupposed) sexual content of each of the three episodes. Though the majority of exegetes have also noted that fornication implicitly connects these verses (see, for example, Kelly, *A Commentary*, 253–259, Bauckham, *Jude, 2 Peter*, 54–55, and Wisse, "The Epistle of Jude," 138), Charles would disagree.

52. These same three examples are referred to in Sir 16.7–10, *CD* 2:17–3:12, and 3 Macc 2:4–7 to illustrate God's judgment upon the ungodly. See Watson, *Invention*, 488.

53. Throughout the Septuagint, false prophets were said to "dream dreams" and to mislead the people. So, according to Deuteronomy, false prophets, dreaming dreams (LXX), encourage Israel to follow other gods. Such prophets must be rejected, even killed, for their words lead Israel astray (Deut 13:2–4, 6, LXX). Jeremiah laments that false prophets "dreaming dreams" cause the people to forget their God, just as their ancestors did when they worshiped Baal (Jer 23:25–28): The false prophets, saying "I have dreamed dreams!" (LXX) try to lead the people to forget the name of God, "just as their fathers forgot my name for Baal." Zechariah worries that the lying dreams of the dreamers guide the people falsely (Zech 10:2). Thus, by accusing them of "dreaming," Jude compares the current false prophets with the false dreamers of old. Still, dreaming could also be depicted as a positive channel of divine revelation across the cultures of the Mediterranean world. Old men who "dream dreams" were offered as a sign of God's restoration of Israel in Joel 2:28. See Patricia Cox Miller, *Dreams in Late Antiquity: Studies in the Imagination of a Culture* (Princeton, N.J.: Princeton University Press, 1994).

54. Most contemporary scholars read κυριότης as referring to "lordship" or "divine sovereignty," on analogy with *Did.* 4.1 and Herm. *Sim.* 5.6.1 (e.g., Kelly, *A Commentary*, 262 and Bauckham, *Jude, 2 Peter*, 54–55). Other options include that the false teachers reject ecclesiastical authority or that the false teachers reject a class of angels known as "κυριότητες" (analogous

to Col 1:16; Eph. 1:21). The first option has been largely rejected. The second is difficult given that "κυριότης" is rendered in the singular. As Kelly notes, verse 4 suggests that Christ is the appropriate designation: "[they] deny our only master and lord, Jesus Christ." Bauckham suggests that the author's fondness for catchwords offers further evidence that he intended to pick up the charge he first made in verse four.

55. See Bauckham, *Jude, 2 Peter*, 57.

56. To Bauckham, the charge "slandering the angels" means that the false teachers offended the angels who were in charge of guarding the created order (the position rejected by the Watchers when they lusted after women): "We can well imagine that the false teachers, reproached for conduct which offended the angels as the administrators of the moral order, justified themselves by proclaiming their liberation from bondage to these angels and speaking slightingly of them" (*Jude, 2 Peter*, 58). Watson suggests that the inappropriate behavior of the Sodomites toward the angels is analogous to the "reviling" attributed to the false teachers (489).

57. Pointed out by Bauckham, *Jude, 2 Peter*, 56.

58. Israel's disobedience is repeatedly described as defilement, especially sexual defilement. For example, in Leviticus, God commands Israel not to give their children (lit. "give of his seed") to Molech (Gk. *archonti*, "a ruler") (Lev 20:1, 3, LXX). If they do, they will defile (*miainō*) God's "holy things" (Lev 20:1–5). Jeremiah, denouncing Israel for apostasy, asked, "How can you say, 'I am not defiled [*miainō*] and I have not gone after Baal'?" since this is precisely what unfaithful Israel has done (Jer 2:23, LXX). Indeed, "she" (i.e., Israel) has been handed over to the "lusts of her soul," for "she loved strangers and went after them" (Jer 2:24–25). Recounting the sorry behavior of Israel in the wilderness, Ezekiel notes that, despite God's warnings, the sons of Israel defiled themselves (*miainō*) with the habits of Egypt (Ezek 20:7, 8, LXX). Thus, in Leviticus and the prophets, illicit religious behavior is frequently equated with illicit sexual behavior. Not surprisingly, illicit sexual behavior is also described in terms of defilement (*miainō* and cognates). For example, a woman who commits adultery is said to defile herself (Num 5:13, 14, 20, 27, 29); a man who commits adultery with his neighbor's wife defiles her (Ezek 18:6, 11); and Shechem's rape of Dinah is described as a defilement (Gen 34:5, 13, 27).

59. Noted by Bauckham: "Jude is therefore identifying the sin of the false teachers as corresponding to that of the second and third types" (*Jude, 2 Peter*, 56).

60. Neyrey, comparing Jude to Philo, also notes that "defilement" often refers to sexual immorality in particular and is linked to apostasy (*2 Peter, Jude*, 67–68).

61. Bauckham, *Jude, 2 Peter*, 63. On the idea that sexual indulgence leads to destruction, see also Rom 1:18–32; 1 Tim 5:6 ("She who lives luxuriously is dead while she lives").

62. Joseph *Ant.* 1.52–66.

63. According to Philo, Josephus, and Pseudo-Philo, Balaam led Israel into the apostasy described in Num 25:1–5. See Philo *Mos.* 1.295–300; Joseph *Ant.* 4.126–30; Ps-Philo 18.13. As Bauckham notes, "Jewish tradition remembered Balaam primarily as a man of greed, who for the sake of reward led Israel into debauchery and idolatry" (*Jude, 2 Peter*, 81). See also Neyrey, *2 Peter, Jude*, 73. The author of Revelation accused the church in Pergamum of tolerating members who follow the teaching of Balaam, "who taught Balak to put a stumbling block before the sons of Israel that they eat food sacrificed to idols and fornicate" (Rev 2:14).

64. Num 16:1–35, 26:9–10. For later traditions about Korah, see Psalm 106:16–18; Sir 45.18–19; Ps-Philo 16.1; Joseph *Ant.* 4.12–13. See discussion in Bauckham, *Jude, 2 Peter*, 83–84; and Neyrey, *2 Peter, Jude*, 73.

65. Cain was cursed by God (Gen 4:11–12; according to *T. Benj.* 7.2–5, Cain suffered for two hundred years prior to being destroyed by the Flood); Balaam was put to death (Num 31:8); Korah was swallowed up by the earth (Num 16:30–33).

66. The use of "σπιλάδες" (LSJ "a rock over which the sea dashes; a ledge of rock," s.v. "σπίλας") is puzzling here. Some commentators have preserved the reading "reef" or "sea-rock" and understood Jude to be arguing that the false teachers are like dangerous reefs—"close contact with them will result in [metaphorical] ship-wreck" (Bauckham, *Jude, 2 Peter*, 85. See also Kelly,

A Commentary, 270–71). Others understand "σπίλας" to be equivalent to "σπίλος," meaning "blemish" or "spot": Neyrey, 2 Peter, Jude, 74–75; R. Knopf, Die Briefe Petri und Judä, Kritisch-exegetischer Kommentar über das Neue Testament 12 (Göttingen: Vandenhoeck & Ruprecht, 1912); BDF § 45; the English translations found in the NRSV and the RSV. Jude's earliest interpreter, the author of 2 Peter, read "σπιλάδες" as "stain" or "blemish" (2 Pet 2:13). No matter how one translates "σπιλάδες," however, Jude clearly intends to imply that "these" have spoiled community meals in some way.

67. With the majority of scholars, I am reading "en tais agapais humōn" as a reference to the community meals of the Christians Jude is addressing (cf. 2 Pet 2:13; Ign. Smyrn. 8.2). See Kelly, A Commentary, 269–70; Bauckham, Jude, 2 Peter, 86–7; Neyrey, 2 Peter, Jude, 75; Sidebottom, ed., James, Jude, and 2 Peter, 89; Leaney, Letters of Peter and Jude, 94.

68. "Admiring faces," appears in the LXX as a translation of a Hebrew idiom that seems to mean "show partiality," esp. for the sake of a bribe. See Bauckham, Jude, 2 Peter, 99–100; Kelly, A Commentary, 279.

69. On Jude as a source for the author of 2 Peter, see Bauckham, Jude, 2 Peter, 141–43; Tord Fornberg, An Early Church in a Pluralistic Society: A Study of 2 Peter, Coniectanea biblica New Testament Series 9 (Uppsala: CWK Gleerup, 1977), chap. 3.

70. An early-second-century date for 2 Peter is suggested by the mention of the letters of Paul (considered to be scripture); the recitation of the complaint that "ever since the fathers fell asleep, all things have continued as they were"; and the reminder to the "beloved" that they ought to remember the commandment of the Lord that they received "through your apostles" (3:16, 3:4, 3:2) For discussion, see Frankemölle, 1. und 2. Petrusbrief, 80–82; Fuchs and Reymond, La Deuxième Épitre, 39–40; Senior, 1 and 2 Peter, 99–101. Some scholars suggest an earlier date, however—perhaps late first century: Bauckham, Jude, 2 Peter, 157–58; Ceslas Spicq, Les Épitres de Saint Pierre, Sources Bibliques (Paris: Librairie Lecoffre, 1966), 194–96. Whatever the date, most would agree that 2 Peter is pseudonymous. Jerome, noticing the striking differences between 1 and 2 Peter, attempted to account for the serious differences in style and language between the two letters by suggesting that Peter used two different interpreters to assist him in the composition of the letters (Jerome Ep. 120). This suggestion has proven to be unsatisfactory, however, both to ancient and modern readers. Eusebius, for example, noted that apostolic authorship was not universally accepted by the churches (Hist. Eccl. 3.3.4; 6.35.8). Bauckham pronounces modern attempts to demonstrate a possible literary relationship between 1 and 2 Peter "unsuccessful" (Jude, 2 Peter, 43–44), a sentiment shared by Kelly (A Commentary, 235). Perhaps the most decisive evidence against Peterine authorship is the overwhelming evidence for a late-first-century or early-second-century date. If Peter was martyred circa 64 C.E., as is commonly believed, then he could not have penned this document (noted and discussed by Bauckham, Jude, 2 Peter, 159; Fuchs and Reymond, La Deuxième Épitre, 30–31). Bauckham, noting the relationship of 2 Peter to the testamentary genre, suggests that pseudonymity was an appropriate choice for this author. The author, writing a "testament" in letter form, sought to faithfully interpret the teachings of Peter in light of his own situation, presenting these teachings as the final words of the apostle to the faithful, a strategy he shared with the authors of, for example, the Testament of the Twelve Patriarchs and the Testament of Job (Bauckham, Jude, 2 Peter, 131–32, 161).

71. The biblical anti-examples are found in 2 Peter 4–9; also see Jude 7. On the sexual over-tones of "μίασμα," "μιαίνω," and cognates in the Septuagint, see discussion of Jude 8 above.

72. Reminiscent of warnings in the Septuagint that Israel ought not to follow after (poreuomai) other gods. So, for example, Deut 6:14: "Do not follow other god from among the gods of the Gentiles around you"; Deut 8:19: "If you ... follow after other gods and serve and worship them ... you shall perish"; Jer 13:10: "Wanton [hubris] Judah and wanton Jerusalem ... following after other gods, are enslaved to them and worship them." See also Deut 11:28, 28:14, 30:17; Ezek 5:6–7; 20:18–21.

73. Envisioning adultery, according to one teaching attributed to Jesus, is as bad as actually committing the act (Matt 5:28 and parallels).

74. See discussion of the metaphors "slave to desire" and "slave to sin" in chapter 2.

75. 1 Thess 4:3–7; Rom 1:18–32; Eph 4:17–23; 1 John 2:15–17.

76. Ign. *Eph.* 7.1; Ign. *Smyr.* 4.1. Compare Muson. 10.26–30.

77. Perhaps this interpretation can make sense of the difficult use of the term "ἐμπορεύομαι" ("to sell, to trade") in 2 Pet 2:3. BAGD suggests that this term be translated "they will exploit you," a translation followed in the RSV (s.v. "ἐμπορεύομαι"). Another possibility, suggested by Kelly and Neyrey, is that "to buy" rather than "to sell" is the sense of the term here. Thus, Neyrey translates the verse "in their greed they will buy you with specious arguments" (*2 Peter*, 107). Kelly remarks "their false words are of course the specious arguments or fictitious claims they will use to buy over converts" (*A Commentary*, 329). Alternatively, "Peter" may be implying that the false teachers will sell duped Christians to desire and licentiousness by their pseudo-teachings. They will act as pimps to those who, through their apostasy, become "prostitutes." Later Peter remarks, "They promise freedom, they themselves being ruled by corruption. For whatever overpowers someone, by that he is enslaved" (2 Pet 2:19). The danger to those who listen to the false teachers is that they, too, will become slaves of lust.

78. Bauckham, *Jude, 2 Peter,* 155.

79. Bauckham, *Jude, 2 Peter,* 156. According to Bauckham's reading of Jude, the false teachers Jude opposed were itinerant charismatics resembling the super-apostles who troubled Paul in Corinth. The opponents of the author of 2 Peter, by contrast, promoted a Hellenistic skepticism about the relevance of apocalyptic thought.

80. Kelly, *A Commentary*, 328.

81. Senior, *1 and 2 Peter*, 100. According to Senior, they also boasted about their knowledge and exploited other Christians for economic gain, characteristics they shared with later "gnostic heretics." Still, "we cannot be sure if there is any connection between the two groups." Fuchs and Reymond also suggest that the opponents of 2 Peter were proto-Gnostic in type, though they do not repeat the charges of licentiousness and antinomianism that "Peter" made against them (*La Deuxième Épitre*, 27–29).

82. See, for example, various depictions of Antony: Cass. Dio 51.10–11, 15.2–4; Plut. *Ant.* 25.1. Plutarch suggests that Antony was undone by his love (*erōs*) for Cleopatra: "Such, then, was the nature of Antony, where now as a crowning evil his love for Cleopatra supervened, roused and drove to frenzy many of the passions (*pathē*) that were still hidden and quiescent in him, and dissipated and destroyed whatever good and saving qualities still offered resistance" (Perrin's translation). Antony is further accused of reveling in luxury, engaging in licentious practices, and abandoning his lawful, Roman wife for a foreigner. See esp. *Demetrii cum Antonio comparatio* 4.

83. Aelius Aristides, in *P. Aelii Aristidis Opera quae exstant omnia*, ed. F. W. Lenz and C. A. Behr (Lugduni Batavorum: Brill, 1976), English translation by C. A. Behr, *Aristides: Panathenaic oration and In defence of oratory*, LCL (Cambridge, Mass.: Harvard University Press, 1973), 188. "If they were servants of the desire of the crowds and harangued what the audience approved, it would be impossible for them to have spoken boldly, not to mention to be proud beyond other men. But I think they know in their hearts that they do not serve pleasures, but chastise desires, nor look to the multitude, but the multitude looks to them, nor are ruled by ordinary citizens, but themselves rule the multitude."

84. "Not every king derives his scepter or his royal office from Zeus, but only the good king.... he is not to become licentious or profligate, strutting and gorging with folly, insolence, arrogance, and all manner of lawlessness ... but to the best of his ability he is to devote his attention to himself and his subjects, becoming a guide and a shepherd of his people, not, as someone has said, a caterer and a banqueter at their expense" (Dio Chrys. *Or.* 1.13).

85. See, for example, 1 Thess 4:4–5; Eph 2:1–3; Col 1:21–22; Titus 2:1–2; Justin *2 Apol.*

86. See, for example, 1 Tim 3:1–7, 5:1–21; Titus 2:12; Col 3:18–4:1; Ign. *Pol.* 4–5; Gos. Thom. 22, 79; *Acta Pauli et Theclae,* 5–6; Justin *1 Apol.* 15, 29; Theophilus *Ad Auto.* 3.15; *Thom. Cont.* 139.1–12, 140.1.

87. Chadwick's translation, 66. Still, Clement argues, Christians may marry and, if they do, should not abstain from married sexual intercourse as long as the intercourse is self-controlled and for the sake of begetting children. To claim otherwise is contrary to Scripture and a blasphemy against the law and the Lord (Clement *Strom.* 3.9–12). For discussion, see Brown, *The Body and Society*, 132–39.

88. Martin, *Corinthian Body*, 212–18. For further discussion, see chapter 2.

89. 2 Pet 3:7: "But by the same word [of God that created the heavens and the earth] the present heavens and earth have been reserved for fire, being kept until the day of judgment and destruction of ungodly people [ἀσεβῶν ἀνθρώπων]." Jude 14–15: "Behold, the Lord came with his holy myriads, to execute judgment on all, and to convict the ungodly of all their deeds of ungodliness which they have committed in such an ungodly way" (citing Enoch).

90. Wisse, "The Epistle of Jude," 142.

91. J. Reiling makes a similar observation in his examination of the false prophet who is denounced in Mandate 11 of *The Shepherd*: "The distinction between the false prophets and false teachers ... is of a typological nature and not necessarily an exact description of historical facts," an argument he supports by analogy with Iren. *Adv. Haer.* 1.13 and 4.33. J. Reiling, *Hermas and Christian Prophecy: A Study of the Eleventh Mandate*, Supplements to Novum Testamentum 37 (Leiden: E. J. Brill, 1973), 64.

92. See, for example, Gal 5:13; 1 Clem 30.1; *Herm.* Vis. 1.1.8–9, 3.7.2; Sim. 9.13.7–9.

93. See, for example, Iren. *Adv. Haer.* 1.13.1, 1.25.3–6, 1.26.3; Epiph. *Pan.* 25.1–4. Quoting the same Proverb cited by 2 Peter while denouncing a sect of heretics first mentioned by Revelation (and about which he had not direct knowledge), Epiphanius notes, "He [Nicolaus] had an attractive wife, and had refrained from intercourse as though in imitation of those whom he saw devoted to God. He endured this for a while but in the end could not bear to control his incontinence. Instead, since he wished to return to it like a dog to its vomit, he looked for poor excuses, and invented them in defense of his own state of intemperance ... because he was ashamed of his defeat and suspected that he had been found out, he ventured to say, 'Unless one copulates every day, he cannot have eternal life'" (Williams's translation, 77). Compare Proverbs 26:11; 2 Pet 2:22 (on dogs returning to their vomit); Rev 2:6 (for the first mention of the "Nicolaitans"); Clem. *Strom.* 3.26.6; Iren. *Adv. Haer.* 1.26.3; Hippolytus *Haer.* 7.36.3; Eusebius *Hist. Eccl.* 3.29.2–4.

94. Bauer cites Hermas "who has no heresies in view" as evidence that Rome was initially "spared controversy with the heretics" (Bauer, *Orthodoxy and Heresy*, 114).

95. Though *The Shepherd* does not contain an explicit attack against any specific "false" Christians, I have chosen to include it here to illustrate that the typical false Christian described in this text directly conforms to representations of the "opponents" discussed above and of the "heretics" discussed in more detail below. The close parallels between the ideal type described in *The Shepherd* and the purportedly "real" false prophets, teachers, and heretics described elsewhere further call into question the portrait of pseudo-Christians offered by Jude, 2 Peter, Justin, and Irenaeus, among others.

96. There is little agreement as to the precise date of *The Shepherd of Hermas*. Some have argued that *The Shepherd* was written as early as 80 C.E.: J. Christian Wilson, *Toward a Reassessment of the Shepherd of Hermas: Its Date and Its Pneumatology* (Lewiston, N.Y.: Mellen Biblical Press, 1993), 9–10, 24–61. Discounting the evidence of the Muratorian Fragment, Wilson concludes that internal evidence suggests a late-first-century date. Osiek objects to Wilson's "unhistorical assumptions," however (*The Shepherd of Hermas*, 19 n. 143). Tugwell also prefers an early date, perhaps as early as 60–70 C.E.: Tugwell, *The Apostolic Fathers*, Outstanding Christian Thinkers Series (Harrisburg, Penn.: Morehouse Publishing, 1989), 47. Martin Dibelius argues, based in part on a reference to Clement in Herm. *Vis.* 2.4.3, that the early stage of the work was completed during the first quarter of the second century: Dibelius, *Der Hirt des Hermas*, 453. Still, no one view has held sway. For a helpful overview of the issues involved, see Osiek, *The Shepherd of Hermas*, 18–20; and Bart D. Ehrman, introduction to *The Shepherd of Hermas*, trans. Ehrman, in *Apostolic Fathers*, LCL (Cambridge, Mass.: Harvard University Press, 2003), 2:162–73.

97. In her study of *The Shepherd*, Carolyn Osiek has argued that this document is properly read as conforming to the genre "apocalypse." She concurs with the judgment of Adela Yarbro Collins that "since Herm is characterized both by apocalyptic eschatology and by revelation mediated by otherworldly beings, there is no good reason to exclude it from the genre 'apocalypse'"; Collins, "The Early Christian Apocalypses," *Semeia* 14 (1979): 75; and Osiek, "The Genre and Function of the Shepherd of Hermas," *Semeia* 36, ed. Adela Yarbro Collins (1986): 115. Also see David Hellholm, *Das Visionenbuch des Hermas als Apokalypse*, Coniectanea Biblica, New Testament Series 13, no. 1 (Uppsala: CWK Gleerup, 1980). Others have been more reluctant to accept this designation, however; see P. Vielhauer, "Apokalyptik des Urchristentums 1. Einleitung," in *Neutestamentliche Apokryphen II; Apostolisches, Apokalypsen und Verwantes*, ed. E. Hennecke and W. Schneemelcher (Tübingen: Mohr/Siebeck, 1964), 408–54. By calling *The Shepherd* an "apocalypse," I seek to highlight the importance of eschatology and revelation to this document, not to solve the problem of its genre.

98. Hermas may well be a historical figure, but the text is more allegorical than autobiographical. Doubts about the historical reliability of biographical information offered by the author were raised by Dibelius in his important early commentary (*Hirt des Hermas*, 419–20). To Dibelius, Hermas's family and their sins represent the church and its sins. Particularly troubling to those who want to argue for historical reliability is the opening scene of the text—the bath of Rhoda in the Tiber. See Dibelius, *Hirt des Hermas*, 429–30. Extensive discussion of Dibelius's argument and of the issue of historicity may be found in Martin Leutzsch, *Die Wahrnehmung sozialer Wirklichkeit im "Hirten des Hermas,"* (Göttingen: Vandenhoeck & Ruprecht, 1989), 20–49.

99. The woman-church appears as the principal revealer in the first 4 Visions. The Shepherd is introduced in Vision 5 and remains Hermas's guide throughout the rest of the document. The disappearance of the woman-church from the initial visions, coupled with the existence of ancient text editions of *The Shepherd* that include only Visions 1–4 or Vision 5 and following, suggest that the early visions were first intended to serve as a separate unit. Nevertheless, the relative thematic unity and self-referential qualities of *The Shepherd* suggest a single author. See the helpful discussion of this issue in Edith McEwan Humphrey, *The Ladies and the Cities: Transformation and Apocalyptic Identity in Joseph and Aseneth, 4 Ezra, the Apocalypse, and The Shepherd of Hermas*, Journal for the Study of Pseudepigrapha Supplement Series 17 (Sheffield: Sheffield Academic Press, 1995), 126–29.

100. The Bodmer Papyrus manuscript (P. Bod. 38), for example, probably contained only Visions 1–4. Antonio Carlini, "La tradizione testuale del Pastor di Ermo I nuovi papiri," in *Le Stade del Testo*, ed. Gugielmo Cavallo (Lecce: Adriatica Editrice, 1987), 29. Noted by Osiek, *The Shepherd of Hermas*, 3. See also Humphrey, *The Ladies and the Cities*, 128–29; and Ehrman, introduction, 169–72.

101. Most famously Stanislas Giet, *Hermas et les pasteurs: Les Trois auteurs du Pasteur d'Hermas* (Paris: Presses Universitaires de France, 1963). Geit's thesis is now largely rejected. See Robert Joly, "Hermas et le Pasteur," *Vigiliae Christianae* 21 (1967): 201–18; and Ehrman, introduction, 165–66.

102. Osiek, *The Shepherd of Hermas*, 10.

103. As Osiek rightly points out, the document is self-referential, with Herm. *Sim.*10.1 presupposing Herm. *Vis.* 5 and Herm. *Sim.* 10.3 presupposing Herm. *Sim.* 9.10–3. Moreover, the book is unified in theme and language. Osiek suggests that the loose structure of the book, a structure that has contributed to theories of multiple authorship or multiple redactions, is best explained by the use of the text as a basis for oral proclamation (Osiek, *The Shepherd of Hermas*, 12–16). Whether or not one is satisfied with this explanation, Osiek succeeds in demonstrating the unity of theme that links the book together as it now stands.

104. Aune suggests that repentance is *the* organizing theme of the entire text: David E. Aune, *The New Testament in its Literary Environment*, Library of Early Christianity (Philadelphia: Westminster Press, 1987), 247. Humphrey objects, arguing that it is a mistake to seek "either a

dogmatic or thematic 'core' passage which overshadows the rest of the work" (*The Ladies and the Cities*, 125). Osiek accepts the view that μετάνοια is the major theme but notes: "It is a mistake to look for perfect overall consistency in the text.... Each story or unit must be taken primarily on its own merits, with a glance to possible relationships with other passages, but without expecting overall consonance of details" (Osiek, *The Shepherd of Hermas*, 28–38).

105. All in all, the terms "μετάνοια," "μετανοεῖν," or "*paenitentia*" occur 156 times. See Ingrid Goldhahn-Müller, *Die Grenze der Gemeinde: Studien zum Problem der Zweiten Busse im Neuen Testament unter Berucksichtigung der Entwicklung im 2. Jh. bis Tertullian*, Gottinger theologische Arbeiten 39 (Göttingen: Vandenhoeck & Ruprecht, 1989), 245. Cited in Osiek, *The Shepherd of Hermas*, 28 n. 218.

106. For more on the importance of *dipsuchia* to *The Shepherd*, see Reiling, *Hermas and Christian Prophecy*, 32–33. Reiling suggests, rather convincingly in my opinion, that *dipsuchia* is best understood as "the opposite of ἐξ ὅλης καρδίας: a divided allegiance; they have the Lord on their lips, not in their heart." It is also the opposite of *pistis* (faith).

107. Young has argued that "becoming a real man" is the organizing theme of the *Shepherd*. Hermas, Young notes, becomes ever more "manly" as the text progresses. At the beginning of the text, he is convicted of failing to control his household/church. By the end, he takes his place as the "man," supported by the virgins who become his assistants. According to Young's interpretation, the fitness of a church and its members is measured on a trajectory of "maleness" where to be male is to be in control of oneself (exhibited through sexual purity) and one's household (which in the case of Hermas includes the church): Steve Young, "'Being a Man': The Pursuit of Manliness in *The Shepherd of Hermas*," *JECS* 2, no. 3 (1994): 237–55. Young's provocative exegesis fits well with my own reading. Still, I would add that the enkrateia promoted—and the "manliness" that this enkrateia implies—is constituted by the control of *epithymia*. If one is plagued by wicked desire, one has not truly achieved self-control nor has one found true faith. *The Shepherd* repeatedly drives home this point when describing the failures of weak Christians or the wickedness of false Christians and apostates. The author's concern for *metanoia* and the critique of *dipsuchia* are not superseded. Rather, the urgent need for repentance is created, in part, by problems associated with desire. Moreover, double-mindedness leaves Christians open to the temptations of wicked desire and the machinations of the devil—especially to the seductions of false prophets or false spirits that seek to lead astray the slaves of God.

108. See also Herm. *Vis.* 1 (a Christian ought not to sin in his heart); Herm. *Vis.* 3 (Christian "stones" are rejected for disobedience, hypocrisy, wickedness, wavering faith, divisiveness, loving the riches of the world); Herm. *Mand.* 4 (Christians must be pure, avoiding *porneia* and thoughts of *porneia*); Herm. *Mand.* 6 (an angel of wickedness seeks to lead Christians to sin); Herm. *Mand.* 12 (evil desire must be cast off); Herm. *Sim.* 5.7 (keep your flesh and your mind pure); Herm. *Sim.* 6.2 (the angel of luxury and pleasure seeks to beguile the faithfull with wicked desires); Herm. *Sim.* 7.5.4 (apostate Christians surrender to desire and the devil).

109. Compare Herm. *Mand* 6.2 (the angel of evil causes people to desire extravagant food and drink, reveling, delicacies, and women); Herm. *Sim.* 6.2 (angels of luxury and pleasure beguile the faithful with wicked desires). Note also that the personified vices in Herm. *Sim.* 9 are called "evil spirits."

110. See also Herm. *Mand* 4; 6; Herm. *Sim* 6.2, 7.5, 9.19.

111. Reiling suggests that the author of *Hermas* utilized technical language of ("pagan") magical divination to describe the "emptiness" of the divinatory acts engaged in by the "ψσευδοπροφήτης," thereby suggesting that false prophecy was meant to be seen as a "pagan intrusion" into the Christian community (*Hermas and Christian Prophecy*, 45–47).

112. "Luxury" and "indulgence" are also denounced in Herm. *Sim.* 6.4.4; Herm. *Mand.* 6.2.5; 12.2.1, often appearing as τρυφὴ πονηρά.

113. This charge is especially important to *The Shepherd*; See Reiling, *Hermas and Christian Prophecy*, 52; Osiek, *The Shepherd of Hermas*, 145.

114. Crescens, Justin suggests, denounced the Christians just to satisfy the mob (*hoi polloi*).

115. Hence the "double-minded" make the mistake of seeking out false prophets who fulfill their desires. Herm. *Mand.* 11.1 (see Reiling, *Hermas and Christian Prophecy,* 32–34).

116. For a summary of the chief differences between the two visions, see Osiek, *The Shepherd of Hermas,* 220.

117. In Herm. *Vis* 3.8.3–8, there are seven women/personified virtues who hold up the tower.

118. The significance of the clothing of the virgins or vices is clear. The virgins wear linen and are dressed εὐπρεπῶς (i.e., seemingly, becomingly, in a fitting way): Herm. *Sim.* 9.2.4. The vices wear black, a sign of impurity and sin throughout this Similitude, and are wild (ἄγριαι): Herm. *Sim.* 9.6.4, 8.1, 4–5, 19.1. Compare Herm. *Vis.* 4.2.1, where the world is described as the black markings on a terrible beast. The red markings show that this world must be destroyed in blood and fire. For further discussion of the significance of the color black in Christian discourse, see Byron, *Symbolic Blackness,* esp. 17–28, 77–103.

119. Reminiscent of the view that God handed over (*paradidōmi*) non-Christians to lust in Rom. 1:18–32.

120. This kind of moralizing call to repentance seems to be quite different from the suggestion of Jude and 2 Peter that one is either faithful and thus self-controlled or faithless and therefore licentious. Indeed, the seemingly loose standards of *The Shepherd* earned the work the designation "lover of adulterers" and "shepherd of adulterers" from Tertullian (*Pud.* 10). Many Christian authors held *The Shepherd* in high regard, however, esp. Origen; see Origen, *De principiis,* in *Traité des principes. Origène; introduction, texte critique de la version de Rufin, traduction, commentaire et fragments,* Latin translation of *Peri archon,* by Rufinus, edited with French translation by Henri Crouzel and Manlio Simonetti, 5 vols., Sources chretiennes 252–253, 268–269, 312 (Paris: Editions du Cerf, 1978–1984), 4.2.4; Iren. *Adv. Haer.* 4.20.2; Clement *Strom.* 1.181; 2.3; 2.55–59. Robin Lane Fox suggests that it was precisely this teaching on "one further chance of repentence" that ensured the future popularity of the work: Fox, *Pagans and Christians* (New York: Alfred A. Knopf, 1987), 389. Still, the μετανοία (repentance) that *The Shepherd* calls for is offered only once and in light of the eschatological situation (see, for example, Herm. *Vis.* 1.3.2, 3. 7.6, 8.9; Herm. *Mand.* 4.7–8. Osiek remarks: "It is not a question of ritual or repeated action, not a discipline or an expectation, but personal and corporate transformation through the power of the good spirit" (*The Shepherd of Hermas,* 30). Furthermore, apocalyptic warnings about the coming exclusion of all sinners—be they guilty of διψυχία, a wicked thought, or worse—from the eternal life promised to the saints are found throughout. Such warnings suggest that in the end the standard for inclusion in the kingdom of God will actually be quite high. Hermas's own transformation from one who commits adultery in his heart to one who, assisted by the virtues, experiences no wicked desire at all is paradigmatic of the kind of μετανοία that is required.

121. Pagels, *The Origin of Satan,* 47–60. She identifies the Essenes as the sectarian Jews who began this process. Foreign occupation of Palestine was, to the Jews of Qumran, "evidence that the forces of evil had taken over the world and … infiltrated and taken over God's own people, turning them into allies of the Evil One" (57).

122. Pagels, *The Origin of Satan,* 112–181, esp. 150: "Many Christians believed that even more dangerous were Satan's forays among the most intimate enemies of all—other Christians, or, as most said of those with whom they disagreed, among heretics."

123. Bernard McGinn, *Antichrist: Two Thousand Years of the Human Fascination with Evil* (San Fancisco: HarperSanFrancisco, 1994), 4.

124. This special punishment is referred to in Jude 6; 2 Pet 2:4; Rev 20:10–15; and alluded to in Herm. *Vis.*4.3.6, 5.7; Herm. *Mand.* 8.3–4; Herm. *Sim.* 6.7, 8.11.3–4, 9.33.1, 10.4. The persuasive possibilities of these sorts of arguments are readily apparent; see discussion in O'Leary, *Arguing the Apocalypse,* esp. 4–61.

125. Justin *1 Apol.* 36; Iren. *Adv. Haer.* 1.21.3; Epiph. *Pan.* 26.4–5.

126. Iren. *Adv. Haer.* 6.3, 1.13.2–6.

127. Iren. *Adv. Haer.* 1.25.3.

128. Iren. *Adv. Haer.* 1.24.2, 1.28.1; Clement *Strom.* 3.3.12, 3.9.63, 3.12.80–81. But see 1 Tim 4:3 for an earlier example, with discussion in Margaret MacDonald, *The Pauline Churches*, 179–83 and Dennis MacDonald, *The Legend and The Apostle.*

129. Justin *1 Apol.* 15; Iren. *Adv. Haer.* 3.12.13, 4.16.5, 5.8.2; Clement *Strom.* 3.1.4, 3.5.41, 3.7.59.

5. ILLICIT SEX, WICKED DESIRE, AND THE DEMONIZED HERETIC

1. Justin's *1 Apology* is commonly thought to have been written in 156 C.E. Irenaeus wrote the first five books of *Adversus haereses* sometime between 175 and 189 C.E. See Grant, *Greek Apologists*, 52–53 and Grant, *Irenaeus of Lyons*, Early Church Fathers (London: Routledge, 1997), 6–7.

2. In his first "apology," Justin mentions a treatise that he composed against all heresies that he promises to make available to the emperor, should he be interested (*1 Apol.* 26; see also Justin *Dial.* 35.2–7, 80.1–5). The reference to this treatise against heresies is usually understood to refer to a heresiological work—the first of its kind—written by Justin but now lost. See Jean-Daniel Dubois, "Polémiques, pouvoir et exégèse l'exemple des gnostiques anciens en monde Grec," in *Inventer L'Hérésie? Discours polémiques et pouvoirs avand l'inquisition*, ed. Monique Zerner, Collection du Centre d'Etudes Médiévales de Nice 2 (Nice: Centre d'Études Médiévales, 1998), 41; le Boulluec, *La notion d'hérésie*, 1:40–91.

3. English translation my own. Irenaeus goes on to note that some, while pretending to live chastely with these women as sisters, are exposed when the "sister" turns out to be pregnant by her "brother."

4. English translation my own.

5. Unger's translation.

6. Compare Rev 2:6, 14–15.

7. English translation my own.

8. I borrow the terms "heresiological representation" from le Boulluec (*La notion d'hérésie*, 1:19). My arguments here would not be possible without the invaluable contributions to the study of heresiology and Christian identity formation by Alain le Boulluec, Denise Kimber Buell, Virginia Burrus, Elizabeth Clark, Bart Ehrman, Karen King, and Michael Allen Williams. I rely heavily on their important work throughout this chapter.

9. Earlier generations of scholars tended to read Justin's and Irenaeus' polemics as historical reports in a manner similar to some interpreters of Jude and 2 Peter, often joining their ecclesiastical forbears in an energetic denunciation of those who would dare to promote sexual immorality in the name of Christ. This argument appears even after the important intervention of Walter Bauer in 1934, an intervention that challenged scholars to avoid simple repetition of the antiheretical views of the church fathers (Bauer, *Orthodoxy and Heresy*; on the reception of Bauer's work, see appendix 2 to the English edition, "The Reception of the Book," written by George Strecker, revised and expanded by Robert A. Kraft, 286–316; also see Michel Desjardins, "Bauer and Beyond: On Recent Scholarly Discussions of Αἵρεσις in the Early Christian Era," *Second Century* 8, no. 2 [1991]: 65–82"). Though few contemporary scholars uncritically accept the evidence offered by Justin, Irenaeus, and the heresiologists that followed their lead, the view that there were at least some Christians who experimented with "free love" or something like it persists (see Brown, *Body and Society*, 61, for the "free love" suggestion; Wilken, *The Christians as the Romans Saw Them*, 19–20; Benko, *Pagan Rome*, 63–67), as do attempts to reconstruct the beliefs and practices of the Simonian "Gnostics"; see, for example, Roukema, *Gnosis and Faith*, 22; see also Beyschlag, *Simon Magus*, 193–201; but compare Gerd Lüdemann, *Untersuchungen zur simonianischen Gnosis* (Göttingen: Vandenhoek & Ruprecht, 1975), 84–85; Kurt Rudolph, *Gnosis: The Nature and History of an Ancient Religion*, trans. Robert McL. Wilson (Edinburgh: T & T Clark, 1983), 296. Karen King has written a comprehensive and, to my mind, devastating

critique of scholarship that takes heresiology at its word, examining the content of ancient Christian polemical construction of heresy and observing the repetition of these ancient categories and their politics in the works of modern scholars (*What is Gnosticism?*).

10. Clark, *Reading Renunciation*, 39–42. See also Guila Sfameni Gasparro, "Asceticism and Anthropology: *Enkrateia* and 'Double Creation' in Early Christianity," in *Asceticism*, ed. Vincent L. Wimbush and Richard Valantasis (New York: Oxford University Press, 1995), 130.

11. Heresiology seeks to impose a certain image of the adversary so that, when one speaks of another, one also speaks of himself (le Boulluec, *La notion d'hérésie*, 1:11–19).

12. As Cameron has observed regarding Byzantine heresiology: "[Heresiology] *names* the many heresies it wishes to condemn; in so doing it *differentiates* them from a stated norm, and thereby defines the nature of that norm; it *classifies*, that is, it imposes an ordering on things according to the principles of the writer; it lays down a virtual *hierarchy* of heresies according to their own origins; and finally it *prescribes* their nature, and thereby defines and lays down the structure of knowledge": Averil Cameron, "How to Read Heresiology," *Journal of Medieval and Early Modern Studies* 33, no. 3 (2003): 477, emphasis in the original. Cameron is here describing the heresiological contribution of Epiphanius of Salamis. For further discussion, see Aline Pourkier, *L'Hérésiologie*, 29–52; J. Rebecca Lyman, "Ascetics and Bishops: Epiphanius on Orthodoxy," in *Orthodoxy, Christianity, History*, ed. Susanna Elm, Éric Rebillard, and Antonella Romano, Collection de l'École Française de Rome 270 (Paris: de Boccard, 2000), 149–61; Frances M. Young, "Did Epiphanius Know What He Meant by Heresy?," *Studia Patristica* 17 (1982): 199–205; Gerard Vallée, *A Study in Anti-Gnostic Polemic: Irenaeus, Hippolytus, and Epiphanius* (Waterloo, Ont.: Wilfrid Laurier University Press, 1981).

13. On the illegitimate-succession argument, see esp. le Boulluec, *La notion d'hérésie*, 114–57; Denise Kimber Buell, *Making Christians: Clement of Alexandria and the Rhetoric of Legitimacy* (Princeton, N.J.: Princeton University Press, 1999); King, *What is Gnosticism?*, 31–39; Bart D. Ehrman, *Lost Christianities: The Battles for Scripture and the Faiths We Never Knew* (New York: Oxford University Press, 2003), 189, 192–93. On this argument in the writings of later heresiologists, see Virginia Burrus, *The Making of a Heretic: Gender, Authority, and the Priscillianist Controversy* (Berkeley: University of California Press, 1995); Averil Cameron, "Jews and Heretics—a Category Error?" in *The Ways That Never Parted*, ed. Adam H. Becker and Annette Yoshiko Reed, Texts and Studies in Ancient Judaism (Tübingen: Mohr/Siebeck, 2003), 350–51; Susanna Elm, "The Polemical Use of Genealogies: Jerome's Classification of Pelagius and Evagrius Ponticus," *Studia Patristica* 33 (1997): 311–18.

14. According to Jude, current pseudo-prophets resembled the Hebrew fornicators in the wilderness, the angels who lusted after women, and the men of Sodom who sought intercourse with angels; according to 2 Peter, his targets were like the disobedient angels, the sex-crazed generation destroyed by the flood, and the people of Sodom and Gomorrah.

15. In their writings, the Jews were accused of being congenitally sinful and hard of heart and the deeds of their infamous ancestors were taken as a proof of the argument. As Justin put it, "[you Jews] eagerly committed fornication with the daughters of foreigners, and committed idolatry, and did so again afterwards, when the land had been entrusted to you"; Irenaeus repeated the charge: "they turned to make a calf and turned back to Egypt in their minds, desiring to be slaves rather than free men," forcing God to give them a law "conformed to their desire" that could enslave them and, therefore, control their illicit, idolatrous impulses" (Justin *Dial.* 132.1; Iren. *Adv. Haer.* 4.14.3–15.2, quote from 15.1). On the use of the golden calf episode as a supposed proof of Jewish obstinacy, see Pier Cesare Bori, *The Golden Calf and the Origins of the Anti-Jewish Controversy*, trans. David Ward, South Florida Studies in the History of Judaism 16 (Atlanta: Scholars Press, 1990), esp. 29–33.

16. For further discussion of early Christian claims regarding their superior "race" or "ethnos," see esp. Denise Kimber Buell, "Race and Universalism in Early Christianity," *JECS* 10, no. 4 (2002): 429–68; Buell, "Rethinking the Relevance of Race," 449–76; Caroline Johnson Hodge, "If Sons, Then Heirs.'"

17. A note on the word "γένος [*genos*]": The term implies descent from a common ancestor; it can be translated as "nation," "race," "kind," "people," "family," "kin," and even "stock" or "breed," depending on the context. Following Buell, I argue that Justin uses the term to construct the Christians as a distinct ethnic group, a "people" and a "family" separate from others, characterized by their religious and moral practices as well as their kinship to one another. I will often leave the term untranslated to indicate that it is a technical term with a culture-specific meaning. Buell has argued that the most appropriate translation of the term may well be "race" since, as she rightly points out, the rejection of the term "race" among contemporary scholars presupposes an early Christian rejection of race or ethnicity in favor of universalism over particularity, a rejection that never occurred. Indeed, as Buell and Hodge have shown, ethnoracial thinking was central to the construction of Christian identity, whether by Paul, who viewed the gentiles as joining the lineage of Abraham by means of adoption, or Clement of Alexandria, who sought to classify the Christians as "the one *genos* of the saved people [*laos*]," separate from others (*Strom.* 6.42.2; cited by Buell, "Rethinking Race," 461; on Paul's use of kinship language and metaphors, see Hodge, "'If Sons, Then Heirs,'" 56–138).

18. In Justin's and Irenaeus' reading, biblical tales of apostasy predict a just, foreordained separation of those from the "seed of Abraham," the Jews, from "true Israel," that is, the church. The Christians, they assert, have now become the true race (*genos*) of God (Justin *Dial.* 120.1, 135.3–6; Iren. *Adv. Haer.* 4.23.1, 26.1).

19. English translation my own.

20. Justin and Irenaeus, then, participated in a long standing tradition in Greco-Roman antiquity of identifying one's ultimate progenitor as divine. See Jonathan M. Hall, *Ethnic Identity*.

21. Numerous scholars have noted a peculiar redefinition of the term "αἵρεσις" among Christian authors. Already in his letter to the Galatians, Paul asserts that the "heresies" (*haireseis*) ought to be counted among the "works of the flesh" (Gal 5:20), yet the view that "heresies" are a negative phenomenon was not present in the writings of Paul's Greek contemporaries. See discussion in Simon, "From Greek Hairesis"; H. von Staden, "Hairesis and Heresy: The Case of the *haireseis iatrikai*," in *Jewish and Christian Self-Definition*, vol. 3, *Self-Definition in the Greco-Roman World*, ed. B. Meyer and E. P. Sanders (Philadelphia: Fortress Press, 1982), 76–81; and the helpful overview by Michel Desjardins, "Bauer and Beyond," 65–82. Le Boulluec attributes the invention of the entirely negative, Christian meaning of the term to Justin (*La notion d'hérésie*, 40–91).

22. Arr. *Epct. diss.* 2.19.20. See also Diog. Laert., a summary of earlier summaries of the philosophical schools known as περί αἱρέσεων (*Peri Haireseōn* [On schools of thought]).

23. Stoics (Justin *2 Apol.* 8, 13; Justin *Dial.* 2.1–3); Peripatetics (*Dial.* 2.1); Cynics (*2 Apol.* 3) Socrates (*1 Apol.* 5, 18; *2 Apol.* 10; *Dial.* 1.1); Plato (*1 Apol.* 18, 59–60; *2 Apol.* 13; *Dial.* 4.1); Pythagoras (*2 Apol.* 18; *Dial.* 4.1). On the "heresies" of the Jews, Justin offers the following comment: "do not suppose that [these so-called Christians] are Christians, any more than if one examined the matter rightly he would acknowledge as Jews those who are Sadducees, or similar sects of Genistae, and Meristae, and Galileans, and Hellenians, and Pharisees, and Baptists" (*Dial.* 88.4).

24. Barnard's translation. On the "seed of the Logos" in Justin, especially as this concept is applied to Socrates, see Michel Fédou, "La Figure de Socrate selon Justin," in *Les Apologistes chrétiens et la culture greque*, ed. Bernard Pouderon and Joseph Doré, Théologie Historique 105 (Paris: Beauchesne, 1996), 51–66, esp. 60–62. Fédou notes that Justin's theory of the Logos and his inclusion of Socrates among those who received a portion of the Logos admitted both Jews and people from "the nations" (i.e., the gentiles) into the company of those who could be "Christians before Christ." Nevertheless, I would add, only Christians had received the *fullness* of the Logos.

25. Barnard's translation.

26. Compare Justin *Dial.* 5.1–7.3: "For things are not seen nor comprehended of all, save of him whom God, and his Christ, shall have given understanding" (7.3; Williams's translation).

27. I am adopting the now-widespread view that the *Dialogue with Trypo* was primarily directed at Christians. See esp. Michael Mach, "Justin Martyr's *Dialogus cum Tryphone Iudaeo* and

the Development of Christian Anti-Judiasm," in *Contra Iudaeos: Ancient and Medieval Polemics Between Christians and Jews*, ed. Ora Limor and Guy G. Stroumsa (Tübingen: Mohr/Siebeck, 1996), 27–47; Rajak, "Talking at Trypho"; Judith Lieu, *Image and Reality: The Jews in the World of the Christians in the Second Century* (Edinburgh: T. & T. Clark, 1996), 103–9 (though Lieu leaves open the possibility that Jews or at least proselytes were included in Justin's intended audience). The more general comments by Guy Stroumsa and Paula Fredriksen regarding Christian anti-Jewish rhetoric are also very helpful. See Guy G. Stroumsa, "From Anti-Judaism to Antisemitism in early Christianity?" in *Contra Iudaeos: Ancient and Medieval Polemics Between Christians and Jews*, ed. Ora Limor and Guy G. Stroumsa (Tübingen: Mohr/Siebeck, 1996), 1–26 and Paula Fredriksen, "What Parting of the Ways?" in *The Ways That Never Parted: Jews and Christians in Late Antiquity and the Early Middle Ages*, ed. Adam H. Becker and Annette Yoshiko Reed (Tübingen: Mohr/Siebeck, 2003), 35–64.

28. As he put it the *Apology*, the ancestors of Israel were moved by God's "prophetic spirit" to reveal that there would be a "new covenant" (διαθήκη καινή, a new "inheritance") brought by Christ and given to Christians to the exclusion of most Jews (*1 Apol.* 30–45).

29. English translation my own.

30. Thus, the law, the observance of Sabbath, and the sacrifices were given by God as a vain attempt to keep the Judeans from worshipping idols and forgetting God (Justin *Dial.* 19.6, 92.4). In the wilderness, Israel lusted after flesh to eat (*Dial.* 131.6), made a calf, and eagerly committed fornication with the daughters of foreigners (*Dial.*132.1, 19.5). As a nation, Israel sacrificed children to demons (*Dial.* 19.6, 133.2) and practiced polygamy, a practice that continues to this day (*Dial.* 134.1).

31. As Mach has recently observed in his analysis of the *Dialogue*, "the system according to which the whole of the Jewish Bible becomes a Christian book exacts a high price: the polemics against the Jews" (Mach, "Justin Martyr's *Dialogus*," 46). Mach offers a brilliant analysis of Justin's rhetorical procedures and epistemological assumptions, suggesting that Justin's method guarded the church from Marcion's non-Jewish "Christianity" by reinterpreting the law as "God's answer to sinful Israel." On the second-century Christian effort to produce a Jewish Bible that is actually a "book of Christ," see further Hans von Campenhausen, *The Formation of the Christian Bible*, trans. J. A. Baker (Philadelphia: Fortress Press, 1972), 65–102 (with caution regarding Campenhausen's approach to "the Gnostics").

32. Justin's strategy may be compared with the claim in 1 Peter 2:9 that the Christians are a "chosen *genos*" distinct from all others and the suggestion in the *Martyrdom of Polycarp* that the Christians are a "godly and pious *genos*" (*Martyrdom of Polycarp*, 3), as well as several other examples.

33. This could be contrasted with the philosophers, some of whom received a "seed of the Logos" that enabled them to speak truth even before the advent of Christ (*1 Apol.* 46).

34. Williams's translation.

35. Justin's discussion of the Christians as God's "heirs" and "sons" seems also to be quite literal. As Roman inheritance law suggests, privileges and wealth were distributed and controlled on the basis of relations to a common agnate (*D* 5.2.1, Ulpian: "For one's cognates beyond the degree of brother would do better not to trouble themselves with useless expense since they are not in a position to succeed"). Elite Roman women could inherit property from their fathers, but patrilineal control of the family property was viewed as the norm (*D* 5.2.5, Marcellus: "For those who are not descended in the male line also have the power to bring an action, since they do so in respect of a mother's will and are constantly accustomed to win"). On the importance of Roman inheritance law to "fraternal *pietas*" (the Roman ideal of brotherhood), see Cynthia J. Bannon, *The Brothers of Romulus: Fraternal Pietas in Roman Law, Literature, and Society* (Princeton, N.J.: Princeton University Press, 1997). She explains: "While the *sui heredes* [heirs to the household] included all family members under the father's *potestas* at the time of his death, brothers were central in Roman approaches to sustaining the family over the generations. Sisters and brothers alike were *sui heredes*, yet sisters were not so closely associated with *consortium* [joint

family ownership of property] because of the practice of dowry and because of the traditional priority of male relatives in intestate succession" (28). I would suggest that Justin uses terms such as "διαθήκη [*diathēkē*]" (covenant or inheritance) to mean that the members of the Christian household have become the actual heirs to divine privilege.

36. Williams's translation.

37. Christ "came according to the power given to him by the almighty father calling [us] into love and blessing [*eulogian*] and repentance and one shared household [*synoikian*]" (*Dial.* 139.4). *Concordia*/*homonoia* was frequently cited as one of the benefits of empire. Personified *concordia* was worshiped as a goddess and featured on imperial coins from the reign of Augustus onward (Andrew Wallace-Hadrill, "Image and Authority in the Coinage of Augustus," *JRS* 76 [1986]: 66–87, esp. 77). Greek cities advertised their endorsement of good reciprocal relations between themselves, other cities and the empire at large (Swain, *Hellenism and Empire*, 219–20; Swain discusses this emphasis on concord in light of Dio's speech "On Concord with the Nicaeans). The *concordia* enjoyed between rulers and their subjects was an important theme in late-antique imperial representation (see Roger Rees, *Layers of Loyalty in Latin Panegyric, AD 289–307* [Oxford: Oxford University Press, 2002], 56–67).

38. The devastation of Jerusalem was viewed by Justin as a just, divinely ordained punishment (*Dial.* 16.2–18.3, 19).

39. For a more detailed exploration of Justin's arguments here, see Lieu, *Image and Reality*, 136–40.

40. Justin here employs his own form of "ethnic reasoning" (see Buell, "Rethinking the Relevance of Race," 464; and Buell, "Race and Universalism"; but compare Lieu, *Image and Reality*, 136). Buell's discussion of "ethnic reasoning" is inspired by the work of Hall, *Ethnic Identity*, esp. his analysis of "oppositional" and "aggregative" modes of ethnic reasoning. Oppositional reasoning develops binary classifications, primarily for the sake of polemic; aggregative reasoning formulates ethnicity through connections (17–33); see also Jonathan M. Hall, *Hellenicity*, 9–19. Read in this light, Justin clearly engages in both types of argument: the Christians are a *genos* in opposition to other (corrupt) groups; they are also a *genos* that has been incorporated into the line of Abraham, Judah, and Jacob.

41. Before the advent of Christ, God gave the Jews the law in an attempt to keep them from their (purportedly) innate tendency to engage in these "crimes." After Christ came, the Jews continued in their (ancestral) bad behavior, persecuting not only Christ but the Christians, while continuing to practice polygamy and to remain otherwise enslaved to desire.

42. Grant's translation.

43. Unger's translation.

44. Ehrman notes that Acts already portrays the truth as what was given by the apostles to the church on the basis of their eyewitness testimony though in Acts: "Most converts are said to remain true to the apostolic message. And theological issues are readily resolved by an appeal to apostolic authority" (*Lost Christianities*, 167).

45. Irenaeus knew Justin's writings, including his lost work against the heresies, and drew at least some of his arguments from him; he cites Justin's work against Marcion specifically (Iren. *Adv. Haer.* 4.6.2). On the relationship between Justin and Irenaeus, see le Boulluec, *La notion d'hérésie*, 113–14, 157.

46. See Wayne A. Meeks, "Simon Magus in Recent Research," *Religious Studies Review* 3, no. 3 (1977): 137–42; he concludes: "The quest for the historical Simon [and Helena!] is even less promising than the quest for the historical Jesus" (141). Also see Williams, *Rethinking "Gnosticism,"* 165–66. Of course, it is at least possible that there were "Simonians," but neither Justin nor Irenaeus seems to have had access to reliable evidence about them. One of Justin's central claims—that the Romans had allowed a statue to be dedicated to Simon—has turned out to be false (Ehrman, *Lost Christianities*, 165–66; see also Grant, *Greek Apologists*, 46–48). Epiphanius adds still more detail—Simon was "naturally lecherous" and engaged in an "unnatural relationship" with Helena in secret. He called "the whore who was his partner" the Holy Spirit (Epiph.

Pan. 21.2.3). Simon's followers collected seminal emission and menstrual blood, stating that they are the mysteries of life and perfect knowledge (*Pan.* 21.4.1–2.). Simon corrupted marriages to satisfy his own lusts (*Pan.* 21.5.8). Yet, Epiphanius claimed, their sect is nearly extinct, for Christ ended it (*Pan.* 21.7.3, 22.2.4).

47. Williams comments, "The Nicolaitans constitute a textbook example of the birth and evolution of a libertine legend" (*Rethinking "Gnosticism,"* 170).

48. Le Boulluec notes that Irenaeus synthesized a system of scattered traditional polemic, utilizing the work of Justin and Theophilus of Antioch as well as others (*La notion d'hérésie,* 113–14).

49. On Irenaeus' retelling, see McGuire, "Women, Gender, and Gnosis"; Anne McGuire, "Valentinus and the Gnostic Haeresis: Irenaeus, Haer 1.11.1 and the Evidence of Nag Hammadi," *Studia Patristica* 18, no. 1 (1985): 247–52.

50. Irenaeus introduces Marcus as a special example of this phenomenon (1.15.4–20.2).

51. Marcus, a Valentinian, invented a theory of divine origins based in an erroneous, preposterous understanding of the secret meaning of letters (Iren. *Adv. Haer.* 1.1–15.5); Simon thought that Helena was the "Mother of All" and that he himself was an Aeon (*Adv. Haer.* 1.23.2); Saturninus and Basilides "taught still different doctrines" involving angels, archangels, virtues, and powers (*Adv. Haer.* 1.24.1); Carpocrates' myth involved angels too, and he proposed that his followers were divine like Jesus (*Adv. Haer.* 1.25.2); and so on.

52. For example, Marcus' true father is Satan; his power is achieved through one of the fallen angels (Iren. *Adv. Haer.* 1.15.6); Marcus and those like him are inspired by unclean spirits (*Adv. Haer.* 1.16.3); the Carpocratians have been sent by Satan so that the gentiles will slander the church (*Adv. Haer.* 1.25.3); all the heretics present "the bitter and malignant poison of the serpent who introduced apostasy" (*Adv. Haer.* 1.27.4). King explains that Irenaeus "strategically manipulated this genealogy to contrast the demonic origin of heretical groups with the apostolic origin of the true church. His opponents, Irenaeus insisted, were not *really* fellow Christians; they were the agents of the Devil. Their teaching derived from the Devil through his minion Simon and his harlot Helen, whereas the teaching of true Christians came from God through Jesus and his chosen male disciples" (*What is Gnosticism?*, 31).

53. And so he prayed: "I call upon you, Lord God of Abraham and God of Isaac and God of Jacob and Israel, … you who made heaven and earth and rule over all things, you who are the only true God, above whom there is no other God" to keep everyone who reads this work "separate from every heretical doctrine, godless and impious" (Iren. *Adv. Haer.* 3.6.4).

54. Yet these Ebionites cannot be actual "Jews" from Irenaeus' perspective since they share the opinions of Cerinthus and Carpocrates regarding Christ. Moreover, in Irenaeus' genealogical scheme they can only be gentiles pretending to be Jews (Iren. *Adv. Haer.* 4.14.3, 15.1–2). Whether they were "Jews" or simply thought of themselves as such cannot be easily determined (see Ehrman, *Lost Christianities,* 99–102); moreover, if ethnicity is always fictive, as Hall and others have argued, then arguments regarding their "true" identity become moot. The important question is not "Were they Jewish?" but "Did they seek to identify themselves as such?"

55. A particularly sharp rebuke since Marcion seems to have "spurned all things Jewish" (Ehrman, *Lost Christianities,* 103–6).

56. Le Boulluec, *La notion d'hérésie,* 117–57.

57. For example, Justin *1 Apol.* 5, 14, 57; Justin *2 Apol.* 5; Theophilus *Ad. Auto.* 2.2–3. According to Irenaeus, Ptolemaeus claimed that Silence received the seed (σπέρμα) of the Abyss; Logos and Life emitted Man and Church "by pairing" (*coniugationem*/συζυγίαν; *Adv. Haer.* 1.1.2; see also 1.29.1–4, 1.20.2).

58. Valentinus in particular is accused of adapting his theory of the Aeons from the writings of Hesiod (Iren. *Adv. Haer.* 2.21.2). They "propose random hypotheses for themselves and try to treat them from the Homeric verses" (*Adv. Haer.* 1.9.4). Indeed, "do not these people seem to you, O beloved, to have envisioned the Homeric Zeus … rather than the Lord of all?" (*Adv. Haer.* 1.12.2)

59. Irenaeus labels God's work in the world "οἰκονομία," that is, household management (Iren. *Adv. Haer.* 3.18.1; 5.6.1). The heretics reject God's *oikonomia* when they reject certain doctrines deemed essential by Irenaeus, especially the resurrection of the flesh (*Adv. Haer.* 5.2.2). By contrast, the (Hebrew) patriarchs and prophets served God's *oikonomia*, as did those who preached the gospel and transmitted the (Christian) scriptures (*Adv. Haer.* 3.1.1). Grant also notices Irenaeus' fondness for "*oikonomia*," though he interprets the significance of the term rather differently (Grant, *Irenaeus of Lyons*, 49–50).

60. For interesting comparative examples, see Bernard S. Cohen, *Colonialism and Its Forms of Knowledge* (Princeton, N.J.: Princeton University Press, 1996), esp. 3–15, 78–88; Frederick Cooper and Ann L. Stoler, "Introduction to Tensions of Empire: Colonial Control and Visions of Rule," *American Ethnologist* 16, no. 4 (1989): 609–21, esp. 611–13; George W. Stocking Jr., *Victorian Anthropology* (New York: Free Press, 1987), esp. 78–109.

61. Justin's and Irenaeus' genealogical schemes are exclusively patrilineal; knowledge and authority pass from a (male) God to one legitimate son to male disciples to male church leaders, an early form of the theory of apostolic succession. As Nancy Jay has remarked, "This social organization is a truly perfect 'eternal line of patrilineal descent,' in which, as it were, authority descends from father to father, through the 'one Son made perfect forever,' in a line no longer dependent on women's reproductive powers for continuity": Nancy Jay, "Sacrifice as a Remedy for Having Been Born of Woman," in *Women, Gender, Religion: A Reader*, ed. Elizabeth A. Castelli with the assistance of Rosamond C. Rodman (New York: Palgrave, 2001), 181. See also Buell, *Making Christians*, esp. 83–86. Indeed, Christianness in Justin and Irenaeus is dependent on the implantation of the divine Logos, the inspiration of the "prophetic spirit," adoption as God's sons, a mingling with the Logos, and the transmission of tradition as given to the apostles and by them to others (Justin *1 Apol.* 23, 60; Justin *2 Apol.* 13; Justin *Dial.* 120, 138–39; Iren. *Adv. Haer.* 3.19.1, 4.24.2, 5.20.1), a series of procedures that are wholly dependent upon obedience to a male god and his designated heirs.

62. Legitimate (male) prophets, apostles, and evangelists composed certain books requiring an interpretive treatment known only by the members of God's true "family," the Christians. The Jews misinterpreted their books since they deny Christ (Justin *Dial.* 11.1–23.5, 68.1–7, 93.4; Iren. *Adv. Haer.* 4.14.1–15.2, 23.1, 25.1–26.1); the heretics misconstrue both the Jewish (that is, the Christian) Scriptures and the writings of the evangelists, adding to them, ignoring them, or editing them violently (Justin *Dial.* 80.1–4; Iren. *Adv. Haer.* 1.8.1–8, 16.3, 20.1–2, 27.2–4, 29.4, 30.1–14). For discussion of the development of a "canon" in light of Christian controversies, see Ehrman, *Lost Christianities*, 229–43. On the changing understanding of Christian scripture and their use, see Gamble, *Books and Readers*, 215–18. On the impact of these controversies on the New Testament text, see Ehrman, *The Orthodox Corruption*; David Parker, *The Living Text of the Gospels* (Cambridge: Cambridge University Press, 1997); Kim Haines-Eitzen, *Guardians of Letters: Literacy, Power, and the Transmitters of Early Christian Literature* (New York: Oxford University Press, 2000), esp. 105–32.

63. The God of Israel is the God of the Christians; failure to adopt this God as one's "father" leads to moral and religious corruption; "the world" (i.e., the creation) is "good" and will be preserved imperishable at the resurrection (Justin *Dial.* 80.4; Iren. *Adv. Haer.* 4.20.1–2; 5.2.2–5.2, 14.1, 18.3, 31.2). On alternative Christian ideas regarding resurrection, see, for example, Gregory Riley, *Resurrection Reconsidered: Thomas and John in Controversy* (Minneapolis: Fortress Press, 1995); Ehrman, *Lost Christianities*, 131–32.

64. I am borrowing the phrase "language of disqualification" from Cameron. She notes that the "language of binary opposition" is "standard when labeling one's enemies as 'the other,'" noting the "habitual resort" to genealogies of heresy among late antique heresiologists ("Jews and Heretics," 350).

65. See esp. Rom. 3:1–26, 9:1–11:36. Johnson Hodge's work is helpful here: she argues that Paul sought to place gentiles-in-Christ within the *genos* "Judean" through adoption, not to remove Judeans from the "family." See also Stowers, *Rereading Romans*.

66. Irenaeus' strategy would be adopted by later heresiologists, leading to the (intentional) confusion between heretics and Jews (see Cameron, "Jews and Heretics").

67. Hence, "lives" often began with a recitation of the subject's noble birth (*eugeneia*) and with a description of his (or her) illustrious home city, if it was distinguished in some way. Josephus, for example, began his βίος by observing that he had been raised in Jerusalem "our greatest city," by a father who was universally esteemed for his noble birth (*eugeneia*) and his upright character (Joseph *Vit.* 1.7). Further examples include Plut. *Alex.* 2.2–3 (Alexander was a descendant of Heracles); Suet. *Iul.* 6.1 (Julius Caesar was descended from kings and immortal gods, including Venus); Suet. *Aug.* 1–4 (Octavian was the descendant of an old and dignified family that originally came from Velitrae). Noble birth was among the standard topics recommended in rhetorical handbooks (see chapter 1; for late antique practice, see Nixon and Rogers, *In Praise of Later Roman Emperors*, 10–12).

68. See, for example, Hadrian's praise of his adopted father Trajan, "the descendant of Aeneas" (*Anth. Pal.* 6.332; discussed by Ando, *Imperial Ideology*, 37); M. Aur. *Med.* 1.1–4, 16–17 (Marcus Aurelius lists the wonderful virtues he inherited from his grandfather, his father, his mother, his great-grandfather and then from his adopted father Antoninus Pius). For further discussion of imperial claims regarding descent, see Ando, *Imperial Ideology*, 36–40.

69. See esp. Johnson Hodge, "'If Sons, Then Heirs,'" 34–54; Buell, "Race and Universalism," 461–63; Greg Woolf, *Becoming Roman: The Origins of Provincial Civilization in Gaul* (Cambridge: Cambridge University Press, 1997); Hall, *Ethnic Identity*; and Hall, *Hellenicity*.

70. Ezra 9:1–3, 11–12. Compare Tobit 4:12; Pseudo-Aristeas, 139. For further discussion, see chapter 2.

71. "God made the gentiles, who were despaired of, joint heirs and fellow members and joint partakers with the saints" (Iren. *Adv. Haer.* 1.10.3); "people from every quarter, whether slave or free ... are aware that they will be together with [Christ] in that land and will inherit the incorruptible things of eternity" (Justin *Dial.* 39.1).

72. I am borrowing the phrase "sex was about sex" from Ann Stoler. Stoler argues that discourse about sex, when deployed in a British colonial context, could be reflecting real concerns about the consequences of sex between British colonists and the indigenous peoples that these colonists sought to dominate. Therefore, this talk was not entirely metaphorical, though see agrees with Partha Chatterjee that talk about sexual behavior could be employed to specify the contents of "Europeannes." See Cooper and Stoler, "Introduction, "614. See also Ann Laura Stoler, *Carnal Knowledge and Imperial Power: Race and the Intimate in Colonial Rule* (Berkeley and Los Angeles: University of California Press, 2002); and Partha Chatterjee, "Colonialism, Nationalism, and Colonized Women: The Contest in India," *American Ethnologist* 16, no. 4 (1989): 622–33.

73. Clark cites Irenaeus, Tertullian, Theodore of Mopuestia, John Chrysostom, Clement of Alexandria, Origen, Hippolytus, and Jerome.

74. Clark, *Reading Renunciation*, 39–42.

75. Chadwick's translation.

76. Jerome *Adv. Iovinia.* 1.7; 1.8; 1.20; and *Ep.* 49 (48).11. Cited and discussed by Clark, *Reading Renunciation*, 41.

77. Clark observes, "Differentiation became all the more necessary when theories and behaviors were similar" (*Reading Renunciation*, 40). A similar observation was made by Sfameni Gasparro in her discussion of second-century Christian "Encratites." She observes that despite the "wide gulf" that separates "radical" from "moderate" second-century Christian sexual ascetics, both groups shared an "*ethos*" that "ensures substantial homogeneity in the perception of humanity's sexual dimension and sexual activity" (Sfameni Gasparro, "Asceticism and Anthropology," 130). In other words, heresiologists such as Irenaeus and Clement of Alexandria may have sought to distance themselves from a "radical Encratism" that rejects marriage outright, yet, upon closer examination, they appear to have had more in common with their "radical" opponents than they might want to admit. There is a difference of degree rather than of kind

between them, with the "radicals" arguing that sexual abstinence is the only authentic choice for Christians and the "moderates" suggesting that marriage is the appropriate option for "ordinary believers" though sexual abstinence is preferable.

78. Clark, *Reading Renunciation*, 42–370. For Clark, this involved reading strategies capable of interpreting biblical ("Old" and "New" Testament) passages in favor of the sexual renunciation they sought to recommend. In this way, the "fathers" could argue that their practices were preserved in Scripture and recommended by God, Christ, and the apostles.

79. I borrow these terms from Clark and Sfameni Gasparro.

80. On the date of Celsus' invective against the Christians, see Chadwick, introduction to *Contra Celsum*, xxiv–xxix. Chadwick settles for 177–80 C.E. as a conservative estimate. If Grant is correct, Irenaeus composed his books against the Valentinians c. 175–89 C.E. (*Irenaeus*, 6). On Celsus as a representative of standard anti-Christian invective, see Frede, "Origen's Treatise," 133; Droge, *Homer or Moses?*, 72–81; Labriolle, *La Reaction païnne*, 117–27; Grant, *Greek Apologists*, 133–39.

81. See the excellent, straightforward discussion by Margaret Y. MacDonald, "Reading Real Women Through the Undisputed Letters of Paul," in *Women and Christian Origins*, ed. Ross Shepard Kraemer and Mary Rose D'Angelo (New York: Oxford University Press, 1999). The apostle Junia provides a particularly interesting example. Paul mentions her in Rom 16:7, stating that she is "prominent among the apostles," although later Christian scribes and biblical scholars were not quite willing to believe it; see Eldon J. Epp, "Text-Critical, Exegetical, and Socio-Cultural Factors Affecting the Junia/Junias Variation in Romans 16.7," in *New Testament Criticism and Exegesis: Festschrift J. Delobel*, ed. A. Denaux, Bibliotheca Ephemeridum Theologicarum Lovainiensium 161; (Belgium: Leuven University Press, 2002), 287–91.

82. See discussion in chapter 3.

83. For example, Simon shares leadership with the "prostitute" Helena (Iren. *Adv. Haer.* 1.23.2); the followers of the Valentinian Marcus tricked women into joining by pretending to allow them to become prophetesses, only to seduce them by driving them into a sexual and religious frenzy (*Adv. Haer.* 1.13.4); the Carpocratians included a preacher by the name of Marcellina who led multitudes of faithful Christians astray (*Adv. Haer.* 1.25.6).

84. On this possibility, see Karen Jo Torjesen, *When Women Were Priests: Women's Leadership in the Early Church and the Scandal of their Subordination in the Rise of Christianity* (San Francisco: HarperSanFrancisco, 1993). Elaine Pagels associated the one God–one church–one bishop theory with ecclesiastical patriarchy in *The Gnostic Gospels* (New York: Random House, 1979). On the strategy of associating suspect religious groups with "silly women," see MacDonald, *Early Christian Women*.

BIBLIOGRAPHY

PRIMARY SOURCES

1 QS. *Rule of the Community*. In *The Dead Sea Scrolls. Hebrew, Aramaic, and Greek Texts with English Translations*. Vol. 1, *Rule of the Community and Related Documents*, ed. James H. Charlesworth. Tübingen: Mohr /Siebeck, 1994.

4Q166–7. In *Discoveries in the Judaean Desert of Jordon, V:I (4Q158–4Q186)*, ed. J. M. Allegro and A. A. Anderson. Oxford: Oxford University Press, 1968. English translation with commentary by Geza Vermes. *The Complete Dead Sea Scrolls in English*. New York: Penguin Books, 1997. See also John Strugnell. "Notes en marge du volume V des *Discoveries in the Judaean Desert of Jordan*." *RQ* 7 (1970): 163–276.

4Q201–7. *Enoch*. In *The Books of Enoch. Aramaic Fragments of Qumran Cave 4*, ed. with commentary by J. T. Milik with the collaboration of Matthew Black. Oxford: Clarendon Press, 1976.

4Q266–73. *Damascus Document*. In *The Dead Sea Scrolls. Hebrew, Aramaic, and Greek Texts with English Translations*. Vol. 2, *Damascus Document, War Scroll, and Related Documents*, ed. James H. Charlesworth. Tübingen: Mohr/Siebeck, 1994.

Achilles Tatius. *Leucippe et Clitophon*. Ed. and trans. E. Vilborg. Stockholm: Almqvist and Wiksell, 1955. English translation by B. P. Reardon. *Collected Ancient Greek Novels*. Berkeley: University of California Press, 1989.

Acta Andreae. In *Acta Andreae*, ed. with French translation by Jean-Marc Prieur. 2 Vols. Corpus Christianorum Series Apocyphorum 5–6. Turnhout: Brepols 1989. English translation by Dennis R. MacDonald. *The Acts of Andrew and the Acts of Andrew and Matthias in the City of the Cannibals*. SBL Texts and Translations 33. Atlanta: Scholars Press, 1990.

Acta Joannis. Ed. M. Bonnet. In *Acta apostolorum apocrypha*. Vol. 2.1, 151–215. Leipzig: Mendelssohn, 1898. Repr., Hildesheim: Olms, 1972. English translation by J. K. Elliott. *The Apocryphal New Testament: a Collection of Apocryphal Christian Literature in an English Translation*. Oxford: Clarendon Press, 1993.

Acta Pauli et Theclae. Ed. R. Lipsius. In *Acta apostolorum apocrypha*. Vol. 1, 235–71. Leipzig: Mendelssohn, 1891. Repr., Hildesheim: Olms, 1972. English translation by J. K. Elliott. *The Apocryphal New Testament: A Collection of Apocryphal Christian Literature in an English Translation*. Oxford: Clarendon Press, 1993.

Acta Thomae. Ed. M. Bonnet. In *Acta apostolorum apocrypha*. Vol. 2.2, 99–288. Leipzig: Mendessohn, 1903. Repr., Hildescheim: Olms, 1972. English translation by J. K. Elliott. *The Apocryphal New Testament: A Collection of Apocryphal Christian Literature in an English Translation*. Oxford: Clarendon Press, 1993.

Aeschines. *In Timarchus.* In *Eschine: Discours,* ed. with French translation by Victor Martin and Guy de Budé. Collection des Universités de France. Paris: Société d' édition "Les belles lettres," 1927–28.

Aeschylus. *Persae.* In *Aeschyli Persae,* ed. Martin L. West. Bibliotheca scriptorum Graecorum et Latinorum Teubneriana. Stuttgart: Teubner, 1991. English translation in *Aeschylus: Persians,* by Janet Lembke and C. J. Herington. New York: Oxford University Press, 1981.

Anthologia Graeca, ed. with introduction, commentary, and English translation by A. S. F. Gow and D. L. Page. *The Greek Anthology: The Garland of Philip and Some Contemporary Epigrams.* 2 vols. Cambridge: Cambridge University Press, 1968.

Ap(h)thonius. *Progymnasmata.* In *Rhetores Graeci,* ed. L. Spengel. Vol. 10, *Aphthonii. Progymnasmata,* ed. Hugo Rabe. Bibliotheca Scriptorum Graecorum et Romanorum Teubneriana. Leipzig: Teubneri, 1926.

Apocalypse of Peter. In *Apocrypha.* Vol. 1, *Reste des Petrusevangeliums, der Petrusapokalypse und des Kerygma Petri,* edi. E. Klostermann. 2nd ed. Kleine Texte 3. Bonn: Marcus & Weber, 1908. English translation by J. K. Elliott in *The Apocryphal New Testament: A Collection of Apocryphal Christian Literature in an English Translation.* Oxford: Clarendon Press, 1993.

Apuleius. *Apologia.* In *L. Apulei Madaurensis Apologia sive De magia liber,* ed. Gustav Kreuger. Berolini: Apud Weidmannos, 1864. English translation by H. E. Butler. *The Apologia and Florida of Apuleius of Madaura.* Oxford: Clarendon Press, 1909.

Arrian, Flavius. *Alexandri anabasis.* In *Flavii Ariani quae exstant omnia,* ed. A. G. Roos and G. Wirth. 1:1–390. Leipzig: Teubner, 1967. English translation by P. A. Brunt and E. Iliff Robson. *Arrian: Anabasis of Alexander.* 2 vols. LCL. Cambridge, Mass.: Harvard University Press, 1976–1983.

Pseudo-Aristeas. In *Aristeae Ad Philocratum epistula cum ceteris de orignie versions LXX interpretum testimonis,* ed. Paul Wendland. Bibliotheca scriptorum Graecorum et Romanorum Teubneriana. Leipzig: Teubner, 1900.

Aristides. *Apologia.* In "Fragmenta (*P. Oxy.*15.1778, *P. Lond.* 2486)," *L'apologia di Aristide,* ed. C. Vona, 115–26. Rome: Facultas Theologica Pontificii Athenaei Lateranesis, 1950.

Aristides, Aelius. In *P. Aelii Aristidis Opera quae exstant omnia,* ed. F. W. Lenz and C. A. Behr. Lugduni Batavorum: Brill, 1976. English translation by C. A. Behr. *Aristides: Panathenaic oration and In defence of oratory.* LCL. Cambridge, Mass.: Harvard University Press, 1973.

Aristotle. *Ethica Nicomachea.* In *Aristotle. Opera omnia.* Vol. 2, *Ethica. Naturalis auscultationis. De coelo. De generatione ei metaphysica,* ed. J. H. E. Heitz and A. F. Didot. Paris: Firmin-Didot, 1848–74. English translation by H. Rackman. *Aristotle.* Vol. 19, *The Nichomachean Ethics.* Rev. ed. LCL. Cambridge, Mass.: Harvard University Press, 1934; repr., 1975.

——. *Politica.* In *Aristotle. Opera omnia.* Vol. 1, *Organon. Rhetorica Poetica. Politica,* ed. J. H. E. Heitz and A. F. Didot. Paris: Firmin-Didot, 1848–74. English translation by H. Rackman. *Aristotle.* Vol. 21, *Politics.* LCL. Cambridge, Mass.: Harvard University Press, 1967.

——. *Ars Rhetorica.* In *Aristotelis.* Ed. Rudolf Kassel. Berolini, Novi Eboraci: de Gruyter, 1976. English translation by John Henry Freese. *Aristotle.* Vol. 22 of *The "Art" of Rhetoric.* LCL. Cambridge, Mass.: Harvard University Press, 1975.

Athanasius. *Apologia.* In *Athanase d'Alexandrie. Apologie à l Empereur Constance,* ed. with French translation by Jan-M. Szymusiak. Sources Chrétiennes 56. Paris: Éditions du Cerf, 1958.

——. *Contra Gentes.* In *Athanasius. Contra Gentes and De Incarnatione,* ed. with English translation by Robert W. Thompson. Oxford Early Christian Texts. Oxford: Clarendon Press, 1971.

Pseudo-Athanasius. *De virginitate.* Syriac text ed. with English translation by David Braake. *Pseudo-Athanasius on Virginity.* 2 vols. Corpus scriptorum Christianorum Orientalium 592–93, Scriptores Syri 232–33. Louvain: Peeters, 2002.

Athenagoras. *Legatio.* In *Athenagoras: Legatio and De Resurrectione.* Ed. and trans. William R. Schoedel. Oxford Early Christian Texts. Oxford: Clarendon Press, 1972.

Aurelius, Marcus. *Meditations*. In *Marci Aurelii Antonini Ad se ipsum libri XII*, ed. Joachim Dalfen. Bibliotheca scriptorum Graecorum et Latinorum Teubneriana. Leipzig: Teubner, 1979. English translation by A. S. L. Farquharson, *The Meditations of Marcus Aurelius Antoninus and Selections from the Letters of Marcus and Fronto*, intro. and notes by R. B. Rutherford. Oxford: Oxford University Press, 1989.

Baird, Father Pierre. 1611. In *New American World*. Vol. 4, ed. D. B. Quinn. New York: Arno Press and Hector Bye, 1979.

2 Baruch (*Syriac Apocalypse of Baruch*). In *Apocalypse de Baruch. Introduction, Traduction du Syriaque et Commentaire*, ed. with French translation by Pierre Bogaert. 2 Vols. Sources Chrétiennes 144–45. Paris: Éditions du Cerf, 1969.

Berliner Griechische Urkunden (Ägyptische Urkunden aus den Königlichen [later *Staatlichen*] *Mussen zu Berlin, Griechische Urknunken)*. 15 vols. Berlin, 1895–1983.

Book of Thomas the Contender. In *Nag Hammadi Codex II, 2–7*. Vol. 2, *On the Origin of the World, Expository Treatise on the Soul, Book of Thomas the Contender*, ed. Bentley Layton and trans. John D. Turner. Nag Hammadi Studies 21. Leiden: E. J. Brill, 1989.

Caesar, Julius. *Bellum Gallicum*. In *C. Iuli Caesaris Commentarii. Rerum in Gallia Gestarum*, ed. T. Rice Holmes. Oxford: Clarendon Press, 1914. English translation by H. J. Edwards. *Caesar*. Vol. 1, *The Gallic War*. LCL. Cambridge, Mass.: Harvard University Press, 1917; repr., 1970.

Cassius Dio. *Historiae Romanae*. In *Cassii Dionis Cocceiani historiarum Romanarum quae supersunt*, ed. U. P. Boissevain. 3 vols. Berlin: Weidmann, 1895–1901; repr., 1955. English translation by Earnest Cary and Herbert B. Foster. *Dio's Roman History*. 9 vols. LCL. Cambridge, Mass.: Harvard University Press, 1914–27; repr., 1961.

Cicero, Marcus Tullius. *In Catilinam*. In *Cicero. In Catilinam I and II*, ed., intro., and notes in English by H. E. Gould and J. L. Whiteley. London: Bristol Classical Press, 1982. Also consulted: *Cicero*. Vol. 10, *In Catilinam I–IV. Pro Murena. Pro Sulla. Pro Flacco*. English translation by C. MacDonald. LCL. Cambridge, Mass.: Harvard University Press, 1977.

——. *Epistulae ad familiares*. In *Cicero. Letters to Friends*, ed. with English translation by D. R. Shackleton Bailey. 3 vols. LCL. Cambridge, Mass.: Harvard University Press, 2001.

——. *Pro Murena*. In *Cicero*. Vol. 10, In *In Catilinam I–IV. Pro Murena. Pro Sulla. Pro Flacco*, English translation by C. MacDonald. LCL. Cambridge, Mass.: Harvard University Press, 1977

——. *De officiis*. Ed. H. A. Holden. 3rd ed. New York: Harper & Brothers, Publishers, 1877; repr., 1899. English translation by Walter Miller. *Cicero. De officiis*. LCL. Cambridge, Mass.: Harvard University Press, 1928.

——. *De oratore*. Ed. Kazimierz F. Kumaniecki. Bibliotheca scriptorum Graecorum et Romanorum Teubneriana. Leipzig: Teubner, 1969. English translation by E. W. Sutton and H. Rackham. *Cicero*. Vol. 3, *De Oratore*. Vol. 4, *De Oratore Book 3. De Fato. Paradoxa Stoicorum. De Partitione Oratatio*. LCL. Cambridge, Mass.: Harvard University Press, 1942.

——. *Philippicae*. Ed. and trans. D. R. Shackleton Bailey. Chapel Hill: University of North Carolina Press, 1986.

——. *Tusculanae disputations*. Ed. Thomas Wilson Dougan. 2 vols. Cambridge: Cambridge University Press, 1905–1934. English translation by J. E. King. *Cicero*. Vol. 18, *Tusculan Disputations*. Rev. ed. LCL. Cambridge, Mass.: Harvard University Press, 1971.

——. *In Verrum*. English translation by L. H. G. Greenwood. *Cicero*. Vol. 7, *The Verrine Orations 1: Against Caecilius. Against Verres*. Vol. 8, *The Verrine Orations 2: Against Verres Part 2*. LCL. Cambridge, Mass.: Harvard University Press, 1928, 1935.

Clement of Alexandria. *Stromateis*. In *Clemens Alexandrinus*, ed. Otto Stählin, Ludwig Früchtel, and Ursala Treu. 4th ed. Die Griechischen Schriftsteller der ersten Jahrhunderte 2. Berlin: Akademie-Verlag, 1985. English version of *Stromateis*, book 3, ed. and trans. Henry Chadwick and J. Oulton. *Alexandrian Christianity*. Library of Christian Classics 2. London: SCM, 1954.

Clement of Rome. *Epistula i ad Corinthios*. In *Clément de Rome. Épitre aux Corinthiens*, ed. A. Jaubert. Sources Chrétiennes 167, 98–204. Paris: Cerf, 1971. English translation by Bart D. Ehrman. *The Apostolic Fathers*. Vol. 1. LCL. Cambridge, Mass.: Harvard University Press, 2003.

——. *Epistula ii ad Corinthios*. In *Die apostolichen Väter*, ed. K. Bihlmeyer and W. Schneemelcher, 71–81. 3rd ed. Tübingen: Mohr, 1970. English translation by Bart D. Ehrman. *The Apostolic Fathers*. Vol. 1. LCL. Cambridge, Mass.: Harvard University Press, 2003.

Dagron, Gilbert, ed. and French trans. *Vie et miracles de Sainte Thècle: Texte grec, traduction et commentaire*. Subsidia Hagiographica 62. Brusells: Société des bollandistes, 1978.

Demetrius of Phalerum. *De Elocutione* = Περὶ ἑρμηνείας, ed. and trans. W. Rhys Roberts. *Demetrius On Style: The Greek text of Demetrius De Elocutione*. Cambridge: Cambridge University Press, 1902.

Demosthenes. *Demosthenis orationes*, ed. S. H. Butcher. 3 vols. Scriptorum classicorum bibliotheca Oxoniensis. Oxford: Clarendon Press, 1903–1931. English translation by J. H. Vince. *Demosthenes*. 7 vols. LCL. Cambridge, Mass.: Harvard University Press, 1935–1954.

Didache XII Apostolorum. In *La Didachè. Instructions des Apotres*, ed. J. P. Audet, 226–42. Paris: Lecoffre, 1958. English translation by Bart D. Ehrman. *The Apostolic Fathers*. Vol. 1. LCL. Cambridge, Mass.: Harvard University Press, 2003.

Digest of Justinian. Ed. and trans. Alan Watson. 4 vols. Philadelphia: University of Pennsylvania Press, 1985.

Dinarchus. In *Dinarchus and Hyperides*, ed. with English translation by Ian Worthington. Warminster: Aris & Phillips, 1999.

Dio Chrysostomus. *Orationes*. In *Dionis Prusaensis quem vocant Chrysostumum quae exstant omnia*, ed. J. von Arnim. Vols. 1–2. 2nd ed. Berlin: Weidmann, 1893–1896; repr., 1962. English translation by J. W. Cohoon and H. Larmar Crosby. *Dio Chysostom*. 5 vols. LCL. Cambridge, Mass.: Harvard University Press, 1932–1951.

Diodorus Siculus. *Bibliotheca historica*. In *Diodori. Bibliotheca historica*, ed. F. Vogel, C. T. Fischer, L. A. Dindorf, and I. Bekker. 5 vols. Bibliotheca scriptorum Graecorum et Romanorum Teubneriana. Leipzig: Teubner, 1888–1906. English translation by C. H. Oldfather. *Diodorus of Sicily*. 12 vols. LCL. Cambridge, Mass.: Harvard University Press, 1933–1967.

Diogenes Laertius. *Vita philosphorum*. In *Diogenis Laertii vitae philosophorum*, ed. H. S. Long. 2 vols. Oxford: Clarendon Press, 1964. English translation by R. D. Hicks. *Diogenes Laertius*. 2 vols. LCL. Cambridge, Mass.: Harvard University Press, 1925; repr., 1972.

Dionysius of Halicarnassus. *Antiquitates Romanae*. In *Dionysi Halicarnasensis. Antiquitatum romanarum quae supersunt*, ed. C. Jacoby. 4 vols. Bibliotheca scriptorum Graecorum et Romanorum Teubneriana. Leipzig: Teubner, 1885–1905; repr., Stuttgart: 1967. English translation by Earnest Cary. *The Roman Antiquies of Dionysius of Halicarnassus*. 7 vols. LCL. Cambridge, Mass.: Harvard University Press, 1937–1950.

1 Enoch. Ethiopic text trans. Matthew Black. *The Book of Enoch, or, 1 Enoch. A new English edition with critical notes*. Studia in Veteris Testamenti Pseudepigrapha 7. Leiden: Brill, 1985. Greek text edited by Matthew Black. *Apocalypsis henochi graece*. Pseudepigrapha Veteris Testamenti Graece 3. Leiden: Brill, 1970. Ethiopic text ed. Michael A. Knibb. *The Ethiopic Book of Enoch: A New Edition in Light of the Aramaic Dead Sea Fragments*. Vol. 1, *Text and Apparatus*. Oxford: Clarendon Press, 1978.

Epictetus. *Dissertationes ab Arriano digestae*. In *Epicteti dissertationes ab Arriano digestae*, ed. H. Schenkl. Bibliotheca scriptorum Graecorum et Romanorum Teubneriana. Leipzig: Teubner, 1965. English translation by W. A. Oldfather. *Epictetus*. Vol. 1, *Discourses, Books 1–2*. Vol. 2, *Discourses, Books 3–4. Fragments. The Encheiridion*. LCL. Cambridge, Mass.: Harvard University Press, 1925–1928; repr., 2000.

Epiphanius. *Panarion (Adversus haereses)*. In *Epiphanius, Bände 1–3: Ancoratus und Panarion*, ed. K. Holl. 3 vols. Leipzig: Hinrichs, 1915–1933. English translation of book 1 by Frank Williams. *The Panarion of Epiphanius of Salamis: Book 1 (Sects 1–46)*. Nag Hammadi Studies 35. Leiden: E. J. Brill, 1987.

Epistle of Barnabas. In *Épitre de Barnabé,* ed. R. A. Kraft. Sources Chrétiennes 172. Paris: Cerf, 1971. English translation by Bart D. Ehrman. *The Apostolic Fathers.* Vol. 2. LCL. Cambridge, Mass.: Harvard University Press, 2003.

Epistle to Diognetus. In *A Diognète,* ed. H.-I. Marrou. Sources Chrétiennes 33. 2nd ed., 52–84. Paris: Cerf, 1965. English translation by Bart D. Ehrman. *The Apostolic Fathers.* Vol. 2. LCL 25. Cambridge, Mass.: Harvard University Press, 2003.

Eusebius. *Historia ecclesiastica.* In *Eusèbe de Césarée. Histoire ecclésiastique,* ed. G. Bardy. 3 vols. Sources Chrétiennes 31, 41, 55. Paris: Cerf, 1967.

4 Ezra. Latin text in *Die lateinische text der Apokalypse des Esra,* ed. A. F. J. Klijn. Texte und Untersuchungen 131. Berlin: Akademie Verlag, 1983. English translation by Bruce M. Metzger. "The Fourth Book of Ezra." In *Old Testament Pseudepigrapha,* vol. 1, ed. J. H. Charlesworth, 514–59. London: Darton, Longman & Todd, 1983.

Gellius, Aulus. *Noctes Atticae.* In *Les Nuits attiques,* ed. René Marache. 3 vols. Collection des Universités de France. Paris: Les Belles Lettres, 1967. English translation by J. C. Rolfe. *Aulus Gellius: Attic Nights.* 3 vols. LCL. Cambridge, Mass.: Harvard University Press, 1927–28; repr., 1967.

Gospel of the Egyptians. In *Apocrypha II. Evangelien,* ed. E. Klostermann. 2nd ed. Kleine Texte 8. Bonn: Marcus & Weber, 1910. English translation by J. K. Elliott. *The Apocryphal New Testament: A Collection of Apocryphal Christian Literature in an English Translation.* Oxford: Clarendon Press, 1993.

Gospel of Thomas. In *Apocrypha II. Evangelien,* ed. E. Klostermann. 2nd ed. Kleine Texte 8. Bonn: Marcus & Weber, 1910. English translation by J. K. Elliott. *The Apocryphal New Testament: A Collection of Apocryphal Christian Literature in an English Translation.* Oxford: Clarendon Press, 1993.

Greek Papyri in the British Museum. Ed. F. G. Kenyon and H. I. Bell. Vol. 3. London, 1907.

Griechische Ostraka aus Aegypten und Nubien. Ed. U. Wilcken. 2 vols. Leipzig-Berlin, 1899; repr., Amsterdam, 1970.

Horace (Quintus Horatius Flaccus). *Carmina.* In *Horace: Odes and Epodes,* ed. with English translation by Niall Rudd. LCL. Cambridge, Mass.: Harvard University Press, 2004.

Hippolytus. *Refutatio omnium haeresium.* In *Hippolytus. Werke,* vol. 3, ed. Paul Wendland. Die Griechischen Christlichen Schriftsteller der Ersten Drei Jahrhunderte 26. Leipzig: J. C. Hinrichs, 1916.

Ignatius of Antioch. *Epistles.* In *Ignace d'Antioche. Polycarpe de Smyrne. Lettres. Martyre de Polycarpe,* ed. P. T. Camelot, 56–154. Paris: Cerf, 1969. English translation by Bart D. Ehrman. *The Apostolic Fathers.* Vol. 1. LCL. Cambridge, Mass.: Harvard University Press, 2003.

Irenaeus. *Adversus haereses.* In *Irenäus von Lyon. Epideixis. Adversus Haereses,* ed. Norbert Brox. 3 vols. Fontes Christiani 8. Freiburg: Herder, 1993. English translation of book 1 by Dominic J. Unger. *St. Irenaeus of Lyons Against the Heresies,* rev. John J. Dillon. Ancient Christian Writers 55. New York: Paulist Press, 1992. English translations of books 1–5 (excerpts) by Robert M. Grant. *Irenaeus of Lyons.* Early Church Fathers. London: Routledge, 1997.

Isocrates. *Orations.* In *Discours,* ed. with French translation by Georges Mathieu and Émile Brémond. 4 vols. Collection des universités de France. Paris: Société d'édition "Les Belles lettres," 1962–1967. English translation by George Norlin. *Isocrates.* 3 vols. LCL. Cambridge, Mass.: Harvard University Press, 1928–1945.

Jerome. *Adversus Iovinianum.* In *Patrologiae cursus completus. Series Latina,* ed. J. P. Migne, 23.221–352. Paris, 1844–55, 1862–1865. Electronic edition, *Patrologia Latina Database.* Version 5.0. Alexandria, Vir.: Chadwick-Healey, Inc., 1995. English translation by W. H. Fremantle with the assistance of G. Lewis and W. B. Martley. *St. Jerome: Letters and Select Works.* Nicene and Post-Nicene Fathers Second Series. Vol. 6. American Edition. United States: Christian Literature Publishing Company, 1893. Reprint, Peabody, Mass.: Hendrickson, 1994.

———. *Epistulae.* In *Sancti Eusebii Hieronymi Epistulae,* ed. Isidorus Hilberg. Corpus Scriptorum Ecclesiasticorum Latinorum 54–55 (*Epistulae I-LXX* and *Epistulae LXXI-CXX*). Vindobonae:

Verlag der österreichischen Akademie der Wissenschften, 1996. English translation by W. H. Fremantle with the assistance of G. Lewis and W. B. Martley. *St. Jerome: Letters and Select Works*. Nicene and Post-Nicene Fathers Second Series. Vol. 6. American Edition. United States: Christian Literature Publishing Company, 1893. Reprint, Peabody, Mass.: Hendrickson, 1994.

Josephus, Flavius. *Antiquitates Judaicae*. In *Flavii Iosephi opera*, ed. B. Niese. Vols. 1–4. 2nd ed. Berlin: Weidmann, 1955. English translation by H. St. J. Thackeray, Ralph Marcus and Allen Wikgren. *Josephus*. Vols. 6 and 10, *Biblical Antiquities*. LCL. Cambridge, Mass.: Harvard University Press, 1998.

——. *Contra Apionem*. In *Flavii Iosephi opera*, ed. B. Niese. Vols. 4–5. 2nd ed. Berlin: Weidmann, 1955. English translation by H. St. J. Thackeray. *Josephus*. Vol. 1, *The Life, Against Apion*. LCL. Cambridge, Mass.: Harvard University Press, 1997.

——. *Vita*. In *Flavii Iosephi opera*, ed. B. Niese. Vol. 4. 2nd ed. Berlin: Weidmann, 1955. English translation by H. St. J. Thackeray. *Josephus*. Vol. 1. *The Life, Against Apion*. LCL. Cambridge, Mass.: Harvard University Press, 1997.

Jubilees. In *The Book of Jubilees*, ed. James C. Vanderkam. 2 vols. Corpus Scriptorum Christianorum Orientalium 510–11. Scriptures Aethiopici 88–89. Louvain: Peeters, 1989. English translation by O. S. Wintermute. "Jubilees." In *Old Testament Pseudepigrapha*, ed. James H. Charlesworth. Vol. 2. New York: Doubleday, 1985.

Justin Martyr. *Apologia Maior and Apologia Minor*. In *Die ältesten Apologeten*, ed. E. J. Goodspeed. Göttingen: Vandenhoek & Ruprecht, 1915. Also consulted: Miroslav Marcovich, ed. *Iustini Martyris. Apologiae pro Christianis*. Patristische Texte und Studien 38. New York: Walter de Gruyter, 1994. English translation of the First and Second Apologies by L. W. Barnard, *Saint Justin Martyr: The First and Second Apologies*. Ancient Christian Writers 56. New York: Paulist Press, 1997.

——. *Dialogue with Trypho*. In *Die ältesten Apologeten*, ed. E. J. Goodspeed. Göttingen: Vandenhoek & Ruprecht, 1915. English translation by A. Lukyn Williams. *Justin Martyr: The Dialogue with Trypho*. Translation of Christian Literature Series 1. London: Society for Promoting Christian Knowledge. New York: Macmillan, 1930.

Juvenal. *Satirae*. In *Juvenal: The Satires*, ed. with introduction, commentary, and bibliography by John Ferguson. New York: St. Martin's Press, 1979; repr., London: Bristol Classical Press, 1999. English translation by G. G. Ramsay. *Juvenal and Persius*. Rev. ed. LCL. Cambridge, Mass.: Harvard University Press, 1940.

Koenen, Ludwig, and Reidhold Merkelbach, ed. "Die Prophezeiungen des 'Töpfers.'" *ZPE* 2, no. 3 (1968): 178–209.

Lucian of Samosata. *De morte peregrini*. In *Luciani. Opera*, ed. M. D. Macleod. 4 vols. Scriptorum classicorum bibliotheca Oxoniensis. Oxford: Clarendon Press, 1972. English translation by A. M. Harmon. *Lucian*, vol. 5. LCL. Cambridge: Harvard University Press, 1913.

——. *Dialogi meretricii*. In *Luciani. Opera*, ed. M. D. Macleod. 4 vols. Scriptorum classicorum bibliotheca Oxoniensis. Oxford: Clarendon Press, 1972–. English translation by M. D. Macleod. *Lucian*. Vol. 7, *Dialogues of the Dead. Dialogues of the Sea-Gods. Dialogues of the Gods. Dialogues of the Courtesans*. LCL. Cambridge, Mass.: Harvard University Press, 1967.

——. *Nigrinus*. In *Luciani. Opera*, ed. M. D. Macleod. 4 vols. Scriptorum classicorum bibliotheca Oxoniensis. Oxford: Clarendon Press, 1972–. English translation by A. M. Harmon. *Lucian*. Vol. 1, *Phalaris. Hippias or The Bath. Dionysus. Heracles. Amber or The Swans. The Fly. Nigrinus. Demonax. The Hall. My Native Land. Octogenarians. A True Story. Slander. The Consonants at Law. The Carousal (Symposium) or The Lapiths*. LCL. Cambridge, Mass.: Harvard University Press, 1913; repr., 1968.

Lysias. In *Lysias. Discourses*, ed. with French translation by Louis Gernet and Marcel Bizet. Collection des Universités de France. Paris: Société de l'édition "Les belles lettres," 1926.

Macrobius, Ambrosius Theodosius. *Saturnalia*, ed. James Willis. 2 vols. 2nd ed. Bibliotheca scriptorum Graecorum et Romanorum Teubneriana. Leipzig: Teubner, 1970.

Malcovati, Enrica. *Oratorum Romanorum fragmenta liberae rei publicae.* 2 vols. 4th ed. Corpus Scriptorum Latinorum Paravianum. Aug. Taurinorum; Mediolani; Patavii: In Oedibus I. B. Paraviae, 1976.

Martial (Marcus Valerius Martialis). *Epigrammata.* In *M. Valerii Martialis Epigrammata,* ed. W. Heraeus and D. R. Schackleton Bailey. Bibliotheca scriptorum Graecorum et Romanorum Teubneriana. Stuttgart: Teubner, 1990. English translation by D. R. Shackleton Bailey. *Martial. Epigrams.* 3 vols. LCL. Cambridge, Mass.: Harvard University Press, 1993.

Martyrdom of Perpetua and Felicitas. In *Passion de Perpétue et de Félicité suivi des Actes,* ed. with French translation by Jacqueline Amat. Sources Chrétiennes 417. Paris: Éditions du Cerf, 1996.

Martyrdom of Polycarp. Ed. and trans. Bart D. Ehrman. *The Apostolic Fathers,* vol. 1. LCL. Cambridge, Mass.: Harvard University Press, 2003.

Martyrs of Lyons (Epistle of the Churches of Lyons and Vienne). Ed. and trans. Herbert Musurillo. *The Acts of the Christian Martyrs.* Oxford: Clarendon Press, 1972.

Menander of Laodicea. *Menander Rhetor.* Ed. with English translation and commentary by D. A. Russell and N. G. Wilson. Oxford: Clarendon Press, 1981.

Minucius Felix. *Octavius.* In *Tertullian and Minucius Felix,* ed. with English translation by G. H. Randall. LCL. Cambridge, Mass.: Harvard University Press, 1953.

Musonius Rufus. *Fragmenta.* In "Musonius Rufus: The Roman Socrates," ed. with English translation by Cora B. Lutz. *Yale Classical Studies* 10 (1947): 3–147.

Nepos, Cornelius. *Vitae excellentium imperatorum. Dion.* Ed. with English commentary by Grace Starry West. Bryn Mawr Latin Commentaries. Bryn Mawr: Thomas Library, Bryn Mawr College, 1985. English translation by J. C. Rolfe. *Cornelius Nepos.* LCL. Cambridge, Mass.: Harvard University Press, 1929; repr., 1994.

Nixon, C. E. V., and Barbara Saylor Rodgers. *In Praise of Later Roman Emperors: The Panegyrici Latini.* Berkeley: University of California Press, 1994.

Novum Testamentum Graece. Ed. Eberhard Nestle and Erwin Nestle, rev. Kurt Aland, et. al. 27th rev. ed. Stuttgart: Deutsche Bibelgeschaftung, 1993.

Oracula Sibyllina. Book 3, ed., intro., and trans. Rieuwerd Buitenwerf. *Book III of the Sibylline Oracles and Its Social Setting.* Studia in Veteris Testamenti Pseudepigrapha 17. Leiden: Brill, 2003.

Origen. *Contra Celsum.* In *Origen: Contra Celsum,* 5 vols., ed. with French translation by Marcel Borret. Sources chrétiennes. Paris: Éditions du Cerf, 1967–76. English translation and introduction by H. E. Chadwick. *Origen: Contra Celsum.* Cambridge: Cambridge University Press, 1965.

———. *De principiis (Peri archon).* In *Traité des principes. Origène: introduction, texte critique de la version de Rufin, traduction, commentaire et fragments,* ed. with French translation of Rufinus' text by Henri Crouzel and Manlio Simonetti. 5 vols. Sources chretiennes 252–53, 268–69, 312. Paris: Editions du Cerf, 1978–1984.

Papyrus grecs d'époque byzantine. Catalogue général des antiquités égyptiennes du Musée du Caire. Ed. J. Maspero. Cairo: 1911.

Petronius Arbiter. *Satyricon.* In *Petronii Arbitri Satyricon,* ed. Konrad Müller. Munich: E. Heimeran, 1961. English translation by Sarah Ruden. *Petronius: Satyricon.* Indiapolis, Ind.: Hackett, 2000.

Philo. *De Abrahamo, de decalogo, de Iosepho, de migratione Abrahami, de posteritate Caini, Quaestiones et solutiones in Genesin, de specialibus legibus, de virtutibus, de vita contemplativa,* and *de vita Mosis.* In *Philonis Alexandrini. Opera Quae Supersunt,* ed. L. Cohn and P. Wendland. 7 vols. Berolini: Typis et impensis Georgii Reimerii, 1896–1930. English translation by F. H. Colson, *Philo.* 10 vols. LCL. Cambridge, Mass.: Harvard University Press, 1935–1950.

———. *Legatio ad Gaium,* ed. and trans. E. Mary Smallwood. Leiden: E. J. Brill, 1961.

Pseudo-Philo. *Liber antiquitatum biblicarum.* In *Pseudo-Philon. Les antiquités bibliques,* ed. with French translation by Daniel J. Harrington, Charles Perrot, and Pierre Bogaert. Sources Chrétiennes, 229–30. Paris: Éditions du Cerf, 1976.

Pseudo-Phocylides. *Admonitions*. In *The Sentences of Pseudo-Phocylides*, ed. and trans. Pieter W. van der Horst. Studia in Veteris Testamenti Pseudepigrapha 4. Leiden: E. J. Brill, 1978.

Plato *Gorgias*. In *Plato*, ed. E. R. Dodds. Oxford: Clarendon Press, 1959; repr., 1990. English translation by Terence Irwin. *Plato: Gorgias*. Oxford: Clarendon Press, 1979.

——. *Leges*. In Platonis *Opera Omnia*, ed. Godofredus Stallbaum. Vol. 10, *Leges et Epinomis*. Leipzig: Teubner, 1877. English translation R. G. Bury. *Plato*. Vols. I–II, *The Laws*. LCL. Cambridge, Mass.: Harvard University Press, 1914–37.

——. *Phaedo*. In *Platonis Opera Omnia*, ed. Godofredus Stallbaum. Vol. 1, *Euthyphro. Apologia. Crito. Phaedo. Theages Erastae. Theaetetus*. Leipzig: Teubner, 1877. English translation by C. J. Rowe. *Plato. Phaedo*. Cambridge: Cambridge University Press, 1993.

——. *Protagoras*. In *Platonis Opera Omnia*, ed. Godofredus Stallbaum. Vol. 2, *Sophista. Euthydemus. Protagoras. Hippias minor. Cratylus*. Leipzig: Teubner, 1879. English translation by C. C. W. Taylor. *Plato: Protagoras*. Oxford: Clarendon Press, 1976.

——. *Republica*. In *Platonis Opera Omnia*, ed. Godofredus Stallbaum. Vol. 5, *De republica, sive, De iusto libri decem*. Leipzig: Teubner, 1880. English translation Paul Shorey. *Plato*. Vols. 5–6, *The Republic*. LCL. Cambridge, Mass.: Harvard University Press, 1914–1937.

——. *Sophista*. In *Platonis Opera Omnia*, ed. Godofredus Stallbaum. Vol. 2, *Sophista. Euthydemus. Protagoras. Hippias minor. Cratylus*. Leipzig: Teubner, 1879. English translation H. N. Fowler. *Plato*. Vol. 7, *Theaetetus. Sophist*. LCL. Cambridge, Mass.: Harvard University Press, 1914–1937.

——. *Timaeus*. In *Platonis Opera Omnia*, ed. Godofredus Stallbaum. Vol. 7, *Timaeus. Timaei locri lib. De anima mundi. Critias. Parmenides. Symposion*. Leipzig: Teubner, 1871. English translation by R. G. Bury. *Plato*. Vol. 10, *Timaeus. Critias. Cleitophon. Menexenus. Epistles*. Cambridge, Mass.: Harvard University Press, 1914–1937.

Pliny (the Elder). *Naturalis historia*. English translation by H. Rackham, W. H. S. Jones, D. E. Eichholz. *Pliny: Natural History*. 10 vols. LCL. Cambridge, Mass.: Harvard University Press, 1967–75.

Pliny (the Younger). *Epistularum*. In *Epistularum libri novem. Epistularum ad Traiainum liber panegyricus*, ed. Mauriz Schuster. Bibliotheca scriptorum Graecorum et Romanorum Teubneriana. Leipzig: Teubner, 1952. English translation by Betty Radice. *Pliny: Letters and Panegyricus*. 2 vols. LCL. Cambridge, Mass.: Harvard University Press, 1972.

——. *Panegyricus*. In *XII Panegyrici Latini*, ed. R. A. B. Mynors. Scriptorum Classicorum bibliotheca Oxoniensis. Oxford: Clarendon Press, 1964.

Plutarch. *Moralia*. In *Plutarchi Chaeronensis Moralia*, ed. Gregorius N. Bernardakis. 7 vols. Bibliotheca scriptorum Graecorum et Romanorum Teubneriana. Leipzig: Teubner, 1888–1896. English translation by Frank Cole Babbitt, W. C. Helmbold, Phillip H. de Lacy, Benedict Einarson, Paul A. Clement, Herbert B. Hoffliet, Edwin L. Minar Jr., F. H. Sandbach, Harold North Fowler, Lionel Pearson, and Harold Cherniss. *Plutarch's Moralia*. 15 vols. LCL. Cambridge: Harvard University Press, 1927–1976.

——. *Vitae parallelae*. In *Plutarchus*. Ed. Claes Lindskog and Konrat Ziegler. 4 vols. Bibliotheca scriptorum Graecorum et Romanorum Teubneriana. Leipzig: Teubner, 1914–39. English translation by Bernadotte Perrin. *Plutarch's Lives*. 11 vols. LCL. Cambridge, Mass.: Harvard University Press, 1926.

Pollux. In *Pollucis Onomasticon: E codicibus ab ipso collatis*, ed. Erich Bethe. Lexicographi graeci recogniti et apparatu critico instructi 9, Sammlung Wissenschaftlicher Commentare. Stuttgart: Teubner, 1967.

Polybius. *Histories*. Ed. Raymond Weil and Claude Nicolet. 4 vols. Collection des Universités de France. Paris: Société d'Édition "Les Belles Lettres," 1977.

Polycarp. *Epistula ad Philippenses*. In *Die apostolischen Väter*, ed. K. Bihlmeyer and W. Schneemelcher, 114–20. Tübingen: Mohr, 1970. English translation by Bart D. Ehrman. *The Apostolic Fathers*. Vol. 1. LCL. Cambridge, Mass.: Harvard University Press, 2003.

Propertius, Sextus. *Carmina*. In *Sexti Properti. Carmina*, ed. E. Aarber. Scriptorum classicorum bibliotheca Oxoniensis. Repr., Oxford: Clarendon Press, 1957.

Protevangelium Iacobi. In *Evangelia Infantiae Apocrypha. Apocryphe Kindheitsevangelien,* ed. with German translation by Gerhard Schneider. Fontes Christiani 18. Basel: Herder, 1995.

Quintilian. *Institutio Oratoria.* In *Quintilian.* Trans. H. E. Butler. 4 vols. LCL. Cambridge, Mass.: Harvard University Press, 1920–1922.

Res gestae divi Augusti. Ed. with commentary by Cynthia Damon. Bryn Mawr Latin Commentaries. Bryn Mawr, Penn.: Bryn Mawr College, 1995. English translation by P. A. Brunt and J. M. Moore in *The Achievements of the Divine Augustus.* London: Oxford University Press, 1967.

Sallust (Gaius Sallustius Crispus). *Bellum Catilinae.* In *Catilina. Iurgutha. Historiarum fragmenta selecta C. Sallusti Crispi,* ed. L. D. Reynolds. Scriptorum classicorum bibliotheca Oxoniensis. Oxford: Clarendon Press, 1991. English translation by J. C. Rolfe. *Sallust: War with Catiline. War with Jugurtha. Selections from the Histories. Doubtful Works.* LCL. Cambridge, Mass.: Harvard University Press, 1921; repr., 1980.

Seneca (the Younger) *De beneficiis. De clementia. Epistulae morales.* In *L. Annaei Senecae opera quae supersunt,* ed. by Carl Hosius et. al. 4 vols. Bibliotheca scriptorum Graecorum et Romanorum Teubneriana. Leipzig: Teubner, 1923–. English translation by John W. Basore. *Seneca: Moral Essays.* 3 vols. LCL. Cambridge, Mass.: Harvard Univserity Press, 1935. English translation of *Epistulae morales* by Richard M. Gummere. *Seneca: Moral Epistles.* 2 vols. LCL. Cambridge, Mass.: Harvard University Press, 1925.

Seneca (the Elder). *Controversiae.* In *The Elder Seneca. Declamations,* ed. and trans. M. Winterbottom. 2 vols. LCL. Cambridge, Mass.: Harvard University Press, 1974.

——. *Suasoriae,* ed. William A. Edward. London: Bristol Classical Press, 1996.

Septuagint. Ed. Alfred Rahlfs. Stuttgart: Deutsche Bibelgellschaft, 1935; repr., 1979.

Sepúlveda, Juan Ginés de. *Democrates secundus.* In *Demócrates segundo. Apología en favor del libro sobre las justas causas de la guerra.* Ed. Jamie Brafau Prats with Spanish translation by A. Coroleu Lletget. Pozoblanco, Spain: Excmo. Ayuntamiento de Pozoblanco, 1997.

Suetonius. *De vita Caesarum.* English translation by J. C. Rolfe. *Suetonius.* 2 vols. Rev. ed. LCL. Cambridge, Mass.: Harvard University Press, 1997–1998.

The Shepherd of Hermas. In *Die apostolischen Väter I. Der Hirt des Hermas,* ed. Molly Whittaker, 1–115. Berlin: Akademie-Verlag, 1956. English translation by Bart D. Ehrman. *The Apostolic Fathers.* 2:175–473. LCL. Cambridge, Mass.: Harvard University Press, 2003.

Tacitus, Cornelius. *Historiarum.* In *P. Cornelii Taciti Libri qui supersunt,* ed. Heinz Heubner. 2 vols. Bibliotheca scriptorum Graecorum et Romanorum Teubneriana. Stuttgart: Teubner, 1978–1983. English translation by Clifford H. Moore. *Tacitus. Histories.* 4 vols. LCL. Cambridge, Mass.: Harvard University Press, 1925–1937.

——. *Annals.* In *Cornelius Tacitus. Annalen,* ed. Erich Koestermann. 4 vols. Wissenschaftliche Kommentare zu griechischen und lateinishen Schriftstellern. Heidelberg: C. Winter, 1963–68. English translation by M. Hutton, revised by R. M Ogilvie. *Tacitus. Annals.* 2 vols. LCL. Cambridge, Mass.: Harvard University Press, 1914–37.

Tatian. *Oratio ad Graecos.* In *Tatian: Oratio ad Graecos and Fragments,* ed. and trans. Molly Whittaker. Oxford: Clarendon Press, 1982.

Tertullian. *Ad nations.* Book 1. Ed. with French translation by André Schneider. Bibliotheca Helvetica Romana 9. Rome: Institut Suisse, 1968.

——. *Apologeticum, de cultu feminarum, de praescriptione haereticorum,* and *de virginibus velandis.* In *Tertulliani Opera,* ed. E. Dekkers and E. Kroymann. Corpus Christianorum, Series Latina 1–2. Turnhout: Brepols, 1954.

——. *De pudicitia.* In *Tertullian. La pudicité,* ed. with French translation by Charles Munier, introduction, index, and commentary by Claudio Micaelli. 2 vols. Sources chretiennes 394–95. Paris: Editions du Cerf, 1993.

Testament of Job. In *The Testament of Job,* ed. with English translation by Robert A. Kraft, Harold Attridge, Russell Spittler, and Janet Timbie. Text and Translations Series 5, Pseudepigrapha Series 4. Society of Biblical Literature, Missoula, Mont.: Scholars Press, 1974.

Testamenta XII Patriarcharum. [Includes *Testaments* of Asher, Benjamin, Dan, Gas, Issacher, Joseph, Judah, Levi, Naphthali, Reuben, Simeon, and Zebulun]. In *The Testaments of the Twelve Patriarchs. A Critical Edition of the Greek Text,* ed. M. de Jonge. Pseudepigrapha Veteris Testamenti Graece 1.2. Leiden: E.J. Brill, 1978.

Theon. *Progymnasmata.* In *Rhetores Graeci,* ed. Leonardi Spengel. Vol. 2. Bibliotheca Scriptorum Graecorum et Romanorum Teubneriana. Leipzig: Teubner, 1854–1885.

Theophilus of Antioch. *Ad Autolycum.* In *Theophilus of Antioch: Ad Autolycum,* ed. and trans. Robert M. Grant. Oxford: Clarendon Press, 1970.

Valerius Maximus. *Factorum et dictorum memorabilium,* ed. and trans. D.R. Shackleton Bailey. *Valerius Maximus. Memorable Deeds and Sayings.* 2 vols. LCL. Cambridge, Mass.: Harvard University Press, 2000.

Xenophon. *Oeconomicus,* ed. with English translation by E.C. Marchant. LCL. Cambridge, Mass.: Harvard University Press, 1923; repr., 1968.

SECONDARY SOURCES

Adams, J.N. *The Latin Sexual Vocabulary.* Baltimore, Md.: Johns Hopkins University Press, 1982.

Ahl, Frederick. "The Art of Safe Criticism in Greece and Rome." *American Journal of Philology* 105, no. 2 (1984): 174–208.

Alexandre, Monique. "Apologétique judéo-hellénistique et premières apologies chrétiennes." In *Les apologistes chrétiens et la culture greque,* ed. Bernard Pouderon and Joseph Doré, 1–40. Paris: Beauchesnes, 1998.

Alföldy, Géza. *The Social History of Rome.* Trans. David Braund and Frank Pollock. London: Croom Helm, 1985.

Alonso, Ana Maria. "Gender, Power, and Historical Memory: Discourses of *Serrano* Resistance." In *Feminists Theorize the Political,* ed. Judith Butler and Joan Wallach Scott, 404–25. New York: Routledge, 1992.

Alpert, Rebbeca. *Like Bread on the Seder Plate: Jewish Lesbians and the Transformation of Traditions.* New York: Columbia University Press, 1997.

Althusser, Louis. *Lenin and Philosophy and Other Essays.* New York: Monthly Review Press, 1971.

Amaru, Betsy Halpern. *The Empowerment of Women in the Book of Jubilees.* Supplements to the Journal for the Study of Judaism 60. Leiden: E.J. Brill, 1999.

——. "Portraits of Biblical Women in Josephus' *Antiquities.*" *Journal of Jewish Studies* 39 (1988): 143–70.

Anderson, Graham. *Lucian: Theme and Variation in the Second Sophistic.* Netherlands: E.J. Brill, 1976.

——. *The Second Sophistic: A Cultural Phenomenon in the Roman Empire.* New York: Routledge, 1993.

Anderson, R. Dean, Jr. *Ancient Rhetorical Theory and Paul.* Rev. ed. Leuven: Peeters, 1998.

Ando, Clifford. *Imperial Ideology and Provincial Loyalty.* Classics and Contemporary Thought 6. Berkeley: University of California Press, 2000.

Antonelli, Judith S. *In the Image of God: A Feminist Commentary on the Torah.* Northvale, N.J.: Jason Aronson Inc., 1995.

Ariès, Philippe, and André Béjin, eds. *Western Sexuality: Practice and Precept in Past and Present Times.* Trans. Anthony Foster. Oxford: Basil Blackwell, 1985.

Arieti, James A. "Rape and Livy's View of Roman History." In *Rape in Antiquity,* ed. Susan Deacy and Karen F. Pierce, 209–29. London: Duckworth, 1997.

Asad, Talal. *Genealogies of Religion: Discipline and Reasons of Power in Christianity and Islam.* Baltimore: Johns Hopkins University Press, 1993.

Astin, Alan E. "*Regimen Morum.*" *JRS* 78 (1988): 14–34.

Attridge, Harold W. *The Epistle to the Hebrews.* Hermeneia. Philadelphia: Fortress Press, 1989.

Aune, David. "Romans as a Logos Protreptikos in the Context of Ancient Religious and Philosophical Propaganda." In *Paulus und das antike Judentum,* ed. Martin Hengel and Ulrich Heckel, 91–121. Tübingen: Mohr/Siebeck, 1992.

——. *The New Testament in its Literary Environment.* Library of Early Christianity. Philadelphia: Westminster Press, 1987.

Babcock, William S. ed. *Paul and the Legacies of Paul.* Dallas, Tex.: Southern Methodist University Press, 1990.

Bach, Alice. *Women, Seduction, and Betrayal in Biblical Narrative.* Cambridge: Cambridge University Press, 1997.

Bagnall, Roger S. *Egypt in Late Antiquity.* Princeton, N.J.: Princeton University Press, 1993.

——. "A Trick a Day to Keep the Tax Man at Bay? The Prostitute Tax in Roman Egypt." *Bulletin of the American Society of Papyrologists* 28 (1991): 5–12.

Baile, David. *Eros and the Jews: From Biblical Israel to Contemporary America.* New York: Basic-Books, 1992.

Baker, Peter. *The Breach: Inside the Impeachment and Trial of William Jefferson Clinton.* New York: Berkley, 2000.

Balch, David. *Let Wives be Submissive: The Domestic Code in 1 Peter.* SBL Monograph Series 26. Chico, Calif.: Scholars Press, 1981.

Bannon, Cynthia J. *The Brothers of Romulus: Fraternal Pietas in Roman Law, Literature, and Society.* Princeton, N.J.: Princeton University Press, 1997.

Barnard, L. W. *Athenagoras: A Study in Second Century Christian Apologetic.* Théologie Historique 18. Paris: Beauchesne, 1972.

——. *Justin Martyr: His Life and Thought.* Cambridge: Cambridge University Press, 1967.

——. *St. Justin Martyr: The First and Second Apologies.* Ancient Christian Writers 56. New York: Paulist Press, 1997.

Barnes, Timothy David. *Tertullian: A Historical and Literary Study.*Oxford: Clarendon Press, 1971.

Barrett, Anthony A. *Caligula: The Corruption of Power.* New Haven, Conn.: Yale University Press, 1989.

Barrett, C. K. *A Commentary on the Epistle to the Romans.* 2nd ed. London: Black, 1991.

Baskin, Judith R. "Rabbinic Judaism and the Creation of Woman." In *Judaism Since Gender,* ed. Miriam Peskowitz and Laura Levitt, 125–30. New York: Routledge, 1997.

Bassler, Joette. "1 Corinthians." In *The Women's Bible Commentary,* ed. Carol A. Newsom and Sharon H. Ringe, 321–29. London: SPCK, 1992.

Bauckham, Richard J. *Jude, 2 Peter.* Word Biblical Commentaries 50. Waco, Tex.: Word Books, 1983.

Bauer, Walter. *Orthodoxy and Heresy in Earliest Christianity.* 2nd German ed. Ed. George Strecker. Trans. Philadelphia Seminar on Christian Origins. Philadelphia: Fortress Press, 1971. Originally published as *Rechgläubigkeit und Ketzerei im ältesten Christentum.* Beiträge zur historischen Theologie 10. Tübingen: Mohr/Siebeck, 1934.

Bauer, W., W. F. Arndt, F. W. Gingrich, and F.W. Danker. *Greek-English Lexicon of the New Testament and Other Early Christian Literature.* 2nd ed. Chicago, 1979.

Beard, Mary, John North, and Simon Price. *Religions of Rome.* Vol. 1, *A History.* Cambridge: Cambridge University Press, 1998.

Beaucamp, Joëlle. *Le Statut de la femme à Byzance (4e–7e siècle).* 2 vols. Paris: De Boccard, 1990.

Beauvoir, Simone de. *The Second Sex.* Trans. H.M. Parshley. New York: Vintage Books, 1952.

BeDuhn, Jason. "'Because of the Angels': Unveiling Paul's Anthropology in 1 Corinthians 11." *JBL* 118 (1999): 295–320.

Beker, J. Christaan. *Paul's Apocalyptic Gospel.* Philadelphia: Fortress Press, 1982.

——. *Paul the Apostle: The Triumph of God in Life and Thought.* Philadelphia: Fortress Press, 1980.

Benko, Stephen. *Pagan Rome and the Early Christians*. Bloomington: Indiana University Press, 1986.

Betz, Hans Dieter. *Galatians: A Commentary on Paul's Letter to the Churches of Galatia*. Hermeneia. Philadelphia: Fortress Press, 1979.

———, ed. *Plutarch's Ethical Writings and Early Christian Literature*. Leiden: E. J. Brill, 1978.

Beyschlag, Karlmann. *Simon Magus und die christliche Gnosis*. Wissenschaftliche Untersuchungen zum Alten und Neuen Testament 16. Tübingen: Mohr (Siebeck), 1975.

Biale, David. *Eros and the Jews: From Biblical Israel to Contemporary America*. New York: Basic Books, 1992.

Biale, Rachel. *Women and Jewish Law: The Essential Texts, Their History, and Their Relevance for Today*. New York: Schocken Books, 1995.

Biblia Patristica: Index des citations et allusions bibliques dans la littérature patristique. 3 vols. Paris: Université des science humaines de Strasbourg, 1975.

The Bible and Culture Collective. *The Postmodern Bible*. New Haven, Conn.: Yale University Press, 1995.

Bigg, Charles. *A Critical and Exegetical Commentary on the Epistles of St. Peter and St. Jude*. International Critical Commentaries. New York: Scribner, 1922.

Bilde, Per, Troels Engberg-Pedersen, Lise Hannestad, and Jan Zahle, eds. *Aspects of Hellenistic Kingship*. Studies in Hellenistic Civilization 7. Aarhus: Aarhus University Press, 1986.

Billows, Richard A. *Kings and Colonists: Aspects of Macedonian Imperialism*. Columbia Studies in the Classical Tradition 22. Leiden: E. J. Brill, 1995.

Bird, Phyllis A. "The Harlot as Heroine: Narrative Art and Social Presupposition in Three Old Testament Texts." In *Missing Persons and Mistaken Identities*, 197–218. Minneapolis: Fortress Press, 1997.

———. "'To Play the Harlot': An Inquiry into an Old Testament Metaphor." In *Gender Difference in Ancient Israel*, ed. Peggy L. Day, 75–94. Minneapolis: Fortress Press, 1989.

Blass, F., A. Debrunner, and R. W. Funk. *A Greek Grammar of the New Testament and Other Early Christian Literature*. Chicago, 1961.

Boatwright, Mary T. *Hadrian and the Cities of the Roman Empire*. Princeton, N.J.: Princeton University Press, 2000.

Bori, Pier Cesare. *The Golden Calf and the Origins of the Anti-Jewish Controversy*. Trans. David Ward. South Florida Studies in the History of Judaism 16. Atlanta: Scholars Press, 1990.

Boswell, John. *Christianity, Social Tolerance, and Homosexuality: Gay People in Western Europe from the Beginning of the Christian Era to the Fourteenth Century*. Chicago: University of Chicago Press, 1980.

Bosworth, A. B. *From Arrian to Alexander: Studies in Historical Interpretation*. Oxford: Clarendon Press, 1988.

———. "Augustus, the *Res Gestae* and Hellenistic Theories of Apotheosis." *JRS* 89 (1999): 1–18.

Boughton, Lynne C. "From Pious Legend to Feminist Fantasy: Distinguishing Hagiographical License from Apostolic Practice in the *Acts of Paul/Acts of Thecla*." *JAAR* 71 (1991): 362–83.

Bourdieu, Pierre. *Language and Symbolic Power*, edit. J. B. Thompson, trans. Gino Raymond and Matthew Adamson. Cambridge: Cambridge University Press, 1991.

Bové, Paul A. *Mastering Discourse: The Politics of Intellectual Culture*. Durham, N.C.: Duke University Press, 1992.

Bowman, Alan K., and Greg Woolf, ed. *Literacy and Power in the Ancient World*. Cambridge: Cambridge University Press, 1994.

Boyarin, Daniel. *Carnal Israel: Reading Sex in Talmudic Culture*. The New Historicism 25. Berkeley: University of California Press, 1993.

———. *Dying for God: Martyrdom and the Making of Christianity and Judaism*. Stanford, Calif.: Stanford University Press, 1999.

———. *A Radical Jew: Paul and the Politics of Identity*. Berkeley: University of California Press, 1994.

Bradley, Keith. "Legal Privilege in the Roman Empire." In *Studies in Ancient Society*, ed. Moses I. Finley. London: Routlege and Kegan Paul, 1974.

——. "On the Roman Slave Supply and Slavebreeding." *Slavery and Abolition* 8 (1987): 42–64.

——. *Slave and Society at Rome.* Cambridge: Cambridge University Press, 1994.

Braund, Susanna H. "Juvenal—Misogynist or Misogamist?" *JRS* 82 (1992): 71–86.

——. "A Woman's Voice? Laronia's Role in Juvenal *Satire* 2." In *Women in Antiquity: New Assessments*, ed. Richard Hawley and Barbara Levick, 207–19. London: Routledge, 1995.

Bronner, Leila Leah. "Esther Revisited: An Aggadic Approach." In *A Feminist Companion to Esther, Judith and Susanna*, ed. Athalya Brenner, 176–97. Feminist Companion to the Bible 7. Sheffield: Sheffield Academic Press, 1995.

Brooten, Bernadette J. *Love Between Women: Early Christian Responses to Female Homoeroticism.* Chicago: University of Chicago Press, 1996.

Brown, Peter. *Authority and the Sacred: Aspects of the Christianisation of the Roman World.* Cambridge: Cambridge University Press, 1995.

——. *The Body and Society: Men, Women, and Sexual Renunciation in Early Christianity.* New York: Columbia University Press, 1988.

——. "The Notion of Virginity in the Early Church." In *Christian Spirituality: Origins to the Twelfth Century*, ed. B. McGinn and J. Meyendorff, 426–43. New York: Crossroad, 1985.

——. *Power and Persuasion in Late Antiquity: Towards a Christian Empire.* Madison: University of Wisconsin Press, 1992.

Brundage, James A. *Law, Sex, and Christian Society in Medieval Europe.* Chicago: University of Chicago Press, 1987.

Brunt, P. A. "Marcus Aurelius in his *Meditations*." *JRS* 64 (1974): 1–20.

Buckley, J. J. "Libertines or Not: Fruit, Bread, Semen, and Other Bodily Fluids in Gnosticism." *JECS* 2 (1994): 15–34.

Buell, Denise Kimber. "Race and Univsersalism in Early Christianity." *JECS* 10, no. 4 (2002): 429–68.

——. "Rethinking the Relevance of Race for Early Christian Self-Definition." *Harvard Theological Review* 94, no. 4 (2001): 449–76.

——. *Making Christians: Clement of Alexandria and the Rhetoric of Legitimacy.* Princeton, N.J.: Princeton University Press, 1999.

Bultmann, Rudolf. "Christ the End of the Law." *Beiträge zur Evangelischen Theologie* 1 (1940): 3–27.

——. *Der Stil der Paulischen Predigt und die kynische-stoische Diatribe.* Göttingen: Vandenhoeck & Ruprecht, 1910.

Burgess, Theodore C. "Epideictic Literature." *University of Chicago Studies in Classical Philology* 3 (1902): 89–102.

Burrus, Virginia. *Chastity as Autonomy: Women in the Stories of the Apocryphal Acts.* Studies in Women and Religion 23. Lewiston, N.Y.: Edwin Mellen Press, 1987.

——. "The Heretical Woman as a Symbol in Alexander, Athanasius, Epiphanius, and Jerome." *Harvard Theological Review* 84 (1991): 229–48

——. *The Making of a Heretic: Gender, Authority, and the Priscillianist Controversy.* Berkeley: University of California Press, 1995.

——. "Reading Agnes: the Rhetoric of Gender in Ambrose and Prudentius." *JECS* 3 (1995): 25–46.

——. "In the Theater of this Life: The Performance of Orthodoxy in Ancient Christianity." In *The Limits of Ancient Christianity: Essays on Late Antique Thought and Culture in Honor of R. A. Markus*, ed. William E. Klingshirn and Mark Vessey, 80–96. Ann Arbor: University of Michigan Press, 1999.

Butler, Judith. "Contingent Foundations: Feminism and the Question of 'Postmodernism.'" In *Feminists Theorize the Political*, ed. Judith Butler and Joan W. Scott, 3–21. New York: Routledge, 1992.

———. *Gender Trouble: Feminism and the Subversion of Identity.* New York: Routledge, 1990.

Byron, Gay L. *Symbolic Blackness and Ethnic Difference in Early Christian Literature.* London: Routledge, 2002.

Cameron, Averil. *Christianity and the Rhetoric of Empire.* Sather Classical Lectures 55. Berkeley: University of California Press, 1991.

———. "How to Read Heresiology." *Journal of Medieval and Early Modern Studies* 33, no. 3 (2003): 471–92.

———. "Jews and Heretics—a Category Error?" In *The Ways That Never Parted,* ed. Adam H. Becker and Annette Yoshiko Reed. Texts and Studies in Ancient Judaism. Tübingen: Mohr/Siebeck, 2003.

———. "Redrawing the Map: Early Christian Territory After Foucault." *JRS* 76 (1986): 266–71.

———. "Virginity as Metaphor: Women and the Rhetoric of Early Christianity." In *The Writing of Ancient History,* ed. Averil Cameron, 175–205. London: Duckworth, 1989.

Camp, Claudia V. *Wise, Strange, and Holy: The Strange Woman and the Making of the Bible.* JSOT Supplement Series 320. Sheffield: Sheffield Academic Press, 2000.

Campenhausen, Hans von. *The Formation of the Christian Bible.* Trans. J. A. Becker. Philadelphia: Fortress Press, 1972.

Cantarella, Eva. *Bisexuality in the Ancient World.* Trans. Cormac Ó Cuilleanáin. New Haven, Conn.: Yale University Press, 1992.

———. *Pandora's Daughters: The Role and Status of Women in Greek and Roman Antiquity.* Trans. Maureen B. Fant. Baltimore: Johns Hopkins University Press, 1987.

Carey, D., and R. A. Reid, eds. *Demosthenes: Selected Private Speeches.* Cambridge: Cambridge University Press, 1985.

Carlini, Antonio. "La tradizione testuale del Pastor di Ermo I nuovi papiri." In *Le Stade del Testo.* ed. Gugielmo Cavello. Lecce: Adriatica Editrice, 1987.

Castelli, Elizabeth A. "Gender, Theory, and *The Rise of Christianity*: A Response to Rodney Stark." *JECS* 6 (1998): 227–57.

———. *Imitating Paul: A Discourse of Power.* Louisville, Ky.: Westminster/John Knox Press, 1991.

———. "Interpretations of Power in 1 Corinthians." *Semeia* 54 (1992): 197–222.

———. *Martyrdom and Memory: Early Christian Culture Making.* New York: Columbia University Press, 2004.

———. "Romans." In *A Feminist Commentary.* Vol. 2, *Searching the Scriptures,* ed. Elizabeth Schüssler Fiorenza, 272–300. New York: Crossroad, 1996.

———. "Virginity and its Meaning for Women's Sexuality in Early Christianity." *Journal of Feminist Studies in Religions* 2 (1986): 61–88.

———. *Visions and Voyeurism: The Politics of Sight in Early Christianity.* Protocol of the Colloquy of the Center for Hemeneutical Studies. Berkeley: Center for Hermeneutical Studies, 1995.

———., ed. "Lesbian Historiography Before the Name?" *GLQ* 4 (1998).

Chadwick, Henry. "Justin Martyr's Defence of Christianity." *Bulletin of the John Rylands Library* 47 (Manchester, 1965): 275–97. Also in *History and Thought of the Early Church.* London: Variorum Reprints, 1982.

Chadwick, H. E., trans. and intro. *Origen: Contra Celsum.* Cambridge: Cambridge University Press, 1965.

Charles, J. Daryl. *Literary Strategy in the Epistle of Jude.* Scranton, Penn.: University of Scranton Press, 1993.

Chatterjee, Partha. "Colonialism, Nationalism, and Colonized Women: The Contest in India." *American Ethnologist* 16, no. 4 (1989): 622–33.

Clark, Elizabeth A. *Ascetic Piety and Women's Faith: Essays on Late Ancient Christianity.* Studies in Women and Religion 20. Lewiston: Edwin Mellen Press, 1986.

———. "Foucault, The Fathers, and Sex." *JAAR* 56 (1988): 619–41.

———. "Ideology, History, and the Construction of Woman." *JECS* 2 (1994): 155–84.

——. *Reading Renunciation: Asceticism and Scripture in Early Christianity.* Princeton, N.J.: Princeton University Press, 1999.

——. "Sex, Shame, and Rhetoric: En-Gendering Early Christian Ethics." *JAAR* 59 (1991): 221–45.

Clark, Gillian. "Women and Asceticism in Late Antiquity: The Refusal of Status and Gender." In *Asceticism*, ed. Vincent L. Wimbush and Richard Valantasis, 33–48. New York: Oxford University Press, 1995.

——. *Women in Late Antiquity.* New York: Oxford University Press, 1993.

Clarke, M. L. *Rhetoric at Rome: A Historical Survey.* London: Cohen & West, 1953.

Cohen, Bernard S. *Colonialism and Its Forms of Knowledge.* Princeton, N.J.: Princeton University Press, 1996.

Cohen, David, and Richard Saller. "Foucault on Sexuality in Greco-Roman Antiquity." In *Foucault and the Writing of History*, ed. Jan Goldstein, 35–59. Oxford: Blackwell, 1994.

Cohen, Shaye J. D. *The Beginnings of Jewishness: Boundaries, Varieties, Uncertainties.* Berkeley and Los Angeles: University of California Press, 1999.

Coleman, Kathleen M. "Fatal Charades: Roman Executions Staged as Mythological Enactments." *JRS* 80 (1990): 44–73.

——. "Informers on Parade." In *The Art of Ancient Spectacle*, ed. Bettina Berhmann and Christine Kondoleon, 231–45. National Gallery of Art Studies in the History of Art 56, Center for Advanced Study in the Visual Arts Symposium Papers 34. New Haven, Conn.: Yale University Press, 1999.

Collins, Adela Yarbro. "Early Christian Apocalypses." *Semeia* 14 (1979): 61–121.

——., ed. "Early Christian Apocalypticism: Genre and Social Setting." *Semeia* 36 (1986): 1–174.

Collins, John J., ed. "Apocalypse: The Morphology of a Genre." *Semeia* 14 (1979).

——. *The Apocalyptic Imagination: An Introduction to Jewish Apocalyptic Literature.* 2nd ed. Grand Rapids, Mich.: William B. Eerdmans Publishing Co., 1998.

Collins, Raymond F. *First Corinthians.* Sacra Pagina Series 7. Collegeville, Minn.: Liturgical Press, 1999.

Conzelmann, Hans. *1 Corinthians.* Trans. James W. Leitch. Hermeneia. Philadelphia: Fortress Press, 1975.

Cooper, Frederick, and Ann L. Stoler. "Introduction to Tensions of Empire: Colonial Control and Visions of Rule." *American Ethnologist* 16, no. 4 (1989): 609–21.

Cooper, Kate. "Apostles, Ascetic Women, and Questions of Audience: New Reflections on the Rhetoric of Gender in the Apocryphal Acts." *SBL Seminar Papers* (1992): 147–53.

——. "Insinuations of Womanly Influence: An Aspect of Christianization of the Roman Aristocracy." *JRS* 72 (1992): 150–64.

——. *The Virgin and the Bride: Idealized Womanhood in Late Antiquity.* Cambridge, Mass.: Harvard University Press, 1996.

Corley, Kathleen. *Private Women, Public Meals: Social Conflict in the Synoptic Tradition.* Peabody, Mass.: Hendrickson, 1992.

Corrington Streete, Gail. "Askesis and Resistance in the Pastoral Epistles." In *The New Testament and Asceticism*, ed. Leif E. Vaage and Vincent L. Wimbush, 299–316. Routledge: New York, 1998.

Courtney, E. *A Commentary on the Satires of Juvenal.* London: Athlone Press, 1980.

Damon, Cynthia. *The Mask of the Parasite: A Pathology of Roman Patronage.* Ann Arbor: University of Michigan Press, 1997.

D'Angelo, Mary Rose. "Εὐσέβεια: Roman Imperial Family Values and the Sexual Politics of 4 Maccabees and the Pastorals." *Biblical Interpretation* 11, no. 2 (2003): 139–65.

——. "Veils, Virgins, and the Tongues of Men and Angels: Women's Heads in Early Christianity." In *Off with Her Head! The Denial of Women's Identity in Myth, Religion, and Culture*, ed. Howard Eilberg-Schwartz and Wendy Doniger, 131–64. Berkeley: University of California Press, 1998.

Davidson, Maxwell J. *Angels at Qumran: A Comparative Study of 1 Enoch 1–36 and Sectarian Writings from Qumran.* Journal for the Study of the Pseudepigrapha Supplement Series 11. Sheffield: JSOT Press, 1992.

Davies, Stevan. *The Revolt of the Widows: The Social World of the Apocryphal Acts.* Carbondale: Southern Illinois University Press, 1980.

Davis, Stephen J. *The Cult of Saint Thecla: A Tradition of Women's Piety in Late Antiquity.* New York: Oxford University Press, 2001.

Delcor, M. "Le Mythe de la chute des anges et de l'origine des géants comme explication du mal dans le monde dans l'apocalyptique juive. Histoire des traditions." *Revue d'histoire des religions* 190 (1976): 3–53.

Deloria, Vine, Jr. *Custer Died for Your Sins: An Indian Manifesto.* New York: Macmillan, 1969.

Denis, Albert-Marie. *Introduction aux pseudépigraphes grecs d'Ancien Testament.* Studia in Veteris Testamenti Pseudepigrapha. Leiden: E. J. Brill, 1970.

Desjardins, Michel. "Bauer and Beyond: On Recent Scholarly Discussions of Αἵρεσις in the Early Christian Era." *Second Century* 8, no. 2 (1991): 65–82.

Diamond, Irene, and Lee Quinby, eds. *Feminism and Foucault: Reflections on Resistance.* Boston: Northeastern University Press, 1988.

Dibelius, Martin. *Der Hirt des Hermas.* Vol. 4 of *Die apostolischen Väter.* Handbuch zum Neuen Testament. Tübingen: Mohr/Siebeck, 1923.

———. *An die Kolosser, an die Epheser, an Philemon.* 3rd ed. HNT 12. Tübingin: J. C. B. Mohr, 1953.

Dibelius, Martin, and Hans Conzelmann. *A Commentary on the Pastoral Epistles.* Trans. P. Buttolph, A. Yarbro, and H. Koester. Hermenaeia. Philadelphia: Fortress Press, 1972.

Dickey, Eleanor. *Greek Forms of Address from Herodotus to Lucian.* Oxford: Clarendon Press, 1996.

Diethart, Johannes, and Ewald Kislinger. "Papyrologisches zur Prostitution im Byzantinischen Ägypten." *Jahrbuch der Österreichishen Byzantinistik* 41 (1991): 15–23.

Dijk-Hemmes, Fokkelien van. "The Metaphorization of Women in Prophetic Speech: An Analysis of Ezekiel 23." In *On Gendering Texts: Female and Male Voices in the Hebrew Bible,* ed. Athalya Brenner and F. van Dijk-Hemmes, 167–76. Biblical Interpretation Series 1. Leiden: E. J. Brill, 1993.

Dixon, Suzanne. *The Roman Family.* Baltimore, Md.: Johns Hopkins University Press, 1992.

———. "The Sentimental Ideal of the Roman Family." In *Marriage, Divorce, and Children in Ancient Rome,* ed. Beryl Rawson, 99–113. Oxford: Clarendon Press, 1991.

Donelson, Lewis R. *Pseudepigraphy and Ethical Argument in the Pastoral Epistles.* Tübingen: Mohr/Siebeck, 1986.

Donfried, Karl Paul. "False Presuppositions in the Study of Romans." *Catholic Biblical Quarterly* 36 (1974): 232–55.

———, ed. *The Romans Debate.* Rev. ed. Peabody, Mass.: Hendrickson, 1991.

Dover, Kenneth J. *Greek Homosexuality.* Cambridge, Mass.: Harvard University Press, 1978.

———. *Greek Popular Morality in the Time of Plato and Aristotle.* Oxford: Basil Blackwell, 1974.

Droge, Arthur J. *Homer or Moses? Early Christian Interpretations of the History of Culture.* Tübingen: Mohr/Siebeck, 1989.

———. "Josephus between Greeks and Barbarians." In *Josephus' Contra Apionem,* ed. Louis H. Feldman and John R. Levison, 115–42. Leiden: E.J. Brill, 1996.

Dubois, Jean-Daniel. "Polémiques, pouvoir et exégèse l'example des gnostiques anciens en monde Grec." In *Inventer l'hérésie? Discours polémiques et pouvoirs avant l'Inquisition,* ed. Monique Zerner. Collection du Centre d'études médiévales de Nice 2. Nice: Centre d'etudes médiévales, 1998.

Dulles, Avery. *A History of Apologetic.* Theological Resources. Philadelphia: Westminster Press, 1971.

Dunn, James G. *Romans 1–8.* Word Biblical Commentary 38. Dallas, Tex.: Word Books, 1988.

Earl, Donald. *The Moral and Political Tradition of Rome.* London: Thames and Hudson, 1967.

Edwards, Catherine. *The Politics of Immorality in Ancient Rome.* Cambridge: Cambridge University Press, 1993.

——. "Unspeakable Professions: Public Performance and Prostitution in Ancient Rome." In *Roman Sexualities*, ed. Judith P. Hallett and Marilyn B. Skinner, 66–98. Princeton, N.J.: Princeton University Press, 1997.

Edwards, Mark J. "Justin's Logos and the Word of God." *JECS* 3 (1995): 261–80.

——. "On the Platonic Schooling of Justin Martyr." *Journal of Theological Studies* 42 (1991): 17–34.

Edwards, Mark J., Martin Goodman, S. R. F. Price, and Christopher Rowland, eds. *Apologetics in the Roman Empire: Pagans, Jews, and Christians.* Oxford: Clarendon Press, 1999.

Ehrman, Bart D. Introduction to *The Shepherd of Hermas*, trans. Bart D. Ehrman. In *The Apostolic Fathers*, 2:162–73. LCL. Cambridge, Mass.: Harvard University Press, 2003.

——. *Lost Christianities: The Battles for Scripture and the Faiths We Never Knew.* New York: Oxford University Press, 2003.

——. *The Orthodox Corruption of Scripture: The Effect of Early Christological Controversies on the Text of the New Testament.* New York: Oxford University Press, 1993.

Eilberg-Schwartz, Howard. *God's Phallus and Other Problems for Men and Monotheism.* Boston: Beacon Press, 1994.

Elliott, Neil. *Liberating Paul: The Justice of God and the Politics of the Apostle.* Maryknoll, N.Y.: Orbis Books, 1994.

Elm, Susanna. "The Polemical use of Genealogies: Jerome's Classification of Pelagius and Evagrius Ponticus." *Studia Patristica* 33 (1997): 311–18.

——. *Virgins of God: The Making of Asceticism in Late Antiquity.* Oxford: Clarendon Press, 1994.

Elsner, Jaś. *Imperial Rome and Christian Triumph: The Art of the Roman Empire, 100–450.* Oxford: Oxford University Press, 1998.

Elsner, Jaś, and Jamie Masters, eds. *Reflections of Nero: Culture, History, and Representation.* Chapel Hill: University of North Carolina Press, 1994.

Epp, Eldon J. "Text-Critical, Exegetical, and Socio-Cultural Factors Affecting the Junia/Junias Variation in Romans 17.7." In *New Testament Criticism and Exegesis: Festschrift J. Delobel*, ed. A. Denaux, 287–91. Bibliotheca Ephemeridum Theologicarum Lovaniensium 161. Belgium: Leuven University Press, 2002.

Eskenazi, Tamara C., and Eleanore P. Judd. "Marriage to a Stranger in Ezra 9–10." In *Second Temple Studies.* Vol. 2., *Temple Community in the Persian Period*, ed. Tamara C. Eskenazi and Kent H. Richards, 266–72. JSOT Supplement Series 175. Sheffield: JSOT Press, 1994.

Esler, Philip. "Ezra-Nehemiah as a Narrative of (Re-invented) Israelite Identity." *Biblical Interpretation* 11 (2003): 413–26.

Evans Grubbs, Judith. "Constantine and Imperial Legislation on the Family." In *The Theodosian Code*, ed. Jill Harries and Ian Wood, 120–42. Ithaca, N.Y.: Cornell University Press, 1993.

——. *Law and Family in Late Antiquity.* Oxford: Clarendon Press, 1995.

Fears, J. Rufus. "The Cult of the Virtues and Roman Imperial Ideology." *ANRW* II.17.2 (1981): 827–948.

Fédou, Michel. "La Figure de Socrate selon Justin." In *Les Apologistes chrétiens et la culture greque*, ed. Bernard Pouderon and Joseph Doré, 51–66. Théologie Historique 105. Paris: Beuchesne, 1996.

Feeney, D. C. "*Silicit et fastest*: Ovid's *Fasti* and the Problem of Free Speech Under the Principate." In *Roman Poetry and Propaganda in the Age of Augustus*, ed. Anton Powell, 1–25. London: Bristol Classical Press, 1992.

Fekkes, Jan. "'His Bride Has Prepared Herself': Revelation 12–21 and Isaian Nuptial Imagery." *JBL* 109 (1990): 269–87.

Feldman, Louis H. *Jew and Gentile in the Ancient World.* Princeton, N.J.: Princeton University Press, 1993.

——. *Studies in Hellenistic Judaism*. Leiden: E. J. Brill, 1996.

Feldman, Louis H., and John R. Levison. "An Ass in the Jerusalem Temple: The Origins and Development of the Slander." In *Josephus' Contra Apionem: Studies in its Character and Context with a Latin Concordance to the Portion Missing in Greek*, ed. by Louis H. Feldman and John R. Levison, 310–26. Arbeiten zur Geschichte des antiken Judentums und des Urchristentums 34. Leiden: E. J. Brill, 1996.

Ferguson, Everett. *Demonology of the Early Christian World*. Symposium Series 12. New York: Edwin Mellen Press, 1980.

Ferrill, Arthur. *Caligula: Emperor of Rome*. London: Thames and Hudson, 1991.

Festugière, A.-J. *Freedom and Civilization Among the Greeks*. Trans. P. T. Brannan. Princeton Theological Monograph Series 11. Allison Park, Penn.: Pickwick, 1987.

Fields, Weston W. *Sodom and Gomorrah: History and Motif in Biblical Narrative*. JSOT Supplement Series 231. Sheffield: Sheffield Academic Press, 1997.

Finley, Moses I. *The Ancient Economy*. Berkeley: University of California Press, 1973.

Fiore, Benjamin. "Passion in Paul and Plutarch: 1 Corinthians 5–6 and the Polemic Against Epicureans." In *Greeks, Romans, and Christians*, ed. Everett Ferguson, D. L. Balch, and W. A. Meeks, 133–43. Minneapolis: Fortress Press, 1990.

Fisk, Bruce N. "ΠΟΡΝΕΥΕΙΝ as Bodily Violation: The Unique Nature of Sexual Sin in 1 Corinthians 6.18." *New Testament Studies* 42 (1996): 540–58.

Fitzmyer, Joseph A. "Another Look at KEPHALE in 1 Corinthians 11:3." *New Testament Studies* 35 (1989): 503–11.

——. *Romans*. Anchor Bible. New York: Doubleday, 1993.

Flory, Maureen. "Livia and the History of Public Honorific Statues for Women in Rome." *Transactions of the Americal Philological Association* 123 (1993): 287–308.

——. "*Sic exempla parantur*: Livia's Shrine to Concordia and the Porticus Liviae." *Historia* 33 (1984): 309–30.

Forbis, Elizabeth. *Municipal Virtues in the Roman Empire*. Stuttgart and Leipzig: B. G. Teubner, 1996.

Fornberg, Tord. *An Early Church in a Pluralistic Society: A Study of 2 Peter*. Coniectanea biblica New Testament Series 9. Uppsala: CWK Gleerup, 1977.

Foucault, Michel. *Discipline and Punish*. Trans. Alan Sheridan. New York: Vintage Books, 1979.

——. *Ethics, Subjectivity, and Truth*. Vol. 1 of *The Essential Works of Michel Foucault*, ed. Paul Rabinow. Trans. Robert Hurley et al. New York: New Press, 1994.

——. *Foucault Live*, ed. S. Lotringer. New York: Semiotexte, 1989.

——. "On the Genealogy of Ethics: An Overview of Work in Progress." In *Ethics, Subjectivity, and Truth*. Vol. 1 of *The Essential Works of Michel Foucault*, ed. Paul Rabinow. Trans. Robert Hurley et al., 253–80. New York: New Press, 1994.

——. *History of Sexuality*. Vol. 1, *An Introduction*. Trans. Robert Hurley. New York: Vintage Books, 1985.

——. *History of Sexuality*. Vol. 2, *The Use of Pleasure*. Trans. Robert Hurley. New York: Vintage Books, 1985.

——. *History of Sexuality*. Vol. 3, *The Care of the Self*. Trans. Robert Hurley. New York: Vintage Books, 1985.

——. "The Subject and Power." In *Michel Foucault: Beyond Structuralism and Hermeneutics*, ed. Herbert Dreyfuss and Paul Rabinow, 208–28. Chicago: University of Chicago Press, 1982.

Fox, Robin Lane. *Pagans and Christians*. New York: Alfred A. Knopf, 1987.

Francis, James A. *Subversive Virtue: Asceticism and Authority in the Second-Century Pagan World*. University Park: Pennsylvania State University Press, 1995.

Frankemölle, Hubert. *1. und 2. Petrusbrief, Judasbrief*. Die Neue Echter Bibel. Würtzburg: Echter Verlag, 1987.

Frede, Michael. "Origen's Treatise *Against Celsus*." In *Apologetics in the Roman Empire: Pagans,*

Jews, and Christians, ed. Mark Edwards, Martin Goodman, and Simon Price, 131–55. Oxford: Oxford University Press, 1999.

Fredriksen, Paula. "What Parting of the Ways?" In *The Ways That Never Parted: Jews and Christians in Late Antiquity and the Early Middle Ages*, ed. Adam H. Becker and Annette Toshiko Reed, 35–64. Tübingen: Mohr/Siebeck, 2003.

French, Dorthea R. "Maintaining Boundaries: The Status of Actresses in Early Christian Society." *Vigiliae Christianae* 52 (1998): 293–318.

Freymer-Kensky, Tikva. "Law and Philosophy: The Case of Sex in the Bible." In *Women in the Hebrew Bible: A Reader*, ed. Alice Bach, 293–304. New York: Routledge, 1999.

Fuchs, Eric, and Pierre Reymond. *La Deuxième Épître de Saint Pierre, l'Épître de Saint Jude.* Commentaire de Noveau Testament 13b. Paris: Delachaux & Niestlé, 1980.

Gaca, Kathy L. *The Making of Fornication: Eros, Ethics, and Political Reform in Greek Philosophy and Early Christianity*. Hellenistic Culture and Society 40. Berkeley and Los Angeles: University of California Press, 2003.

Gager, John. *Reinventing Paul*. Oxford: Oxford University Press, 2000.

Gamble, Harry Y. *Books and Readers in the Early Church: A History of Early Christian Texts*. New Haven, Conn.: Yale University Press, 1995.

Gardner, Jane F. *Women in Roman Law and Society*. Bloomington: University of Indiana Press, 1991.

Garlan, Yvon. *Slavery in Ancient Greece*. Trans. Janet Lloyd. Ithaca, N.Y.: Cornell University Press, 1988.

Garnsey, Peter. "Legal Privilege in the Roman Empire." In *Studies in Ancient Society*, ed. Moses I. Finley, 141–65. London: Routlege and Kegan Paul, 1974.

——. *Social Status and Legal Privilege in the Roman Empire*. Oxford: Clarendon Press, 1970.

Gaston. Lloyd. *Paul and the Torah*. Vancouver: University of British Columbia Press, 1987.

Gaventa, Beverly. *From Darkness to Light*. Philadelphia: Fortress Press, 1986.

Georgi, Dieter. *The Opponents of Paul in 2 Corinthians: A Study of Religious Propaganda in Antiquity*. Philadelphia: Fortress Press, 1986.

——. "Who Is the True Prophet?" *Harvard Theological Review* 79 (1986): 100–126.

Gero, Stephen. "With Walter Bauer on the Tigris: Encratite Orthodoxy and Libertine Heresy in Syro-Mesopotamian Christianity." In *Nag Hammadi, Gnosticism, and Early Christianity*, ed. Charles W. Hedrick and Rogert Hodgson Jr., 287–309. Peabody, Mass.: Hendrickson, 1986.

Giet, Stanislas. *Hermas et les pasteurs: Les Trois auteurs du Pasteur d'Hermas*. Paris: Presses Universitaires de France, 1963.

Gilbert, Maurice. *La Critique des dieux dans le Livre de la Sagesse*. Analecta Biblica 53. Rome: Biblical Institute Press, 1973.

Glancy, Jennifer A. "Obstacles to Slaves' Participation in the Corinthian Church." *JBL* 117 (1998): 481–501.

——. *Slavery in Early Christianity*. Oxford: Oxford University Press, 2002.

Gleason, Maude W. *Making Men: Sophists and Self-Presentation in Ancient Rome*. Princeton, N.J.: Princeton University Press, 1995.

——. "The Semiotics of Gender: Physiognomy and Self-Fashioning in the Second Century C.E." In *Before Sexuality: The Construction Erotic Experience in the Ancient Greek World*, ed. David Halperin, John J. Winkler, and Froma L. Zeitlin, 389–416. Princeton, N.J.: Princeton University Press, 1990.

Goehring, James E. "Libertine or Liberated: Women in the So-called Libertine Gnostic Communities." In *Images of the Feminine in Gnosticism*, ed. Karen L. King, 329–44. Philadelphia: Fortress Press, 1988.

Goessler, Lisette. "Advice to the Bride and Groom: Plutarch Gives a Detailed Account of His Views on Marriage." In *Plutarch's Advice to the Bride and Groom and A Consolation to his Wife*, trans. Hazel Harvey, ed. Sarah B. Pomeroy, 97–115. Oxford: Oxford University Press, 1999.

Goldhahn-Müller, Ingrid. *Die Grenze der Gemeinde: Studien zum Problem der Zweiten Busse in Neuen Testament unter Berücksichtigung der Entwicklung im 2 Jh. bis Tertullian.* Göttinger theologische Arbeiten 39. Göttingen: Vandenhoeck & Ruprecht, 1989.

Goldhill, Simon. *Foucault's Virginity: Ancient Erotic Fiction and the History of Sexuality.* Cambridge: Cambridge University Press, 1995.

——, ed. *Being Greek Under Rome: Cultural Identity, the Second Sophistic, and the Development of Empire.* Cambridge: Cambridge University Press, 2001.

Good, Deirdre. "Commentary on *Love Between Women,* by Bernadette Brooten." In "Lesbian Historiography Before the Name?" ed. Elizabeth A. Castelli, *GLQ* 4 (1998): 601–6.

Goodman, Martin. "Josephus' Treatise *Against Apion.*" In *Apologetics in the Roman Empire: Pagans, Jews, and Christians,* ed. Mark Edwards, Martin Goodman, and Simon Price, 45–58. New York: Oxford University Press, 1999.

Grant, Robert M. "Five Apologists and Marcus Aurelius." *Vigiliae Christianae* 42 (1988): 1–17.

——. *Greek Apologists of the Second Century.* Philadelphia: Westminster Press, 1988.

——. *Irenaeus of Lyons.* Early Church Fathers. London: Routledge, 1997.

Graves, Robert. *I, Claudius.* New York: R. Smith and R. Haas, 1934.

Gruen, Erich S. "Jews, Greeks, and Romans in the Third Sibyline Oracle." In *Jews in a Graeco-Roman World,* ed. Martin Goodman, 15–36. Oxford: Clarendon Press, 1998.

Guerra, Anthony J. "The Conversion of Marcus Aurelius and Justin Martyr: The Purpose, Genre, and Content of the First Apology." *Second Century* 9 (1992): 171–87.

——. *Romans and the Apologetic Tradition: The Purpose, Genre, and Audience of Paul's Letter.* Society for New Testament Studies Monograph Series 81. Cambridge: Cambridge University Press, 1995.

Guthrie, W. K. C. *A History of Greek Philosophy.* Vol. 3, *The Fifth-Century Enlightenment.* Cambridge: Cambridge University Press, 1969.

Haarhoff, T. J. *The Stranger at the Gate: Aspects of Isolationism and Cooperation in Ancient Greece and Rome.* 2nd ed. Oxford: Oxford University Press, 1948.

Haines-Eitzen, Kim. *Guardians of Letters: Literacy, Power, and the Transmitters of Early Christian Literature.* New York: Oxford University Press, 2000.

Hall, Jonathan M. *Ethnic Identity in Greek Antiquity.* Cambridge: Cambridge University Press, 1997.

——. *Hellenicity: Between Ethnic Identity and Culture.* Chicago: University of Chicago Press, 2002.

Halperin, David M. "Commentary on *Love Between Women,* by Bernadette J. Brooten." In "Lesbian Historiography Before the Name?" ed. Elizabeth A. Castelli, *GLQ* 4 (1998): 559–78.

——. *How to Do the History of Homosexuality.* Chicago: University of Chicago Press, 2002.

——. *One Hundred Years of Homosexuality and Other Essays on Greek Love.* New York: Routledge, 1990.

Hamel, Debra. *Trying Neaira: The True Story of a Courtesan's Scandalous Life in Ancient Greece.* New Haven, Conn.: Yale University Press, 2003.

Hargis, Jeffrey W. *Against the Christians: The Rise of Early Christian Polemic.* Patristic Studies 1. New York: Peter Lang, 1999.

Harris, William V. *Ancient Literacy.* Cambridge, Mass.: Harvard University Press, 1989.

——. "Child Exposure in the Roman Empire." *JRS* 84 (1994): 1–22.

——. "On the Applicability of the Concept of Class in Roman History." In *Forms of Control and Subordination in Antiquity,* ed. Toru Yuge and Masaoki Doi, 598–610. New York: E. J. Brill, 1988.

——. *Restraining Rage: The Ideology of Anger Control in Classical Antiquity.* Cambridge, Mass.: Harvard University Press, 2001.

Harrison, Verna E. F. "The Allegorization of Gender: Plato and Philo on Spiritual Childbearing." In *Asceticism,* ed. Vincent L. Wimbush and Richard Valantasis, 520–34. New York: Oxford University Press, 1995.

Hartsock, Nancy C. M. *Money, Sex, and Power*. Boston: Northeastern University Press, 1983.

———. "Postmodernism and Political Change: Issues for Feminist Theory." In *Feminist Interpretations of Michel Foucault*, ed. Susan Hekman, 39–55. University Park: Pennsylvania State University Press, 1996.

Hauptman, Judith. "Images of Women in the Talmud." In *Religion and Sexism*, ed. Rosemary Radford Ruether. New York: Simon & Schuster, 1974.

Hawley, Richard. "Practicing What You Preach: Plutarch's Sources and Treatment." In *Plutarch's Advice to the Bride and Groom and a Consolation to his Wife*, ed. Sarah B. Pomeroy, 116–27. Oxford: Oxford University Press, 1999.

Hayes, Christine. "Intermarriage and Impurity in Ancient Jewish Sources." *Harvard Theological Review* 92, no. 1 (1999): 3–36.

Hays, Richard B. *The Moral Vision of the New Testament: A Contemporary Introduction to New Testament Ethics*. San Francisco: HarperCollins, 1996.

Hefner, Robert W. "The Rationality of Conversion." In *Conversion to Christianity: Historical and Anthropological Perspectives on a Great Transformation*, ed. Robert W. Hefner, 3–44. Berkeley: University of California Press, 1993.

Hekman, Susan J., ed. *Feminist Interpretations of Michel Foucault*. University Park: Pennsylvania State University Press, 1996.

Hellholm, David. *Das Visionenbuch des Hermas als Apokalypse*. Coniectanea Biblica, New Testament Series 13, no. 1. Uppsala: CWK Gleerup, 1980.

Henrichs, Albert. "Pagan Ritual and the Alleged Crimes of the Early Christians: A Reconsideration." In *Kyriakon: Festschrift Johannes Questen*, ed. Patrick Granfield and Josef A. Jangmann, 1:18–35. Münster: Verlag Aschendorff, 1970.

Himmelfarb, Martha. *Ascent to Heaven in Jewish and Christian Apocalypses*. New York: Oxford University Press, 1993.

———. *Tours of Hell: An Apocalyptic Form in Jewish and Christian Literature*. Philadelphia: University of Pennsylvania Press, 1983.

Hodge, Caroline Johnson. " 'If Sons, Then Heirs': A Study of Kinship and Ethnicity in Paul's Letters." Ph. D. diss., Brown University, 2001.

Hollander, H. W., and M. de Jonge. *The Testaments of the Twelve Patriarchs*. Studia in Veteris Testamenti Pseudepigrapha. Leiden: E. J. Brill, 1985.

Holzberg, Niklas. *The Ancient Novel: An Introduction*. Trans. Christine Jackson-Holzberg. New York: Routledge, 1995.

Hopkins, (M.) Keith. "The Age of Roman Girls at Marriage." *Population Studies* 18 (1965): 309–27.

———. "Christian Number and Its Implications." *JECS* 6 (1998): 185–226.

Horrell, David. "From *adelphoi* to *oikos theou*: Social Transformation in Pauline Christianity." *JBL* 120, no. 2 (2001): 293–311.

Horsley, Richard A. *1 Corinthians*. Nashville: Abingdon Press, 1998.

———., ed. *Paul and Empire: Religion and Power in Roman Imperial Society*. Harrisburg, Penn.: Trinity Press International, 1997.

Hughes, F. W. *Early Christian Rhetoric and 2 Thessalonians*. Sheffield: JSOT Press, 1989.

———. "The Rhetoric of 1 Thessalonians." In *The Thessalonian Correspondence*, ed. Raymond F. Collins, 94–116. Belgium: Leuven University Press, 1990.

Hughes-Hallett, Lucy. *Cleopatra: Histories, Dreams, and Distortions*. New York: Harper & Row, 1990.

Humphrey, Edith McEwan. *The Ladies and the Cities: Transformation and Apocalyptic Identity in Joseph and Aseneth, 4 Ezra, the Apocalypse, and The Shepherd of Hermas*. Journal for the Study of the Pseudepigrapha 17. Sheffield: Sheffield Academic Press, 1995.

Humphrey, J. H., ed. *Literacy in the Roman World*. Journal of Roman Archaeology Supplementary Series 3. Ann Arbor, Mich.: Journal of Roman Archaeology, 1991.

Hunt, Emily J. *Christianity in the Second Century: The Case of Tatian*. London: Routledge, 2003.

Hunter, Virginia. *Policing Athens: Social Control in the Attic Lawsuits, 420–320 B.C.* Princeton, N.J.: Princeton University Press, 1994.

Hurd, John Coolige, Jr. *The Origin of 1 Corinthians.* London: S.P.C.K., 1965. Repr., Atlanta: Mercer University Press, 1983.

Hurley, Donna W. *A Historical and Historiographical Commentary on Suetonius' Life of Caligula.* Atlanta: Scholars Press, 1993.

Ilan, Tal. *Mine and Yours Are Hers: Retrieving Women's History from Rabbinic Literature.* Leiden: E. J. Brill, 1997.

Isaac, E. Introduction to the Ethiopic Apocalypse of Enoch. In *The Old Testament Pseudepigrapha*, vol. 1, ed. James H. Charlesworth, 5–12. New York: Doubleday, 1983.

Jaeger, Werner. *Early Christianity and Greek Paideia.* Cambridge, Mass.: Harvard University Press, 1961.

Jay, Nancy. "Sacrifice as a Remedy for Having been Born of Woman." In *Women, Gender, Religion: A Reader*, ed. Elizabeth A. Castelli with the assistance of Rosamond C. Rodman. New York: Palgrave, 2001.

Jenks, Gregory C. *The Origins and Early Development of the Antichrist Myth.* Beihefte zur Zeitschrift für die neutestamentliche Wissenschaft 59. Berlin: Walter de Gruyter, 1991.

Jewett, Robert. "Following the Argument of Romans." In *The Romans Debate*, ed. Karl Donfried, 265–77. Rev. ed. Peabody, Mass.: Hendrickson, 1991.

——. "Romans as an Ambassadorial Letter." *Interpretation* 36 (1982): 5–20.

——. *The Thessalonian Correspondence: Pauline Rhetoric and Millenarian Piety.* Philadelphia: Fortress Press, 1986.

Johnson, Luke Timothy. "The New Testament's Anti-Jewish Slander and the Conventions of Ancient Polemic." *JBL* 108 (1989): 419–41.

Joly, Robert. *Christianism et philosophie: Études sur Justin et les Apologistes grecs due deuxìeme sìecle.* Paris: Editions de L'Universite de Bruxelles, 1973.

——. "Hermas et le Pasteur." *Vigiliae Christianae* 21 (1967): 201–18.

Jonas, Hans. *Gnosis und spätaniker Geist.* Vol. 1. Göttingen: Vandenhoeck und Ruprecht, 1934.

Jones, Amos, Jr. *Paul's Message of Freedom: What Does It Mean to the Black Church?* Valley Forge, Penn.: Judson Press, 1992.

Jordan, Mark D. "Ancient Philosophic Protreptic and the Problem of Persuasive Genres." *Rhetorica* 4 (1986): 309–33.

Kappeler, Suzanne. *The Pornography of Representation.* Minneapolis: University of Minnesota Press, 1986.

Karras, Ruth Mazo. "Active/Passive, Acts/Passions: Greek and Roman Sexualities." *The American Historical Review* 105, no. 4 (2000): 1–42.

Käsemann, Ernest. *Commentary on Romans.* Trans. Geoffrey W. Bromily. Grand Rapids, Mich.: William B. Eerdmans, 1980.

Kasher, Aryeh. "Polemic and Apologetic Methods of Writing in *Contra Apionem*." In *Josephus' Contra Apionem: Studies in its Character with a Latin Concordance to the Portions Missing in Greek*, ed. Louis H. Feldman and John R. Levison, 143–86. Arbeiten zur Geschichte des antiken Judentums und des Urchristentums 34. Leiden: E. J. Brill, 1996.

Kaster, Robert A. *Guardians of Language: The Grammarian and Society in Late Antiquity.* Berkeley: University of California Press, 1988.

Kautsky, John H. *The Politics of Aristocratic Empires.* Chapel Hill: University of North Carolina Press, 1982.

Keller, Catherine. *Apocalypse Now and Then: A Feminist Guide to the End of the World.* Boston: Beacon Press, 1996.

Kelly, J. N. D. *A Commentary on the Epistles of Peter and Jude.* Black's New Testament Commentaries. London: Adam and Charles Black, 1969.

Kennedy, Duncan F. *The Arts of Love: Five Studies in the Discourse of Roman Love Elegy.* Cambridge: Cambridge University Press, 1993.

Kennedy, George A. *The Art of Persuasion in Greece.* Princeton, N.J.: Princeton University Press, 1963.

——. *The Art of Rhetoric in the Roman World.* Princeton, N.J.: Princeton University Press, 1972.

——. *Classical Rhetoric and Its Christian and Secular Traditions from Ancient to Modern Times.* Chapel Hill: University of North Carolina Press, 1987.

——. *Greek Rhetoric Under Christian Emperors.* Princeton, N.J.: Princeton University Press, 1983.

——. *A New History of Classical Rhetoric.* Princeton, N.J.: Princeton University Press, 1994.

——. *New Testament Interpretation through Rhetorical Criticism.* Chapel Hill: University of North Carolina Press, 1984.

——. *Quintilian.* New York: Twayne Publishers, Inc.,1969.

Keuls, Eva. *The Reign of the Phallus: Sexual Politics in Ancient Athens.* Berkeley: University of California Press, 1985.

Kilgallen, John J. *First Corinthians: An Introduction and Study Guide.* New York: Paulist Press, 1987.

King, Karen. *What is Gnosticism?* Cambridge, Mass.: Harvard University Press, 2003.

Kittredge, Cynthia Briggs. *Community and Authority: The Rhetoric of Obedience in the Pauline Tradition.* Harvard Theological Studies 45. Harrisburg, Penn.: Trinity Press International, 1998.

Klawans, Jonathan. *Impurity and Sin in Ancient Judaism.* Oxford: Oxford University Press, 2000.

Knopf, R. *Die Briefe Petri und Judä.* Kritisch-exegetischer Kommentar über das Neue Testament 12. Göttingen: Vandenhoeck & Ruprecht, 1912.

Koenen, Ludwig. "The Prophecies of a Potter: A Prophecy of World Renewal Becomes and Apocalypse." In *Proceedings of the Twelfth International Congress of Papyrology,* ed. Deborah H. Samuel, 249–54. Toronto: Hakkert, 1970.

Konstan, David. *Sexual Symmetry: Love in the Ancient Novel and Related Genres.* Princeton, N.J.: Princeton University Press, 1994.

Koster, Severin. *Die Invektive in der griechischen und römischen Literatur.* Beiträge zur Klassichen Philologie 99. Meisenheim am Glan: Verlag Anton Hain, 1980.

Kraemer, Ross Shepard. *Her Share of the Blessings: Women's Religions Among Pagans, Jews, and Christians in the Greco-Roman World.* New York: Oxford University Press, 1992.

——. "The Conversion of Women to Ascetic Forms of Christianity." *Signs* 6 (1980): 298–307.

Kümmel, Walter G. *Introduction to the New Testament.* 14th ed. New York: Abingdon, 1966.

Kuntzman, Raymond. *Le Livre de Thomas (NH II, 7).* Bibliotheque Copte de Nag Hammadi. Quebec: Les Presses de l'Université Laval, 1986.

Labriolle, Pierre de. *La Réaction païnne: Étude sur la polémique antichrétinne du Ier au IVe siècle.* Paris: L'Artisan du Livre, 1934.

Laqueur, Thomas Walter. *Making Sex: Body and Gender from the Greeks to Freud.* Cambridge, Mass.: Harvard University Press, 1990.

Larmour, David H. J., Paul Allen Miller, and Charles Platter, eds. *Rethinking Sexuality: Foucault and Classical Antiquity.* Princeton, N.J.: Princeton University Press, 1997.

Lawlor, H. J. "Early Citations from the Book of Enoch." *Journal of Philology* 25 (1987): 164–225.

Leaney, A. R. C. *The Letters of Peter and Jude: A Commentary on the First Letter of Peter, a Letter of Jude, and the Second Letter of Peter.* Cambridge Bible Commentary. Cambridge: Cambridge University Press, 1967.

Le Boulluec, Alain . *La notion d'hérésie dans la littérature greque, IIe–IIIe siècles.* Vol. 1, *De Justin à Irénée.* Paris: Études Augustiniennes, 1985.

Leutzsch, Martin. *Die Wahrnehmung sozialer Wirklichkeit im "Hirten des Hermas."* Göttingen: Vandenhoeck & Ruprecht, 1989.

Levine, Amy-Jill. "Diaspora as Metaphor: Bodies and Boundaries in the Book of Tobit." In *Diaspora Jews and Judaism: Essays in Honor of and in Dialogue with Thomas A. Kraabel*, ed. J. Andrew Overman and Robers S. MacLenham, 105–17. Atlanta: Scholars Press, 1992.

——. "'Hemmed in on Every Side': Jews and Women in the Book of Susanna." In *A Feminist Companion to Esther, Judith, and Susanna*, ed. Athalya Brenner, 303–23. Feminist Companion to the Bible 7. Sheffield: Sheffield Academic Press, 1995.

——, ed. *"Women Like This": New Perspectives on Jewish Women in the Greco-Roman World*. Atlanta: Scholars Press, 1991.

Liddell, H.G., R. Scott, H.S. Jones. *A Greek English Lexicon*. 9th ed. with revised supplement. Oxford: Oxford University Press, 1996.

Lietzmann, Hans. *An die Römer*. HNT 9. Tübingen: J.C.B. Mohr, 1906.

Lieu, Judith. *Image and Reality: The Jews in the World of the Christians in the Second Century*. Edinburgh: T. & T. Clark, 1996.

Lincoln, Bruce. *Authority: Construction and Corrosion*. Chicago: University of Chicago Press, 1994.

——. *Discourse and the Construction of Society: Comparative Studies of Myth, Ritual, and Classification*. Oxford: Oxford University Press, 1989.

Lindemann, Andreas. "Paul in the Writings of the Apostolic Fathers." In *Paul and the Legacies of Paul*, ed. William Babcock, 25–45. Dallas: Southern Methodist University Press, 1990.

——. *Paulus im ältesten Christentum: Das Bild des Apostels und die Rezeption der paulinischen Theologie in der früchristlichen Litteratur bis Marcion*. Beiträge zur historischen Theologie 58. Tübingen: J. P. Mohr, 1979.

Lohse, Bernhard. *Askese und Mönchtum in der Antike und der alten Kirche*. Religion und Kultur der alten Mittelmeerwelt in Parallelforschungen 1. Munich: R. Oldenbourg, 1969.

——. *Colossians and Philemon*. Trans. W.R. Poehlmann and R.J. Karris. Philadelphia: Fortress Press, 1971.

Long, A.A., and D.N. Long *The Hellenistic Philosophers*. 2 vols. Cambridge: Cambridge University Press, 1987.

Long, Jacqueline Flint. *Claudian's In Eutropium: Or, How, When, and Why to Slander a Eunuch*. Chapel Hill: University of North Carolina Press, 1996.

Lüdemann, Gerd. *Untersuchungen zur simonianischen Gnosis*. Göttingen: Vandenhoeck & Ruprecht, 1975.

Lund, Helen S. *Lysimachus: A Study in Early Hellenistic Kingship*. London: Routledge, 1992.

Luther, Martin. "Admonition to Peace, A Reply to the Twelve Articles of the Peasants of Swabia, 1525." In *Luther's Works*, trans. Charles M. Jacobs, rev. and ed. Robert C. Schultz. American Edition. Vol. 46. Philadelphia: Fortress Press, 1967.

——. "On Temporal Authority." In *Luther's Works*, trans. Charles M. Jacobs, rev. and ed. Robert C. Schultz. American Edition. Vol. 46. Philadelphia: Fortress Press, 1967.

Lyman, Rebecca. "Ascetics and Bishops: Epiphanius on Orthodoxy." In *Orthodoxy, Christianity, History*, ed. Susanna Elm, Eric Rebillard, and Antonella Romano, 149–61. Collection de l'École française de Rome 270. Paris: de Boccard, 2000.

——. "2002 NAPS Presidential Address: Hellenism and Heresy." *JECS* 11, no. 2 (2003): 209–22.

MacDonald, Dennis R. *The Legend and The Apostle: The Battle for Paul in Story and Canon*. Philadelphia: Westminster Press, 1983.

MacDonald, Margaret Y. *Early Christian Women and Pagan Opinion: The Power of the Hysterical Woman*. Cambridge: Cambridge University Press, 1996.

——. *The Pauline Churches: A Socio-Historical Study of Institutionalization in the Pauline and Deutero-Pauline Churches*. SNTS Monograph Series 60. Cambridge: Cambridge University Press, 1988.

——. "Reading Real Women Through the Undisputed Letters of Paul." In *Women and Christian Origins*, ed. Ross Shepard Kraemer and Mary Rose D'Angelo, 199–220. Oxford: Oxford University Press, 1999.

——. "Rereading Paul: Early Interpreters of Paul on Women and Gender." In *Women and Christian Origins*, ed. Ross Shepard Kraemer and Mary Rose D'Angelo, 236–53. Oxford: Oxford University Press, 1999.

——. "The Social Setting of 1 Corinthians 7." *New Testament Studies* 36 (1990): 169–73.

Mach, Michael. "Justin Martyr's *Dialogue cum Tryphone Iudaeo* and the Development of Christian Anti-Judaism." In *Contra Iudaeos: Ancient and Medieval Polemics Between Christians and Jews*, ed. Ora Limor and Guy G. Stroumsa, 27–47. Tübingen: Mohr/Siebeck, 1996.

Mack, Burton L. *Rhetoric and the New Testament*. Minneapolis: Fortress Press, 1990.

MacKinnon, Catherine A. "Does Sexuality Have a History?" In *Discourses of Sexuality: From Aristotle to AIDS*, ed. Domna C. Stanton, 117–36. Ann Arbor: University of Michigan Press, 1992.

MacMullen Ramsay. *Enemies of the Roman Order: Treason, Unrest, and Alienation in the Empire*. London: Routledge, 1966.

Malherbe, Abraham J. *Ancient Epistolary Theorists*. SBL Sources for Biblical Study 19. Atlanta: Scholars Press, 1988.

——. "Gentle as a Nurse: The Cynic Background of 1 Thess 2." *NovT* 12 (1970): 203–17.

——. *Paul and the Popular Philosophers*. Minneapolis: Fortress Press, 1989.

——. *Social Aspects of Earlier Christianity*. 2nd ed. Philadelphia: Fortress Press, 1983.

Malina, Bruce. *The New Testament World: Insights from Cultural Anthropology*. Rev. ed. Atlanta: John Knox Press, 1993.

Marrou, H. I. *A History of Education in Antiquity*. Trans. George Lamb. Madison: University of Wisconisn Press, 1956.

Martin, Dale B. *The Corinthian Body*. New Haven, Conn.: Yale University Press, 1995.

——. "Paul Without Passion: On Paul's Rejection of Desire in Sex and Marriage." In *Constructing Early Christian Families*, ed. Halvor Moxnes, 201–15. London: Routledge, 1997.

——. *Slavery as Salvation: The Metaphor of Slavery in Pauline Christianity*. New Haven, Conn.: Yale University Press, 1990.

Matthews, Shelly. "Thinking of Thecla: Issues in Feminist Historiography." *JFSR* 17, no. 2 (2001): 39–55.

McCallum, E. L. "Technologies of Truth and the Function of Gender in Foucault." In *Feminist Interpretations of Michel Foucault*, ed. Susan J. Hekman, 77–98. University Park: Pennsylvania State University Press, 1996.

McGehee, Michael. "Why Tatian Never 'Apologized' to the Greeks." *JECS* 1 (1993): 143–58.

McGinn, Thomas A. J. *Prostitution, Sexuality, and the Law in Ancient Rome*. Oxford: Oxford University Press, 1998.

——. "The Taxation of Roman Prostitutes." *Helios* 16 (1989): 79–111.

McGinn, Bernard. *Antichrist: Two Thousand Years of Human Fascination with Evil*. San Francisco: HarperSanFrancisco, 1994.

McGowan, Andrew. "Eating People: Accusations of Cannibalism Against Christians in the Second Century." *JECS* 2 (1994): 413–42.

McGuire, Anne. "Valentinus and the Gnostic Haeresis: Irenaeus, Haer 1.11.1 and the Evidence of Nag Hammadi." *Studia Patristica* 18, no. 1 (1985): 247–52.

——. "Women, Gender, and Gnosis in Gnostic Texts and Traditions." In *Women and Christian Origins*, ed. Ross Shepard Kraemer and Mary Rose D'Angelo, 257–99. Oxford: Oxford University Press, 1999.

McNamara, Jo Ann. "Gendering Virtue." In *Plutarch's Advice to the Bride and Groom and A Consolation to His Wife*, ed. Sarah B. Pomeroy, 151–61. Oxford: Oxford University Press, 1999.

Meeks, Wayne. *First Urban Christians: The Social World of the Apostle Paul*. New Haven, Conn.: Yale University Press, 1983.

——. "Image of the Androgyne: Some Uses of a Symbol in Earliest Christianity." *History of Religions* 3 (1974): 165–208.

——. *The Moral World of the First Christians*. Library of Early Christianity. Philadelphia: Westminster Press, 1986.

——. "Simon Magus in Recent Research." *Religious Studies Review* 3, no. 3 (1977): 137–42.

Miles, Margaret R. *Carnal Knowing: Female Nakedness and Religious Meaning in the Christian West*. Boston: Beacon Press, 1989.

Millar, Fergus. *The Emperor in the Roman World*. Ithaca, N.Y.: Cornell University Press, 1977.

Miller, Patricia Cox. *Dreams in Late Antiquity: Studies in the Imagination of a Culture*. Princeton, N.J.: Princeton University Press, 1994.

Miller, William Ian. *Humiliation: And Other Essays on Honor, Social Discomfort, and Violence*. Ithaca, N.Y.: Cornell University Press, 1993.

Momigliano, A. *On Pagans, Jews, and Christians*. Middletown, Conn.: Wesleyan University Press, 1987.

Moo, Douglas J. *The Epistle to the Romans*. Grand Rapids, Mich.: Eerdmans, 1996.

Murphy, Frederick J. *Fallen Is Babylon: The Revelation to John*. Harrisburg: Trinity Press International, 1998.

——. *Pseudo-Philo: Rewriting the Bible*. Oxford: Oxford University Press, 1993.

Murphy-O'Conner, Jerome. *1 Corinthians*. New Testament Message 10. Wilmington, N.C.: Michael Glazier, 1979.

Musurillo, Herbert. *The Acts of the Christian Martyrs*. Oxford: Clarendon Press, 1972.

Mydans, Seth. "Malaysian Police Break Up Protests on Arrest." *New York Times*, 22 September 1998.

——. "Top Opposition Leader in Malaysia is Jailed in Sex Case," *New York Times*, 21 September 1998.

——. "Using a Sexual Slur, Malaysian Calls Ex-Deputy Unacceptable," *New York Times*, 23 September 1998.

Newsom, Carol A., and Sharon H. Ringe, eds. *The Women's Bible Commentary*. Louisville, Ky.: Westminster/John Knox Press, 1992.

Neyrey, Jerome. *2 Peter, Jude: A New Translation with Introduction and Commentary*. Anchor Bible 37c. New York: Doubleday, 1993.

Nickelsburg, George W. E. *Jewish Literature Between the Bible and the Mishnah: A Historical and Literary Introduction*. Philadelphia: Fortress Press, 1981.

Nisbet, R. M. "The *in Pisonem* as an Invective." Appendix 6 to *Cicero: In L. Campurnium Pisonem*. Oxford: Clarendon Press, 1961.

——. "Piso and the *Invectiva in Ciceronem*." Appendix 7 to *Cicero: In L. Campurnium Pisonem*. Oxford: Clarendon Press, 1961.

Nixon, C. E. V., and Barbara Saylor Rodgers. *In Praise of Later Roman Emperors: The Panegyrici Latini*. Berkeley: University of California Press, 1994.

North, Helen. "Canons and Hierarchies of the Cardinal Virtues in Greek and Latin Literature." In *The Classical Tradition: Literary and Historical Studies in Honor of Harry Caplan*, ed. Luitpold Wallach, 165–83. Ithaca, N.Y.: Cornell University Press, 1966.

——. *From Myth to Icon: Reflections of Greek Ethical Doctrine in Literature and Art*. Ithaca, N.Y.: Cornell University Press, 1979.

——. *Sophrosyne: Self-Knowledge and Self-Restraint in Greek Literature*. Ithaca, N.Y.: Cornell University Press, 1966.

Ogden, Daniel, "Rape, Adultery, and the Protection of Bloodlines in Classical Athens." In *Rape in Antiquity*, ed. by Susan Deacy and Karen F. Pierce, 25–41. London: Duckworth, 1997.

O'Leary, Stephen D. *Arguing the Apocalypse: A Theory of Millennial Rhetoric*. Oxford: Oxford University Press, 1994.

Omitowoju, Rosanna. "Regulating Rape: Soap Operas and Self-Interest in the Athenian Courts." In *Rape in Antiquity*, ed. Susan Deacy and Karen F. Pierce, 1–24. London: Duckworth, 1997.

Opelt, Ilona. *Die lateinischen Schimpfwörter und verwandte sprachliche Erscheinungen. Eine Typologie*. Heidelberg: Carl Winter Universitätsverlag, 1965.

——. *Die Polemik in der christlichen lateinischen Literatur von Tertullian bis Augustin.* Heidelberg: Carl Winter Universitätsverlag, 1980.

Osiek, Carolyn. "The Genre and Function of the Shepherd of Hermas." In "Early Christian Apocalypticism," *Semeia* 36, ed. Adela Yarbro Collins (1986): 113–22.

——. *The Shepherd of Hermas.* Hermenaeia. Minneapolis: Fortress Press, 1999.

Pagden, Anthony. *Lords of All the World: Ideologies of Empire in Spain, Britain, and France, c. 1500–1800.* New Haven, Conn.: Yale University Press, 1995.

Pagels, Elaine. "Adam, Eve, Christ, and the Church: A Survey of Second-Century Controversies Concerning Marriage." In *The New Testament and Gnosis: Essays in Honour of Robert McL. Wilson,* ed. A. H. B. Logan and A. J. M. Wedderburn, 147–75. Edinburgh: T & T Clark, 1983.

——. *Adam, Eve, and the Serpent.* New York: Random House, 1988.

——. "Christian Apologists and the 'Fall of the Angels': An Attack on Roman Imperial Power." *Harvard Theological Review* 78 (1985): 301–25.

——. *The Gnostic Gospels.* New York: Random House, 1979.

——. *The Gnostic Paul: Gnostic Exegesis of the Pauline Letters.* Philadelphia: Fortress Press, 1975.

——. *The Origin of Satan.* New York: Random House, 1995.

Parker, David C. *The Living Text of the Gospels.* Cambridge: Cambridge University Press, 1997.

Parker, Holt N. "The Observed of All Observers: Spectacle, Applause, and Cultural Poetics in the Roman Theater Audience." In *The Art of Ancient Spectacle,* ed. Bettina Berhmann and Christine Kondoleon, 163–79. National Gallery of Art Studies in the History of Art 56, Center for Advanced Study in the Visual Arts Symposium Papers 34. New Haven, Conn.: Yale University Press, 1999.

Parkin, Tim G. *Demography and Roman Society.* Baltimore, Md.: Johns Hopkins University Press, 1992.

Peerbolte, L. J. Lietaert. *The Antecedents of Antichrist: A Traditio-Historical Study of the Earliest Christian Views on Eschatological Opponents.* Supplements to the Journal for the Study of Judaism 49. Leiden: E. J. Brill, 1996.

Pellegrini, Ann. "Commentary on *Love Between Women,* by Bernadette J. Brooten." In "Lesbian Historiography Before the Name?" ed. Elizabeth A. Castelli, *GLQ* 4 (1998): 578–89.

Perkins, Judith. *The Suffering Self: Pain and Narrative Representation in the Early Christian Era.* New York: Routledge, 1995.

Perkins, Pheme. *Ephesians.* Nashville: Abingdon Press, 1997.

——. *The Gnostic Dialogue: The Early Church and the Crisis of Gnosticism.* Theological Inquiries. New York: Paulist Press, 1980.

Pilgrim, Walter E. *Uneasy Neighbors: Church and State in the New Testament.* Minneapolis: Fortress Press, 1999.

Plaskow, Judith. "Anti-Judaism in Feminist Christian Interpretation." In *A Feminist Introduction.* Vol. 1, *Searching the Scriptures,* ed. Elizabeth Schüssler Fiorenza, 117–29. New York: Crossroad Publishing Company, 1997.

——. *Standing Again at Sinai: Judaism from a Feminist Perspective.* San Francisco: HarperCollins, 1990.

Pomeroy, Sarah B. *Families in Classical and Hellenistic Greece.* Oxford: Clarendon Press, 1997.

——, ed. *Plutarch's Advice to the Bride and Groom and A Consolation to his Wife.* Oxford: Oxford University Press, 1999.

Potter, David. "Martyrdom as Spectacle." In *Theater and Society in the Classical World,* ed. Ruth Scodel, 53–88. Ann Arbor: University of Michigan Press, 1993.

Pourkier, Aline. *L'Hérésiologie chez Épiphane de Salamine.* Christianisme Antique 4. Paris: Beauchesne, 1992.

Price, R. M. "Are There 'Holy Pagans' in Justin Martyr?" *Studia Patristica* 31 (1997): 153–69.

Price, Simon. "From Noble Funerals to Divine Cult: The Consecration of Roman Emperors."

In *Rituals of Royalty: Power and Ceremonial in Traditional Societies*, ed. D. Cannadine and S. Price, 56–105. Cambridge: Cambridge University Press, 1987.

———. "Latin Christian Apologetics: Minucius Felix, Tertullian, and Cyprian." In *Apologetics in the Roman Empire: Pagans, Jews, and Christians*, ed. Mark Edwards, Martin Goodman, and Simon Price, 105–29. New York: Oxford University Press, 1999.

———. *Rituals and Power: The Roman Imperial Cult in Asia Minor*. Cambridge: Cambridge University Press, 1984.

Quasten, Johannes. *Patrology*. 3 vols. Utrecht: Spectrum, 1966.

Raditsa, L. F. "Augustus' Legislation Concerning Marriage, Procreation, Love Affairs and Adultery." *ANRW* II.13 (1980): 278–339.

Rae, J. R. "P. Lond. inv. 1562 verso: Market Taxes in Oxyrhynchus." *ZPE* 46 (1982): 191–209.

Rajak, Tessa. "Talking at Trypho: Christian Apologetic as Anti-Judaism in Justin's *Dialogue with Trypho the Jew*." In *Apologetics in the Roman Empire*, ed. Mark J. Edwards, Martin Goodman, and Simon Price, 58–80. Oxford: Clarendon Press, 1999.

Rawson, Beryl. "From 'Daily Life' to 'Demography.'" In *Women in Antiquity: New Assessments*, ed. Richard Hawley and Barbara Levick, 1–20. London: Routledge, 1995.

———. "Family Life Among the Lower Classes at Rome in the First Two Centuries of the Empire." *Classical Philology* 61 (1966): 71–83.

Reardon, B. P. *The Form of Greek Romance*. Princeton, N.J.: Princeton University Press, 1991.

Rees, Roger. *Layers of Loyalty in Latin Panegyric, AD 289–304*. Oxford: Oxford University Press, 2002.

Reiling, J. *Hermas and Christian Prophecy: A Study of the Eleventh Mandate*. Supplements to Novum Testamentum 37. Leiden: E. J. Brill, 1973.

Richlin, Amy. *The Garden of Priapus: Sexuality and Aggression in Roman Humor*. New Haven, Conn.: Yale University Press, 1983.

———. "Julia's Jokes, Galla Placidia, and the Roman Use of Women as Political Icons." In *Stereotypes of Women in Power*, ed. Barbara Glicken, Suzanne Dixon, and Pauline Allen, 65–84. New York: Greenwood Press, 1992.

———. "Making Up a Woman: The Face of Roman Gender." In *Off with Her Head! The Denial of Women's Identity in Myth, Religion, and Culture*, ed. Howard Eilberg-Schwartz and Wendy Doniger, 185–213. Berkeley: University of California Press, 1998.

———. "Not Before Homosexuality: The Materiality of the *Cinaedus* and the Roman Law Against Love Between Men." *Journal of the History of Sexuality* 3 (1992–93): 523–73.

———. "Towards a History of Body History." In *Inventing Ancient Culture: Historicism, Periodization and the Ancient World*, ed. Mark Golden and Peter Toohey, 16–35. London and New York: Routledge, 1997.

Riley, Gregory. *Resurrection Reconsidered: Thomas and John in Controversy*. Minneapolis: Fortress Press, 1995.

Rist, James M. *Stoic Philosophy*. Cambridge: Cambridge University Press, 1969.

Rives, James. "The Decree of Decius and the Religion of Empire." *JRS* 89 (1999): 135–54.

———. "Human Sacrifice Among Pagans and Christians." *JRS* 85 (1995): 65–85.

———. "The Piety of a Persecutor." *JECS* 4, no. 1 (1996): 1–25.

———. "Roman Religion Revisited." *Phoenix* 52 (1998): 345–65.

Rodman, Rosamond C. "Who's on Third? Reading *Acts of Andrew* as a Rhetoric of Resistance." In "Rhetorics of Resistance: A Colloquy on Early Christianity as Rhetorical Formation," ed. Vincent L. Wimbush. *Semeia* 79 (1997): 27–43.

Roetzel, Calvin J. *The Letters of Paul: Conversations in Context*. Atlanta: John Knox Press, 1975.

Rossing, Barbara R. *The Choice Between Two Cities: Whore, Bride, and Empire in the Apocalypse*. Harvard Theological Studies 48. Harrisburg: Trinity Press, International, 1999.

Roukema, Riemer. *Gnosis and Faith in Early Christianity: An Introduction to Gnosticism*. Trans. John Bowden. Harrisburg, Penn.: Trinity Press International, 1999.

Rousselle, Aline. *Porneia: On Desire and the Body in Antiquity*. Trans. Felicia Pheasant. London: Basil Blackwell, 1988.

Rowland, Christopher. "Apocalyptic and the New Testament." In *Apocalypse Theory and the Ends of the World*, ed. Malcolm Bull, 38–57. Oxford: Blackwell, 1995.

Rudolph, Kurt. *Gnosis: The Nature and History of an Ancient Religion*. Trans. Robert McL. Wilson. Edinburgh: T & T Clark, 1983.

Ruether, Rosemary Radford. "Misogynism and Virginal Feminism in the Fathers of the Church." In *Religion and Sexism: Images of Women in the Jewish and Christian Traditions*, ed. Rosemary Radford Reuther, 150–79. New York: Simon and Schuster, 1974.

Russell, D. A. "Greek and Latin in Antonine Literature." In *Antonine Literature*. Oxford: Clarendon Press, 1990.

Russell, D. S. *Divine Disclosure: An Introduction to Jewish Apocalyptic*. Minneapolis: Fortress Press, 1992.

Rutherford, R. B. *The Meditations of Marcus Aurelius: A Study*. Oxford: Clarendon Press, 1989.

Saller, Richard. "Anecdotes as Historical Evidence for the Principate." *Greece and Rome* 27 (1980): 69–83.

Sanders, E. P. *Paul, the Law, and the Jewish People*. Philadelphia: Fortress Press, 1983.

Satlow, Michael L. *Jewish Marriage in Antiquity*. Princeton, N.J.: Princeton University Press, 2001.

——. "Rhetoric and Assumptions: Romans and Rabbis on Sex." In *Jews in a Graeco-Roman World*, ed. Martin Goodman, 135–44. Oxford: Clarendon Press, 1998.

——. *Tasting the Dish: Rabbinic Rhetorics of Sexuality*. Brown Judaic Studies 33. Atlanta: Scholars Press, 1995.

Saussure, Ferdinand de. *Cours de Linguistique Générale*, ed. Charles Bally and Albert Sechehaye. 3rd ed. Paris: Payot, 1931. English translation, *Course in General Linguistics*. Trans. Wade Baskin. New York: Philosophical Library, 1959.

Sawicki, Jana. *Disciplining Foucault: Feminism, Power, and the Body*. New York: Routledge, 1991.

Schäfer, Peter. *Judeophobia: Attitudes Toward the Jews in the Ancient World*. Cambridge, Mass.: Harvard University Press, 1997.

Schenkeveld, D. M. *Studies in Demetrius*. Amsterdam: Adolf M. Hakkert, 1964.

Schmithals, Walther. *Gnosticism in Corinth*. Trans. J. Steely. Nashville: Abingdon Press, 1971.

——. *Paul and the Gnostics*. Trans. John E. Steely. Nashville: Abingdon Press, 1972.

Schoedel, William R. "Christian Atheism and the Peace of the Roman Empire." *Church History* 42 (1973): 309–19.

——. *A Commentary on the Letters of Ignatius of Antioch*. Philadelphia: Fortress Press, 1985.

Schürer, Emil. *The History of the Jewish People in the Age of Jesus Christ (175 B.C.–A.D. 135)*. 3 vols. in 4. Ed. Geza Vermes and Fergus Millar. Edinburgh: T. & T. Clark, 1973.

Schüssler Fiorenza, Elisabeth. *Bread Not Stone*. Boston: Beacon Press, 1984.

——. *In Memory of Her: A Feminist Theological Reconstruction of Christian Origins*. New York: Crossroad, 1983.

——. *The Book of Revelation: Justice and Judgement* . Philadelphia: Fortress Press, 1985

——. *Revelation: Vision of a Just World*. Proclamation Commentaries. Minneapolis: Fortress Press, 1991.

——, ed. *Searching the Scriptures*. 2 vols. New York: Crossroad Press, 1993.

Schwartz, Seth. *Imperialism and Jewish Society, 200 B.C.E. to 640 C.E.* Princeton, N.J.: Princeton University Press, 2001.

Scott, James C. *Domination and the Arts of Resistance: Hidden Transcripts*. New Haven, Conn.: Yale University Press, 1990.

Scott, Joan W. "Experience." In *Feminists Theorize the Political*, ed. Judith Butler and Joan Wallach Scott, 22–40. New York: Routledge, 1992.

——. *Gender and the Politics of History*. New York: Columbia University Press, 1988.

Scroggs, Robin. *The New Testament and Homosexuality*. Philadelphia: Fortress Press, 1983.
———. "Paul and the Eschatological Woman." In *The Text and the Times: New Testament Essays for Today*, 69–95. Minneapolis: Fortress Press, 1993.
Segal, Alan F. *Paul the Convert: The Apostolate and Apostasy of Saul the Pharisee*. New Haven, Conn.: Yale University Press, 1990.
Senior, Donald. *1 and 2 Peter*. New Testament Message 20. Wilmington, N.C.: Glazier, 1980.
Sfameni Gasparro, Giulia. "Asceticism and Anthropology: *Enkrateia* and 'Double Creation' in Early Christianity." In *Asceticism*, ed. Vincent L. Wimbush and Richard Valantasis, 127–46. New York: Oxford University Press, 1995.
Shaw, Brent. "Body/Power/Identity: Passions of the Martyrs." *JECS* 4 (1990): 269–312.
Shaw, Teresa M. "Practical, Theoretical and Cultural Tracings in Late Antique Asceticism: Response to the Three Preceeding Papers." In *Asceticism*, ed. Vincent L. Wimbush and Richard Valantasis, 75–79. New York and Oxford: Oxford University Press, 1995.
Sherwood, Yvonne. *The Prostitute and the Prophet: Hosea's Marriage in Literary and Theoretical Perspective*. JSOT Supplement Series 212. Sheffield: Sheffield Academic Press, 1996.
Sidebottom, E. M., ed. *James, Jude, and 2 Peter*. The Century Bible. London: Thomas Nelson and Sons, 1967.
Sider, Robert Dick. *Ancient Rhetoric and the Art of Tertullian*. London: Oxford University Press, 1971.
Simon, Marcel. "From Greek Hairesis to Christian Heresy." In *Early Christian Literature and the Classical Intellectual Tradition: In Honorem Robert M. Grant*, ed. William R. Schoedel and Robert L. Wilken, 101–16. Théologie Historique 54. Paris: Éditions Beauchesne, 1979.
Sissa, Giulia. "Maidenhood Without Maidenhead: The Female Body in Ancient Greece." In *Before Sexuality*, ed. David M. Halperin, John J. Winkler, and Froma I. Zeitlin, 339–64. Princeton, N.J.: Princeton University Press, 1990.
Skarsuane, Oskar. *The Proof from Prophecy: A Study of Justin Martyr's Proof-Text Tradition: Text-Type, Provenance, Theological Profile*. Supplements to Novum Testamentum 56. Leiden: E. J. Brill, 1987.
Slingerland, H. D. *The Testaments of the Twelve Patriarchs: A Critical History of Research*. Missoula, Mont.: Scholars Press, 1977.
Smallwood, E. Mary. Introduction to *Philonis Alexandrini: Legatio ad Gaium*. Leiden: E. J. Brill, 1961.
Smith, Mark D. "Ancient Bisexuality and the Interpretation of Romans 1:26–27." *JAAR* 64 (1996): 223–56.
Smith, Morton. "On the History of ΑΠΟΚΑΛΥΠΤΩ and ΑΠΟΚΑΛΥΨΙΣ." In *Apocalypticism in the Mediterranean World and the New East*, ed. David Hellholm, 9–20. 2nd ed. Proceedings of the International Colloquium on Apocalypticism. Tübingen: Mohr/Siebeck, 1989.
Smith-Christopher, Daniel L. "The Mixed Marriage Crisis in Ezra 9–10 and Nehemiah 13: A Study of the Sociology of the Post-Exilic Judaean Community." In *Second Temple Studies*. Volume 2, *Temple Community in the Persian Period*, ed. Tamara C. Eskenazi and Kent H. Richards, 243–65. JSOT Supplement Series 175. Sheffield: JSOT Press, 1994.
Spanneut, Michael. *Le Stoïcisme des pères de l'église: De Clément de Rome à Clément d'Alexandrie*. Patristica Sorbonensia 1. Paris: Éditions du Seuil, 1957.
Spengler, Oswald. *The Decline of the West*. Trans. Charles Francis Atkinson. 2 vols. New York: Knopf, 1976. Originally published as *Der Untergang des Abendlandes: Umrisse einer Morphologie der Weltgeschichte*. München: Beck, 1922–23.
Spicq, Ceslas. *Les Épîtres de Saint Pierre*. Sources Bibliques. Paris: Librarie Lecoffre, 1966.
Staden, H. von. "Hairesis and Heresy: The Case of the *haireseis iatrikai*." In *Jewish and Christian Self-Definition*. Vol. 3, *Self-Definition in the Greco-Roman World*, ed. B. Meyer and E. P. Sanders, 76–81. Philadelphia: Fortress Press, 1982.
Ste. Croix, G. E. M. de. *The Class Struggle in the Ancient Greek World*. London: Duckworth, 1981.

Stendahl, Krister. *Paul Among Jews and Gentiles.* Philadelphia: Fortress Press, 1976.

Stern, Sacha. *Jewish Identity in Early Rabbinic Writings.* Arbeiten zur Geschichte des antiken Judentums und des Urchristentums 23. Leiden: E. J. Brill, 1994.

Stocking, George W., Jr. *Victorian Anthropology.* New York: Free Press, 1987.

Stoler, Ann L. *Carnal Knowledge and Imperial Power: Race and the Intimate in Colonial Rule.* Berkeley and Los Angeles: University of California Press, 2002.

Stowers, Stanley. *The Diatribe and Paul's Letter to the Romans.* SBL Dissertation Series 57. Atlanta: Scholars Press, 1981.

——. *Letter Writing in Greco-Roman Antiquity.* Library of Early Christianity. Philadelphia: Westminster Press, 1986.

——. *A Rereading of Romans: Justice, Jews, and Gentiles.* New Haven, Conn.: Yale University Press, 1994.

Strecker. George. "The Reception of the Book." Revised and augmented by Robert A. Kraft. In *Orthodoxy and Heresy in Earliest Christianity,* by Walter Bauer. Edited by Robert A. Kraft and Gerhard Krodel, 286–316. Trans. the Philadelphia Seminar on Christian Origins. Philadelphia: Fortress Press, 1971.

Stroumsa, Guy G. *Another Seed: Studies in Gnostic Mythology.* Nag Hammadi Studies 24. Leiden: E. J. Brill, 1984.

——. "From Anti-Judaism to Antisemitism in Early Christianity?" In *Contra Iudaeos: Ancient and Medieval Polemics Between Christians and Jews,* ed. Ora Limor and Guy G. Stroumsa, 1–26. Tübingen: Mohr/Siebeck, 1996.

Stylianou, P. J. *A Historical Commentary on Diodorus Siculus Book 15.* Oxford Classical Monographs. Oxford: Clarendon Press, 1998.

Summers, John H. "What Happened to Sex Scandals? Politics and Peccadilloes, Jefferson to Kennedy," *The Journal of American History* 87, no. 3 (December 2000): 825–54.

Süß, Wilhelm. *Ethos. Studien zur älteren griechischen Rhetorik.* Leipzig: B. G. Teubner, 1910.

Swain, Simon. *Hellenism and Empire: Language, Classicism, and Power in the Greek World, A.D. 50–250.* Oxford: Clarendon Press, 1996.

Syme Ronald. "The Crisis of 2 BC." *Bayerische Akademie der Wissenschaften* 7 (1974): 3–34.

——. *The Roman Revolution.* Oxford: Oxford University Press, 1939.

Taylor, Lily Ross. *Party Politics in the Age of Caesar.* Sather Classical Lectures 22. Berkeley: University of California Press 1949.

Terry, Ralph Bruce. *A Discourse Analysis of First Corinthians.* Arlington, Tex.: Summer Institute of Linguistics, 1995.

Thomas, Rosalind. *Literacy and Orality in Ancient Greece..* Key Themes in Ancient History. Cambridge: Cambridge University Press, 1992.

Thompson, Leonard L. *The Book of Revelation: Apocalypse and Empire.* Oxford: Oxford University Press, 1990.

Thornton, Bruce. *Eros: The Myth of Ancient Greek Sexuality.* Boulder, Colo.: Westview Press, 1997.

Torjesen, Karen J. "In Praise of Noble Women: Gender and Honor in Ascetic Texts." *Semeia* 57 (1992): 41–64.

——. *When Women Were Priests: Women's Leadership in the Early Church and the Scandal of Their Subordination in the Rise of Christianity.* San Francisco: HarperSanFrancisco, 1993.

Treggiari, Susan. *Roman Marriage: Iusti Coniuges from the Time of Cicero to the Time of Ulpian.* Oxford: Clarendon Press, 1991.

Trevett, Christine. "Ignatius and the Monstrous Regiment of Women." *Studia Patristica* 21, ed. Elizabeth Livingstone (1989): 202–14.

Trible, Phyllis. *God and the Rhetoric of Sexuality.* Philadelphia: Fortress Press, 1978.

Tugwell, Simon. *The Apostolic Fathers.* Outstanding Christian Thinkers Series. Harrisburg, Penn.: Morehouse, 1989.

Turner, N. "The Literary Character of New Testament Greek." *New Testament Studies* 20 (1974): 107–14.

Vaage, Leif E., and Vincent L. Wimbush, eds. *The New Testament and Asceticism*. New York: Routledge, 1998.

Valantasis, Richard. "Competing Ascetic Subjectivities in the Letter to the Galatians." In *The New Testament and Asceticism*, ed. Leif E. Vaage and Vincent Wimbush, 211–25. New York: Routledge, 1999.

———. "Constructions of Power in Asceticism." *JAAR* 63 (1995): 775–821.

———. *The Gospel of Thomas*. New York: Routledge, 1997.

———. "A Theory of the Social Function of Asceticism." In *Asceticism*, ed. Vincent L. Wimbush and Richard Valantasis, 544–52. New York: Oxford University Press, 1995.

Vallée, Gérard. *A Study in Anti-Gnostic Polemic: Irenaeus, Hippolytus, and Epiphanius*. Waterloo, Ont.: Wilfrid Laurier University Press, 1981.

VanderKam, James C. "1 Enoch, Enochic Motifs, and Enoch in Early Christian Literature." In *The Jewish Apocalyptic Heritage in Early Christianity*, ed. James C. VanderKam and William Adler, 33–101. Compendia Rerum Iudaicarum ad Novum Testamentum 4. Minneapolis: Fortress Press, 1996.

Vasaly, Ann. *Representations: Images of the World in Ciceronian Oratory*. Berkeley: University of California Press, 1993.

Verhey, Allen. *Remembering Jesus: Christian Community, Scripture, and the Moral Life*. Grand Rapids, Mich.: Eerdmans, 2002.

Vermes, Geza. "The Story of Balaam." In *Scripture and Tradition in Judaism*. 127–77. Leiden: E. J. Brill, 1973.

Veyne, Paul. "La Famille et l'amour sous le Haut-Empire romain." *Annales ESC* 33 (1978): 35–63.

———. "Homosexuality in Ancient Rome." In *Western Sexuality*, ed. Philipppe Ariès and André Béjin, trans. Anthony Forster, 26–35. Oxford: Basil Blackwell, 1985.

Vielhauer, P. "Apokalyptik des Urchristentums 1. Einleitung." In *Neutestamentliche Apokryphen II; Apostolisches, Apokalypsen und Verwantes*, ed. E. Hennecke and W. Schneemelcher, 408–54. Tübingen: Mohr/Siebeck, 1964.

Vogel, Lise. *The Column of Antoninus Pius*. Cambridge, Mass.: Harvard University Press, 1973.

Vögtle, Anton. *Die Tugend- und Lasterkataloge im Neuen Testament*. Neutestamentliche Abhandlungen 16. Münster: Aschendorffschen, 1936.

Wallace, D. H. "The Semitic Origin of the Assumption of Moses." *Theologische Zeitschrift* 11 (1955): 321–28.

Wallace-Hadrill, Andrew. "Image and Authority in the Coinage of Augustus." *JRS* 76 (1986): 66–87.

———. "Roman Arches and Greek Honours: The Language of Power at Rome." *Proceedings of the Cambridge Philological Society* 216, no. 36 (1990): 143–81.

———. *Suetonius: The Scholar and His Caesars*. London: Duckworth, 1983.

Wardman, Alan. *Plutarch's Lives*. Berkeley: University of California Press, 1974.

———. *Rome's Debt to Greece*. London: Paul Elek, 1976.

Washington, Harold C. "Israel's Holy Seed and the Foreign Women of Ezra-Nehemiah: A Kristevan Reading." *Biblical Interpretation* 11 (2003): 427–37.

Watson, Duane F. "The Letter of Jude." In *The New Interpreter's Bible*. 12:471–500. Nashville: Abingdon Press, 1998.

———. *Invention, Arrangement, and Style: Rhetorical Criticism of Jude and 2 Peter*. SBL Dissertation Series 104. Atlanta: Scholars Press, 1988.

Weaver, P. R. C. "Children of Freedmen (and Freedwomen)." In *Marriage, Divorce, and Children in Ancient Rome*, ed. Beryl Rawson, 166–90. Oxford: Clarendon Press, 1991.

———. "Social Mobility in the Early Roman Empire: The Evidence of Imperial Freedmen and Slaves." *Past and Present* 37 (1967): 3–20.

Wegner, Judith Romney. *Chattel or Person: The Status of Women in the Mishnah*. New York: Oxford University Press, 1988.

——. "Philo's Portrayal of Women—Hebraic or Hellenic." In *Women Like This: New Perspectives on Jewish Women in the Greco-Roman World*, ed. Amy-Jill Levine, 41–66. Atlanta: Scholars Press, 1991.

Welch, Katherine. "Negotiating Roman Spectacle: Architecture in the Greek World: Athens and Corinth." In *The Art of Ancient Spectacle*, ed. Bettina Berhmann and Christine Kondoleon, 125–45. National Gallery of Art Studies in the History of Art 56. Center for Advanced Study in the Visual Arts Symposium Papers 34. New Haven, Conn.: Yale University Press, 1999.

Wengst, Klaus. *Pax Romana*. Trans. John Bowden. Philadelphia: Fortress Press, 1987.

Westermann, William L. *The Slave Systems of Greek and Roman Antiquity*. Philadelphia: American Philosophical Society, 1955.

Wheeldon, M. J. " 'True Stories': The Reception of Historiography in Antiquity." In *History as Text*, ed. Averil Cameron, 33–63. Chapel Hill: University of North Carolina Press, 1989.

Whitmarsh, Tim. *Greek Literature and the Roman Empire: The Politics of Imitation*. New York: Oxford University Press, 2001.

Wilken, Robert L. *The Christians as the Romans Saw Them*. New Haven, Conn.: Yale University Press, 1984.

Williams, Craig A. *Roman Homosexuality: Ideologies of Masculinity in Classical Antiquity*. Oxford: Oxford University Press, 1999.

Williams, Michael Allen. *Rethinking "Gnosticism": An Argument for Dismantling a Dubious Category*. Princeton, N.J.: Princeton University Press, 1996.

Wilson, Bryan R. *Magic and the Millennium*. New York: Harper and Row, 1973.

——. "A Typology of Sects." In *Sociology of Religion*, ed. Roland Robertson, 361–83. Baltimore, Md.: Penguin Books, 1969.

Wilson, J. Christian. *Toward a Reassessment of the Shepherd of Hermas: Its Date and Its Pneumatology*. Lewiston, N.Y.: Mellen Biblical Press, 1993.

Wimbush, Vincent L. *Paul: The Worldly Ascetic: Response to the World and Self-Understanding According to I Corinthians 7*. Macon, Ga.: Mercer University Press, 1987.

——. "Reading Texts Through Worlds, Worlds Through Texts." *Semeia* 62 (1993): 129–39.

——. *Renunciation Towards Social Engineering: An Apologia for the Study of Asceticism in Greco-Roman Antiquity*. Occasional Papers of the Institute for Antiquity and Christianity 8. Claremont: Institute for Antiquity and Christianity, 1986.

Wimbush, Vincent, and Richard Valantasis, eds. *Asceticism*. New York: Oxford University Press, 1995.

Winkler, John J. *Constraints of Desire*. New York: Routledge, 1990.

——. "Laying Down the Law: The Oversight of Men's Sexual Behavior in Classical Athens." In *Before Sexuality: The Construction of Erotic Experience in the Ancient Greek World*, ed. David M. Halperin, John J. Winkler, and Froma I. Zeitlin, 171–209. Princeton, N.J.: Princton Univerity Press, 1990.

Winterbottom, M. "Quintilian and Rhetoric." In *Empire and Aftermath*, ed. T. A. Dorey, 79–97. London: Routlege and Kegan Paul, 1975.

Wire, Antoinette Clark. *The Corinthian Women Prophets: A Historical Reconstruction through Paul's Rhetoric*. Minneapolis: Fortress Press, 1990.

——. "1 Corinthians." In *A Feminist Commentary*. Vol. 2, *Searching the Scriptures*, ed. Elisabeth Schüssler Fiorenza, 153–95. New York: Crossroad, 1996.

Wisse, Frederik. "The Epistle of Jude in the History of Heresiology." In *Essays on the Nag Hammadi Texts in Honour of Alexander Böhlig*, ed. Martin Krause, 133–43. Nag Hammadi Studies 3. Leiden: E. J. Brill, 1972.

Witherington, Ben, III. *Conflict and Community in Corinth: A Socio-Rhetorical Commentary on 1 and 2 Corinthians*. Grand Rapids, Mich.: Eerdmans, 1995.

Woolf, Greg. *Becoming Roman: The Origins of Provincial Civilization in Gaul*. Cambridge: Cambridge University Press, 1997.

Worthington, Ian. "The Canon of the Ten Attic Orators." In *Persuasion: Greek Rhetoric in Action*, ed. Ian Worthington, 244–63. London: Routledge, 1994.

——. *A Historical Commentary on Dinarchus: Rhetoric and Conspiracy in Later Fourth-Century Athens*. Ann Arbor: University of Michigan Press, 1992.

Wuellner, W. "The Argumentative Structure of 1 Thessalonians as Paradoxical Encomium." In *The Thessalonian Correspondence*, ed. Raymond F. Collins, 117–36. Belgium: Leuven University Press, 1990.

——. "Greek Rhetoric and Pauline Argumentation." In *Early Christian Literature and the Classical Tradition*, ed. W. R. Schoedel and R. L. Wilken, 177–88. Paris: Beauchesne, 1979.

——. "Paul's Rhetoric of Argumentation in Romans: An Alternative to the Donfried-Karris Debate Over Romans." *Catholic Biblical Quarterly* 38 (1976): 330–51.

Wyke, Maria. "Augustan Cleopatras: Female Power and Poetic Authority." In *Roman Poetry and Propaganda in the Age of Augustus*, ed. Anton Powell, 98–140. London: Bristol Classical Press, 1992.

Yarbrough, O. Larry. *Not Like the Gentiles: Marriage Rules in the Letters of Paul*. SBL Dissertation Series 80. Atlanta: Scholars Press, 1985.

Young, Frances. "Did Epiphanius Know What He Meant by Heresy?" *Studia Patristica* 17 (1982): 199–205.

——. "Greek Apologists of the Second Century." In *Apologetics in the Roman Empire: Pagans, Jews, and Christians*, ed. Mark Edwards, Martin Goodman, and Simon Price, 81–104. Oxford: Oxford University Press, 1999.

Young, Steve. " 'Being a Man': The Pursuit of Manliness in *The Shepherd of Hermas*." *JECS* 2, no. 3 (1994): 237–55.

Zanker, Paul. *The Power of Images in the Age of Augustus*. Trans. Alan Shapiro. Ann Arbor: University of Michigan Press, 1988.

Ziesler, John. *Paul's Letter to the Romans*. London: SCM Press; Philadelphia: Trinity Press International, 1989.

INDEX

Actium, battle of, 15, 16
active/passive paradigm, 29–31, 83, 204–5n.
    155; effeminacy, accusations of, 35–37;
    gentiles and homosexuality, 58–59
actors, 91, 190n. 3
Acts of Paul and Thecla, 96–97, 208n. 37
Acts of the Apostles, 153, 154
Adams, Robert M., 166n. 9
adoption metaphors, 152, 159, 234nn. 61, 65,
    235n. 68
adultery, 44–47; as demonstration of virility,
    46–47, 189n. 204; legislation, 39–42; for
    political purposes, 46, 189n. 204
Aelius Aristides, 131
Aemilianus, 36
Aeschines, 5, 23–24, 32, 35, 48, 169n. 27, 181n.
    95, 188n. 197; misquotes law, 45–46
Ahab, King, 61
Ahl, Frederick, 198n. 71
Alexander, 172n. 57, 184n. 137
Althusser, Louis, 28
angels, 121–24, 210n. 53, 220n. 50, 221n. 56
animal worship, 66
Antinous, 103–4, 210–11n. 60
Antiochus IV Epiphanes, 60
Antoninus Pius, 89, 100, 103, 104, 108
Antony, 15–17, 34, 36, 46, 49, 181n. 99, 187n.
    174, 223n. 81
Ap(h)thonius, 19
apocalypse, 113, 119–22, 130, 215nn. 2, 4, 224n.
    89; false Christians as sign of, 115–16, 119,
    126
Apocryphal Acts, 8, 208n. 39
Apocryphal literature, 61–62
apologists, 89–90, 103; offensive defense used
    by, 90–94, 98, 99–100; philosophy, use

of, 92–93, 104, 206nn. 18, 20, 207nn.
    22, 25
Apuleius, 36
Aristides, 8
aristocratic societies, values of, 177n. 55
Aristotle, 17–18, 19, 37, 48
Astin, Alan, 181–82n. 107
Athenagoras, 8, 90–91, 105–6, 110, 190n. 2,
    205n. 2, 206n. 18, 214n. 93
Athenians, 22–23, 44, 170n. 35, 178n. 67,
    188n. 199. *See also* Greeks
Attic orators, 22, 24, 176n. 38
audience, 195–96n. 57; in-group, 91–92,
    111–12, 173–74n. 74, 206n. 12
Augustus, 11–12, 16, 34, 49, 72–73, 172n. 61,
    186n. 170, 210n. 54; adultery of, 46, 47;
    anger and, 109; daughter and grand-
    daughter of, 42–43; marriage legislation,
    39–41, 77; as restorer of morality, 41–42
authority, 128, 173n. 66, 189n. 216; over
    desire, 80, 83–85; of Paul, 75–78, 84, 85;
    submission to, 71–74, 200n. 95; veiling of
    women and, 83–85
Autolychus, 90

Bacchanalian scandal, 40
Baker, Peter, 1
Balaam, 116, 121, 125, 221n. 63
Barnabas, Epistle of, 137
Basilides, 116
Basilidians, 116–1 17
Bauckham, Richard, 130, 132, 169n. 26, 219n.
    39, 220nn. 46, 48, 221nn. 54, 56, 222n. 70
Bauer, Walter, 116–17, 217nn. 14, 17, 22
Beard, Mary, 91
Betz, Hans Dieter, 199n. 91

gender (*continued*)
151; as hierarchical, 31, 179–80n. 82; martyrdom and, 106–7, 179–80n. 82, 213nn. 83, 87; natural, 66, 197n. 67; as type, 30–31. *See also* women
gendered disciplinary apparatus, 13
Genesis, 84
genos, 146, 148–52, 159, 230n. 17, 231n. 32. *See also* lineage
genre: apocalyptic, 215n. 4; in Paul, 64; petition, 89–90; praise/blame speeches, 89–90; testamentary, 222n. 70
gentiles: depravity of, 62–65, 195n. 53; homoerotic sex as disorder of, 58–59, 62, 195n. 53; moral impurity as inherent in, 56–57; as suppressors of truth, 66–67
Gleason, Maude, 30, 182n. 115
Gnostics, 116–17
gods, Greek and Roman, 90, 99, 100, 206n. 6
Goehring, James, 217n. 23
Gomorrah, 121, 123
Greco-Roman rhetoric, 51, 95–96, 208n. 34; in letter of Jude, 119–20, 218n. 32, 220n. 46; Paul's use of, 53–54, 64–65, 69
Greeks, 4–5, 10, 29–30, 33, 34. *See also* Athenians
Guerra, Anthony, 200n. 103

Hadrian, 103–4, 210n. 57
hairstyle, gender and, 81–85, 183n. 121
Halperin, David, 29, 167n. 15, 182n. 113
Harris, William V., 109, 175n. 17, 209n. 46
Hefner, Robert W., 174n. 75
Helena (Simonian), 153, 154, 232n. 46, 233n. 51, 236n. 83
Henrichs, Albert, 168n. 17
heresiologies, 134–35, 228n. 2, 229nn. 11, 12; identity formation and, 145–46; impact of outsider critique on, 161–62
heresy: categorization of, 117–18, 147–52, 157–58; as innovation, 117, 217n . 18; as term, 168–69n. 24, 230n. 21
heretics (false Christians), 112–14, 169n. 26, 216nn. 8, 9; accused of demonic influence, 114–15, 134, 143; apostates, 126–27; categorization of, 147–52, 157–58; Christian writers' disagreement about, 161–62; compared to false prophets of old, 126–27, 128; diversity of as proof of error, 154–56; dreaming/revelatory visions, 124, 220n. 53; equated with false prophets, 126–28, 135, 136–38; gentile nature of,

156–57; lack of information about, 145, 160, 228–29n. 9; as libertines, 117–20, 217n. 23; lineage of the ungodly, 121–24, 146–52, 157–58; list of vices, 21, 32, 115–16, 180n. 84, 191n. 12, 216n. 10; 2 Peter on, 127–30; pseudo-teachers, 128–29, 134; as sign of apocalypse, 115–16, 119, 126; stereotypical descriptions of, 134–35, 143–44; as ungodly, 120–21
Hermas, 119, 135
Hilarianus, 212n. 79
historical events, moral explanation for, 16–17, 181n. 105
History of Sexuality (Foucault), 29, 180n. 83
Hodge, Caroline Johnson, 171n. 49, 199n. 93
Holiness Code, 56–57, 62–63
Holofernes, 60
Homer, 10–11
homosexuality, 178n. 69, 179n. 72; ancient Greece, 29–30; as disorder of gentiles, 58–59, 62, 195n. 53; effeminacy, 35–36; violation of freeborn youths, 36, 37, 47, 183n. 122, 188nn. 189, 192. *See also* masculinity; unnatural lusts
Hopkins, Keith, 106
Horace, 11–12, 41, 43, 72
Hosea, 55, 56
household codes, 12, 208n. 34; Christians and, 95–98, 207nn. 31, 32, 207–8n. 33
hubris, 46, 176n. 40
human sacrifice, accusations of, 4, 6–7, 55, 105, 144, 145, 151, 158, 161
humor, 2–3, 49, 166n. 9
Humphrey, Edith McEwan, 225–26n. 104
Hunter, Virginia, 7, 178n. 67
Hurley, Donna, 166n. 14, 181n. 101

Ibrahim, Anwar, 165n. 1
ideal man, 24, 28–29
identity production, 9–10, 55, 57; heresiology as central to, 145–46; sexual slander and, 13, 160–63
idolaters, as category of others, 5, 6
idolatry, linked with fornication, 53–55, 66, 103, 122, 126, 154, 190n. 4
Ignatius of Antioch, 8, 130, 191n. 13, 209n. 45
inheritance, 231n. 35
invective, 20, 22; appropriated by Christian writers, 50, 131–32; as rhetorical tradition, 5–6, 16, 48–50. *See also* sexual slander
Irenaeus of Lyons, 5, 8–9, 117, 144–46, 229n. 15; categorization of heresies, 152, 157–58;